The Men Behind Monty

The Men Behind Monty

The Staff and HQs of Eighth Army and 21st Army Group

Richard Mead

Foreword by The Viscount Montgomery
of Alamein CMG CBE

Pen & Sword
MILITARY

First published in Great Britain in 2015 by
Pen & Sword Military
an imprint of
Pen & Sword Books Ltd
47 Church Street
Barnsley
South Yorkshire
S70 2AS

ISBN 978 1 47382 716 5

A CIP catalogue record for this book is available from the British
Library

Typeset in Ehrhardt by
Mac Style Ltd, Bridlington, East Yorkshire
Printed and bound in the UK by CPI Group (UK) Ltd,
Croydon, CRO 4YY

Pen & Sword Books Ltd incorporates the imprints of Pen & Sword
Archaeology, Atlas, Aviation, Battleground, Discovery, Family
History, History, Maritime, Military, Naval, Politics, Railways, Select,
Transport, True Crime, and Fiction, Frontline Books, Leo Cooper,
Praetorian Press, Seaforth Publishing and Wharncliffe.

For a complete list of Pen & Sword titles please contact
PEN & SWORD BOOKS LIMITED
47 Church Street, Barnsley, South Yorkshire, S70 2AS, England
E-mail: enquiries@pen-and-sword.co.uk
Website: www.pen-and-sword.co.uk

Contents

List of Maps

Foreword

by The Viscount Montgomery of Alamein CMG CBE

Richard Mead and I first met when he was researching his book on my father-in-law, 'Boy' Browning. The book, *General 'Boy'*, turned out to be an immensely readable and sympathetic account of a difficult life.

When he subsequently mentioned that he was proposing to write about my father, I had some reservations that there was nothing new that could be said. However, he has proved me quite wrong and written a fascinating story of the many talented officers who served on Monty's staff at various times. Although Monty was very self-centred, he had an extraordinary talent for choosing subordinates and commanding their absolute loyalty. Richard Mead brings all this out in flowing prose which illustrates how these young men in their different ways contributed to the successful outcome of the war.

He has also covered the difficult relationship Monty had with Eisenhower. I have always felt that this stemmed from the latter's lack of battlefield experience. Whereas Monty had commanded every unit and formation from an infantry unit to an army group, Eisenhower had risen through the Washington staff with no understanding of actual warfare. Reconciliation took place when Monty became the Military Deputy to Eisenhower as Supreme Commander of NATO, and was further consolidated when Ike became President and invited Monty to stay at the White House.

Introduction

Early on the morning of 12 August 1942 Lieutenant General Bernard Montgomery arrived in Cairo by plane from England, in response to an urgent summons. The previous nine days had been momentous ones in terms of Great Britain's conduct of the Second World War. Both the Prime Minister and the Chief of the Imperial General Staff had been in the Egyptian capital with the express purpose of finding a solution to what the former considered to be serious deficiencies in the command of the British and Empire forces in the Western Desert. A calamitous defeat in June and a retreat to a line some 70 miles west of Alexandria, the furthest the Axis armies had advanced since the beginning of the war, had created a huge threat to Britain's strategic position in the Middle East and even, by extension, to India.

Although the enemy army had been halted, there was little evidence in Churchill's opinion of any plans to defeat it comprehensively. His remedy was change at the top. General Sir Claude Auchinleck was replaced as C-in-C Middle East by General Sir Harold Alexander, who arrived in Cairo only three days before Montgomery. Auchinleck's Chief of Staff and his Deputy were also dismissed. A more difficult question arose over the selection of a new leader for the Eighth Army, which Auchinleck himself had been commanding since the end of June. Alan Brooke, the CIGS, strongly favoured Montgomery, but Churchill insisted on the appointment of Lieutenant General 'Strafer' Gott, a corps commander in the Army with considerable experience in the desert. Against his better judgement Brooke agreed, but on 7 August Gott was killed when the transport plane in which he was returning to Cairo was shot down by German fighters. Montgomery, at this time by no means a favourite of Churchill's, was duly summoned.

By the time Montgomery arrived, Churchill and Brooke had moved on to a meeting with Stalin in Moscow, although they were to reappear in Egypt five days later. Montgomery was thus briefed initially by Auchinleck and then by Alexander before leaving for his first visit to Eighth Army early the next morning. By a happy chance the Brigadier General Staff at Army HQ was a friend of many years' standing, Freddie de Guingand, who had himself been in the post for less than three weeks. Montgomery signalled de Guingand to meet him at the crossroads outside Alexandria and accompany him to Eighth Army's Advanced HQ, situated not far behind the front line. By the time they arrived he was well briefed on the situation, which he found inherently unsatisfactory, so much so that he took immediate command of the Army, notwithstanding an agreement with Auchinleck that this should not happen for another two days. That evening he addressed Eighth Army staff in terms that all of them would remember for the rest of their lives.

Other than de Guingand and Brian Robertson, the Deputy Adjutant and Quartermaster General, the senior members of the staff were all new to Montgomery. The reputation which preceded him was of a man who had strong views on the capabilities of individual officers. He divided them into two categories, 'absolutely first class' and 'quite useless', and was both ruthless in weeding out those in the latter category and highly skilled in engineering their replacement by others in whom he reposed confidence. It is extraordinary, therefore, that a significant number of the key staff officers not only survived the first few weeks but continued to work for Montgomery throughout his time at Eighth Army and then followed him to 21st Army Group on his appointment as its C-in-C. On VE Day many of the senior officers at Army Group HQ could remember vividly that first electrifying address outside the Mess Tent on the Ruweisat Ridge.

Military histories and biographies seldom dwell at any length on the staff, preferring to focus attention on those either determining strategy or doing the actual fighting. Yet in twentieth and twenty-first century warfare, with all its complexities, excellent staff work at all levels has been fundamental to success, and was never more so than in the Second World War. The armies and army groups in the Great War may have been as large as or even larger than those in the subsequent conflict, but they were all too often static. The Second World War, by contrast, saw enormous bodies of men move great distances, often on long lines of communication, in successions of multifaceted operations involving not only ground, but also naval and air forces. Putting these armies into the field, controlling their actions and then sustaining them over long periods of time required organizational skills of a high order and on a scale hitherto unknown.

The staff came away from the Great War with a poor reputation. The image of red-tabbed officers living comfortably in French chateaux far behind the front is an enduring one. At higher HQs this was often the case, and Montgomery himself was struck by the lack of connection between their staff and those doing the fighting, a state of affairs which strongly influenced his own military philosophy. At divisional and brigade HQs this was far from the truth, but the standard of staff work was inevitably affected by the decision to close the staff colleges for the duration of the War, in retrospect a great mistake. By the start of the Second World War, the situation had changed. Almost every general officer who would hold high command or a senior staff position had been through the two-year course at one of the two staff colleges at Camberley and Quetta, whilst many of the best had also taught there; and although some of them might have been disinclined to pursue a career in staff work, they had a very good idea of what it involved. Just as importantly, not only did the two staff colleges remain open for the duration of the war, but they were joined by a third, at Haifa in Palestine. The courses were cut down from two years to less than six months and focused exclusively on preparing officers for staff work at General Staff Officer Grade 2 and Deputy Assistant Quartermaster General or Adjutant General level, appointments holding the rank of major. The supply of trained officers was thus maintained and, as many of them had also seen active service, they came with added credibility and attracted less resentment from their brother officers at the front than their Great War forebears.

As a military historian and biographer I had, like most of my fellow authors, focused on field commanders. Whilst casting around for a suitable subject for a new book, however, I was offered access to the papers of General Sir Charles Richardson. Richardson was one of those who had been at Eighth Army HQ on 13 August 1942 and had then accompanied Montgomery all the way from El Alamein to the Baltic, except for a brief period when he was lent to General Mark Clark. He had written his own autobiography and, just as importantly, was the biographer of Freddie de Guingand; his papers were thus of potentially considerable value. The germ of an idea began to take shape that I could explore many aspects of the staff in the field, built around the figure of Britain's best known general of the twentieth century. I took the idea in the first instance to David Montgomery, not only because he was an authority on his father, but also because he had met many of the key members of his staff. His considerable enthusiasm encouraged me to believe that this would be an excellent subject.

Further investigation showed that there was no lack of source material. As they were required to do, each of the staff branches and sub-branches kept war diaries, which are varying in quality but nevertheless full of day-to-day information which throws some light on their activities. There is no lack of other official and semi-official documents bearing on the subject. Perhaps more importantly, many of those who had belonged to the HQs subsequently went into print: de Guingand, Richardson and several more by way of published autobiographies, others through rather more informal reminiscences. The officers at Montgomery's Tactical HQ ('Tac HQ') were particularly prolific, possibly because their very closeness to the C-in-C meant that their experiences went well beyond those of the average staff officer. Many of the key figures also recorded interviews, now in the archives of the Imperial War Museum, the majority of which were conducted by Nigel Hamilton during the writing of his magisterial three-volume biography of Montgomery.

Monty, as he was familiarly known and will henceforward be called in this book, was fortunate to have inherited a talented group of individuals at Eighth Army HQ. That they had yet to be welded into a cohesive team was the result both of weak command in the past and, more recently, of extreme confusion.

Monty, for his part, knew a great deal about staff work, both theoretical and practical. He had served on the Western Front in the Great War as a Brigade Major, as a GSO2 in both a division and a corps and briefly as the GSO1 of another division. He had attended the post-war course at Camberley in 1920, when it still lasted for a single year, and followed this with three successive staff appointments. He was on the Directing Staff at Camberley for three years in the late 1920s and Chief Instructor at Quetta in the mid-1930s. He had commanded, successively, a brigade, two divisions (one of them in action), two corps and a Home Forces command, the last the equivalent of an army and referred to as such by Monty. There was little he did not know about the work of the General Staff branch, but he was also very familiar with A and Q, the Adjutant General's and Quartermaster General's branches, and had strong views on administration.

This might have been intimidating within his HQs, but in fact Monty, or 'Master' as he was called behind his back, never interfered with staff work. His style of leadership was to select the best people, inform them fully of his plans and then let them get on with the job. If they were good, and most of them were, they survived. If not, and there are relatively few examples, they left. His insistence on running his campaigns from a small Tac HQ meant that he actually distanced himself physically from what was happening at his Main and Rear HQs. The key members of the staff were required to visit him frequently, but even in North Africa, once the army was on the move, Monty rarely spent time at his Main HQ and almost never visited his Rear HQ, whilst at 21st Army Group he knew few below the heads of branches and those at Tac HQ.

While the main objective of this book is to shine a light on Monty's staff, the book is inevitably just as much about him. The story of the staff can only be told in the context of the events in which he played the leading part, but what it attempts to do is to describe how those events were influenced by the work and advice of his staff. Several thousand officers and men served in the HQs of Eighth Army and 21st Army Group between 1942 and 1945, but the focus must inevitably alight on relatively few of them, broadly divided into two groups. The first of these consists of the major players, headed by de Guingand and including the heads of the various staff branches and functions and the senior advisers. The second group contains those much more junior officers who were physically close to Monty, his personal staff and personal liaison officers, the latter something of an innovation and a most important ingredient of Monty's approach to running a campaign.

In order to appreciate how all these men made their individual contributions, it is also necessary to understand something about their work. The organization of Eighth Army HQ was relatively straightforward. Its strength fluctuated, rather depending on what the Army was doing at the time. At its peak it contained over 200 officers and 1200 other ranks, but in the quiet patch between the end of the Tunisian campaign and the invasion of Sicily, the numbers dropped to 67 and 323 respectively. There was always a superior HQ – in order of succession, Middle East Command, 18th Army Group and 15th Army Group – to look after much of the logistics and take over the rear areas once these were liberated.

By contrast, 21st Army Group HQ was huge. It was itself the superior HQ for between two and four armies and, although SHAEF sat above it, in practice it handled all its own administrative requirements, which were highly complex. In addition to its armies it ran a large Line of Communications organization. It had branches and departments which were unheard of in the Eighth Army, such as Publicity & Psychological Warfare, Airfield Construction and Survey. Among many other activities it constructed and ran long pipelines to carry petroleum and aviation fuel, and it operated its own general hospitals. Unlike in Italy, where an organization divorced from military command relieved those doing the fighting as early as possible, 21st Army Group remained directly responsible for Civil Affairs in its rear areas and, from early 1945, for Military Government in its sector of Germany. It is hardly surprising, therefore, that by VE Day the combined Tac, Main and Rear HQs of the Army Group numbered over 1,000 officers and 3,500 other ranks.

In this book there is an inherent bias amongst the senior officers towards the general staff, as its work tended to have the greatest impact on events, but I have not ignored the logistical side which made such a huge contribution to victory. The A, or personnel, staff gets less attention, but it was as vital as the others in the overall scheme of things and I have covered it in general, particularly in 21st Army Group, although there are few mentions of individuals.

It is also essential to look at Eighth Army before Monty's arrival. Although he was the agent of considerable change in the army itself, at Army HQ the detailed staff work continued much as before and there were few changes in personnel. The contrast between the ways in which Auchinleck and Monty used their staff, on the other hand, was substantial.

Whilst Monty dominates the story, the 'hero' of the book is really de Guingand, the man who made it all happen. He was the antithesis of 'Master', most noticeably because of his emollient character: if Monty ruffled feathers, de Guingand smoothed them, and on at least one occasion he saved Monty from the potentially disastrous consequences of his actions. The members of the staff were devoted to him on a much more personal level than they were to Monty. They also admired him hugely for his professionalism and dedication. As the second dominant personality in this story from mid-1942 onwards, he is referred to throughout by the name by which he was known to everyone, superiors, peers and subordinates, British and Allies – 'Freddie'.

On 8 June 1946, a great Victory Parade was held in London, with representatives of the Armed Forces and Civilian Services and detachments from the British Empire and most of the United Nations. The members of the

Chiefs of Staff Committee had a prominent role both in the parade and on the saluting base, whilst field commanders were present in abundance, including Monty, who was rapturously received by the crowd. There were, however, no representatives of the staff of any of the various formations which had done the fighting. Lieutenant General Sandy Galloway, who had not only served as the very first BGS of Eighth Army, but had also succeeded Freddie as Chief of Staff of 21st Army Group immediately after the end of the war, wrote to him two days earlier:

> I should have thought that they might have included some of the staff who played a part in all the immense work that went on. This war has not only been a war of commanders, but of intense and brilliant staff work.[*]

My hope is that this book will help to demonstrate the truth of Galloway's words.

---

[*] Letter from Galloway to de Guingand, 6.11.46.

Chapter One

Prelude in the Desert

War came to the Western Desert of North Africa on 10 June 1940, when Benito Mussolini cast his hat into the ring alongside his fellow dictator in Germany. Mussolini was motivated by both greed and vainglory. He coveted the territory which he might now be able to obtain for Italy, notably British colonies or areas of influence in North and East Africa, and he was desperate to have a seat at the top table in the new European order.

The British, close to being driven from the continent of Europe and with their French allies looking increasing shaky, were understandably apprehensive about their position in Egypt, in which country they were far from popular and where there were signs of growing sympathy for the Axis. Egypt had been technically an independent state since 1922, but Great Britain remained responsible for its defence and security. Although the Anglo–Egyptian Treaty of 1936 handed over control of the Egyptian Army to local commanders, a sizeable body of British troops had remained in the country, critical as it was to Britain's control of the short route to India through the Suez Canal.

The threat from the Italians was not new. In October 1935 Italy had invaded Ethiopia, causing a crisis in which the League of Nations finally revealed its ineffectiveness and which ended with the de facto Italian occupation of that country. The British were more concerned about the danger from Libya, an Italian colony since 1912, and they temporarily augmented their military establishment in Egypt until the crisis subsided. With the coming of war against Germany and with concerns growing about Mussolini's plans for the expansion of his empire, steps were taken again to increase the British forces in the Middle East. By June 1940 there was a powerful fleet based at Alexandria, whilst British Troops in Egypt ('BTE'), the organization responsible for ground forces, had grown significantly from its three peacetime brigades.

The longest established formation in Egypt was 7 Armoured Division, formerly the Mobile Division (Egypt), comprising two armoured brigades and a support group of artillery and infantry, together with divisional troops. In July 1940 the division had 175 light tanks, armed with machine guns, and 75 cruiser tanks with 2-pounder guns. New arrivals since the beginning of the war were 4 Indian Division, whose two Indian brigades had been augmented by a British brigade, and 6 Australian Division, whilst 2 New Zealand Division was due to disembark shortly. Churchill, who from the beginning regarded the defence of Egypt as of vital importance, despatched a convoy containing fifty Matilda

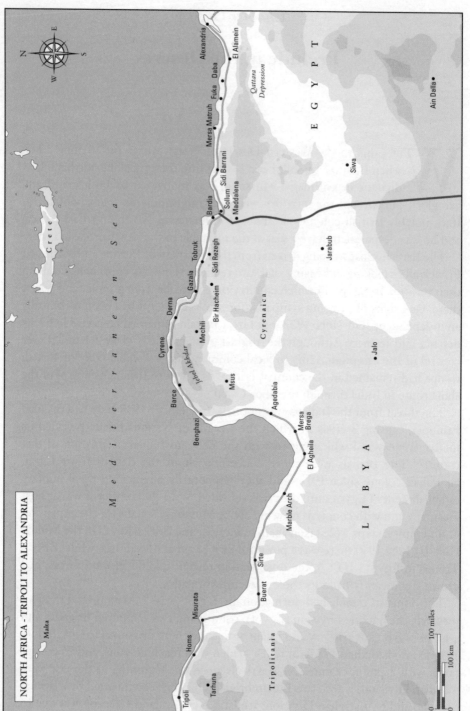

Map 1.

infantry tanks, about half the number available in Britain, a bold decision for a premier expecting invasion at any moment. Well armoured, albeit slow moving, they were to prove their worth in the months to come.

Three days before the declaration of war by Italy, Lieutenant General Richard O'Connor was summoned from Palestine to take command of the new Western Desert Force, a corps-sized formation consisting of 7 Armoured Division and 4 Indian Division, with its HQ at Mersa Matruh. On the instructions of General Sir Archibald Wavell, C-in-C Middle East, O'Connor immediately went on the attack, capturing the frontier positions at Forts Capuzzo and Maddalena, but the Italians then advanced in force with the whole of their Tenth Army, moving ponderously into Egypt until they reached Sidi Barrani, where they stopped and constructed defensive positions. O'Connor, grateful for this pause, conserved his tanks and trained his men for a future offensive.

Both Wavell and O'Connor were thoroughly offensively minded and, in November 1940, plans were drawn up for a new attack. BTE, now under Lieutenant General Henry Maitland 'Jumbo' Wilson, still sat in between Middle East Command and Western Desert Force and this plethora of HQs might have introduced unnecessary duplication into the process, but by good fortune both the commanders and their chief staff officers were men of good sense. Wilson's BGS, Sandy Galloway, was lent to O'Connor to work on the planning with the latter's BGS, Rupert Hobday, and when Galloway fell ill he was replaced by John Harding, at the time a GSO1 at GHQ Middle East. As events progressed, it was found more effective for O'Connor to report directly to Wavell. For the remainder of the war, BTE remained in command of the static troops in the base area of Egypt, whilst responsibility for those doing the fighting was delegated by the C-in-C Middle East first to Western Desert Force and then to Eighth Army.

Operation COMPASS was originally conceived and planned as a five-day raid. A full-scale training exercise was carried out by way of preparation, and on 9 December, as the troops advanced on what had been billed as a second exercise, they were told that it was the real thing. The attack was totally successful, the Italian fortified positions south of Sidi Barrani being overrun, whilst a left hook around the town to the sea cut off large numbers of the enemy, the remainder of whom retreated in some confusion to the frontier. At just this point 4 Indian Division was withdrawn for service in East Africa, to be replaced by 6 Australian Division. O'Connor, with Harding replacing Hobday as his BGS, did not let this throw him off his stride, but instead immediately capitalized on the enemy's confusion, bringing his new division into action as soon as it arrived. The Australians, together with 7 Armoured Division, went on to mount successful attacks on Bardia and Tobruk. By the end of January 1941, Western Desert Force had taken Derna on the coast road and Mechili, astride the main track across the desert south of the hilly Jebel Akhdar.

There then took place the outstanding action of the campaign, in which the Australians pressed forward from Derna to Benghazi, whilst mobile forces from 7 Armoured Division raced across the desert to cut the main road from Benghazi to Tripoli at Beda Fomm, trapping what remained of Tenth Army. It was a very complete victory, in which Western Desert Force, never much more than 30,000 strong, had taken 130,000 prisoners and captured or destroyed 400 tanks, 850 guns and large quantities of soft transport. Great Britain's position in North Africa looked secure.

At this juncture Wavell would probably have been able to mount an advance from O'Connor's forward position at El Agheila all the way to Tripoli, seizing the whole of Libya, bringing the lightning campaign to an ultimate conclusion and shortening the war in North Africa by two years. Instead, his attention was diverted to another theatre of war, Greece. The Greeks had themselves dealt the Italians a bloody nose over the winter, but they were now under serious threat from a drive into the Balkans by the Germans to protect their flank prior to launching Operation BARBAROSSA against the Soviet Union. Churchill was obsessed with bolstering Greece and he brought Wavell, initially sceptical, around to his viewpoint. W Force, commanded by Wilson and comprising 2 New Zealand Division, 6 Australian Division and 1 Armoured Brigade, was duly despatched, only to be soundly defeated when the Germans invaded.

The Australians were replaced in Western Desert Force by their countrymen in the keen but untested 9 Australian Division, from which some of the best trained units had been withdrawn for service in Greece and replaced by newly arrived and greener troops. Then 7 Armoured Division was withdrawn to Egypt to refit, relieved by the newly arrived and as yet untrained 2 Armoured Division, now shorn of 1 Armoured Brigade. Of the three regiments in its other armoured brigade, one was equipped with light tanks with no anti-tank capability, one had only half its proper establishment of cruiser tanks and the third was equipped entirely with Italian tanks captured at Beda Fomm. The support group was also short of its full establishment. In the meantime, O'Connor had also gone, stepping into Wilson's job at BTE. He was replaced by Philip Neame, now styled Military Governor of Cyrenaica, which became a static district.

On the other side of the front line, a highly significant development now took place. Concerned by his ally's failure to hold on to Cyrenaica, Hitler sent to Libya one of his most experienced generals, Erwin Rommel, who had proved his quality as a divisional commander during the blitzkrieg in France in May and June 1940. Using the newly arrived 5 German Light Division and two fresh Italian divisions, with two German panzer divisions under orders to follow as soon as they landed in Libya, Rommel went on to the offensive on 24 March, taking 2 Armoured Division by surprise, capturing El Agheila and sweeping forward along the very track that O'Connor had used to reach Beda Fomm. Wavell sent O'Connor back to the battlefield to act as an adviser to Neame, but in the confusion of retreat both men were captured, as was Michael Gambier-Parry, GOC of 2 Armoured Division, which soon ceased to exist as a coherent formation.

Together with 9 Australian Division, sundry British units, including some much needed artillery, withdrew in good order to Tobruk. The Australian commander, Leslie Morshead, was a vigorous and determined soldier and he and John Harding, who had stayed with Neame as BGS when O'Connor returned to Cairo but had avoided capture, resolved to stand fast there, swiftly siting strong defensive positions around the town. As the Axis troops swept past on their way to the Egyptian frontier, the Australians and British found themselves under siege.

By the end of April, Wavell was in trouble on several fronts. Rommel's force had entered Egypt, W Force had been expelled from Greece and the same fate would shortly be in store for the British, Australian and New Zealand troops in Crete. There were also problems in Iraq, where a pro-Axis clique had taken power and threatened to cut off the air route to India. No sooner had this been satisfactorily resolved than Wavell was forced to undertake the invasion of Vichy French Syria to prevent the Germans establishing themselves there. A brief but unpleasant little campaign ensued which secured the Levant but distracted Wavell from his most important task, recovering the lost ground in the Western Desert.

On 15 May Wavell mounted Operation BREVITY, its objective being to take the Halfaya Pass and Sollum on the Egyptian side of the frontier and then exploit as far as possible towards Tobruk. The weakness of the force resulted in withdrawal two days later, with modest initial gains quickly lost. The more ambitious Operation BATTLEAXE was mounted by XIII Corps, Western Desert Force's new name, with the objective not only of taking the Axis frontier positions but also of relieving Tobruk. On paper this reunited the original two divisions of the desert war, 7 Armoured and 4 Indian, the former refitted, the latter returned from East Africa. In practice, the Indian Division had only a single brigade and was given temporary command of 22 Guards Brigade. Although 7 Armoured Division had the benefit of new cruiser tanks which had arrived in a recent convoy from England, one of its brigades was still equipped entirely with Matildas, which had served well against the Italians but were obsolete in the face of German tanks and anti-tank guns. With the attack opening on 15 June, there was initial success on the escarpment, where 7 Armoured Division took Fort Capuzzo; but Rommel held the vital Halfaya Pass, where the British armour met the lethal German 88s for the first time. The commander of XIII Corps, Noel Beresford-Peirse, was inexperienced in the use of armour and his force found itself in serious trouble when faced with 15 Panzer Division. The commander of 4 Indian Division, Frank Messervy, ordered a retreat from Halfaya and Sollum, 7 Armoured Division was forced to conform and the operation was over three days after it began.

The failure of BATTLEAXE proved to be the last straw for Churchill, who had lost patience with Wavell. On 2 June it was announced that he had exchanged appointments with the C-in-C India, General Sir Claude Auchinleck.

Chapter Two

Eighth Army Enters the Field

Auchinleck came to the Middle East with his reputation standing high, in Churchill's eyes at least. Whereas Wavell had been slow to respond to the crisis in Iraq and had seemed to the Prime Minister almost reluctant to commit troops there, Auchinleck had reacted vigorously, despatching a division from India and reinforcing by air the small garrison at Habbaniya sufficiently strongly to drive away the threatening Iraqis, even before Wavell's relieving column arrived from Palestine.

Unusually for an officer of the Indian Army, 'the Auk', as he was popularly known, had held a corps command in the UK at the beginning of the war, taking part of his HQ to Norway in April 1940 in the closing stages of the short campaign there, which he had quickly recognized was a lost cause. He had organized the inevitable evacuation skilfully and was rewarded on his return with Southern Command, where he succeeded Brooke. There he attracted the favourable attention of the Prime Minister, but also the scorn of Montgomery, one of his corps commanders, with whom he completely failed to establish a good relationship. Both men were delighted when Auchinleck became C-in-C India, an appointment which the latter regarded at the time as both the pinnacle and the likely finale of his career. Now he found himself back where the action was the hottest.

The Prime Minister did not allow the new man time to settle in. On the contrary, he began where he had left off with Wavell, applying considerable pressure for a new offensive to be undertaken immediately. Like Wavell, Auchinleck was a consummate professional soldier and he resisted any attempt to make him attack before he was ready. First the Syrian campaign required to be finished. In Egypt new formations were arriving, but they all required time for acclimatization and training, whilst the tanks sent from the UK had to be modified for desert conditions. Auchinleck did, however, begin to plan a major operation and travelled to London in late July to present his preliminary plans to the Prime Minister and the CIGS, General Sir John Dill.

Auchinleck's new offensive was to employ both the existing XIII Corps and a new XXX Corps. An Army would be required to control the whole battlefield, and this was to the first field formation of such a size to see action since the demise of the British Expeditionary Force in June 1940. The choice of its commander was the first of many matters over which Auchinleck and Churchill disagreed.

The Prime Minister favoured 'Jumbo' Wilson, although he had never met him, whilst Auchinleck preferred Alan Cunningham. On the evidence, this was the right decision. Wilson had been resoundingly defeated in Greece and had made heavier weather than anticipated in Syria. He was also, although this might not have weighed heavily with the 66-year old Prime Minister, approaching his sixtieth birthday. Cunningham, on the other hand, had recently conducted a successful campaign against the Italians in Somaliland and Ethiopia and was familiar with desert conditions. Churchill accepted Auchinleck's choice rather grumpily, but it was to come back to bite the C-in-C in due course. The Prime Minister was also forced to give in to Auchinleck's insistence that he would be unable to mount the offensive until November.

It was on 10 September 1941 that HQ Western Army was formed at Pirbright Camp, Abbasia, and on 27 September that its designation was changed to HQ Eighth Army. Even to Auchinleck, who hardly knew Cunningham, the appointment of the Army Commander must have seemed something of a risk, so the choice of a first-class Brigadier General Staff was seen by many as an insurance policy. The man selected was Sandy Galloway. Galloway already had considerable experience as a general staff officer. He had served in Egypt in the 1930s as the Brigade Major of the Canal Brigade and had been on the Directing Staff at Camberley. Possibly as a result of the latter appointment, he was chosen to open the new Staff College at Haifa as its Commandant in February 1940. That August he became Wilson's BGS at BTE, in which capacity he was involved in the planning for Operation COMPASS, before following Wilson to Greece, where he was instrumental in organizing the successful evacuation of the bulk of W Force from ports in the Peloponnese. With a reputation for both common sense and decisiveness, he was trusted by Arthur Smith, formerly Wavell's and now Auchinleck's Chief of Staff, and by other senior officers at GHQ Egypt and in the War Office.

Galloway began to assemble his side of the staff, selecting, where possible, officers he knew. The staff of Western Desert Force, with Harding still the BGS, had mostly continued with XIII Corps, so he had to look outside. One of the first men Galloway picked was David Belchem, a young officer from the Royal Tank Regiment who had been in the first intake at Haifa before progressing to Wavell's Intelligence Staff in Cairo. Hoping to return to his regiment, Belchem had found himself posted instead as GSO2 (Ops) at W Force, where he worked for Galloway and acted as his right-hand man during the evacuation. Back in Cairo, with clear ideas as to how a campaign should not be fought, he once again applied to return to regimental duty, only to be picked by Galloway as GSO1 (Staff Duties), which at least meant promotion to acting lieutenant colonel.

'Staff Duties' is a misnomer for what is a key General Staff branch. Lieutenant General Sir Ronald Weeks, Deputy CIGS from 1942 to 1945, was to say later that the Director of Staff Duties at the War Office should have been called the

Director of Organization, and the same applied further down the line. In an army HQ the GSO1 (SD) acted as the main link between the GSO1 (Ops) and the A & Q staff. The former translated the plans of the commander into action, whilst the latter provided the necessary manning (A) and the provisioning and movement (Q). The SD branch acted as co-ordinator between them, organizing the allocation and deployment, and sometimes even the creation, of formations and units to meet the requirements of the order of battle. Belchem excelled at the job: Charles Richardson, who joined the HQ in the following summer, described him as 'sharp as a knife ... clear, accurate and decisive in every emergency'.[1]

Galloway's opposite number on the administrative side of the HQ was the Deputy Adjutant and Quartermaster General, Charles Miller, a cavalryman and an exact contemporary of Galloway's at Camberley, who arrived from holding the same position at BTE. Miller's Q branch was led by Brian Robertson, the Assistant Quartermaster General. The son of Field Marshal Sir William Robertson, the CIGS in the Great War from 1915 to 1918, Robertson had served in the Royal Engineers on the Western Front but had left the Army in 1934 due to what he saw as the lack of career prospects. He accepted a management position in South Africa with Dunlop, at the time one of the largest British companies, and was still there when war broke out in 1939. His attempts to rejoin the British Army were rebuffed – at 43 he was considered too old – and he volunteered instead for the Union Defence Force.[2] As an AQMG in the South African Expeditionary Force he accompanied his adopted countrymen to Kenya, whence they provided the backbone of Cunningham's campaign to drive the Italians out of first Somaliland and then Ethiopia, culminating in the capture of Addis Ababa. The success of the campaign was due in large part to the efforts of Robertson and his colleagues to keep the supply lines going, straightforward enough whilst the force remained close to the coast, especially when the ports of Kismayu and Mogadishu were opened up, but vastly more difficult when Cunningham split up his force, both arms of which had to cross difficult country and one of them the Ogaden desert. Cunningham not only gave full credit to Robertson in his despatches, but invited him to become AQMG at Eighth Army, making a direct appeal to the Chief of Staff of the Union of South Africa, who was most reluctant to let him go. Once in place, Robertson began to pull together a talented team, which included two officers from very different social backgrounds: Oliver Poole, an old Etonian who had arrived in the Middle East with the Warwickshire Yeomanry and who very quickly showed an affinity for complex planning, and Rimmel 'Rim' Lymer, a Lancastrian who had joined the Royal Army Service Corps as a Territorial and who was to specialize in supply and transport.

Galloway and Miller both held the rank of brigadier, as did a small number of officers who acted as advisers to the army commander on the activities of the various combat arms, including the Brigadiers Royal Artillery and Anti-Aircraft and the Deputy Directors of Supply and Transport, Ordnance Services and Medical Services. In charge of communications was Brigadier 'Slap' White, the Chief Signals Officer, who had commanded the Divisional Signals of 4 Indian Division in the Western Desert and Eritrea and then served briefly as CSO in East Africa Command prior to his move to Eighth Army. With wireless notoriously unreliable at this stage of the war, particularly in the armoured divisions, and fixed lines only really practicable when the army was at a standstill, his work was cut out to ensure that formations and units could communicate with each other and, most importantly at army level, with the RAF. It was as well, in the words of Charles Richardson, that White was 'efficient, imperturbable and charming'.[3] Eighth Army Signals directly employed more men than any other branch of the HQ.

Perhaps the most unusual of the senior officers was the Chief Royal Engineer, Brigadier Frederick Kisch. At 53, Fred Kisch was much older than most of his colleagues. He had served with distinction during the Great War in Flanders and Mesopotamia and had been a member of the British delegation to the Paris Peace Conference in 1919. Leaving the Army shortly afterwards, he joined the Zionist Commission (later the Jewish Agency) in Palestine, becoming its head for the Jerusalem region. His background enabled him to form excellent relationships with the British military authorities and he was one of the few leading Jews to be on good terms with Arab leaders in Jordan and elsewhere. He was both popular and exceptionally capable at his job.

Whilst Galloway and the General Staff at the Advanced HQ focused on planning the forthcoming operation, Miller, Robertson and the Q Staff at the Main and Rear HQs organized dumps for stores, fuel and ammunition. The prevailing feature of the Desert War was the existence of only one metalled road between Tripoli and Alexandria, running parallel to the coast. The Western Desert Railway had reached Mersa Matruh by April 1936 and work began on extending it in October 1940. By November 1941 it had reached Misheifa, 93 miles west of Marsa Matruh, on the escarpment due south of Sidi Barrani, where extensive marshalling yards, loops and spurs were constructed. However, the railhead was still 60 miles from the frontier and the onward journey was by lorry or tanker across the desert. Much of the front could only be reached by rough tracks, including the Advanced HQ near Fort Maddalena.

The plan developed by Cunningham and Galloway involved the advance of both corps, with the defeat of the German armour as the primary objective, followed only once this had happened by the relief of Tobruk and the expulsion of Axis forces from Cyrenaica. The main thrust would come from XXX Corps, substantially an armoured formation and commanded by a cavalryman who was new to the desert, Willoughby Norrie. Its spearhead was 7 Armoured Division, under the command of 'Strafer' Gott, one of the most experienced desert leaders and the man who had taken the Support Group across the desert to cut off the Italians at Beda Fomm. Of the division's two armoured brigades, 22 Armoured Brigade had recently arrived in the Middle East ahead of its original parent, 1 Armoured Division. As it was equipped with the new Crusader cruiser tank, of whose performance hopes ran high and whose name was given to the whole operation, it temporarily replaced 4 Armoured Brigade for the operation. Meanwhile, 7 Armoured Brigade for the most part retained its old A13 tanks. The division's plan was to drive to the north-west from its positions near Fort Maddalena, to dominate the desert tracks leading to the Axis lines around Gabr Saleh and, by so doing, to bring to battle Rommel's armour, which it outnumbered. Once it had defeated the panzers, it would take the key German airfield at Sidi Rezegh, south of Tobruk. Additional support would be provided by the two brigades of 1 South African Division and by 22 Guards (Motor) Brigade. In the meantime, 4 Armoured Brigade, equipped with American Stuart light tanks, very fast but lightly armed and armoured, would move forward independently at the same time as and parallel to 7 Armoured Division, but its main task was to provide left flank protection for XIII Corps.

XIII Corps in the north, with its front lying between the escarpment just east of Halfaya Pass and a position opposite a group of fortified Axis positions south-west of Fort Capuzzo known as the Omars, was substantially an infantry formation. It comprised 2 New Zealand and 4 Indian Divisions, supported by 1 Army Tank Brigade, still equipped with Matilda infantry tanks. Its role was to envelop the Axis defences around Bardia and the Omars and, only when the armoured battle had been won, to advance along to coast road towards Tobruk. Its GOC was Reade Godwin-Austen, who had commanded a division under Cunningham in East Africa.

Also included in the plan was the garrison of Tobruk, now consisting of the Polish Carpathian Brigade and 70 Division, which had relieved the Australians. Under the command of Ronald Scobie, it was to hold its position until such time as an opportunity emerged to break out to meet the relieving forces.

The XXX Corps advance began on 18 November and initially achieved complete surprise: 7 Armoured Division made good progress, reaching its objective at Gabr Saleh without being detected. Cunningham was puzzled at the lack of response, but now decided that the larger part of the division, comprising the HQ, 7 Armoured Brigade and the Support Group, should press on to take Sidi Rezegh airfield, detaching 22 Armoured Brigade to deal with an Italian force known to be at Bir Gubi to the west, while 4 Armoured Brigade remained at Gabr Saleh, initially seeing off a German battle group. However, both it and 22 Armoured Brigade suffered significant tank losses in their engagements.

Norrie's armour was now dangerously dispersed. On 20 November, 15 Panzer Division attacked 4 Armoured Brigade, causing further serious losses, and 22 Armoured Brigade was ordered to assist. The Germans withdrew, but only to join 21 Panzer Division in a combined attack on Sidi Rezegh, where the rest of Gott's division was drawn into vicious fighting on 21 and 22 November. Although 22 Armoured Brigade and 4 Armoured Brigade arrived at the battle, they lost many tanks in the process and the latter's HQ was overrun. Not for the last time, the British proved unable to deal with the enemy's tactics, being all too easily drawn on to the lethal German 88mm anti-tank guns. The British solution to the lack of penetration of their shells at any but the closest range, especially where the Stuarts were concerned, was to charge, usually with disastrous results.

At Cunningham's Advanced HQ, intelligence on XXX Corps' activities had been poor, indeed the initial armoured success had led the army commander to believe that all was going well, so much so that he authorized XIII Corps to begin its advance. On 23 November he learnt to his horror that not only had his armour been decimated, but that 5 South African Brigade, coming up behind it, had been destroyed. His flank was now effectively unprotected. Believing that there was no alternative to withdrawal, he ordered the HQ to move back and drafted signals to the corps commanders to do likewise. Galloway, who disagreed strongly with this decision, spoke immediately by phone to Jock Whiteley, Auchinleck's BGS (Operations), briefing him on the situation and recommending that the C-in-C should fly up as soon as possible, at the same time delaying the order to the HQ staff to move. Cunningham also sent a signal asking for Auchinleck to come immediately.

Whilst waiting for Auchinleck to arrive, Galloway went on his own initiative to Norrie's HQ, where he met Godwin-Austen. Having described the situation, he asked for the corps commanders' views. Godwin-Austin was totally against calling off his own operation, whilst Norrie, who was away but spoke to Godwin-Austen by phone, confirmed that he could hold on for at least another day. At the subsequent conference back at Eighth Army HQ, Galloway was asked for his opinion and said firmly that the offensive should continue, offering the corps commanders' views in support. Auchinleck also saw Miller alone and asked him what he thought of the situation. Miller replied that Eighth Army had the resources to keep going for at least another week, whereas it was his understanding that Rommel was running short of supplies. Auchinleck agreed with the two staff officers and ordered Cunningham to press the attacks both on Sidi Rezegh and on the Axis forces around Tobruk.

Rommel chose this moment to disengage from the battle at Sidi Rezegh and 'dash to the wire', his counter-attack on Eighth Army's lines of communication on the Egyptian frontier. On the morning of 24 November it looked as if he might succeed, as his thrust sent hundreds of British soft-skinned vehicles fleeing back to the frontier in confusion, whilst he also overran XXX Corps HQ, forcing Cunningham, who was visiting it, to leave in undignified haste. However, this allowed Gott time to regroup, whilst the artillery of 4 Indian

Division stopped the Germans only a few miles from Robertson's supply dumps. Cunningham had by now lost Auchinleck's confidence and was replaced by Neil Ritchie, Auchinleck's DCGS and also his former BGS at Southern Command in 1940, whilst Auchinleck himself assumed tactical control until the outcome was assured. Although there was much hard fighting to come, in due course the Axis army was forced to retreat and Tobruk was relieved.

Galloway's role in the moment of crisis during Operation CRUSADER had been vital. It became clear subsequently that Auchinleck, armed with intelligence from ULTRA that the Axis forces were under considerable strain and likely to have to withdraw if the pressure on them could be maintained, was determined to continue. However, it was Galloway's action in asking for the C-in-C to come up immediately while at the same time delaying the withdrawal of the HQ and canvassing the two corps commanders, which prevented a precipitate retreat and allowed Auchinleck time to take control. Auchinleck was also strengthened in his decision to carry on by the confidence expressed by Miller and Robertson that the supply situation remained good.

Eighth Army's advance to the west was contested, but the Axis forces were both outnumbered and suffering from severe supply problems and retreated back into Tripolitania. Ritchie remained in command. There were those who thought at the time, and most historians have agreed subsequently, that Auchinleck should have used the brief pause to replace Ritchie, possibly with Godwin-Austen, who had proved his resolve in CRUSADER, possibly with Wilson, or possibly with a completely new commander brought out from the UK. Auchinleck decided against a change, notwithstanding that Ritchie's reputation was as a staff officer[4] and that he had no experience as a field commander,

It was perhaps unfortunate that Galloway immediately took over Ritchie's job as Deputy Chief of the General Staff at GHQ Middle East, before returning to the UK in the following May to become Director of Staff Duties at the War Office. His successor as BGS at Eighth Army was Harold 'Dixie' Redman, who was to have a successful career as a staff officer[5] but was probably not what Ritchie needed, especially when Rommel struck back unexpectedly on 21 January 1942. The first formation he encountered was 1 Armoured Division, which was new to the desert, as 22 Armoured Brigade, originally one of its components, was refitting after CRUSADER. David Belchem, a tank man himself, visited the division shortly after it reached the front to see if he could provide it with any assistance and 'came away with great misgivings',[6] which turned out to be only too well founded. Its GOC, Herbert Lumsden, had been wounded and was temporarily relieved by Frank Messervy, who had no time to get to know his command. Four days into Rommel's advance it was no longer an effective fighting force. Francis Tuker, Messervy's replacement at 4 Indian Division, agreed with Godwin-Austen that he should withdraw in good order from his position around Benghazi along the coast road, only to have the latter overruled directly by Ritchie, who ordered Tuker to mount a defence. This proved impracticable and, although the Indians managed to extract themselves without heavy losses, Godwin-Austen, one of the best commanders on the British side, asked to be relieved of his command as he felt that Ritchie had displayed a lack of confidence in him. The highly capable and longstanding BGS of XIII Corps, John Harding, left at much the same time to take up the position of Director of Military Training at GHQ Middle East. Gott replaced Godwin-Austen, whilst his new BGS was a fellow 60th Rifleman, Bobby Erskine.

Rommel's attack had been opportunistic and successful, but his force remained weakened after CRUSADER and the best he could do was push Ritchie back to a line running south from Gazala, which both sides settled down to fortify.

Chapter Three

Auchinleck Takes Control

With Eighth Army safely behind hastily laid minefields at Gazala, and in the likelihood that there would be no further immediate advance by Rommel, Auchinleck decided to commission an enquiry into its command and control, particularly in the light of the recent reverse. The man he chose to conduct this enquiry was one of the more controversial officers in the British Army, Brigadier Eric 'Chink' Dorman-Smith. Dorman-Smith had a reputation for intellectual brilliance combined with personal arrogance which made him unpopular with many of his peers and even more of his superiors. However, he had a very good relationship with Auchinleck, with whom he had worked closely when he had been Director of Military Training in India during Auchinleck's tenure there as DCGS. He had had a frustrating war thus far, succeeding Galloway as Commandant of the Staff College at Haifa and becoming involved on the fringes of the planning for Operation COMPASS and, in its latter stages, as a liaison officer to O'Connor from Wavell. Both Wavell and Auchinleck had used him in a number of capacities since then, none of which was more than temporary, and he was desperate to obtain an important position in the heart of the action. His new job hardly achieved that goal, but he realized its potential significance.

Having interviewed a disgruntled Godwin-Austen in Cairo, Dorman-Smith set out for the front, where he met Ritchie, Gott, Norrie and the divisional commanders, together with a number of the more junior officers known to him. The common message was that there was little confidence in Ritchie. Bringing this back to Auchinleck, he found the C-in-C still reluctant to replace the Eighth Army commander, partly because he did not want to get a reputation for sacking officers at the first sign of a reverse and partly because he feared that he would have another commander imposed on him by the War Office; it was possible that this would be Montgomery, whom he knew to be a protégé of Alan Brooke, now the CIGS. If Ritchie was to remain in command, Dorman-Smith advised that he would need a stronger BGS and volunteered himself, but Auchinleck decided that he was too abrasive for the army commander. The compromise was to send Jock Whiteley, Auchinleck's BGS (Ops), whilst Dorman-Smith himself would relieve Galloway as Auchinleck's DCGS. This followed the replacement of Arthur Smith as CGS Middle East by Tom Corbett, an Indian Army officer who came to be widely regarded as ineffectual by both staff and commanders.

Whiteley was a Royal Engineer and a contemporary at Camberley of both Dorman-Smith and Galloway. He had been BGS (Ops) at GHQ Egypt since May 1940, in which role he played an important part in the planning of Operation COMPASS. Wavell regarded him sufficiently highly to send him to the United States in May 1941 to brief President Roosevelt and members of the US Government and armed forces on the military situation in the Middle East, which at the time looked very bleak. After discharging this duty very capably he had returned via London, where he was interviewed by the Prime Minister, who was losing patience with Wavell at the time and who subjected Whiteley to a tirade about the number of men on the ration strength and the poor results they had delivered. Widely regarded as a safe pair of hands in both London and Cairo, he was retained by Auchinleck after Wavell's departure. He knew Ritchie well as his former superior at GHQ.

Another new arrival at HQ Eighth Army was the GSO1 (Ops), Hugh Mainwaring. Among the small number of Grade 1 General Staff officers at an Army HQ, the others being those responsible for Planning, Intelligence, Staff Duties and Air, the GSO1 (Ops) was often regarded as the *primus inter pares*, sitting as he did at the centre of the web of activity. Mainwaring had been commissioned as a regular officer into the 10th Hussars, but had left the Army in 1935, becoming a Territorial and in due course converting to the artillery. He quickly built up a reputation as an original thinker and had already conceived one highly innovative idea, which was in due course significantly to improve intelligence from the battlefield: a dedicated team at Army HQ was directly linked into the radio network of the armoured regiments, thereby providing information which was immediate and thus much quicker than the subsequent reports from corps and divisions. This proved to be particularly valuable for ground/air cooperation, as the locations for their attacks could be transmitted to the RAF instantly, rather than after the need had passed, as had so often previously been the case. Although the concept, which became known as the J Service and was extended to cover infantry units as well, took some time to develop, it would make a material contribution to the rest of the North African campaign.

Once again Auchinleck found himself under considerable pressure from the Prime Minister to strike back at Rommel and once again he resisted until he was fully prepared. The two corps in Eighth Army retained their previous characteristics. XIII Corps comprised most of the infantry, which it deployed along the Gazala Line behind the minefields. The front for 15 miles inland from the coast was held by 1 South African Division and 32 Army Tank Brigade, whilst 50 Division and 1 Army Tank Brigade extended it further south for a similar distance. There was then a gap of some 10 miles, albeit protected by a large minefield, before a strongly fortified 'box' held by 1 Free French Brigade at Bir Hacheim. Also in the corps were the two brigades of 2 South African Division, augmented by 9 Indian Brigade, as the garrison of Tobruk.

XXX Corps once again contained most of the armour, with both 1 and 7 Armoured Divisions located behind the line, ready to strike in whatever direction proved necessary, and 201 Guards Brigade in a static box to the rear, which covered the intersection of two important desert tracks and was given the name of Knightsbridge. Meanwhile, 3 Indian Motor Brigade and 29 Indian Brigade were located in unfortified positions in the desert to the south in order to intercept any attempt by Rommel to hook round Bir Hacheim.

After four months of inaction, it was Rommel who did precisely that, committing all his armour – 15 and 21 Panzer Divisions and the Italian Ariete Division – to an audacious movement on the night of 26/27 May around the end of the Gazala Line. Ritchie's dispositions proved ill-prepared to meet such a concentration of force. The two independent brigades to the south were overwhelmed or pushed back, whilst Norrie's armour received a severe battering at first. However, it had a new weapon in the shape of the American Grant tank, provided with good armour and an effective 70mm gun, although it was mounted in a sponson not a turret and thus had a limited traverse. The German commander had set himself too large a task, that of breaking through to the sea, and as Norrie's scattered tanks began to reform, they were able to take a significant toll of the panzers, bringing them to a halt. Rommel's way to the sea was blocked by the British armour and Knightsbridge, but instead of retreating he did the unexpected, attacking and destroying 150 Brigade of 50 Division from its rear, where there were no minefields. He then set himself the task of clearing both the Allied and Axis minefields and creating a route through them to his own supply lines.

Rommel was in potentially serious trouble at this point in the battle, and if Ritchie had reacted fast and attacked with all his available forces in the first few days of June, the Axis armour would quite possibly have been annihilated before it could re-supply itself. Ritchie, however, initially did nothing to eliminate the salient, now known as 'the Cauldron'. Conference after conference took place, but no decision was taken. By the time he had agreed to a joint attack under his own command on the night of 5/6 June by elements of 7 Armoured Division and a newly arrived brigade from 5 Indian Division, the Germans were far too strong and the operation was a disaster.

Further south, the heroic resistance of the Free French at Bir Hacheim came to an end when Ritchie gave permission for them to break out on the night of 10/11 June. With the threat to his flank thus reduced, Rommel emerged from the Cauldron on 11 June, driving XXX Corps in front of him and isolating Knightsbridge, which had to be evacuated. Ritchie now ordered Gott to send 1 South African Division and 50 Division back to the frontier, the former along the coast, the latter through the open desert. Auchinleck, who was unaware of this, in the meantime ordered him to form a new line just west of Tobruk; but with XXX Corps no longer capable of action and the two infantry divisions retreating towards Egypt, this was impossible. XIII Corps' retreat also meant that Ritchie had no realistic alternative but to abandon Tobruk, which surrendered on 21 June. To Churchill, at the time in Washington meeting Roosevelt, this was the single most crushing blow of the campaign and did more than anything else to harden his opinion against Auchinleck.

Although there were defences on the frontier, they were very exposed to an outflanking movement through the desert. Ritchie therefore proposed to withdraw to Mersa Matruh, where he determined to make a stand with XIII Corps and the newly arrived X Corps. Auchinleck, however, had now totally lost confidence in him and decided to take control of Eighth Army personally. On the afternoon of 25 June, he arrived at Eighth Army's Advanced HQ at Maaten Bagush and relieved Ritchie of his command.

By this time Rommel had momentum on his side and Eighth Army's position was not promising. Even the arrival of 2 New Zealand Division and several Indian brigades under the command of 5 and 10 Indian Divisions failed to stem the tide, and Auchinleck was forced to concede that the only sensible option was a further withdrawal to the potentially much stronger position at El Alamein, which Norrie had been sent back to hold. This was helped to a considerable extent by the foresight of Robertson, who had recently succeeded Miller as DA&QMG. Unknown to either Auchinleck or Ritchie, he had prepared for just such an eventuality by drawing up contingency plans. When the moment came, it proved to be a relatively easy matter to backload the stores, whilst the shortening of the supply lines also began to have a beneficial effect.

Whiteley was by this time exhausted, having been effectively managing a round-the-clock crisis ever since Rommel's breakout. Auchinleck, however, had brought Dorman-Smith with him to the front, on the grounds that, as he remained C-in-C, he would need a senior staff officer alongside him to consult on matters relating to his wider command. In the event, in addition to fulfilling this function, Dorman-Smith began to usurp Whiteley's role as BGS, his closeness to Auchinleck giving him an influence that the titular holder of the position did not possess.

As the retreating Eighth Army's Advanced HQ paused briefly at Fuka it was joined by Charles Richardson, who had been appointed GSO1 (Plans). Richardson was, like Whiteley, a Royal Engineer. He had served in the BEF and been evacuated from Dunkirk, before being posted to the Middle East as an instructor at the Staff College, where by this time Dorman-Smith was the Commandant. He already knew Dorman-Smith from his earlier career in England and India and was sceptical about his abilities:

> To most of us he became a figure of fun. Though gifted with a sharp intelligence and a creative, unconventional mind, his rhetoric, amply larded with his native blarney, seemed seldom based on any sustained

study of the problem. He was certainly not a good tutor for young majors who were about to face the full force of the Afrika Korps.[1]

Having been greeted effusively by Dorman-Smith and having reported to Whiteley, who in spite of his weariness was able to give him a coherent picture of the situation, Richardson was sent back to El Alamein to see Norrie, who had been ordered to reconnoitre the defensive position and who vouchsafed his opinion that holding a line there would require sixteen divisions. Having passed on Auchinleck's orders that Norrie would have to plan for only six divisions, Richardson moved on. His destination was a junction of camel tracks on the Ruweisat Ridge, a key feature in the forthcoming battles, rising as it did above the surrounding desert. The ridge ran not north to south, where it would have been capable of fortification, but east to west, where it bisected what would become the front line.

This was to be the new Advanced HQ of Eighth Army, housing much of the General Staff and representatives of the Q Staff. Situated as it was on well-trodden tracks, it was liberally strewn with camel dung, which attracted even more flies than were generally encountered in the desert. It was not far from the front line and thus vulnerable both to shelling and to any success the Axis forces might have in penetration, whilst being a long way from the HQ of the Desert Air Force at Burg el Arab, next to the sea and closer to Alexandria than to El Alamein. Neither Richardson nor any of his immediate colleagues understood why it was chosen by Auchinleck, but it might have been that the C-in-C wished to demonstrate his commitment to withdraw no further. He was, in any event, dismissive of the comforts generally required by army commanders: although he had a caravan he was quite content to sleep on the ground beside it.[2] The Main HQ was positioned about 20 miles further back behind another key feature, the Alam Halfa Ridge.

The El Alamein Line had been identified long before the war as the only position in Egypt to have its landward flank protected by a significant feature, the Qattara Depression. Reconnaissance expeditions mounted in the 1920s and '30s had all confirmed that the Depression could not be crossed other than by small parties in light vehicles; so if a strong line could be constructed between there and the nearest point on the sea at El Alamein itself, it would prevent the traditional hook through the desert, used with varying success in all previous engagements. The land in between was mostly flat desert, but was dotted with features, some of which were raised above the plain, such as the Ruweisat, Alam Halfa and Miteirya Ridges, Tel el Eisa near the coast and Qaret el Himeimat at the southern end, whilst others were below it, including not only the Depression itself, but much smaller areas of low ground such as Deir el Munassib and Deir el Shein.

It was on the very last of these, at the western end of the Ruweisat Ridge, that the weight of the Afrika Korps fell on 1 July, as Eighth Army turned to face the enemy. The unlucky recipient of the attack was the newly arrived and inexperienced 18 Indian Brigade, which had little opportunity to fortify its position. Nevertheless, it put up a heroic resistance and, even though annihilated in the end, bought time for the army to consolidate elsewhere. When Rommel tried to pass 90 Light Division (formerly 5 Light Division) between the ridge and the sea, he was halted by the well emplaced artillery of 1 South African Division.

In the meantime, Belchem was sent by Auchinleck with an urgent message for Morshead of 9 Australian Division, now at Alexandria and fully refitted after its losses during the siege of Tobruk. The division was galvanised into immediate action and was in position by 2 July, shoring up the defences and, ten days later, taking Tel el Eisa in an aggressive action.

There followed over the next few weeks the confused series of engagements which have come to be known, erroneously in the eyes of many, including most of those at Eighth Army HQ, as the First Battle of El Alamein. They were characterised on both sides by the application of insufficient force to create a breakthrough or, if one looked likely, insufficient reserves to exploit it. On the British side, the outstanding problem was the inability of the armour to work in close cooperation with the infantry, to the extent that the latter lost all trust in the former. The British obsession with destroying the enemy's tanks as they moved about the battlefield, rather than with seizing and dominating ground of their own choosing, was no match for the German tactic of luring the British on to anti-tank guns and hull-down tanks. On the other hand, the Germans now lacked the strength to do more than defend, short as they were rapidly becoming of supplies and equipment at the end of their very long lines of communication. By the end of July Auchinleck had fought Rommel to a standstill, but was incapable of any further effort himself.

There were those who thought that Auchinleck was bereft of ideas, but the truth was that there were too many, most of which emanated from Dorman-Smith. As Richardson was to write later:

Ideas in plenty from the top of his head were liberally distributed, larded with Irish 'blarney', to any listeners available in our small group, more particularly at the 'Evening Prayer' session which six of us attended every evening in General Auchinleck's caravan. The unfortunate Jock Whiteley, as the accredited subordinate of the C-in-C holding executive authority, seldom knew which hare of Chink's was running at the moment; and I felt sure he realized, as I did, that Chink's intellectual dominance of the Auk was such that it was not possible to arrange the removal of this dangerous supernumerary adviser.[3]

Some of the ideas were quite radical, notably those involving the deployment of the armour, which all agreed was unsatisfactory. Dorman-Smith came up with two proposals. One was to increase the number of squadrons in an armoured regiment from three to four, to enable a quicker recovery from losses in any engagement. The second was to convert infantry divisions to mobile divisions by the inclusion in each of an armoured brigade. Both had their merits, but both were untenable in the middle of a battle, as they would require a long period of training for the formations and units involved. As such they fell foul of Auchinleck's chief adviser on armour, Major General Richard McCreery, who was resolutely opposed to them. His opposition was not well received by Auchinleck, who lost his temper on more than one occasion and threatened to sack McCreery if he did not fall into line; this he refused to do, bolstered by the support of most of the divisional commanders and many senior staff officers at GHQ.

There was also a general tendency towards employing troops in any attack in brigade groups incorporating all arms, rather than using complete divisions. This played particularly badly with the Australian, New Zealand and South African commanders, all of whom wished to see their formations employed as one rather than have their strength dissipated.

Richardson's own depression at the lack of sensible ideas at 'Evening Prayer' was heightened when he was instructed to draw up a plan for the retreat of the Eighth Army down the Nile to Khartoum. He felt that his effort, based on a school atlas purchased in Alexandria, was deeply unconvincing. Whiteley sympathised and told him to lock it away in a box.

As July drew to a close, it was clear that Whiteley would have to go. Auchinleck continued to rate him highly, but considered him suitable for a superior headquarters, not as the most senior General Staff officer in a field formation.[4] After consulting with Dorman-Smith, he decided that the man for the job was his Director of Military Intelligence at GHQ Middle East, Freddie de Guingand, who relieved Whiteley on 27 July.

Chapter Four

Freddie

Francis Wilfred de Guingand, always known as Freddie, was born in London on 28 February 1900 into a family which had strong French roots, but which had become thoroughly English. His father was in the business of the manufacture and sale of briar pipes, and the family was comfortably off. This allowed Freddie to be privately educated at Ampleforth, where he developed a love of sailing, encouraged by his father, who was an enthusiastic yachtsman. Freddie's first choice of career was thus, unsurprisingly, the Royal Navy. The medical examination, however, ruined his hopes when it was discovered that he was colour blind, so he turned to the Army instead. He entered the Royal Military College, Sandhurst, as a cadet in 1918, passing in fifteenth, which said something for his intellect. His choice of regiment was the West Yorkshires, on the strength of their sponsoring the OTC at Ampleforth. He was commissioned on 17 December 1919 and immediately joined the second battalion in India.

Freddie did not enjoy his early days as a regimental officer, partly because cantonment life lacked excitement and partly because he suffered the first occurrence of a medical condition which was to be a continuing problem, gallstones. By 1922 he was seriously ill and was invalided home, where the initial prognosis for his career in the Army was poor. However, he made a good recovery and was able to rejoin his battalion, which was by then in Ireland, in the closing year of 'the Troubles'. It was whilst he was there that he first became aware of Brevet Major Bernard Montgomery, Brigade Major of 17 (Cork) Brigade, although the two men did not meet. This situation was remedied shortly afterwards, when Freddie was posted to the regimental depot at York, where his job was to train NCOs. As Monty wrote many years later:

In 1922 I was appointed GSO2 to the 49th (West Yorkshire) Division of the Territorial Army, i.e. senior G.S. officer since in those days a T.A. Division was not allowed a GSO1. The Div. H.Q. was at York, and, being a bachelor, I lived in the depot of the West Yorkshires in Fulford Barracks. Freddie was a 2nd Lieutenant on the Depot strength, and was O i/c the Training Cadre. I quickly spotted him as a very intelligent young officer, and made use of him and his Cadre to help me with the T.A Division by giving demonstrations of platoon tactics.

His life in those days revolved around wine, women, and gambling – in all of which he excelled! I reckon he was about 22; I was a Captain (Bt. Major) and about 35. We became great friends. We played a lot of golf together, and bridge most evenings in the Mess.

When I saw his potentialities, I urged him to work for the staff college – or rather to begin a serious study of his profession, and to read widely, because he was too young then to take the exam.[1]

Monty and Freddie both moved on in 1925, Monty to command a battalion of his own regiment, Freddie to return to his battalion, albeit only for a short time. In early 1926 he volunteered to join the King's African Rifles on secondment. Such an opportunity, popularly known as 'bushwhacking', was attractive to officers with little hope of fast promotion in the inter-war years and expectations of a relatively unexciting life in one of the two battalions of their regiment, in the UK receiving and training recruits or overseas in some dreary posting in India or the Middle East. Service in one of the colonial regiments such as the KAR offered more responsibility and much more excitement as well as being better paid.

To Freddie the life was highly congenial and it left him with a lasting love of Africa. He began his tour as Adjutant of the 1st Battalion of the KAR in Nyasaland, becoming a temporary Captain in 1929, with substantive promotion the following year. The regimental life was itself more energetic than he had been accustomed to, with marches and exercises taking place around the country; but more attractive still were the significant opportunities for big game shooting and fishing, both of which he took to with enthusiasm. When his Commanding Officer moved on to become Officer Commanding Troops, Nyasaland, Freddie accompanied him as his Staff Officer.

His tour ended in 1931 and he returned to the home battalion of the West Yorkshires. Depressed, like many of his seniority, at the prospect of regimental soldiering in England, he was persuaded to stay on only by a transfer in the following year to the overseas battalion, which was then in Egypt. Once again he became the Adjutant, and this time his CO was Harold Franklyn, a highly competent officer who subsequently had an outstanding career and under whom Freddie enjoyed serving.[2] One of Franklyn's fellow COs in the Canal Brigade was Monty, commanding the 1st Battalion of the Royal Warwickshire Regiment, and he and Freddie renewed their friendship. On a brigade exercise Monty was appointed to its temporary command and selected Freddie as his Brigade Major. In Monty's words, 'We completely defeated the enemy in the desert in the Mena House area!'[3]

Two years later, both men found themselves in Quetta, Freddie still the Adjutant of his battalion, Monty now the Chief Instructor at the Staff College. Freddie had qualified for the Staff College course by passing the exam, but had failed to secure the necessary nomination and, in terms of his age, had left it rather late to do so. Monty took it on himself to badger the CGS India to nominate him, which duly happened. In reply to Freddie's letter of thanks, Monty wrote:

> I am not used to backing the wrong horse when it comes to asking favours of people in high places; it would only result in one's own undoing! You ought to do well at Camberley. I know many of the instructors there, some of them quite well ... I will write & commend you to them in due course.[4]

Freddie duly returned to England to take the two-year course at Camberley, which passed uneventfully. A further spell in his regiment, latterly as a company commander, was followed by a posting as Brigade Major of the Small Arms School at Netheravon, during which he managed to visit both its French and its German equivalent. He found the French school deeply depressing and the German school most impressive.

In June 1939 Freddie was selected to be Military Assistant to the Secretary of State for War, Leslie Hore-Belisha. The role was a demanding one. Although the Secretary of State had, like all his colleagues, a number of Civil Service aides, including a Principal Private Secretary, he also needed someone with a good knowledge of the Army to give him an informed view on military matters, to assist with his speeches in the House of Commons and elsewhere, to accompany him on his many visits to units, formations and military establishments and, above all, to act as a personal confidant.

Hore-Belisha was an unusual character as a government minister, on the one hand exceptionally clever, on the other flamboyant in his personal life, and he was far from popular with his Cabinet colleagues. He was, moreover, a reformer, which often made him equally unpopular with the senior officers of the Army, especially when he brought forward their retirement ages, sweeping out much of the dead wood. Freddie did not care much for him at first, but grew to hold him in both high regard and affection. This was his first experience of the corridors of power at the War Office, where he had never served before and where he was able to use his considerable charm to deflect some of the barbs aimed at his master. This was particularly important as Hore-Belisha and Lord Gort, the CIGS, were not on speaking terms; and once Hore-Belisha had engineered Gort into command of the BEF on the outbreak of war, he was to experience similar difficulties initially with his successor, General Sir Edmund Ironside. That these were overcome was due in some measure to Freddie's diplomacy, but the knives were out for Hore-Belisha in both the Army and the Government, and in January 1940 he was forced to resign.

Freddie immediately asked to be transferred back to his regiment, only to be appointed as an instructor at the newly established Staff College at Haifa.

The Commandant when he arrived was Sandy Galloway, but he was succeeded shortly afterwards by Chink Dorman-Smith, whom Freddie had known as an instructor at Camberley whilst he himself had been a student there. Freddie was in due course appointed Chief Instructor, in which post he made a considerable impression on the students and the other members of the Directing Staff, who included Charles Richardson and Gerry Duke, another Royal Engineer who would serve under Freddie later in the war. Duke was later to recall that he and a small party from the college were on a weekend expedition to Damascus when the news arrived that Paris had fallen to the Germans. The gloom that this inspired was quickly dispelled by Freddie's wit and humour.

Freddie had actually predicted the fall of France some time beforehand in one of the weekly talks he gave to the students on the overall military situation. Dorman-Smith was so incensed by what he saw as defeatism that he ordered him off the platform, but Freddie, with his assessment of the relative military capability of the French and Germans still relatively fresh in his mind from his pre-war visits to their military schools, refused to budge until he was placed under arrest. Dorman-Smith relented, but he did change the weekly speaker!

With Dorman-Smith frequently absent in order to involve himself as much as possible with the more interesting action taking place in Cairo or, better still, on the battlefield, Freddie found himself jointly running the college in tandem with John Tiarks, the Deputy Commandant. He was briefly diverted to set up a School of Combined Operations, with himself as the proposed commandant, only to be ordered in December 1940 to take up an appointment as GSO1 at GHQ Middle East as part of the Joint Planning Staff. He was also to act concurrently as the secretary to the C-in-Cs' Committee, on which sat Wavell for the Army, Sir Andrew Cunningham for the Royal Navy and Sir Arthur Longmore for the RAF, thus establishing vital contacts with the other two services at the most senior level. By this time Operation COMPASS was well into its stride and would soon result in the expulsion of the Italians from Cyrenaica.

The Joint Planners were convinced that a swift advance to Tripoli would be possible, but instead they were diverted to planning the intervention in Greece. They were overruled in their objections to the latter operation by purely political considerations, and Freddie accompanied Wavell, Sir John Dill, the CIGS, and Anthony Eden, the Secretary of State for War, to Athens for conferences with the King and General Papagos, the Greek C-in-C. Whilst in the country he was sent off to reconnoitre the much vaunted Aliakmon Line, the main defensive position in the north, of which he thought little, experiencing an earthquake and being arrested as a spy during the journey. Freddie's confidence in the venture remained low and, contrary to the orders of and initially unknown to Wavell and his CGS, Arthur Smith, he and his team prepared a plan for evacuation of W Force if things transpired as they feared. Although Wavell and Smith subsequently gave their approval to the evacuation plan, it was on the explicit instruction that no one outside GHQ should know of it. When it became necessary to implement it, all the components were in place and many more Allied soldiers were saved than would otherwise have been the case.

Freddie's first experience of the battlefield came when he accompanied Air Marshal Sir Arthur Tedder, then Longmore's deputy but soon to become his successor, to Tobruk in April 1941 as the Germans began to invest the town. There he found chaos and confusion, but also a cheerful John Harding, confident in the ability of the Australians and British to hold on. Back in Cairo the planners were kept hard at work on Crete, Iraq and Syria, one disaster and two modest but important successes. These were followed by Operations BREVITY and BATTLEAXE. Freddie thought that the latter in particular had no chance of success. 'The aim', he wrote later, 'was a laudable one, but the tools with which to carry it out were terribly weak.'[5]

Auchinleck's arrival led to a further bout of planning for the new Eighth Army. The first proposal was to hold the enemy on the frontier close to the sea, whilst sending the main force across the desert in a huge hook to take Benghazi. This foundered on the lack of knowledge of the 'going', as surface conditions in the desert were called. Whilst the Long Range Desert Group had done excellent work on surveying parts of the route, there was insufficient information to give any confidence of its viability and the plan was shelved for what became Operation CRUSADER. Freddie himself was diverted into a study of the defence of Iraq, Syria and Persia against a possible German thrust through the Caucasus, flying to Teheran to meet Great Britain's new Russian Allies, whom he found exceptionally uncooperative.

In late February 1942 Freddie was suddenly and unexpectedly summoned by Auchinleck to be told that he was being appointed Director of Military Intelligence, Middle East. In his own words, 'This was a shattering thing for a lieutenant-colonel with no previous Intelligence experience to be told. When I recovered my breath I replied: "But I have never done anything of that sort before, sir." "Excellent," said the Auk, "that's just why I've chosen you, you'll do all right. I want you to take over at once. Good night."'[6]

This development arose as the result of the sudden departure of Freddie's predecessor, John Shearer. Rommel's counter-attack so quickly after his setback in CRUSADER came as a considerable shock in both Cairo and London, and Shearer was blamed for an over-optimistic assessment of Axis capabilities. This had been queried at the time in London, and Brooke wrote to Auchinleck suggesting that he might be replaced. Auchinleck was nothing if not loyal to his staff, but the lack of confidence in Shearer at the War Office and the fact that he had also made enemies in the Middle East compelled him to act. The C-in-C consulted Dorman-Smith, who strongly recommended Freddie for Shearer's job.

Freddie's first task was to rebuild confidence in GHQ's Intelligence branch, primarily at Eighth Army. This he was able to do largely through his own sharp intellect, his congenial personality and his willingness to go up to the front as often as required. That he knew little about intelligence work proved to be of no consequence, as Auchinleck had foretold; indeed, bringing a fresh mind to the subject was just what was needed. As luck would have it, he found some excellent subordinates in place. Two of them, Major Joe Ewart and Captain Edgar Williams, were university dons who proved to have outstanding brains which attuned very easily to intelligence work. Ewart, who had served as an officer in the Royal Scots in France, was also a fluent German speaker. He was to stay on at GHQ Middle East, but to develop close links with Eighth Army before being recruited by Freddie for the campaign in North-West Europe, at the very end of which he found himself at the centre of momentous events.

Williams was to become one of Freddie's closest confidants, part of his inner circle for the rest of the war. Known to all as 'Bill', he was still only 29 years old when Freddie became DMI. He had read Modern History at Merton College, Oxford, where he obtained a first class degree and subsequently became a research fellow. Unlike many at the university, he was strongly opposed to appeasement, joining the Supplementary Reserve as an officer in the 1st King's Dragoon Guards, which in due course became the armoured car regiment of 2 Armoured Division. It was his armoured car, in the van of the newly arrived division, which was the first to detect the presence of Germans in the desert in March 1941. During the various confused encounters that ensued Williams found that his already weak eyesight was adversely affected by the strong sun and he was posted back to GHQ. There both he and Ewart became privy to one of the great secrets of the war, ULTRA, which was already providing excellent intelligence, although its interpretation was not always straightforward, as Shearer had found to his cost.

The immediate focus of the I Staff at GHQ was on Rommel's intentions at Gazala, and a list was prepared of the signs which would indicate his intention to attack. In addition to ULTRA, Freddie made considerable use of the Long Range Desert Group, which provided some direct confirmation of intelligence from other sources. To one idea of Dorman-Smith's, the setting-up of a small body of officers to act as the enemy, he was instinctively opposed, as it would be outside his control and potentially offer conflicting advice to the C-in-C. By playing for time, claiming difficulties with selecting the right officers and identifying other practical problems, he managed to have the idea dropped.

As May 1942 passed by, the indicators of an attack by Rommel were crossed off Freddie's list one by one and, when it came, it was as no surprise to the Intelligence Staff. The next few weeks were highly confused until Eighth Army made its stand on the Alamein Line. In early July, Freddie was asked by Auchinleck to spend ten days at his HQ, which gave him a very good idea of the unsatisfactory state of affairs there. Back in Cairo, he carried on strengthening contacts which would serve him well in the future, notably with Cunningham,

Tedder and Richard Casey, Churchill's representative as Minister of State Resident in the Middle East, to whom Freddie took a liking.

Back at Eighth Army HQ Auchinleck had by now come to the conclusion that Whiteley would have to be replaced and, with the concurrence of Dorman-Smith, who was not interested in the job in spite of having effectively carried it out for weeks, selected Freddie to relieve him. Freddie was concerned that, lacking any experience in the field, he would be unsuitable for the role, and consulted the Deputy Military Secretary, Angus Collier, who agreed to fly up to see Auchinleck about it. On the following day, 27 July, a sharp telegram arrived ordering Freddie to report for duty. Tedder lent him an aircraft and he was at Army Advanced HQ within hours.

Whiteley was helpfulness itself and stayed on for three days to give Freddie the benefit of his advice, before leaving for the UK and a senior position for the rest of the war on the staff of General Eisenhower. Dorman-Smith continued to be an annoyance, producing numerous ideas for evaluation, most of which Freddie thought were a waste of time which prevented him from carrying out his proper duties. In due course he persuaded Auchinleck that the duplication of roles was no longer necessary and, with Dorman-Smith himself welcoming a return to GHQ as the Auk's DCGS, the authority of the BGS was fully restored. Freddie could now concentrate fully on the General Staff team, his immediate subordinates being Belchem, Mainwaring, Richardson and the GSO1 (Intelligence), Lieutenant Colonel L. M. 'Spud' Murphy, an Indian Army officer. To assist Murphy as one of his GSO2s, Freddie brought in Bill Williams from GHQ.

At the same time Freddie began to build close relationships with his opposite number on the 'Q' side, Brian Robertson, and with Robertson's newly arrived AQMG, Miles Graham. Graham had served in the 2nd Life Guards in the Great War, acting for a time as the regiment's adjutant, but left in 1919 for a highly successful career in industry, whilst remaining on the Reserve of Officers. In 1939 he rejoined the regiment as a captain, the same rank that he had held twenty years earlier. The Life Guards were merged with the Royal Horse Guards as the Household Cavalry Regiment for the duration of the war, and it was as the Adjutant of the composite regiment, still equipped with horses as a component of 1 Cavalry Division, that Graham arrived in the Middle East. The skills which he had developed in industry were to lead him into Q work and he was in due course to form a pairing with Freddie which was to become the lynch-pin of success of the HQs of both Eighth Army and 21st Army Group.

Auchinleck continued to combine the roles of C-in-C and Army Commander, but it was evident to him and to others that this was an inherently unsatisfactory situation. Freddie, when consulted by the Auk on possible successors, recommended two, Monty and Bill Slim, the latter having impressed him greatly as an instructor at Camberley. Foremost amongst the others considering the problem were the Prime Minister and the CIGS, Alan Brooke, and the latter decided that he would have to visit Cairo in person. Churchill, his confidence in Auchinleck seriously eroded by the C-in-C's poor choices as Eighth Army Commander and more recently by the events of the last two months, felt equally strongly that the question of command in the Middle East required his presence on the spot. As a meeting with Stalin was also high on his agenda, he decided to kill two birds with one stone and stop off in Egypt en route to Moscow. Churchill and Brooke travelled separately to Cairo, but arrived within an hour of each other on 3 August.

The next day was taken up with discussions between Churchill, Brooke and Auchinleck. Wavell, summoned from India, Cunningham, Tedder and Casey joined in, together with Field Marshal Smuts, an old friend of the Prime Minister and, in spite of his age, a man with an acute brain. Various permutations of command were considered, one of which had Monty in command of Eighth Army, with Auchinleck remaining as C-in-C. Brooke was championing Monty but, as he was to write later, 'I felt some very serious doubts as to whether an Auk-Monty combination would work. I felt that the Auk would interfere too much with Monty, would ride him on a very tight rein, and would consequently be liable to put him out of his stride.'[7] He was apparently not fully aware of the antipathy which Monty had shown towards Auchinleck in 1940, but he still judged the characters of the two men correctly.

Brooke and Churchill visited Eighth Army on 5 August and took soundings from the various formation commanders. The following day became what the CIGS described as one of the most difficult of his life, with Churchill now insisting on the removal of Auchinleck. Brooke himself was offered the position of C-in-C, which he declined as he felt that his current role, arduous and exasperating as it often was, would render the best service to Great Britain; in retrospect, he was absolutely correct. The Prime Minister then insisted on breaking up Middle East Command by detaching Iraq and Persia under Auchinleck, whilst General Sir Harold Alexander would be summoned to take over the reduced Middle East Command. On the previous day Churchill had been most favourably impressed by Gott, who was still in command of XIII Corps, and now insisted that he should move to command Eighth Army. In spite of having been told by Gott that he was tired and had run out of ideas, Brooke could find no arguments to oppose his appointment.

On the next day, Gott boarded a slow-moving Bristol Bombay transport aircraft at Burg el Arab for Cairo and a few days rest before assuming command of Eighth Army. The route was well behind the lines and considered so safe that no escort was ever provided. As bad luck would have it, the aircraft was pounced on by two German fighters and shot down. One pilot died in the attack, but the other managed to make a crash landing. Soon afterwards the plane caught fire and most of the passengers, including Gott, were killed.

As soon as the news broke in Cairo a signal was sent to Monty, ordering him to Egypt immediately to assume command of Eighth Army.

Chapter Five

The Making of Monty

Bernard Law Montgomery was born on 17 November 1887 in Kennington, South London, where his father was vicar of St Mark's Church. The Montgomerys traced their descent back to the Norman Conquest, but settled later in Scotland and then, in the early seventeenth century, in Northern Ireland, where they were solidly upper-middle class members of the Protestant Ascendancy. Monty's paternal grandfather achieved renown in India for his conduct at the siege of Lucknow during the Indian Mutiny and eventually became Sir Robert Montgomery, Lieutenant Governor of the Punjab. His father, a second son who went into the church, married the daughter of another famous Victorian, Frederic Farrar. Dean Farrar was the author of *Eric, or Little by Little*, a novel set in a British public school, whose moralizing tone made it a best seller of its time.

The fourth of nine children – six boys and three girls – the young Monty was only two when his father was appointed Bishop of Tasmania and took his family there with him. Monty was later to describe his childhood as unhappy, and the root cause of the problem was his mother, who ruled the family with an iron rod. Not a person to take such discipline lightly, Monty rebelled and was duly chastised. He developed a strong antipathy towards his mother, albeit tempered with a degree of respect, reserving all his affection for his father, whom he worshipped. Whilst in Tasmania his education was in the hands of a series of tutors, but when he arrived back in London in 1901 at the end of his father's appointment, he was sent to St Paul's School as a day boy, throwing himself enthusiastically into sport and in due course becoming Captain of both the Rugby XV and the Cricket XI. He showed little promise scholastically until, having decided against his mother's wishes that he would join the Army, he was told that he would need to apply himself considerably harder to have any chance of gaining entrance to the Royal Military College, Sandhurst. Neither hard work nor application was ever a problem to Monty once he had set his sights on a particular goal, and he passed into Sandhurst comfortably.

Monty's Sandhurst career was hardly free from controversy. One of the leaders of a particularly rowdy company, an incident occurred in which he set light to the shirt-tails of an unpopular cadet, who suffered serious burns as a consequence. He was reduced from lance corporal to gentleman cadet and very nearly expelled. Only his mother's intervention, the victim's silence and an agreement by the college to hush up the affair saved him from a precipitate departure. Now a reformed character, he worked hard and passed out 36th, well above his entry level and only just out of the running for entry into the Indian Army, which he had sought as he had no private income and it was much better paid. Disappointed but undaunted, he was commissioned instead into the Royal Warwickshire Regiment on 19 September 1908

Notwithstanding his joining the British Army, it was to India that he was posted initially, to the 1st Battalion of his regiment. There he stayed, apart from one leave, until 1912, when the battalion returned to England. By this time he was a full lieutenant, had served as Regimental Quartermaster and was shortly to become Assistant Adjutant, both appointments which would give him an idea of staff activities at unit level. On 22 August 1914, three weeks after the declaration of war on Germany, the battalion sailed from Southampton to join the British Expeditionary Force.

Over the following two months Monty was to experience the chaos and confusion of an army entering a war unprepared and the bloody start of nearly four years of stalemate on the Western Front. The Royal Warwicks were in the thick of the retreat from Mons, the Battle of the Aisne and the First Battle of Ypres. It was at Ypres, leading his platoon in a bayonet charge, that Monty was shot in the knee and chest, the bullet in the case of the latter wound passing though his right lung. By the time he recovered full consciousness he was in hospital at Woolwich. It was the lung which posed the immediate problem for the doctors and, although the wound healed satisfactorily, it was to leave him with a weakness for the rest of his life, although he took care to remain extremely fit which largely compensated for the disability. For his gallantry Monty was promoted to captain in the field and later awarded the DSO, a decoration which, in the case of a subaltern, was not far short of a Victoria Cross.

Monty spent less than four months recuperating before being passed by a medical board for home duties and appointed Brigade Major of 112 Brigade, then training near Manchester. This swift advancement was remarkable, even though the high rate of casualties at Ypres had seen many other regular soldiers promoted. His Brigade Commander fell into the 'quite useless' category, and Monty later claimed that he ran the formation himself during its training in North Wales. His superior may have been useless as a soldier, but he was no fool and gave his Brigade Major free rein, commending him to his superiors when the brigade, now redesignated 104 Brigade, arrived in France at the end of January 1916. It joined the line in early March and saw constant action from then onwards. The Brigade Commander was relieved by another, this time in the 'first-class' category, who began to show Monty how a brigade fitted into the chain of command and related to the other arms with which it cooperated, the artillery and engineers.

Just over a week after the great battle started on 1 July 1916, 104 Brigade was moved to the Somme. That it missed the initial carnage came as no comfort, as the fighting was still exceptionally hard. At the end of the month it had to withdraw in the light of heavy losses before being moved to a quieter sector near Arras. It was there, in January 1917, that Monty took up a new appointment, as GSO2 at 33 Division. Unlike in the Second World War, when the duties of the GSO2 in a divisional HQ were well defined and there were two GSO3s to assist him, one for Operations, the other for Intelligence, in the Great War the GSO2 shared the overall duties with the GSO1, other than Intelligence, which was delegated to a single GSO3. This required a high degree of mutual understanding, lest any matter fall between two stools.

The Battle of Arras that April was not as bloody as the Somme, but it led to the same result, as the advance stalled against impenetrable defences. On 6 July 1917 Monty was posted as a GSO2 on the staff of IX Corps, part of General Sir Herbert Plumer's Second Army. Plumer was one of the most able British generals of the Great War and much of his philosophy and practice of command rubbed off on Monty. Constantly seeking new ideas to break the deadlock on the Western Front, Plumer was a meticulous planner, never launching an operation until he was fully prepared, training his men specifically for the tasks ahead of them and closely coordinating his infantry, artillery and engineers; this would be an accurate description of Monty twenty-five years later. Shortly before Monty arrived at IX Corps, Plumer had scored one of the few Allied successes of 1917 at Messines, a battle which was notable for beginning with the simultaneous detonation of nineteen enormous mines in tunnels below the German trenches, causing the loudest explosion in history to that date.

Plumer was no less successful in the early stages of the Battle of Passchendaele, but Haig's insistence on extending the operation beyond what was militarily sensible led to the usual carnage, and the offensive petered out in the thick mud. He was sent shortly afterwards to Italy to shore up Britain's Italian allies after the disaster at Caporetto, only returning to Second Army in the following spring. IX Corps, in the meantime, relieved a French corps in the seemingly quiet Chemin des Dames sector north-east of Soissons. On 27 May the Germans attacked strongly, forcing the corps and its French counterparts back to the Marne with enormous casualties. IX Corps was effectively reduced to a single division.

Throughout this period Monty had given a good account of himself and was rewarded on 16 July 1918 by being made a brevet major and temporary lieutenant colonel and appointed GSO1 of 47 (London) Division. The GOC was Major General G. F. Gorringe, whom Monty knew already as the Warwicks' former brigade commander in India. This was a big step up for Monty and with it came enlightenment. Gorringe adopted a most unusual approach, much more German than British, making his GSO1 the Chief of Staff of the whole division, responsible not only for the general staff but also for the administrative staff in the Q and A branches, and delegating to him the responsibility for preparing all the detailed orders. Monty not only took to this like a duck to water, but adopted the system himself as soon as he was in a position to do so. His new role gave him the opportunity at divisional level to apply Plumer's practices of training the troops for specific operations and coordinating attacks closely with the artillery. He was lucky in some respects that the great offensive which was to push back the Germans now took place and, although 47 Division engaged in much hard fighting and suffered some setbacks, it was a beneficiary of the overall strength of the Allied advance and the crumbling of enemy resistance.

Monty learnt much from the Great War and not only how to run a brigade, a division and a corps. Like most of his contemporaries he was appalled by the casualties and determined to do his utmost to mitigate these in future. He was particularly critical of the lack of contact between the higher command and the front line troops. He also arrived at a very clear conclusion on the role of the staff:

> The higher staffs were out of touch with the regimental officers and with the troops. The former lived in comfort, which became the greater as the distance of their headquarters behind the lines increased. There was no harm in this provided that there was touch and sympathy between the staff and the troops. This was often lacking. At most large headquarters in back areas the doctrine seemed to be that the troops existed for the benefit of the staff. My war experience led me to believe that the staff must be the servant of the troops, and that a good staff officer must serve his commander and the troops but himself be anonymous.[1]

Monty was now determined to add the theory of staff work to the practice which he had experienced during the Great War. Failing to get on to the 1919 course at Camberley, he actively lobbied the C-in-C of the British Army of Occupation in Germany, General Sir William Robertson, who obliged with the requisite nomination. The 1920 course lasted for a single year and Monty did not rate it particularly highly, John Dill being the only one of the instructors whom he admired. His fellow students included a number who would achieve high command in the next war, notably Richard O'Connor, with whom he formed a solid friendship, and Bernard Paget, but also many who would not last long in the Army.

Monty understood that he had left the Staff College with a good report, although this was never formally communicated to him. It must have been the case, however, because he received one of the plum staff appointments for his rank – like so many of his contemporaries he had taken off the badges of a lieutenant colonel and reverted to brevet major – as the Brigade Major of

17 (Cork) Brigade. It was here that he first came to the attention of the young Lieutenant de Guingand. Although Monty was well suited to what was a most demanding job, he disliked intensely the background in which he had to carry it out. The Irish 'Troubles' were reaching a vicious peak, with murder being commonplace on both sides. Monty thought that the conflict was bad for both officers and men, was in favour of leaving Ireland to its own devices and was delighted when this happened in 1922.

A brief spell as Brigade Major of 8 Brigade was followed by Monty's posting as GSO2 at 47 Division at York, where he messed with the West Yorkshires and befriended Freddie. Monty enjoyed training the TA, developing a deep respect for its officers and men, whom he thought were often more committed than their regular colleagues. His GOC gave him a free rein and he was able to use the division as a test bed for some of his theories.

At the end of his term at 47 Division, Monty returned to his regiment for nine months as a company commander before being appointed as an Instructor at Camberley, with promotion to local lieutenant colonel. Now, for the first time, Monty was able to develop contacts which would benefit him at the highest level in the future and, more importantly, to influence the next generation of officers who would attain high rank in the next war and thereafter. His colleagues on the Directing Staff included Alan Brooke, Harold Franklyn, Wilfred Lindsell and Henry Pownall, together with Paget and O'Connor, both of whom he already knew from his time as a student. Amongst the students who would cross his path subsequently were Harold Alexander, Evelyn Barker, Gerry Bucknall, Eric Dorman-Smith, Sandy Galloway, John Harding, Oliver Leese, Richard McCreery, Gordon MacMillan, Brian Robertson, Gerald Templer, John Whiteley and Douglas Wimberley. Monty made a strong impression on all the students during his lectures on tactics, but it was one of the instructors who most impressed him. This was Brooke, a man he quickly came to admire unequivocally, both for his professionalism and for his strong character.

It was whilst serving at Camberley that one of the most significant events in Monty's life took place. Whilst no misogynist, Monty had never had much time for women, except perhaps for one of his sisters, Winsome. He was staying at Lenk in Switzerland for winter sports shortly before joining the Staff College when he met Betty Carver, a widow with two sons, John, aged 13, and Dick, aged 11. Her first husband had been a Royal Engineer who was killed at Gallipoli, her brother Stanley Hobart had been a student at the Staff College in Monty's year and her other brother, Percy Hobart, was an officer in the Royal Tank Regiment, so she understood something of the Army. She and Monty were quite unalike. She was vivacious, sociable, tolerant, possessed of a fine sense of humour and much given to laughter; he was awkward in mixed company, tightly self-disciplined, egocentric, judgemental and often ruthless in pursuit of a goal. She was cultured and talented, an excellent painter and sculptor; he was only interested in his profession. Nevertheless, there was a mutual attraction, and when they both returned to Lenk a year later he fell head over heels in love, which she reciprocated. They married in July 1927.

The next ten years were happy ones for Monty. He took his stepsons under his wing immediately and his and Betty's own son David was born in 1928. He returned to his regiment in early 1929, but there was no real job for him there so he was offered the job of Secretary to the committee charged with revising the *Infantry Training Manual*. Monty accepted with enthusiasm. Although the manual was a committee responsibility, in practice he did the drafting himself which gave him the opportunity to put many of his own ideas on paper and thereby influence the training of future generations of infantrymen. When published it was generally well received and remained the bible for the infantry right up to the next war.

In January 1931 Monty became the Commanding Officer of the 1st Battalion of the Royal Warwicks, which he took to Palestine, Egypt and then to Poona in India and in 1934 he was appointed Chief Instructor of the Staff College in Quetta, in the rank of colonel. Once again Monty was much admired by the students, the majority of whom were from the Indian Army. Betty was in her element. In Egypt she had excelled as the Colonel's lady, leading the other wives in a number of activities. In Quetta there were no such obligations but there was a very full social life, as there was a large cantonment in addition to the Staff College. This was all rudely interrupted on 31 May 1935 by one of the great natural disasters of the century, the Quetta earthquake. The college was virtually untouched, but the old town was destroyed and there was severe damage to a number of other military installations. It was decided that Betty should be evacuated to England with the wives and children, although she later returned.

In August 1937 Monty was appointed to the command of 9 Brigade, his first of a field formation. The brigade formed part of 3 Division, one of the four standing divisions of the British Army in the United Kingdom and thus a certain component of any expeditionary force sent abroad in the event of war. The GOC was Major General Denis Bernard, whilst the GOC-in-C of the superior formation, Southern Command, was General Sir John Burnett-Stuart, who had commanded British Troops in Egypt during Monty's time there and thought highly of him.

The incumbent Brigade Major was a man who would become close to Monty during the period of his command and remain one of his most important confidants thereafter. Major Frank 'Simbo' Simpson was a 38-year-old Royal Engineer who had seen action on the Western Front in the last year of the Great War, when he had been mentioned in despatches, before going on to serve on the North-West Frontier. He had joined 3 Division after a two-year spell as a GSO3 at the War Office. Simpson was astonished by the contrast between

Monty and his predecessor, especially in the matter of training, on which the new Brigadier had very firm ideas. These included night exercises, which were not always popular with the troops; but Monty insisted that a deep familiarity with all aspects of fighting at night should be ingrained in everyone under his command.

Less than three months after joining 9 Brigade, Monty was struck by personal tragedy. Betty was stung or bitten by some insect whilst on a beach, and her leg began to swell. In great pain she was hospitalized, but her condition deteriorated. Her leg was amputated, but although she survived the operation she developed pneumonia and died in Monty's arms on 19 October.

Monty was devastated. She had been the bright beacon of his personal life, adding a dimension which he could not reproduce elsewhere. Somehow her presence made him more human and approachable. His two stepsons were adults by now, but he was left with full responsibility for bringing up David.

To those around him Monty recovered well and refused to let his very deep hurt show. Less than twenty-four hours after the funeral he told Simpson, who was too close not to know how he really felt and would prove to be an enormous support, that they were back in business. From then onwards he threw himself body and soul into his work, devoting himself single-mindedly to his profession. His reputation grew, and a year later, in October 1938, he was promoted to major general and appointed GOC of 8 Division in Palestine.

Chapter Six

Monty the General

By virtue of the combination of his rank and appointment, Monty was for the first time entitled to an aide-de-camp. A divisional commander rated a single ADC, but as Monty's responsibilities grew, his personal staff would increase in number, until by 1944 it would consist of a Military Assistant, a Personal Assistant and three ADCs.

An ADC is a personal staff officer, whose responsibility is solely and directly to the individual he serves. His function is very simply to smooth the path for his master. Among a myriad of tasks, this involves keeping his diary, coordinating his detailed itinerary for each day and liaising with those whom he is meeting, accompanying him whenever and wherever he so wishes, arranging social occasions and taking notes of his decisions for future action. He must be an excellent organizer and is required to have a detailed knowledge of the units and formations under his master's command, including their key personnel and their locations.

During the Second World War, ADCs to field commanders for the most part held the rank of captain, whilst Military Assistants and Personal Assistants were lieutenant colonels or majors. The officer whom Monty took with him to Palestine was a lowly lieutenant, Louis Sanderson, known as 'Fuzzy' to his brother officers. Sanderson, who was serving with the 1st King's Owns Scottish Borderers in 9 Brigade, had no idea why he was chosen. He was summoned to appear before Monty, terrified that he had committed some serious misdemeanour, to be asked simply if he wanted the job. As soon as he had accepted, he was given a fortnight's notice of departure and the interview was at an end. He and Monty travelled by ship to Haifa, accompanied only by Colonels Douglas McConnel and Eric Nares, the incoming GSO1 and AA&QMG, and Captain Adrian Hope, formerly the Adjutant of Sanderson's regiment, who was joining the divisional HQ as a Staff Captain (Q).[1]

For Sanderson there were few duties to perform whilst they were at sea, so he focused on getting to know Monty better. His assessment was very similar to others by Monty's personal staff over many years:

... there were two sides to his character. One was the stern, dedicated, ambitious and at times ruthless, professional Officer whilst, on the other hand, he was a caring, compassionate and humorous human being with an intense loyalty to all his subordinates, always provided that they carried out their duties satisfactorily … Meals were always a pleasure because he had the knack of steering the conversation to some subject concerning one of us or mutual acquaintances and then dwelling on it, pulling the leg of the individual unmercifully to the amusement of the others, never however, vindictively. Likewise he never took offence if the tables were turned on him regardless of the rank of his tormentor; yet I cannot recall any occasion on which he did not get the better of his teaser before the conversation moved on to another subject.[2]

Palestine had been under military control since 1936, when a nationalist uprising by the Palestinian Arabs had begun in response to mass Jewish immigration. Initially taking the form of strikes and civil disobedience, the failure of such actions to have much effect on the British authorities gave way in 1937 to armed rebellion, with attacks by bands of Arabs against both Jewish settlements and the British military. Both responded vigorously, the former, under the leadership of an enthusiastic Zionist, Major Orde Wingate, by instituting Special Night Squads to take direct action against the Arabs, the latter by ruthless suppression of the revolt, imprisonment of the ringleaders and the destruction of villages believed to harbour rebels.

By this time there were two complete divisions in the country. Monty's 8 Division was based in Haifa and responsible for North Palestine. The other, 7 Division, under his friend Richard O'Connor, who had arrived in the country shortly beforehand, played the same role in the South. The GOC-in-C was General Sir Robert Haining, who had been a senior instructor at Camberley at the same time as both his subordinates, so there was close and cordial cooperation between the three most senior officers in the country.

Monty was in his element in this, his first opportunity for active service since he had left Ireland in 1922. In Palestine he found a not dissimilar situation, although the response to what was perceived as terrorism was even more ruthless than it had been in Ireland. Monty immediately began a tour of all his brigades and units in his Humber Snipe staff car, accompanied by Sanderson and a personal bodyguard, who followed about 25 yards behind Monty carrying a sub-machine gun. Monty focused as always on training as well as on operations, but he was also insistent on high standards of administration and especially on hygiene in the tented and hutted camps which he considered vital to the operational efficiency of his troops. Outside his own command he also paid visits to the French Army in Syria and to the Transjordan Frontier Force, the latter playing a key role by preventing the rebels from accessing safe harbour on the east bank of the River Jordan. The other force involved was the Palestine Police, of whose senior officers Monty was highly critical, although he admired their men. Within months, the combination of Monty and O'Connor, with the active assistance of the Jews, had taken such a toll of the Arabs that the rebellion petered out.

Even before he left for Palestine, Monty knew that he would be required to return to England by the end of July 1939 to relieve Denis Bernard as the GOC of 3 Division. During the early summer, however, whilst still in Palestine, he became seriously ill, with severe pains in his chest and a high fever. Until this time he had been a light smoker and drank alcohol on occasion, but on being told that he had suspected tuberculosis, possibly exacerbated by his war wound, he gave up smoking entirely and only drank on very rare occasions. The doctors decided that he should be evacuated by sea, accompanied by two army nurses, two medical orderlies and his sister Winsome, who had been in the Middle East and was coincidentally on her way home. He was carried on to the ship on 3 July as a stretcher case and walked off ten days later declaring himself 'as fit as a fiddle'. A medical board found no signs of TB or any other infection, but he was still sent on sick leave.

In the meantime, the war clouds were gathering in Europe and Monty was desperate to take command of 3 Division. There was initial confusion at the War Office about the relief, but towards the end of August Bernard departed for his new job as Governor of Bermuda, allowing the fully recovered Monty to achieve his heart's desire, command of a regular division designated for inclusion in the British Expeditionary Force, exactly a week before war was declared on Germany.

Sanderson had initially remained behind in Palestine, where he acted in a temporary capacity as ADC to Monty's successor, Reade Godwin-Austen. Once it was confirmed that Monty would be able to assume his new appointment, Sanderson was ordered to return to the UK to assume his previous role. One of the first duties at 3 Division was to act as guide to the party accompanying King George VI on his inspection of the division prior to its leaving for France. This involved him leading the small convoy on his motorbike, whilst Monty and the commander of II Corps, Alan Brooke, accompanied the King in his car.

Sanderson was allotted the task of taking the HQ vehicles to France, the Camp Commandant, who would normally have fulfilled the role, having been sent in advance to requisition accommodation. He was astonished to find that only two of the vehicles were obviously military by design, the others being a rag-tag collection of civilian origin, including a butcher's van. On arrival at their destination, he found that the accommodation chosen for the GOC was a small French chateau, one half of which remained in the possession of its owner, whilst the other housed the members of Monty's A Mess. In addition to Monty and Sanderson this numbered six officers, the senior member of whom was the GSO1, Colonel 'Marino' Brown, so called because he was, somewhat unusually in a British Army formation, a Royal Marine. Brown was highly capable and very well respected in the division, but he lacked a well-developed sense of humour and thus became the butt of Monty's typical teasing at meals.

A new arrival in the mess in January 1940 was Captain C. P. 'Kit' Dawnay, who replaced the GSO3 (Intelligence), of whom Monty had a low opinion. Dawnay, who was a merchant banker by profession, was aged 30, had been called up as a reservist in the Coldstream Guards and was serving in the division with the 1st Battalion of his regiment. He had been selected by his commanding officer and sent to see Monty, to be told to his surprise that he would be a member of the GOC's mess, as Monty needed to know how he thought and vice versa. His experience was similar to Sanderson's:

> Monty always dominated the proceedings at dinner, directing conversation to any topic which currently interested him. Everyone, however junior, was encouraged to express a point of view, provided that it was not too laboured, since he had a great loathing of prolixity. Any loose or ill-considered statement would be sharply pounced on – 'That's nonsense, my dear fellow!' The subjects discussed were extremely diverse and demanded quick verbal reflexes. It somehow resembled a very fast moving ball game with the ball flying all over the place.[3]

Another new member of the mess was Sanderson's replacement. In mid-February 1940 Monty told Sanderson that he had learnt all that he could in his job and that he should return to his regiment, where the possibilities for advancement would be greater. 'This action', wrote Sanderson later, 'was typical of his consideration and concern for those who served him closely and whose interests he put before his own.'[4] His name was entered into Monty's little black book as an officer whose career would be watched and who, if the opportunity arose, would be employed again in another capacity. The new ADC was Charles Sweeny of the Royal Ulster Rifles, which was serving in the division in Monty's old 9 Brigade. He, like Sanderson, turned out to be outstanding at his job.

Monty was far from satisfied with 3 Division's readiness for battle. Whilst the focus of the rest of the BEF was on preparing fixed defences along the Belgian frontier in expectation of a German attack at some unspecified future date, Monty's own concentration was on dexterity in attack and retreat. He organized a series of exercises, each lasting several days, during which the division would advance to take a specific objective, usually a river line, find itself under attack, and withdraw to another position, often behind a second river. The movements in both directions usually took place at night and without any but the most minimal lighting. By the late spring of 1940 the division was the most agile in the BEF, something which would stand it in good stead. It was known by then that the Allies would execute the C-in-C General Gamelin's Plan D, whereby the Allies would advance far into Belgium and take up positions on the River

Dyle as soon as the Germans attacked. Unlike his corps commander, Alan Brooke, who was deeply unhappy with Plan D, Monty was unconcerned, as he was confident that his division would respond well to a war of movement.

Respond well it did. On 10 May 3 Division entered Belgium in the immediate aftermath of the German attack and moved up to its planned position near Louvain. The insistence of the local Belgian commander that he should have the overall command was countered by Monty placing himself unreservedly under the Belgian's orders, only to take control as soon as the Germans approached. It was during this campaign that he was to adopt what became his unfailing practice of retiring to bed promptly at 21.30 each night with a standing order, rarely disobeyed, that he should not be disturbed.

Although 3 Division saw less fighting than many others in the BEF, with its thoroughly rehearsed and well-disciplined movements it was always in the right place at the right time during the withdrawal back into France. On 27 May, as the Belgian Army crumbled on the left flank of the BEF, it accomplished one of the most difficult operations in war, the night-time movement from the right to the left of another division and only 2,000 yards behind it, achieved without incident and thereby filling a vulnerable gap in the defensive line. On the night of 29/30 May 3 Division moved into the Dunkirk bridgehead, where Monty relieved Brooke, who had been ordered back to the UK, as GOC II Corps. Whilst standing near Monty on the beach, Sweeny was lightly wounded in the head by a shell splinter and was berated by Monty for not wearing his helmet. When Sweeny pointed out to Monty that neither was he, the admonishment was graciously accepted. By the morning of 1 June the two of them were back at Dover, the last of II Corps to leave Dunkirk. One of the fatalities had been 'Marino' Brown, shot at a traffic block en route to the corps HQ during the retreat, probably by a sentry.

Reverting to his former role, Monty re-assembled 3 Division in Somerset. As the most complete division to be evacuated from France, it was immediately nominated to return there to join the 'Second BEF' in Normandy. Monty stopped all leave, but on hearing that it would take some time to re-equip, he changed his mind and allowed all ranks 48 hours. However, following advice to the Prime Minister by Brooke, who had been sent over to command the Second BEF, that the situation in France was hopeless and that all troops remaining there should be evacuated, the division was stood down from its planned role and instead focused on defending against what was widely expected to be an imminent invasion of the UK. On his return, Brooke became C-in-C Home Forces and one of his first actions was to ensure the promotion of Monty to a corps command.

Monty was appointed GOC of V Corps on 21 July. Responsible for Hampshire and Dorset, including a long and strategically important coastline stretching from Lyme Regis to Hayling Island, the corps consisted of 4 and

50 Divisions; but in November Monty persuaded the GOC of VIII Corps to exchange 50 Division for his old 3 Division so that he could have under his command the same formations which had constituted II Corps in the BEF. At much the same time he received 210 Independent Brigade, newly formed and completely untrained but under the command of Gerald Templer, an officer who had impressed Monty as one of his students at Staff College and on whom he would keep a close eye in the future.

Monty was not yet in a position to populate his staff with his favourites, instead inheriting the incumbents. There were two exceptions, the first of whom was Simbo Simpson, his former brigade major at 9 Brigade. Simpson had some months earlier incurred Monty's wrath when the AA&QMG at 3 Division had been posted away. At the time Simpson was working in the Military Secretary's Department at the War Office and was thus himself closely involved with officer appointments, but he was taken aback when Monty peremptorily ordered him to take on the role. Unsure about his ability to hold down an administrative staff appointment, Simpson demurred, and Monty reacted very adversely, threatening to block his promotion in future. Monty did subsequently reluctantly agree that Simpson's decision was the right one and welcomed his later appointment as GSO1 of 4 Division. By the time that he was appointed BGS of V Corps in December 1940, he was fully restored to favour.

The other key officer whom Monty managed to bring into V Corps HQ was Randle Feilden, always known as 'Gerry'. Feilden had been Adjutant of the 1st Battalion of the Coldstream Guards, prior to becoming Brigade Major of 7 Brigade, where he had caught Monty's eye. Initially transferred to 3 Division HQ as DAQMG, he was now appointed AQMG at V Corps, where he impressed Monty with his skill at administration.

Monty particularly wanted to take Dawnay with him but was denied. As 3 Division was still under his command, however, he sought regular intelligence appreciations from his former GSO3 (I) and invited him frequently to his HQ to discuss them. All his attempts failed to persuade the Military Secretary to transfer Dawnay permanently to V Corps as GSO2 (I). 'As you know (or perhaps you don't)', he wrote to Dawnay on 20 August, 'I have a very high opinion of your abilities and am trying to take you along with me wherever I may go … Charles (Sweeny) and I would like to have you with us; if they let you come you will become a major and Charles will have to call you sir.'[5] Five days later he wrote again: 'I fought hard to get you but have been defeated … I may "push out" the fellow they send me and ask for you again and go on doing this with each succeeding G2 until the MS is exhausted.'[6]

On 20 September he wrote again to thank Dawnay for another appreciation, but there was further bad news: 'I have lost my Charles; I really do miss him terribly and life seems quite different without him. We have been through a great deal together and I have a very great and real affection for him; I had to let him go though. He is a dear lad and I do hope and pray no harm comes to him in this war.'[7] As he did with Sanderson, Monty was to keep an eye on Sweeny's progress and, as soon as he had both the power and the opportunity to do so, to bring him back under his wing. None of his subsequent ADCs during his service in Home Forces was to establish himself as a permanent fixture. This would have to wait for the Desert.

Dawnay was a lost cause for the time being as far as Monty's staff was concerned, but the personal relationship remained strong, Monty asking Dawnay to address him less formally as 'General Monty': 'After all I regard you as one of my real friends.'[8] To cement the connection he agreed to become godfather to Dawnay's son and, when all his attempts to have him transferred to HQ V Corps had failed, succeeded instead in getting him on to the wartime Staff College course beginning in early 1941, in the hope of being able to secure him on its completion. In the meantime, the correspondence between the two men continued uninterrupted.

Monty's first five months at V Corps were dogged by his poor relationship with his immediate superior, the GOC-in-C of Southern Command, who was Auchinleck. 'I cannot recall', he wrote later, 'that we ever agreed on anything.'[9] Some of their differences were purely military in nature, Auchinleck having adopted a strategy of defeating the enemy on the beaches, whilst Monty preferred a thin crust of Home Guard beach brigades at the likely landing sites and a highly mobile response thereafter. The issue over which the two men really came into conflict, however, was precisely the one of Monty attempting to have personnel transferred in and out of V Corps. In so doing he had actively lobbied the Adjutant General and members of his department at the War Office, achieving some success in field command appointments, whilst at the same time failing when it came to his own staff. Auchinleck pointed out that many of these appointments were the responsibility of his own HQ and asked Monty to stop going over his head and those of his fellow corps commanders, whose officers he was attempting to poach. Not for the last time, Monty was demonstrating a degree of insubordination to a senior officer which he would never have tolerated himself. It was doubtless a great relief to both men when Auchinleck was appointed C-in-C India and replaced by the altogether more emollient Harold Alexander.

As always, the focus of Monty's attention was on training, and V Corps was subjected to his methods, involving frequent and strenuous exercises, usually carried out at night. The result was a highly serviceable corps and, when Brooke needed a new corps commander for XII Corps in April 1941, it was to Monty that he turned. If the invasion was mounted, it was on the Kent coast in XII Corps' area that it was most likely to descend. Here Monty found much the same situation that he had experienced in V Corps, with two divisions, 43 and 56, employed directly behind the beaches, and the much weaker 44 Division in reserve. Once again he changed the priorities, leaving the coast to static brigades whilst deploying his divisions to strike wherever the threat emerged.

Monty's impact on XII Corps was as immediate as always, especially when it came to weeding out unsatisfactory personnel, which included not only the officers whom he regarded as professionally incompetent, but also those who were physically unfit. His popularity plummeted when he ordered that all wives and families should leave the corps area, as it was an operational zone. He had little success, yet again, with bringing in all those he wanted on his staff, the major exception being Simpson, who accompanied him as BGS, being succeeded at V Corps by Templer. However, that summer Monty at last secured the services of Dawnay, once the Staff College course had finished. On the other hand, he failed with Feilden, who remained behind, shortly afterwards going to the newly formed Guards Armoured Division as its AA&QMG.

Monty had greater success in poaching a number of brigade commanders to replace those found wanting, much to the irritation of V Corps. His greatest triumph, however, was the appointment of Brian Horrocks to lead 44 Division. Horrocks had commanded the machine gun battalion in 3 Division in France and Belgium, where he had seen Monty almost every day during the retreat and had impressed him with his cool cheerfulness in all situations. On their return to England Monty had Horrocks promoted to command 9 Brigade in 3 Division, from where he had been posted as BGS at Eastern Command. When a vacancy suddenly emerged in his most inexperienced division, Monty moved fast to secure Horrocks's services.

One officer who attracted his attention was the Commander Royal Artillery of 56 Division, Sydney Kirkman. Kirkman had the temerity to tell Monty that he had missed a couple of important points in a speech following a cloth-model exercise. Far from taking offence, Monty listened carefully to what Kirkman had to say, then returned immediately to the audience to remedy the deficiency – albeit without any attribution to Kirkman! He was so impressed that he had Kirkman transferred to become his Brigadier Royal Artillery at XII Corps. It soon became evident that it was the man who mattered, not the advice which he was tendering: soon after he arrived, Kirkman suggested three changes which had previously been proposed by his predecessor and rejected by Monty, to find that they were now accepted without question. Like many others, Kirkman discovered that once an officer had secured Monty's confidence, he could be trusted to get on with his job with minimal interference.

His ADC at XII Corps was Colin Drury, a 21-year-old gunner working as Liaison Officer in 56 Division, who had written a report on the anti-tank defence of Romney Marsh, a particularly vulnerable sector. Monty read it, was impressed and asked for him. Drury later wrote:

For me there was no relaxing. There was ever the feeling that Monty, even in the friendliest of conversations, was noting, testing, leading up to something. In the staff car I always sat in the front, knowing that the "back-seat driver" was watching that we took the shortest route.

In the Senior Mess there would be no real relaxation. He would tease and prod the other members, mostly Brigadiers, constantly bowling awkward questions; ranging from whether they had taken their early morning run (he could usually tell without asking) to the current level of VD in the ATS.

To me he was always kindness itself, as indeed he was to all who worked closely for and with him. One did not stay long in his orbit without a dedication to work. Devotion to our General followed as a matter of course.[10]

In November Monty came out as one of the winners in a series of changes at the most senior levels of the British Army. John Dill lost the confidence of the Prime Minister as CIGS and was replaced by Brooke. Bernard Paget moved into his place to command Home Forces and was himself succeeded at South Eastern Command by Monty, one of whose first actions was to rename it South Eastern Army. His two formations were XII Corps, where the new GOC was Lieutenant General James Gammell, who had also followed him at 3 Division, and I Canadian Corps, responsible for Surrey and Sussex and quite new to him. Monty found dealing with the senior Canadian commanders, Andrew McNaughton followed by Henry Crerar, very difficult: neither of them liked him much, whilst he placed them in the 'useless' category. Unlike an equivalent British formation, however, he had little control over their appointments, as they remained responsible to the Government of Canada. Monty reluctantly realized that he would have to live with this situation, much as he might complain to Paget and Brooke. He did, however, think very highly of their BGS, Guy Simonds, who caught his eye at the massive Home Forces Exercise BUMPER, which Monty umpired, and at the subsequent South East Army Exercise TIGER, marking him down as a star of the future.

As an Army Commander, Monty was now entitled to two ADCs and he decided to employ a Canadian as one of them. Captain Trumbull Warren of the 48th Highlanders of Canada, serving at the time as a staff officer in one of the Canadian brigades and with recent experience from a posting with 'Phantom', the GHQ Liaison Regiment, was the man chosen for a three-month posting and was duly introduced to and approved by Monty. Having been warned that his new boss was a very difficult man, Warren reported at South Eastern Army HQ with some trepidation. Monty was in bed with a heavy cold, but Warren was told to go to his room, where he found him heavily wrapped up but with all the windows wide open, letting in the freezing air. There followed two hours of questioning on a wide range of topics, focusing on Warren's family, friends, school, regiment and other aspects of his life. Undaunted by this, Warren recognized that he was dealing with a very human person and by no means the martinet of his reputation.

In their relatively short time together, Monty was much taken with Warren. This was not least because his new ADC had instinctively recognized that Monty would not tolerate any dissembling. He was asked soon after his arrival to arrange for Dick McCreery, then Monty's armoured adviser, to attend a meeting the following afternoon. In the midst of his other duties, Warren completely forgot to do this. Instead of producing some sort of lame excuse, he went to Monty and told him very simply that McCreery would not be coming and why. 'Do you think we can win a war if you do this sort of stuff?' asked Monty. Warren admitted that this was unlikely. 'I'm glad you told me', said Monty, 'now we won't mention it again.'[11]

Monty found Warren to be an excellent confidant with whom to share his difficulties with the senior Canadian commanders and resolved to have him back as soon as possible. When Warren left, Monty wrote:

> You need have no fear as to how you did your work here, you are far and away the best A.D.C I have ever had and you are a real loss to my mess. As for myself, personally, I will miss you more than I can say. I had got used to having you with me, you were exactly what I wanted, and I had become very attached to you. So much so that I used to discuss with you confidential matters that I would never have done with any A.D.C. before, and probably will never do again.[12]

As he had with Dawnay, Monty asked Warren to consider himself a real friend and to call him 'General Monty', and resolved to get him back as soon as he was in a position to do so. In the knowledge that Warren had never seen his newborn child, he arranged for him to return temporarily to Canada, as a student at the Staff College in Kingston, Ontario.

TIGER was the culmination of all the exercises which Monty had devised during his career and on which he placed so much emphasis. This time it pitted one of his corps against the other over ten days and across a massive slice of country. A number of senior visitors appeared, including Brooke, Paget and a recent arrival from Washington, Major General Dwight D. Eisenhower, whose first experience this was of the man who was to play a considerable role in his subsequent wartime career. As always, Monty gave a speech after the exercise, which not only summed up the results but also gave some idea of the development of his own thinking. He rejected the use of brigade groups, at this time popular in the Middle East, in favour of complete divisions. He was equally clear that each corps should be capable of controlling a combination of infantry and armoured divisions. His speeches, preceded by two minutes for coughing, after which it was strictly banned, were considered long-winded by some, occasionally running over two hours, but to his audience they were models of clarity.

In early August 1942 Monty was in Scotland with Paget, observing another Home Forces exercise, when he received an urgent call from the War Office. He was to take up an immediate appointment as commander of the British element for Operation TORCH, the invasion of French North Africa being planned for the autumn, as the previously designated commander, Alexander, had been called away to become C-in-C Middle East. Returning to his HQ at Reigate, Monty had not even had time to hand over to his successor when his orders were countermanded and he was instructed instead to proceed with all despatch to Egypt to assume command of Eighth Army. He had just time to make sure that his son David was to be well looked after whilst he was overseas, before flying out from Lyneham on the evening of 10 August, taking with him only one of his current ADCs, Captain Kenneth Spooner of the Royal Norfolk Regiment. After a brief stopover at Gibraltar he landed in Cairo early on the morning of the second day.

Chapter Seven

The New Broom

Monty blew into Cairo like a whirlwind. Pausing briefly at the Mena House Hotel for a bath and breakfast, he sent Spooner off to obtain a uniform appropriate to the climate, before hastening to meet Auchinleck. According to Monty, Auchinleck told him that if Rommel were to attack in force, he proposed to withdraw Eighth Army to the Delta and, if that could not be held, up the Nile. This was subsequently denied by Auchinleck when Monty's *Memoirs* appeared and, although a rudimentary plan certainly existed, based on the school atlas procured by Charles Richardson, and practical steps to implement it if necessary were being taken by Miles Graham amongst others, it does not appear to have formed the basis of the agreed actions at Eighth Army itself in the event of an attack in force. On the other hand, Auchinleck in his capacity as C-in-C Middle East certainly had John Harding prepare a contingency plan at GHQ in the event of a breakthrough by Rommel. Monty kept his silence anyway in what must have been an awkward encounter for both men. Auchinleck was still the C-in-C for another three days and it was as such that he proposed that Monty should visit Eighth Army to get a feel for the situation, prior to taking command on 15 August.

Monty's next meeting was with Alexander, a man he liked and who he felt would make a good superior, although he did not rate him at all highly as a soldier. Whilst on the plane he had been formulating a number of ideas on how he would revitalise Eighth Army, one of which was to create a powerful reserve *corps de chasse* of armoured and mobile divisions, in many respects much like Rommel's Afrika Korps. Alexander was supportive, and Monty went off to see Harding, who had been one of his favourite students at Camberley and was now DCGS at GHQ Middle East. Harding promised to come up with the components of the new formation and by that evening had produced them in the shape of 1, 8 and 10 Armoured Divisions and 2 New Zealand Division, all to be equipped on a fully mobile basis.

Monty also requested that Alexander ask the War Office for a small number of senior officers to be sent out from the UK. These included Brian Horrocks to command a corps, Sydney Kirkman to be his Chief Gunner, Harry Arkwright, who had held a similar job at South-Eastern Army, to be his Armoured Fighting Vehicles Adviser and Frank Simpson for an unspecified role, but most likely as his Chief of Staff. Alexander quickly arranged for a signal to be sent, and

Horrocks, Kirkman and Arkwright were duly despatched, but Simpson, recently appointed DDMO at the War Office, was thought to be too valuable in that position and remained in England, as did two more on Monty's list.

The one other task Monty had set himself for the day was to acquire another ADC, as Spooner had no experience of the desert. Alexander's Military Assistant recommended John Poston, a young officer in the 11th Hussars, an armoured car regiment which had been in North Africa since the beginning of the war and had taken part in almost every subsequent military operation. Poston had been ADC to Gott and was now waiting for a new posting. In the knowledge that his experience of the country would be invaluable, Monty interviewed him, liked him immediately, and offered him the job, which was accepted. It was the beginning of a relationship which would last until the closing days of the war.

Finally, before going to dine with Sir Miles Lampson, the British Ambassador, Monty sent a signal to Freddie de Guingand, instructing him to be waiting at the crossroads outside Alexandria at 7.30 on the following morning. A student of military history, Monty recalled an earlier instance of such a meeting in a letter to Bill Williams after the War:

> When Napoleon left Paris, by carriage, to take command of the Army of Italy, in which army Berthier was Chief of Staff, he sent orders for Berthier to meet him at a rendezvous some miles from H.Q. so that they could travel the last miles together and the C-in-C would get an idea of the situation before he took over.
>
> I did the same with Freddie.[1]

When Monty arrived at the rendezvous, Freddie was there. His first action on joining Monty in the car was to hand over a report he had prepared on Eighth Army's situation. Monty put it aside and asked him to say in his own words what he thought. During the journey Freddie did just that, whilst Monty only spoke to ask questions or to clarify points, so that by the time that they arrived at the Advanced HQ on the Ruweisat Ridge, he had a clear understanding of where matters stood. Monty later claimed that he had by then decided to retain Freddie as his Chief of Staff. This was not the case, as he had not yet heard from the War Office regarding Simpson. Monty knew and liked Freddie and rated him highly, but the only time that the BGS had served directly under him was for a few days of exercises in the Nile Delta eleven years earlier. Simpson, by contrast, had been his right-hand man and confidant at 9 Brigade, V Corps and XII Corps. A few days later, Monty even told Freddie that he had asked for someone else, that Freddie was not to be upset if that person was appointed and that in such circumstances he could have any other job he wanted. This would not have come as a surprise: according to David Belchem, Freddie believed that Monty would not want to retain him because he had never been in action before.[2] In the event, nothing further was said on the matter and in due course Freddie concluded that the job was his. What he could not predict was that he would still be Monty's Chief of Staff nearly three years later.

Monty had already resolved to adopt a system of staff organization which was entirely foreign to the British Army. Since the beginning of the twentieth century the staff of every command and field formation had been divided into three branches, reflecting the organization of the War Office itself – the General Staff, the Adjutant General's Staff and the Quartermaster General's Staff. The General Staff handled Operations, Intelligence, Planning, Staff Duties, Military Training and Air Cooperation. The Adjutant General's Staff looked after all matters relating to personnel, from recruitment to retirement and including pay, education, health and religion. The Quartermaster General's Staff was responsible for logistics and particularly the supply of equipment, provisions and munitions. In most commands and field formations one person, responsible directly to the commander or commander-in-chief, held overall responsibility for both administrative branches, which were then divided at the next level down. There was always, however, just one head of the General Staff, whether a CGS at a command, a BGS at an army or a corps or a GSO1 at a division.

Monty now proposed to adopt the Chief of Staff system, whereby a single officer, in this case Freddie, would be responsible for the whole staff, both general and administrative, would convey all Monty's intentions to them for action and would issue orders on his behalf. Monty felt strongly that this was the only way to run a staff. In this he harked back to the reforms of the Prussian Army carried out by von Moltke under Bismarck in the mid-nineteenth century, and even further to Napoleon and Berthier.

Monty later expressed his thoughts on the subject thus:

There is a need, I reckon, for any leader, military or political, to have a brilliant and devoted chief of staff who will sift all the relevant information, seek out the facts, and relieve his boss of all irrelevant detail. This will enable the leader, the chief, to survey the whole field of endeavour and to keep his finger on the pulse of those things which matter. A man who is always immersed in details is unfit to be a leader in any walk of life. The Chief of Staff must be anonymous and must never attempt to take unto himself the powers of the leader; on the other hand, he must be prepared to give decisions on all matters of detail. He must, therefore, be completely in the mind of his boss, nothing being hidden from him, and being trusted absolutely. A good Chief of Staff is a pearl of very great price. My impression is that political leaders don't like them! But in the highest level of the military world, a Chief of Staff is essential: without one a Commander-in Chief would become hopelessly entangled in detail, as do so many political leaders.[3]

Monty's experience of the Great War and, more recently, of the disastrous campaign prior to Dunkirk, in which Lord Gort had often shown himself to be obsessed by detail at the expense of the wider picture, had reinforced this conclusion. What he was seeking was a structure which would allow him time to think about the whole canvas of the campaign, not just the battle he was preparing to fight or actually fighting, but also the next one ahead, and then to make his own decisions accordingly. Being able to deal for the most part with a single staff officer for the implementation of those decisions simplified his task considerably. He instructed his subordinate commanders to accept orders emanating from Freddie as if they came from himself and he never interfered with staff work; indeed, as long as he had confidence in the members of his staff, he showed very little interest in it.

This approach might have created problems. On the one hand, the top administrative officer was now subordinate to the Chief of Staff. In this case, however, the DA&QMG of Eighth Army, Brian Robertson, was one of the few at HQ who knew Monty, as one of his instructors at Staff College, and he was delighted with his arrival on the scene. He understood Monty's reasoning, had an excellent relationship with Freddie and was happy to go along with the new arrangements, as was his successor in due course, Miles Graham. Both of them, moreover, were among the relatively few officers to be allowed direct access to Monty whenever they asked for it, although in practice this privilege was only exercised on relatively rare occasions. There was also potential for confusion in the General Staff branch, but in practice Freddie exercised direct control over its activities, with the GSO1 (Ops) and later the BGS (Ops) being implicitly recognized as his deputy.

There were some, such as Sydney Kirkman, about to become Eighth Army's BRA, who considered that Monty exaggerated the role of the Chief of Staff and that it was effectively much the same as that of the typical BGS, albeit with more power over the administrative staff. In the field return of officers Freddie continued to be described as BGS and, in any event, he never exercised the same authority as his equivalent in the German Army, even if this had been somewhat diluted from the immensely powerful positions held by Ludendorff and others in the Great War.

Monty arrived with Freddie at Advanced HQ at about 11.00, to be met by Lieutenant General William Ramsden, the commander of XXX Corps and acting commander of Eighth Army. Ramsden had served under Monty as a battalion commander in Palestine, where he had performed perfectly adequately. By this time, however, Monty was so concerned with what he saw as a most unsatisfactory situation that, after he had been fully briefed by Ramsden, he sent him back to his corps and signalled GHQ that he was assuming immediate command of Eighth Army, totally contrary to Auchinleck's instructions. He also issued orders on the spot to all formations that there would be no further withdrawal. In order to avoid any riposte from Auchinleck,[4] he then set off to XIII Corps to meet Bernard Freyberg, who had assumed temporary command there following the death of Gott. He outlined his ideas to both Freyberg and Leslie Morshead of 9 Australian Division, both of whom expressed firm support.

Before leaving to see Freyberg, Monty had told Freddie that he wanted to talk to the HQ staff on his return that evening. The audience consisted of upwards of fifty officers at Advanced HQ, largely from the General Staff but with representatives from the administrative branches. They sat on the sand whilst Monty gave his address.*

Charles Richardson was later to write that those present 'listened with growing amazement'[5] as Monty spelt out his agenda. No withdrawal, fresh divisions arriving, a *corps de chasse*, 300 to 400 new Sherman tanks, a readiness to accept and defeat any attack by Rommel, a new offensive but only when completely ready; all these spoke of a complete and thoroughly welcome contrast to what they had experienced over the last few months. Monty also spoke of the adoption of the Chief of Staff system and announced that he would tolerate no 'bellyaching', a serious misdemeanour in his eyes. Perhaps most welcome to the morale of the assembled officers was the announcement that the HQ would be moving from its insalubrious position on the Ruweisat Ridge to a location at Burg el Arab, two thirds of the way back towards Alexandria, on the sea and next to the HQ of the Desert Air Force. Monty had been appalled by the conditions in the Advanced HQ, which he thought would not inspire good work, and by its separation from the RAF, making ground/air cooperation more difficult than it should be. Since it housed a considerable proportion of the overall HQ, including most of the General Staff, it was also far too close to the front line.

Monty was always against putting his Main HQ in some large building, as had been the practice in the Great War and, indeed, in the BEF in 1939/40, partly because he believed that it was an invitation to be bombed or shelled and partly because he thought that it would create a reluctance to move within a body of people who would, if all went to plan, frequently have to do just that. On the other hand, he found the Spartan conditions demanded by Auchinleck thoroughly counter-productive, with many of the staff sleeping like their C-in-C on the ground and a mess in which all the flies for miles around used to get trapped and which Monty called 'the meat safe'. Instead he demanded caravans for himself and the senior officers and tents for the remainder of the staff, with the offices likewise accommodated and a large and comfortable mess tent 'with a good cook, white tablecloths and shining cutlery'.[6]

---

* Appendix I.

Another signal had been sent off to GHQ on Monty's first day in the desert, this one asking for the best available soldier servant in the Middle East to be sent up at once. In the meantime, Corporal William English, who had worked previously for Neil Ritchie, was lent to Monty by Freddie and was liked by him so much that he stayed in the role for the rest of the war, whilst Freddie took on the new man, Corporal Alfred Lawrence. Another very longstanding non-commissioned member of the staff, with whom Monty had frequent contact and whom he trusted implicitly, was the highly efficient Chief Clerk, Sergeant (later Sergeant Major) Ernest Harwood, who worked for Freddie but was frequently used directly by Monty.

Monty also ordered that all officer postings out of HQ should be cancelled until he had evaluated the quality of the staff. Those concerned included Belchem, who had been due to leave for 9th Army in the Levant only two days later.

Monty could now begin to get to know his command. His approach was simple. Each day he would visit units and formations, on every occasion ordering that the men should gather round whilst he addressed them, introducing himself and then telling them in clear and uncompromising terms what he was proposing to do and where they would fit into the picture. Eighth Army had not been defeated in its current position and its morale was not as low as many have subsequently claimed, not least Monty himself, but it was puzzled at the position in which it found itself and it needed to be told unambiguously what was happening. The message of no further retreat and of new reinforcements went down well with everyone, whilst Monty's policy that battle groups were a thing of the past and that all divisions would now fight as a whole was warmly welcomed by their GOCs. Spirits and confidence rose very quickly all around the Army. To Churchill and Brooke, back in Egypt after meeting Stalin, the change was palpable and the CIGS wrote in his diary for 19 August that Monty 'gave me a wonderful feeling of relief at having got him out here'.[7]

In terms of raising his profile in the Army and to the general public, Monty was helped significantly by the Head of the Army Film & Photo Unit attached to Eighth Army, Captain Geoffrey Keating. A veteran of Norway, Dunkirk, Greece, Crete and Tobruk, Keating was not strictly a member of the staff, but he was in such frequent attendance on the Army Commander, including during dinners in the mess, that he was often treated as one, and was particularly liked by Monty, who regarded him as the court jester. Keating was not just making films and taking photos, he was in the forefront of developing what became a very successful public relations campaign. He was determined that the profile of the Army should be raised by his work and now, suddenly, he was presented with a gift horse in the shape of Monty. Unlike Auchinleck, Monty adored publicity and swiftly allowed Keating to begin the process of building him up into a national figure. Alan Whicker, who was to join AFPU in the field in Tunisia and to work closely with Keating, described Monty's reaction to the cameras: 'I spent some time with him during the war and always, as soon as he saw me, he'd start pointing at nothing in particular, but in a most commanding manner. It was his way and it seemed to work; half-a-century ago he had television-style fame, before television.'[8]

Keating had an initial problem, in that Monty was physically unprepossessing, short and with a rather pointed face and a high, rasping voice. The early photos of him in the desert, wearing shorts and an officer's cap, show him at a disadvantage to those around him. Help was at hand, however. On one of his early visits to 9 Australian Division he was presented with a slouch hat on which was pinned the badge of the Australian Military Force. At his next stop he was offered another badge and then another, until his hat was covered with them, making him instantly recognisable. A British general officer in Australian headgear was just what Keating needed to emphasize the Empire composition of the Army.

The slouch hat, however, turned out to be an impractical item of dress, particularly when getting in and out of vehicles. As the Army prepared for the battles ahead, Monty decided that he should have his own small battle group, composed of a squadron of the 6th Royal Tank Regiment, a troop of South African armoured cars and some infantry, which would allow him mobility around the whole battlefield. His own personal conveyance was to be a Grant tank, with his name painted on it,[9] which he would use on suitable occasions until he left the Mediterranean theatre in December 1943. The squadron commander invited John Poston to dinner and over a great deal of whisky explained that his regiment could not possibly entertain the idea of the Army Commander travelling in one of its tanks wearing a slouch hat. It was agreed that a spare black beret should be kept in the tank and, at the appropriate moment, when the slouch hat blew off, offered in exchange by the driver, Private Jim Fraser. This duly happened, and the black beret, to which was affixed not only his general's badge but also, and totally against regulations, that of the RTR, remained Monty's distinguishing signature garment thereafter. Keating now had the image he needed.

That this PR campaign began to raise the profile of Eighth Army in the UK and the Empire was important, but perhaps more so was its effect on morale in the Army itself. This was seized upon by the editor of the daily *Eighth Army News* and the weekly *Crusader*, Captain Warwick Charlton. Charlton immediately recognized that Monty could have an enormous personal impact and went out of his way to promote him. Monty, for his part, was happy to indulge Charlton and to protect him when some of his articles, and particularly his cartoons, attracted criticism from other senior officers.

Monty had not come to Egypt just to be photographed, however. He had come to fight and, very soon after his arrival and much as he had anticipated, that is just what he had to do.

Chapter Eight

Alam Halfa and After

Monty's first battle was fought less than three weeks after his arrival, much as he had been briefed by Freddie to expect. Although Rommel would be constrained for space by the Qattara Depression, intelligence from ULTRA, which was received on 17 August, confirmed that he would mount an attack from the southern end of his front in the full moon period at the end of the month, using the traditional right hook. There was subsequent controversy as to whether or not Auchinleck and Dorman-Smith had planned much the same battle, and there is certainly evidence that they realized the vital strategic position of the Alam Halfa Ridge. It is equally clear that, apart from digging defences for a brigade on the ridge, no further action had been taken by the time Monty arrived; indeed, two days beforehand Belchem had found only two Cypriot labour companies there.

Monty immediately assessed the situation and, together with Mainwaring and the Operations team and the recently arrived Horrocks, now commanding XIII Corps, began to make his dispositions. The Alam Halfa Ridge, 12 miles behind and almost at a right angle to the British front line, represented an obstacle to any attempt by the enemy to hook widely in a north-easterly direction and a threat to his left flank if he decided to advance directly to the east. Strongly garrisoned and with artillery and tanks covering the exits, it would constitute a considerable barrier. Monty's first move was to ask that 44 Division, newly arrived in Egypt, should be sent up immediately to provide the static garrison. There was some resistance from GHQ on the grounds that the division was still untrained, an observation which went down badly with both Monty and Horrocks, as it had been under their command in both XII Corps and South-Eastern Army. Accounts differ as to what happened, with both Monty and Freddie writing subsequently that Monty telephoned Alexander directly, whilst John Harding, still the DCGS, maintained that it was he who had spoken to the C-in-C and obtained his approval for the move. Either way, 44 Division arrived very quickly, Belchem having spent a whole night making the necessary arrangements, and its infantry brigades were positioned on and to the east of the ridge, with both the divisional artillery and additional guns from XIII Corps placed within the divisional perimeter.

The main fighting force, however, came from Eighth Army's armoured brigades. The most important position, on the south-western end of the ridge, was

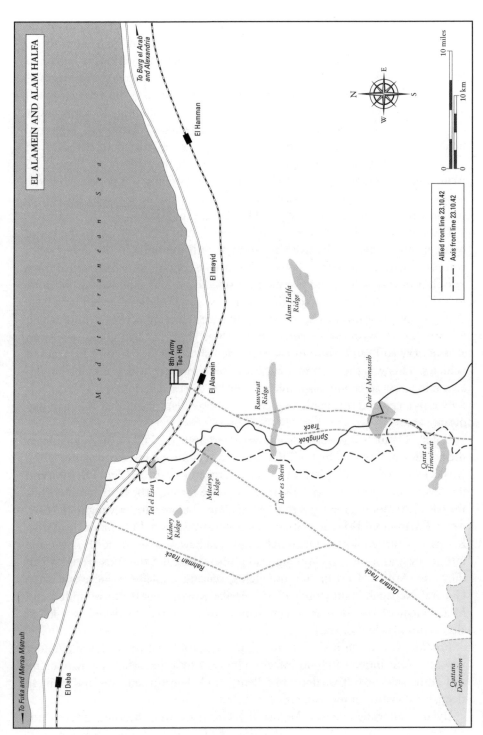

EL ALAMEIN AND ALAM HALFA

Mediterranean Sea

To Fuka and Mersa Matruh

El Daba

To Burg el Arab
and Alexandria

El Hamman

El Imayid

8th Army
Tac HQ

El Alamein

Tel el Eisa

Kidney Ridge

Rahman Track

Miteirya Ridge

Ruweisat Ridge

Deir es Shein

Springbok Track

Alam Halfa Ridge

Deir el Munassib

Qarat el Himeimat

Qattara Track

Qattara Depression

— Allied front line 23.10.42
- - - Axis front line 23.10.42

N
W   E
S

0   10 km
0   10 miles

Map 2.

held by 22 Armoured Brigade, its Grant tanks dug in on broken ground on the slopes, with anti-tank guns concealed on an area of flat ground in front of them. Pip Roberts, the brigade commander, was given explicit instructions to remain in his positions and to resist the temptation to attack if the Germans showed signs of retreating. The Grants of 8 Armoured Brigade were located to the east to forestall any attempt to move around that side of the ridge, and both brigades came under the command of 10 Armoured Division. Meanwhile, 7 Armoured Division, holding the southernmost sector of the front, was instructed to withdraw in the face of an attack, but to harass the attackers as they advanced. Finally, 23 Armoured Brigade, equipped with Valentine infantry tanks, was positioned to the north-west of the ridge to forestall any attempt to reach the sea along the rear of the British front line, as had been tried by Rommel at Gazala.

Freddie now made what proved to be a significant contribution to the battle by deploying a ruse to deceive the Germans. All the units in the desert were equipped with 'going maps' showing the surface conditions, which varied from gravel, providing a firm and fast base for vehicles, to soft sand, which was next to impassable, with variable conditions in between. Freddie arranged for a false 'going map' to be produced, on which one area running across a route which Monty did not wish the Germans to take was shown as bad going, whilst an area of very soft sand south of the ridge was shown as satisfactory for tracked vehicles. This was then left in a rucksack in a scout car, which was 'blown up' on a mine near an enemy position, its crew being evacuated intact. The car was duly ransacked and it was discovered by a subsequent patrol that the map had disappeared.

Rommel launched his offensive in great strength at 23.00 on 30 August from the position anticipated by ULTRA, where a very strong force consisting of the Afrika Korps of 15 and 21 Panzer Divisions, together with 90 Light Division and the Ariete and Littorio Divisions began to move through the British minefields. Initially, 7 Armoured Division put up resistance, before withdrawing to the east, while 4 Armoured Brigade's Stuart tanks harassed the right flank of the Afrika Korps as it turned north. The much improved liaison with the RAF now came into its own as a force of Wellington bombers attacked the Axis troops when they were still tied up in the minefields, scoring immediate successes when General Nehring, commander of the Afrika Korps, was badly wounded and Major General von Bismarck, commander of 21 Panzer Division, was killed along with his chief of staff.

Freddie was woken just after midnight to be told that the attack was under way and went immediately to inform Monty 'I told him what was happening and all he said was "Excellent, excellent," and then turned over and went to sleep, breakfasting at his usual time.'[1]

By mid-afternoon on 31 August the Germans were heading directly for 22 Armoured Brigade, much as Monty had expected. The tank regiment furthest forward suffered significant damage and Roberts was forced to call on his reserve, but by the time that darkness fell, it was clear that the Germans had failed to make any serious penetration. On the following day they tried again, and 23 Armoured Brigade was brought forward to cover a perceived threat, but by that evening all the surviving enemy tanks had withdrawn out of range; of those left on the battlefield a number had become bogged down in soft sand after following the false 'going map'. On the morning of 3 September Rommel decided to withdraw.

In accordance with Monty's strict instructions, no pursuit by the British armour was attempted, but 2 New Zealand Division was ordered to cut off the Axis retreat, supported by a British infantry brigade. Whilst the New Zealand force had some success, the attack of the British brigade, inexperienced in the desert, was a disaster, and the Germans completed their withdrawal in reasonable order. With this exception the battle had been gone entirely to plan. It was a genuine victory, unlike Rommel's withdrawal at the end of Operation CRUSADER, which was largely the result of serious supply problems.

Monty could now turn his attention to preparing Eighth Army for the set-piece offensive operation which he had already worked out clearly in his mind. In the first instance this meant training, invariably a vital ingredient in his recipe for success. Training Memorandum No. 1, issued shortly after his arrival in Egypt to his staff, to the corps commanders for onward transmission to their divisions and to the RAF, set out his ideas very clearly. After emphasizing close cooperation with the RAF from the start, it set out four 'Basic Points': the effective stage management of battles, which had to be understood by all officers; the requirement for individual unit and sub-unit efficiency, emphasizing in particular the need for a high standard of junior leadership; the inculcation of fighting spirit in all ranks and the use of battle drill. The last of these sometimes attracted criticism in that it could lead to the loss of initiative if followed too slavishly, but Monty made the point that it should be the servant and not the master of operations.

These four points were followed by two 'Golden Rules': first, if the situation was vague and indefinite, then reconnaissance, concentration of force and the possession of ground providing an advantage over the enemy were essential; second, gaining and keeping the initiative by vigorous offensive action was vital at all times.

Monty continued by emphasizing that divisions would in future fight as divisions and not in brigade groups, that their artillery would be centralized under one commander, and that infantry, artillery and anti-tank guns should be prepared to hold vital ground as 'pivots', allowing the armour to have greater freedom of action, all with the objective of dominating the battle area. He emphasized 'the intimate cooperation of all arms' in all formations, the effective exercise of command and control, which might demand the use of small tactical

HQs, the absolute need for all troops to be able to operate at night and the duty of COs to train their own officers. He accepted that difficulties would arise during the implementation of his training regime, but concluded with the words, 'bellyaching is definitely forbidden in Eighth Army'.

The emphasis on the role of the COs of individual units, and particularly those on the front line, was central to Monty's philosophy. They were the lynch-pins around whom were developed his concepts of unit efficiency, officer training, junior leadership and fighting spirit. He had long thought that many of those in command at this level were too old for a modern war and, whilst in England, had ruthlessly weeded out the physically unfit. In Eighth Army he took the trouble to get to know not only the commanding officers of battalions and regiments, but also their seconds-in-command and the brigade majors of every brigade. He also began to make a note of those majors who had distinguished themselves in battle so that, when a unit CO was killed, wounded, proved unsatisfactory or was promoted, he would have his own ideas as to the succession. He insisted on all appointments of lieutenant colonel and above being approved personally by him, and thus a key member of his staff was the Deputy Assistant Military Secretary, who was responsible for coming up with recommendations and actioning all officer appointments. At Eighth Army this was Major C. A. R. 'Shrimp' Coghill, who would remain with him for most of the war.

The importance to Monty of lieutenant colonels was emphasized by his insistence on bringing them all into his confidence prior to a battle. As Charles Richardson was to say later:

> Unlike the previous regime, he actually summoned all the officers taking part down to Lt. Col., and told them exactly how he wanted the battle to go, what their individual responsibilities were, how long the battle would last and so on and so on ... Monty you may say over-simplified, but this was very effective for subordinate commanders because they had to follow a simple and well-mapped path throughout that battle.[2]

Alam Halfa was unquestionably Monty's battle in its conception and outline planning, but the detailed dispositions had been made and the battle itself was controlled by Horrocks, who had performed extremely capably. On the other hand, Monty was not satisfied with Ramsden at XXX Corps, and he now asked for Oliver Leese, commanding Guards Armoured Division in the UK, to be sent out. Leese had been one of his students at Staff College and Monty had kept a close eye on his progress subsequently. His appointment as DCGS at HQ BEF on 10 May 1940, the very day that the Germans attacked in the West, had imposed a semblance of order on what Monty considered was a most unsatisfactory organization, and he was subsequently credited with devising the plan which resulted in the successful evacuation of the army at Dunkirk. With XXX Corps destined to play the key role in the forthcoming operation, Monty needed a trusted subordinate at its helm, and Leese fitted the bill admirably.

Monty was not so sure about the command of X Corps, the *corps de chasse* which John Harding had devised on the day of his arrival in Egypt. He had originally identified Horrocks for the role, as he had commanded an armoured division in Home Forces, but Horrocks had been persuaded by Dick McCreery, now Alexander's Chief of Staff, that the job should go to McCreery's fellow 12th Lancer, Herbert Lumsden, who had commanded an armoured division in the desert since late 1941. Monty, whose only experience of Lumsden was as the commander of his regiment of armoured cars in France in 1940, was not entirely convinced but against his better judgement he allowed himself to be swayed by Horrocks.[3]

The much vaunted *corps de chasse* would turn out to be a very different formation from that which Monty had originally conceived, partly through circumstance and partly because of the way in which it was used in due course. Of the four divisions identified by Harding, 2 New Zealand Division was required for the main infantry assault in Monty's forthcoming battle, whilst 8 Armoured Division never had the chance to come up to full strength: it had lost its support group as a result of the general reorganization of armoured divisions in the summer of 1942, but never saw it replaced by an infantry brigade. One by one, other units – notably its armoured car regiment, one of its RE field squadrons and one of its field artillery regiments – were withdrawn to make up numbers elsewhere. This left 1 Armoured Division, from which Lumsden had been promoted, and 10 Armoured Division, the latter having only completed its conversion from horsed cavalry earlier that year.

It was soon evident that Lumsden and Monty were unlikely to see eye to eye. Their different approaches to armoured warfare were demonstrated after Alam Halfa, when Lumsden visited Alec Gatehouse, GOC of 10 Armoured Division, demanding to know why Rommel had not been pursued during his retreat. Gatehouse explained Monty's explicit order to hold firm, which Lumsden refused to believe, leaving the meeting clearly angered. The differences of opinion between Monty and his armoured corps commander would emerge again at a more critical moment.

Matters were much happier when it came to the relationship with the RAF, especially after their performance at Alam Halfa. It is far from the truth to say that Auchinleck had never really understood the importance of ground/air cooperation: he enjoyed very good relations with his opposite number, as had Ritchie with his whilst in command of Eighth Army. He had, however, not accorded it the same priority as Monty, who had written at the beginning of Training Memorandum No. 1 that the air force staff should be brought in on all operations at the very beginning and that the air plan, involving the achievement of air superiority, reconnaissance, the bombing of enemy supply lines and the provision of ground support, required the closest coordination with the military plan.

The two most senior RAF commanders were to remain associated with Monty throughout the rest of the war, but what began as a congenial relationship was to sour dramatically over the next three years. The most senior airman was Air Chief Marshal Sir Arthur Tedder, the Air C-in-C. Tedder had arrived in the Middle East in November 1940 as deputy to the then C-in-C, Air Chief Marshal Longmore, and had succeeded to the top job in June 1941. His experience of the theatre was thus immense and he had been highly successful in building up the air arm from a tiny force, largely equipped with obsolete aircraft, to one which was close to establishing air superiority over the Luftwaffe and the Italian Regia Aeronautica.

Monty's own opposite number was the AOC Western Desert Air Force, Air Vice-Marshal Arthur 'Mary'[4] Coningham, a New Zealander responsible for all tactical operations in conjunction with Eighth Army. Coningham had set out clear priorities: first, to achieve air superiority, then to use that to destroy the enemy's supply lines and finally to provide close support to the Army on the battlefield. Whilst Coningham was as wedded to cooperation as Monty, he jealously guarded the independence of the RAF and insisted on it taking its own decisions. Like Monty he was a prima donna, and their characters were predestined to clash before very long.

A third senior RAF officer would in due course become closer to Monty than either Tedder or Coningham and would remain his strong supporter when the others turned into critics. Air Commodore Harry Broadhurst had just arrived to be Coningham's Senior Air Staff Officer, Freddie's opposite number. Coningham had not wanted him in the role and neither had Tedder, but the Air Ministry had insisted, so the atmosphere was somewhat cool between them, especially when Broadhurst began to question Coningham's continued focus on air superiority, which Broadhurst believed had already been achieved. Monty, on the other hand, who had met Broadhurst at a lecture at Army Air Command in the UK shortly before leaving for Egypt, had taken to him and welcomed him most warmly.

Monty's determination to work hand-in-hand with the RAF had led directly to the siting of his HQ next to theirs at Burg el Arab, and it was there that a new level of close cooperation began, one which would stand the test of time. The GSO1 (Ops) and the Wing Commander (Ops) had their offices next to each other, using the same wireless and maps and relying on the same Intelligence; indeed, the arrangement of the caravans and tents also incorporated the G (I) offices. The improved communication paid dividends at Alam Halfa, during which Mainwaring and his opposite number proved its potential beyond doubt.

The key man on the Eighth Army team was Major Jock McNeill. A gunner by profession, McNeill had been appointed to command No. 2 Army Air

Support Control ('AASC') in the UK in late 1941. The AASCs consisted initially of a GSO2 in command, a Captain (GS) and a Captain (Royal Signals) and approximately 70 men, over a third of whom were signallers. The latter operated wireless tentacles attached to the HQs of divisions and brigades. There was also a RAF signals section which operated a similar network connected to Air Liaison Officers ('ALOs') at the various airfields. McNeill's 2 AASC had arrived in the Middle East when the Army was still on the Gazala Line. It had subsequently been enlarged by absorbing 5 AASC, and it was as 2/5 AASC that it was co-located with the Operations Rooms of Eighth Army and the Western Desert Air Force, effectively fulfilling the duties of what subsequently became the G (Air) branch.

The AASC at Army HQ dealt with target requests from its own signallers with the forward troops and also with changes in bomb lines, tactical reconnaissance reports, reports on enemy aircraft and reports from the RAF on the position of enemy tanks. When target requests were received, G (Ops) was immediately consulted on potential conflicts with current operations and the priorities for air support. Whilst this was happening a warning order was issued to the RAF wings which were placed on stand-by and in which ALOs were available to clarify the situation on the ground to their RAF colleagues. RAF (Ops) would then accept or refuse the target and, if accepted, would receive the estimated time of arrival of the strike from the Wing concerned, which would be transmitted to the originator of the request. The urgency of the requests meant that the messages were often sent in clear rather than code, in spite of the fact that the Germans might be listening in.

The system put in place by McNeill and his RAF colleagues worked well at Alam Halfa and, as the campaign unfolded, ground/air cooperation would steadily become more sophisticated. It would, however, be some time before the tactics were evolved which would go on to make a major impact in North-West Europe in 1944/5 and then only after some serious disagreements within the RAF.

One of Monty's other concerns, the employment of the artillery, was also subject to radical change, following Kirkman's arrival in early September[5] to be his BRA. Kirkman was horrified by what he found, describing it later as 'chaos'.[6] Some divisions still retained brigade groups, with their artillery decentralized and their CRAs unsure at any one time where their units were. There was a serious shortage of wireless sets, so that communication was difficult and sometimes impossible. There was also little understanding of how to cooperate with the armour, not helped by the attitude of Lumsden and some of his divisional commanders. This had been to a significant extent the result of the poor performance of the British 2-pounder anti-tank gun, which had for some time lacked the velocity to penetrate German tanks. The result was that the British infantry wanted their own tanks, with their 75mm guns, to defend them against German attacks, whilst the tanks themselves preferred to be able to manoeuvre and not to be pinned down in static defensive positions. Now, however, the new 6-pounders, with a much improved performance, were arriving in large numbers to equip divisional anti-tank regiments, but there was as yet little understanding of the most effective tactics for deploying them.

Monty's explicit instructions that divisions should fight as such and not be divided into brigade groups meant that Kirkman was able to reassert the authority of the CRAs over all the divisional artillery, but considerable training was required to ensure that the bad habits of the past were forgotten. This fitted in well with Kirkman's overriding order from Monty, which was to ensure that the artillery plan for the forthcoming offensive battle was to be the best possible. Having issued this instruction, Monty never referred to it again. Kirkman raised a number of questions during the process, but Monty never once enquired how the plan was coming along, reposing complete faith in his BRA to do what was necessary.

Kirkman's Royal Engineer counterpart, Fred Kisch, had a different set of problems, which revolved largely around how to tackle the minefields. Any frontal attack, which is just what Monty was proposing, would have to be delivered by the attacking infantry on cleared paths though the formidable defences and by the armour on corridors wide enough to take tanks and self-propelled guns. The general location of the enemy minefields was known, but the distribution of the mines was not, and these would, for the most part, have to be lifted by hand. There was a considerable body of experience available, but it had not been consolidated in any way for dissemination to the RE field squadrons who would have to carry out the job. Kisch called a conference of all the corps and divisional CRE's, the upshot of which was the establishment near the Main HQ at Burg el Arab of the Eighth Army School of Mine Clearance, which held eight-day courses for as many sappers as possible.

A formal drill was introduced, including the use of mine detectors, techniques for lifting mines and laying tapes to mark safe passageways, as well as processes for delineating wider gaps and organizing both signposts and direction by Military Police to steer units through them. For the first time 'flail' tanks were introduced, albeit in small numbers. These were Matildas with drums attached to their fronts from which dangled wire ropes which, as the drums spun, detonated the mines. By the middle of October, most of those selected to be engaged in this highly dangerous work had passed through the School, which dramatically improved the performance of the mine-clearance teams.

Monty now had the HQ where he wanted it in order to prepare for the forthcoming battle and he was broadly satisfied with its composition. There was one missing element, however, which catered for the spiritual rather than the physical well-being of the Army. As the son of a bishop himself, he had very firm views on the value of religion at a time of war and he was determined that this should not be neglected. He believed that God was on his side and frequently alluded to Him in his Orders of the Day, leading one cynic to remark, 'I see that the Almighty, from being "in support", is now firmly "under command"!'[7] Monty himself was to write later:

> I also wanted a first-class chaplain. After considerable investigation we found the man I wanted in Hughes, who was the senior chaplain to a division. I never regretted that choice ... He was the ideal of what an Army padre should be and became one of my greatest friends.[8]

Llewellyn Hughes had served in the Great War, during which he won the MC as an infantry officer, later becoming a Territorial Army chaplain. He was to stay with Monty for the rest of the war.

Chapter Nine

Intelligence and Deception

Intelligence and Deception are two sides of the same coin and both are as old as war itself. In the British Army, Military Intelligence – the obtaining of information on the enemy's intentions and the prediction of his likely actions – had been recognized as a discrete activity in the War Office since 1873, when an Intelligence Branch was set up to pull together information on the major foreign powers. In the reorganization of the War Office at the beginning of the twentieth century, Intelligence was firmly established as one of the key branches of the General Staff, although it was frequently combined with Operations. It also spawned some offshoots, notably MI5, dealing with counter-intelligence, and MI6, dealing with overseas intelligence. The Intelligence Corps was formed in 1914, only to be disbanded in 1929. It was re-formed again in the summer of 1940, but in spite of substantial growth in its numbers, most intelligence officers, and especially those in the field, did not belong to the Corps and had no specialized intelligence background or training, but were appointed from outside. This gave rise to a strong element of amateurishness in the work, exemplified by Auchinleck's appointment of the inexperienced Freddie to the post of DMI Middle East in early 1942. Although some of the basics were taught at Staff College, it seemed to many that all that was required was a keen intellect and an enquiring mind. These qualities were indeed vital, but without the many tedious hours of disciplined sifting and sieving through all the sources, they were not enough in themselves.

In the field there was an Intelligence staff in all formations from army groups to brigades, and there were Intelligence Officers in battalions and regiments. At Eighth Army in September 1942, the establishment consisted of twelve officers and thirty-seven other ranks. The GSO1 (I) was still 'Spud' Murphy, whilst Bill Williams was one of four GSO2s, another of whom was responsible specifically for RAF liaison. The numbers fluctuated slightly, but remained at much the same level throughout the North African campaign.

Monty very quickly identified Williams as an Intelligence officer of some quality and, according to his memoirs, resolved at a very early stage that he would head up his Intelligence staff, although this was not to happen for many months. Newly promoted from captain to major, a mere 29 years old and a 'hostilities-only' officer, he was not ready for such a promotion at the time, but

Monty was never one to let age or background stand in the way of putting the right man in the right job.

Part of the attraction of Williams to Monty was that he was the guardian of ULTRA, having been 'indoctrinated' into the most important secret of the war whilst working at GHQ. How much Monty himself knew about ULTRA before his arrival in Egypt is not known, but his position as an army commander in the UK would almost certainly have put him on the list of recipients. The gift to him, not long after his arrival at Eighth Army, of Rommel's plan for Alam Halfa, which turned out to be correct in every detail other than a two-day delay due to a lack of petrol, made a considerable impression. Quite apart from the blow rendered to the Axis forces, the victory immediately bolstered the new commander's reputation within Eighth Army and lifted morale as only success can do. In fact, although ULTRA continued to produce highly valuable information which had a material impact on Monty's approach to this and future campaigns, on only one future occasion, at Medenine in February 1943, would it be quite so precise in its accuracy.

That ULTRA was never once compromised was one of the great achievements of the war. It was only available to higher commands, army groups and armies, but even then the combined number of people in on the secret was very large. At the army level, the intelligence was handled by a separate group within the Intelligence branch known as the Special Liaison Unit ('SLU').[1] This group had separate offices from the rest of G (I) and was staffed by both officers and other ranks, who included the cipher clerks and signallers. It was the signallers who received the signals from Bletchley Park. The sender and the receiver had identical 'one-time pads', and the former would indicate which of the tear-off sheets on the pad was to be used. The cipher clerks would then use the specific data on the sheet to decipher the signal before destroying the sheet. It was effective and safe, but relatively slow. Later in the war, Typex machines were introduced, which radically improved the speed of deciphering.

It was, however, all too easy to misuse ULTRA. As Williams was later to write:

> It should not be necessary to stress the value of the material in shaping the general intelligence of the war. Yet it should be emphasized from the outset that the material was dangerously valuable not only because we might lose it but also because it seemed the answer to an Intelligence Officer's prayer. Yet by providing this answer it was likely to save the officer from doing Intelligence. Instead of being the best, it tended to become the only, source. There was a tendency at all times to await the next message and, often, to be fascinated by the authenticity of the information into failing to think whether it was significant at the particular level at which it was being considered ... The information purveyed was so remarkable

that it tended, particularly if one was tired or overbusy, to engulf not only all other sources but that very common sense which forms the basis of Intelligence.[2]

Williams's background as an academic now came into play. Accustomed to weighing all the evidence, not just that obtained from a single source, he was well equipped to handle ULTRA with precisely the level of respect it deserved:

At an Army HQ we maintained ... that during battle we had not done our day's work properly unless we had beaten the ULTRA, unless we knew what was happening and could appreciate what would happen before it could arrive. This did not mean that we were not glad of its arrival, for at best it showed that we were wrong, usually it enabled us to tidy up the loose ends and at worst we tumbled into bed with a smug confirmation.[3]

If ULTRA was a gift to Monty, then Monty was a gift to his Intelligence staff. He believed the Intelligence which they were providing, but he made it his own as far as others were concerned, thereby providing just the level of cover needed. Only he and Freddie, who had been indoctrinated whilst serving as DMI at GHQ Middle East, saw the naked material. For further consumption by corps commanders and others, an appropriate gloss was put on the regular Intelligence appreciations received from Army HQ in order to conceal its origins. The only other people aware of it were an equally small number of RAF Intelligence staff, with whom a conference was held nightly to agree how it should be disseminated.

Freddie was only too aware of the way in which ULTRA should be handled from the experiences and eventual fate of his predecessor as DMI, John Shearer. ULTRA had been available from the beginning of the North African campaign and had enabled Shearer to predict accurately the ability of Rommel to attack for the first time in March 1941. On that occasion Wavell had not believed the evidence, based on his own appreciation of the logistical difficulties facing his enemy. Subsequently, Shearer himself had come to grief through an overoptimistic interpretation of ULTRA in early 1942. Freddie was not going to allow the same mistakes to be made.

ULTRA was far from being the only source of Intelligence. A close cousin was the Y-Service, which covered all day-to-day interception of enemy radio and, to a much lesser extent, telephone traffic. In addition to the SLU, there was a dedicated Y-Service detachment at Army HQ, which operated under similar levels of secrecy, although its existence and the nature of its work were widely recognized. Its origins lay in the formation of the Government Code and Cypher School in 1919, known as Station X and more familiarly as Bletchley Park. By late 1942 the school's establishment had grown from some 150 at the outbreak of war to about 3,500 and it was to increase very substantially over the next three years. Always associated with ULTRA, in fact it handled all types of signal intelligence and even had its own cryptanalytical outpost at Middle East Command, known as the Combined Bureau. In both Cairo and Bletchley Y-Service work was carried out on the decryption of German and Italian codes and cyphers.

During the course of a battle the Y-Service tended to become more important than ULTRA, as the Enigma machines were not used to the same extent at the tactical level, where relatively low level codes and cyphers were employed. Moreover, by the use of direction finders, the Y-Service could also monitor the movements of enemy units and formations. Williams considered that it helped significantly to build up the day-to-day knowledge of the enemy which enabled his staff to handle ULTRA with more confidence. For his part he took care to ensure that the Y-Service staff were fully appraised of all other intelligence being received, with the sole exception of ULTRA.

Other sources of intelligence were, in fact, vital. Perhaps the most important of these was aerial photo-reconnaissance. Although it was still some distance from the highly sophisticated activity of the last two years of the war, photo-reconnaissance had come on a long way since 1940. There were as yet no specialized Mosquito aircraft in the theatre, although Tedder had asked for them, but light bombers, particularly the Martin Marylands operated by the South African Air Force, were doing very good high-level strategic reconnaissance work, largely from an altitude of 25,000 feet, whilst low-level tactical reconnaissance was still being carried out by Hurricanes. Between them they managed to contribute significantly to building a picture of the location of the Axis formations and units.

On the ground, the best intelligence had, from the beginning of the campaign, been obtained from the Long Range Desert Group. This was essentially a covert organization, sending its patrols across the wide expanses of desert behind enemy lines to monitor enemy movements whilst concealing its presence, although it did on some occasions attack Axis targets or provide transport for others to do so. During the period up to the end of July 1942 it had kept a watch on the only metalled road between Tripoli and Benghazi, but the rapid German advance to El Alamein had forced it to move its base from the Siwa Oasis, west of the Qattara depression, much further south to the Kufra Oasis, from where such operations, although still carried out, were much more difficult to mount. It would not be until the advance had started in November that the LRDG would come fully into its own once again.

The other major source of intelligence was prisoners of war. Whilst the armies were facing each other across the line at El Alamein, these were relatively few, although patrols would sometimes manage to snatch some, the interrogation of whom would add to the tapestry of Intelligence being patiently built up. Once the battle had begun, they became more plentiful and provided some useful corroboration of other sources.

In the nearly two months between the Battles of Alam Halfa and El Alamein, Eighth Army built up a very accurate picture of the location of the Axis formations. The fear now was that the enemy would also build a similarly accurate picture of Eighth Army, giving them advance notice of where and when a new offensive might strike. A deception plan was required to throw them off the scent, and Monty put Charles Richardson in charge of developing it.

Deception was used at all stages of campaigns, but played a particularly significant role in the run-up to major operations. It would reach its apogee with the highly complex and outstandingly successful Operation FORTITUDE before and immediately after the landings in Normandy in 1944, but even in 1942 it was far from being a new concept. In the Middle East the specialists were concentrated not at Army HQ but at GHQ Middle East, in the persons of Colonel Dudley Clarke, whose 'A' Force had had great success in the past, through a variety of ruses, in persuading the Axis that Eighth Army was much larger than it actually was, and Colonel Geoffrey Barkas, the Director of Camouflage. Richardson and these two men now collaborated on Operation BERTRAM.

The main element of Monty's plan for the next battle was a concentrated attack by four of the five infantry divisions of XXX Corps, through which the two armoured divisions of X Corps would then be passed, all on a front of less than ten miles at the far north of the line. The purpose of Operation BERTRAM was to persuade the enemy that that attack would take place in the south, where Rommel would in any event be more likely to expect it, and that its timing would be two or more days later than it was actually planned to begin. It did so by concealing Eighth Army's real intentions and moves and by providing false information, primarily for the benefit of aerial reconnaissance.

The first problem was the arrival of two new divisions, 51 Highland and 2 New Zealand, in the XXX Corps sector. Long before the date of the attack, the administrative transport of XXX Corps was visibly dispersed in positions which would in due course be occupied by the operational transport of the two divisions, and a gradual switch took place in such a way that the overall numbers did not increase. When the infantry arrived close to D-Day, they were concealed during the day in slit trenches which had been dug a month earlier. Dummy 3-ton lorries were erected in the positions to be occupied by the field artillery, each of which covered a gun and its limber, whilst the quads (gun tractors) were similarly disguised.

The next task was to conceal 2,000 tons of POL (Petrol, Oil & Lubricants), 3,000 tons of ammunition, 1,000 tons of engineer and ordnance stores and 600 tons of other supplies. Most were dealt with by adding very gradually to, but also camouflaging, existing dumps well known to the enemy; but a new site, fully camouflaged, was also constructed on hummocky ground near El Imayid, close to the sea some miles behind the front line. Vehicles and tents on the existing dumps were replaced by supply stacks camouflaged to look the same. POL was hidden in slit trenches which had been in existence for at least a year. At the same time, visible dummy dumps were set up in the southern area.

The most difficult problem was how to conceal six additional tracks leading up to the front from the assembly area 25 miles to the rear, which were being built under the orders of Fred Kisch. There was no good solution other than to delay construction, particularly in the forward areas, to as close as possible to D-Day and to mount constant fighter patrols during daylight hours to deter enemy reconnaissance. All road traffic in the north was strictly controlled by day, whilst traffic in the south was increased. A dummy water pipeline was also constructed to the southern sector, making slow progress, so that by D-Day it was still many miles away.

Notwithstanding that XIII Corps in the south would play a relatively minor role, Monty proposed to attack there to keep the German panzer divisions away from his main thrust. It was thus necessary to increase the artillery establishment in order to break through the minefields. To conceal this, a double bluff was arranged, whereby obviously dummy guns were put in position, to be replaced by the real thing close to D-Day.

The forward move of X Corps from its training area at Wadi el Natrun was staggered. The initial move to a staging area to the south was carried out openly in daylight, which suggested that it might be joining XIII Corps. On the night of D-3 the corps moved north again to an assembly area behind XXX Corps, its place in the staging area filled by exactly the same number of disguised lorries and dummy tanks and guns. Wireless sets were left behind which continued normal working under Clarke's 'A' Force, whilst wireless restrictions were applied to the real divisions.

Richardson was determined that Operation BERTRAM should be highly disciplined. After expressing concern to Freddie that its importance might not be well understood, he was provided with a letter from Monty to each of the corps commanders, explaining what would be happening and instructing them to comply with all of Richardson's plans, regardless of the inconveniences which were likely to be experienced. In the event, all went well, except that a fierce dust storm destroyed a number of the dummy vehicles, literally blowing many away and requiring the camouflage team to work all through the night to restore the situation.

Operation BERTRAM was a successful collaboration between Main HQ Eighth Army and GHQ Middle East and, at the staff level, the relationship between the two was excellent, helped not a little by Freddie's character and that fact that he, and others like Williams, had worked in the latter. There was, however, considerable resentment at GHQ about the way in which Alexander was treated by Monty. Alex was profoundly useful to Monty, both because he kept the politicians in London and Cairo off his back and because he oversaw the organization which provided all the army's material and human resource requirements. The Eighth Army Commander did not, however, rate his superior's military skills at all highly and had not done so since he had taught him at Staff College. Monty tended to treat Alexander as a facilitator, willing and able to provide whatever Eighth Army needed, as the speedy arrival of 44 Division at Alam Halfa had demonstrated. He neither sought nor listened to any advice on how to fight the battle and he could on occasion be abrupt with and sometimes downright rude to Alex. This went down very badly with the senior officers at GHQ, notably Dick McCreery, Alex's Chief of Staff, who had been sacked by Auchinleck for disagreeing with his proposals for the use of armour, only to be selected by Brooke to replace Corbett. McCreery, a strong character, stood up to Monty in a way which Alexander was not prepared to do and incurred his displeasure accordingly.

The relationship between Monty and Alex certainly allowed the former uncommonly free rein. Alex was, if nothing else, a pragmatist. As McCreery wrote after the war, he took the view that, 'There is only one active army in my command and Montgomery is in command of it. The essence of my job here is to support him in every way I can, to handle all the political problems involved with many allies and to let him get on with the battle.' The resentment lingered, but it was narrowly directed at Monty himself. Neither Freddie nor McCreery, outstanding staff officers with a common objective, let it get in the way of their cooperation.

Chapter Ten

Lightfoot and Supercharge

Two days before the start of Monty's offensive, Eighth Army's Tactical HQ – referred to as Tac HQ or simply Tac – opened on a site between the coast road and the sea, about ten miles behind the front line and very close to both the Main HQ of XXX Corps and the Tac HQ of X Corps. There was nothing particularly new about Tactical or Advanced HQs, which had been adopted earlier in the campaign by all the commanders of Eighth Army. This one, however, was organized on a very different basis from that to which the old Eighth Army hands had become accustomed. Cunningham, Ritchie and Auchinleck had included all the key members of the General Staff and some administrative staff at their Advanced Headquarters. Monty wanted none of this. The permanent establishment of officers in the first instance was two GSO2s, one of whom was placed in overall charge, two GSO3s, the officer in command of the signals detachment and the officer in command of an armoured car troop from the Derbyshire Yeomanry, together with Monty's ADCs and Liaison Officers. There were thirty to forty vehicles, including Monty's staff car, jeeps for the ADCs and personal LOs, an Armoured Command Vehicle for the small operations staff, caravans, signal vehicles, mobile cookhouses, lorries and armoured cars. Monty still had his Grant tank, which was good for photo opportunities and morale, but the personal battle group on which he had placed such emphasis soon after he arrived was nowhere to be seen, probably and rightly accepted as too unwieldy a body for an army commander who was intent on making flying visits to all parts of his command.

The officer in charge of Tac was John Oswald, a regular gunner with experience of staff work both at GHQ Middle East and in the field. He had arrived at Eighth Army HQ on the day before Monty took command from his previous appointment as a GSO2 at 5 Indian Division, which had been heavily engaged in the July battles on the Alamein line. One possible reason for his selection to run Tac was that he had once commanded a 'Jock column'[1] and was thus well versed in the sort of mobility which Monty would require once he was on the move.

Two messes were established, one for Monty, his personal staff and Oswald, the other for all the other officers. Only the most distinguished visitors and the most senior staff from Main HQ were entertained in the former; all others, of whatever rank, had to use the latter. Visitors in any event were banned except by invitation from Monty or with the express permission of G (Ops) at Main HQ, on the grounds that Monty did not want any unnecessary distractions.

Tac was the visible expression of Monty's philosophy of battlefield command. He required at all times an up-to-the-minute feel for the battle, and the only way in which he could achieve this was by frequent visits to his subordinate commanders or by sending members of his personal staff, who would report back to him daily. When back at Tac he needed time to think without being disturbed. His only relaxation was dinner with his ADCs and other selected officers, for the most part much younger than himself. From this point onwards he would spend almost no time at his Main HQs, the exceptions being during the brief pauses at Benghazi and Tripoli, the period between the end of the campaign in North Africa and the invasion of Sicily, and the five months of preparation for Operation OVERLORD.

The disadvantage of the system was precisely that Monty was physically and mentally distant from Main HQ, which housed substantially all the G staff, a much smaller proportion of the Q staff and representatives of the A staff responsible for casualties and reinforcements. He was in radio contact with Freddie every day and the Chief of Staff was a frequent visitor to Tac, where he kept a permanent caravan, as did Coningham of the RAF, whilst certain other officers, notably Williams, were regularly called up for meetings; but as the distances between the two HQs were often considerable, this was arguably not a good use of time. Monty met the rest of his senior staff infrequently, and those on the logistics side tended only to be summoned when there was a crisis of supply. To avoid surprises, Freddie charged Oswald with the responsibility for keeping him at all times abreast of 'Master's' actions and intentions.

The system would only have worked with an outstanding Chief of Staff, prepared to accept all the responsibility for the detailed work, and backed up by highly capable subordinates. Monty himself, once he had established confidence in any individual, was the last person to breathe down his neck. To some on the staff this could seem like lack of interest in their work, and indeed there was a strong element of this as far as the detail was concerned, to the extent that only once in the North African campaign was Monty persuaded to enter the Armoured Command Vehicle which housed the operations team at the very centre of Tac. Even then, it was only to shake hands briefly with those who worked there. He almost never appeared at Rear HQ, which housed almost all the A and the majority of the Q staff.

A major ingredient in Monty's system was his personal staff. At El Alamein, with XXX Corps located in a very concentrated area and XIII Corps some distance away but playing a secondary role, only a small number of officers were required. These were the ADCs and an additional Liaison Officer. The latter had received a personal summons shortly after Monty's arrival in Egypt. Lieutenant Carol Mather had been one of the early volunteers for the

Commandos. He had come to the Middle East with No. 8 Commando, which was badly misused and eventually disbanded. Mather then joined Phantom, the GHQ Liaison Regiment, before being recruited into the fledgling SAS by David Stirling, a former comrade in No. 8 Commando. He had participated in a number of exciting operations and was about to take some well-earned leave in August 1942 when he received a peremptory summons from Monty to report to him forthwith.

The association between Mather and Monty went back to early 1927, when the former was only seven years old. His mother was a great friend of Betty Carver and, during a winter sports holiday in Switzerland, the family had skied over to Lenk to meet her and her sons, to find Monty staying in the same hotel. The relationship between the two families flourished during the period of Monty's marriage to the extent that, shortly after Betty's death, Mather was sent down to Portsmouth to keep Monty company for a few days. The bereaved professional soldier and the young school leaver had got on surprisingly well, and in 1938 Monty invited Mather, then in the OTC at Cambridge University, to act as his 'galloper' during exercises on Salisbury Plain. In typical fashion he had followed Mather's subsequent career, to the extent that he knew where to call for him as soon as the opportunity arose.

A similar treatment was accorded to Carol Mather's brother, who was summoned by Monty at much the same time. Older than Carol by five years, Bill Mather had reached the Middle East as an officer of the Cheshire Yeomanry in 1 Cavalry Division. After attending the Staff College at Haifa he was attached to 2 Armoured Brigade as a Liaison Officer, in which capacity he was seriously wounded at Gazala. Recovering in hospital on the Suez Canal, he had just been asked to go as Brigade Major to an armoured brigade when the order arrived to report to HQ Eighth Army as a Liaison Officer. Preferring the first job offer, he asked the hospital commandant to keep him on for a few more days until any fuss about his non-arrival had blown over. Not long afterwards an order went out for his arrest, so he immediately made his way to Burg el Arab, there to be greeted by Monty with the words, 'Mather, you were prevaricating!'[2] On admitting that he would have preferred the job of Brigade Major to that of Liaison Officer, Mather was told by Monty that he was in any event about to convert the armoured brigade into a tank delivery regiment and that he would do better to stay with him; if he performed well, Monty promised, he would be given a job as a Brigade Major in due course. He found himself initially working in Operations and Plans, before being selected for attachment as a Liaison Officer to Herbert Lumsden at X Corps.

Monty had arrived in the Middle East with the plan for Operation LIGHTFOOT already taking shape in his mind. He had discounted the traditional hook through the desert to the south, although he intended to use XIII Corps to threaten this. Instead, the plan was for XXX Corps to advance behind an enormous artillery barrage through the minefields on a narrow seven-mile front running south from Tel el Eisa. The objective for the infantry was a line running along the forward slope of the Miteirya Ridge and extending northwards to the eastern edge of another small feature named the Kidney Ridge. Four of the five divisions of the corps would be committed, which from north to south were 9 Australian, 51 Highland, 2 New Zealand and 1 South African. Meanwhile, 4 Indian Division, established on and around the Ruweisat Ridge, would threaten the Axis centre, whilst XIII Corps would also attack, although its main purpose was to keep 21 Panzer Division in the southern sector.

Monty then intended to launch X Corps through two corridors. The northerly one for 1 Armoured Division passed between the Australians and the Highlanders, the division's objective being to hold Kidney Ridge and dominate the surrounding area. The southerly corridor for 10 Armoured Division, which had orders to break into the open ground on the far side of the Miteirya Ridge, lay between the New Zealanders and the South Africans.

Some days before the battle commenced, Bill Mather was asked to organize a conference of all officers down to the rank of lieutenant colonel in the cinema in Amriya. Monty spoke for two hours without notes, telling his audience in the simplest terms exactly how the battle would go. He envisaged three phases: the 'Break-In' would take place on the first night and would see Eighth Army established on its objectives; the 'Dog Fight' would then ensue, possibly for a number of days, during which the enemy infantry would be progressively ground down through a series of 'crumbling' operations, whilst their tanks, sent in to protect them, would be destroyed by anti-tank guns and the British tanks; this would then lead inevitably to the 'Break-Out', when the collapse of one or more sections of the Axis line would see the British armour through into the open spaces beyond.

There was a fundamental weakness in the plan which was the lack of trust between the infantry and the armour. The latter in particular were highly dubious about their role, which they saw as providing static protection for the infantry and not as the proper use of armoured vehicles, which was to take advantage of their mobility. In the infantry divisions, none of the commanders reposed great confidence in X Corps' ability, or indeed willingness, to follow Monty's orders. Monty, for his part, was already unhappy with the quality of training of the armoured divisions and the resolve of Lumsden and his immediate subordinates, and it was this that had caused him to recast his original plan, which had envisaged a much quicker break-out and which he now knew was impossible with the material which he had to hand. He did, however, repose full confidence in his revised plan, which leant heavily on the 'crumbling' wearing down the Germans to achieve his goal.

On the evening of 23 October 1942 Tac was unusually full of general staff officers from Main HQ. Freddie was there, having established an office in a nearby pill box with good telephone communications to Main HQ, and so were Belchem, Richardson and Williams. Leaving Mainwaring to mind the shop, the four of them had enjoyed a good lunch in Alexandria, washed down with champagne and claret, before going up to join Monty. Monty himself had met his corps and divisional commanders for the last time before the battle, addressing them outside his caravan, where they all sat on the sand. Whilst this was taking place an unusual incident occurred. The Tac HQ armoured cars had taken to shooting with their machine guns at flights of duck which occasionally passed over on their way to the Delta, but had never had any success. As Monty spoke a volley of fire broke out and this time there was a result, one of the ducks spiralling down and hitting the ground not far from where the army commander was delivering his final briefing. Barely pausing for breath, Monty acknowledged the incident by reserving the duck for his own supper that evening!

Content that all was in order, Monty retired to bed as usual at 21.30. The other officers went outside to watch the beginning of the battle. Tac HQ was far enough forward for the artillery to be both in front of and behind them and they had a grandstand view when the barrage opened precisely at 21.40. Kirkman's plan now came into operation. Of the 882 field and medium guns on the strength of Eighth Army, some 600 were on the XXX Corps front, where they had been deployed on the instructions of the CCRA, Meade Dennis. They did not all open fire at once: each gun's distance from its target had been precisely calculated so that its first shell was timed to arrive at exactly the same moment as all the others, thus administering the greatest possible shock to the enemy. This first stage of the plan consisted of counter-battery fire to neutralize the Axis guns, whose positions had been identified in advance by a combination of aerial photography, sound ranging and flash spotting, providing an extremely accurate picture. The firing continued for a full 15 minutes, after which there was a 5-minute pause to rest and re-range the guns.

The second phase began at 21.00 in the shape of an enormous rolling barrage, designed to fall immediately in front of the advancing infantry and thus requiring the highest level of coordination from Forward Observation Officers. The infantry had lain concealed in slit trenches close to their start lines all day, emerging as darkness fell to take up their positions and then advancing behind the rolling barrage. With them went the sappers, but there were not enough of them to clear all the mines, and casualties were incurred both from mines and from mortar fire, as the defenders began to recover from the initial onslaught.

Most of the engineers were engaged in clearing the corridors for the armour, which their recent training enabled them to do with great effectiveness. Like the infantry, the tanks emerged from their hiding places after dark, casting off their camouflage and proceeding to their start lines down the six tracks created by Kisch. Officers from Main HQ Eighth Army, including Bill Mather, were posted on each of the tracks to ensure that the tanks went through smoothly, and at this stage all went to plan. However, as they moved into the corridors, the sand was ground down to a fine dust, creating a thick cloud which reduced visibility to almost nothing and delayed the advance.

It was soon evident that the deception plan had been brilliantly successful. Rommel himself had discounted any possibility of an attack for some days and had gone back to Germany, leaving General Stumme in command. The barrage had stunned the defenders, backed up as it was by bombing from RAF Wellingtons. However, because they were not expecting an attack, their gunners were largely in slit trenches when the bombardment fell and casualties were relatively light. On a piecemeal basis they now began to recover and resistance stiffened, but disaster struck when Stumme suffered a heart attack on the morning of 24 October. He was succeeded temporarily by General von Thoma, commander of the Afrika Korps.

By first light on 24 October, it was clear that much had been achieved. The objectives had been reached by most of the infantry units along the Miteirya Ridge, although the right flank brigade of the Highlanders and the left flank brigade of the Australians, together with 2 Armoured Brigade from 1 Armoured Division, were still a long way from Kidney Ridge. In the left-hand corridor 10 Armoured Division had tried to get over the Miteirya Ridge, but had found strong defences and a minefield extension on the reverse slope and had withdrawn and dug in. In the south XIII Corps had failed to break through the minefields, but had succeeded in keeping 21 Panzer Division in its sector.

Monty was not totally dissatisfied, but gave orders that the armoured divisions must establish themselves on their objectives during the following night. By 02.00 on 25 January, however, it had become clear to Freddie that this was not going to be achieved and that the battle had reached a crisis point. He immediately called a conference for 03.30, to which he summoned Leese and Lumsden, and then, contrary to normal practice, went to wake Monty, who immediately recognized that the situation required his personal intervention. He met the corps commanders in his caravan and listened patiently to their explanations for the situation. He also spoke by telephone to Alec Gatehouse of 10 Armoured Division, ordering him to push his brigades across the Miteirya Ridge. In the end he confirmed that the plan would be unchanged and that, in spite of Lumsden's very obvious unhappiness, the armour should finish the task they had been set.

Without Monty's intervention, the battle might have ground to a complete halt that night. Even as it was, it became clear on the following day that the armour were not going to break through, and Monty reluctantly withdrew them, deciding that it was now up to the infantry to draw in the enemy through a series of 'crumbling' operations whilst he waited for the right moment to exploit any weakness. Not for the last time in such circumstances, Monty would later claim that all had gone to plan. He never seemed to recognize that what actually demonstrated his true capability as a battlefield commander was not that a plan had worked so well, but that he could change it according to circumstances in the middle of a battle.

The 'Dog Fight' developed over the next four days. Monty regrouped XXX Corps, with 2 New Zealand Division taken out of the battle and the South Africans sidestepped into their place, being in turn relieved by 4 Indian Division. There were some successes, notably the repelling of a major attack on 9 Australian Division by 90 Light Division and the defence of 'Snipe', a position to the south of Kidney Ridge, in which 32 enemy tanks from 15 Panzer Division were destroyed and half as many more were disabled. The Australians also began a series of actions which created a salient to the north of Tel el Eisa. At Main HQ the brunt of the activity was falling not only on Mainwaring, but also on Belchem, who was tasked with the reorganization as divisions were shuffled around.

The Tac system was working well. Carol Mather was covering a lot of ground, sometimes with Monty, sometimes on his own. On the first day he visited most of the divisional GOCs: Bernard Freyberg of 2 New Zealand, Douglas Wimberley of 51 Highland, Raymond Briggs of 1 Armoured and Gatehouse of 10 Armoured Divisions, with the HQ of 2 Armoured Brigade thrown in for good measure. On 26 October he was with the Australians and two days later with the South Africans, where he met Leese as well the as GOC, Dan Pienaar. On 29th and 30th he was back with the Australians, who were at the time the most active division on the whole front. As his diary recorded, he was not entirely happy with his lot, possibly because it compared unfavourably with the excitement generated by the SAS:

> My job is really very soft. I usually take Monty out each morning to a Division, come back for lunch and then maybe set out myself in the afternoon to find out some particular piece of information about the front. It is not dangerous as no realistic information can be gained right up in the fighting line, except in Armoured Bde Tac HQ ... It is quite amusing driving the great open Humber with the AC alongside being saluted by everyone, but one feels rather a stooge.[3]

Freddie remained for the most part at Tac HQ and was now thinking ahead. On 26 September he presented a brief appreciation, which concluded that the enemy would in due course be forced to bring 21 Panzer Division north, a decision which the newly returned Rommel would, in the event, take that very evening. Once there, he argued, the Italians in the south would be unlikely to attempt any offensive action and it would be safe to bring 7 Armoured Division north to join X Corps to provide the necessary concentration of force for a break-out. This was the first step towards shaping the plan for the new Operation

SUPERCHARGE, an attack by 2 New Zealand Division and 9 Armoured Brigade along the coast road, with the augmented X Corps poised to break out as soon as a gap had been created.

Whilst Monty and those around him remained confident of success, in London and Cairo there was considerable concern that the battle was not proceeding to plan. On 29 October a deputation arrived at Tac HQ, consisting of Alexander, McCreery and Richard Casey, who as Minister of State for the Middle East was Churchill's representative on the spot. Casey took Freddie aside and warned him of the possible need to send a signal to Churchill warning of a potential stalemate. Whilst Freddie was an admirer of Casey's, he was greatly alarmed by this possibility, which would stir up a hornet's nest quite unnecessarily. He reacted strongly, even threatening to have Casey hounded out of public life if he did so.[4] In the event, no such signal was ever sent.

When Monty had explained his plan for SUPERCHARGE, McCreery, with the benefit of recent decrypts from ULTRA, argued that it would be better to strike not along the coast but further south, where there was a potentially vulnerable junction between German and Italian formations. As it happened, just such a proposal had already been advanced by Williams and accepted by Freddie, but Monty had thus far been unmoved. In a separate discussion between McCreery and the senior Eighth Army staff officers, McCreery offered to discuss it further with Monty, but was warned off by Freddie, who knew that Monty would not accept it from a man with whom he had at best a cool relationship and whom he was inclined to disparage to his staff.

What Freddie knew was that the idea would have no chance of success unless Monty adopted it as his own. He now used his own brand of persuasion, backed up by the intelligence provided by Williams, whom Monty respected highly; and later on the same afternoon he was able to signal McCreery that he had succeeded. Tedder was visiting Tac HQ on the same day. Whilst acknowledging the great improvement in the relationship between the Army and the RAF, he was concerned by what he saw as the slow tempo of operations. Notwithstanding the considerable successes of the RAF in interdicting supplies of fuel to the Axis forces, which were becoming desperately short, he thought that it was only a matter of time before a shipment got through. He was also worried about the situation in Malta, which was still under siege and had not received a supply convoy since mid-August: the position on the island could only be relieved by the RAF establishing air cover from Cyrenaica. He was thus gloomy about the prospects of another slogging match, which was what appeared to be promised by SUPERCHARGE. Monty could offer no comfort until the new direction was adopted, when there was suddenly a complete and most welcome change of attitude and a new sense of urgency.

SUPERCHARGE kicked off with a rolling barrage at 01.05 on 2 November, followed by an advance on a 4,000-yard front. The operation was controlled at a tactical level by the New Zealand Division's HQ, but other than the 28th Maori Battalion, the infantry was provided by 151 Brigade from 50 Division, which had had a quiet time in XIII Corps, and 152 Brigade from 51 Highland Division, which hitherto had been only lightly committed to the battle. Once the brigades had reached their objective, 9 Armoured Brigade would pass through to reach the Rahman Track, a key route running from north to south behind the Axis lines. The commander of 9 Armoured Brigade was told by Freyberg that he should be prepared to accept very high losses.

This is indeed what happened, 9 Armoured Brigade passing through the infantry and drawing on to itself the full remaining might of 15 and 21 Panzer Divisions. Although 2 Armoured Brigade, coming up behind in the van of 1 Armoured Division, was delayed and ground to a halt when it arrived, it was followed by 8 Armoured Brigade and both engaged in a huge tank battle with the Germans. There was as yet no break-through, but a strong salient had been thrust into the enemy line. Then 7 Motor Brigade was brought forward to try to expand the salient, followed by 5 Indian Brigade, which mounted an attack to the south-west on the night of 3/4 November. Rommel now realized that he would have to retreat if his army was to survive in any form. By dawn on 4 November the armoured cars of the 4th South African Armoured Car Regiment and the King's Dragoon Guards were out into the open, followed later that morning by the fresh 7 Armoured Division. On the evening of 3 November, XIII Corps had also reported a withdrawal on its front. The Battle of El Alamein was over.

Among the many prisoners was General von Thoma, who was brought to Tac HQ, where Geoffrey Keating was given the job of tidying him up. Monty invited him to dinner, with Joe Ewart, a fluent German speaker, brought in from GHQ to translate. Monty was on very fine form according to Carol Mather, who recorded the event in his diary. On being told that Eighth Army already had troops in Fuka, Von Thoma, shaken by the news, went on to say, 'In the German army they have a character sketch of you.'

'Oh do they? Do they now? How interesting. And what do they say?' asked Monty.

'They say you are a very hard and ruthless man.'

'Oh,' said Monty, clearly pleased, 'hard and ruthless? Not a bit of it!'[5]

In many ways Monty was quite right. He was certainly not ruthless when it came to minimizing casualties among his men, although he had accepted at El Alamein that they would be high. Richardson was asked to give an estimate to enable the Royal Army Medical Corps to prepare. This he was unable to do, as was Freddie. Monty, on the other hand, confidently produced a number of 13,000, which turned out to be very accurate.

Monty was also far from ruthless in the pursuit, which now began.

Chapter Eleven

The Pursuit

The battle had been comprehensively won. The pursuit was bungled, at least in the vital few days after the break-out.

This was not the fault of the staff. For some time Freddie had been thinking about how to cut off the retreating Germans – the Italian infantry divisions were immobile and abandoned, surrendering in tens of thousands, whilst the two Italian Armoured Divisions were also effectively sacrificed – and had asked Richardson to put together a force which would be sufficiently strong and provided with enough fuel to carry out the job. To meet the requirements of Operation GRAPESHOT, as this venture was called, Richardson assembled 96 tanks, to be brought forward by transporters, 45 armoured cars, two batteries of 25-pounders and three of light anti-aircraft guns, two battalions of infantry and soft transport carrying enough fuel and other supplies to be self-sufficient for at least a week. The units came largely from what remained of 8 Armoured Division and the force was to be commanded by the latter's GOC, Charles Gairdner, whom Freddie met almost daily, and controlled by its HQ, to which was added the necessary RAF and RN liaison staff.

Monty was having none of it, preferring to use all the divisions which had participated in the break-out. These were the same as those which had comprised the *corps de chasse* put together on paper by John Harding on 12 August, except that 7 Armoured Division, now commanded by Harding himself, replaced 8 Armoured Division. These four divisions were now all sent forward simultaneously on 5 November to cut off the enemy at different points between El Alamein and Fuka, but 1 and 10 Armoured Divisions only arrived on the coast road after the enemy rearguard had passed through, whilst 7 Armoured and 2 New Zealand Divisions were delayed by a dummy minefield,[1] allowing the Germans to withdraw with minimal contact.

Monty now ordered the four divisions to envelop the next objective, Mersa Matruh, but both 1 and 7 Armoured Divisions ran out of fuel, whilst late on 6 November it began to rain heavily and by the following morning all the pursuers were bogged down, leaving Rommel to withdraw once again in good order. To cap it all, the RAF was largely ineffective, preferring to offer ground support to the advancing British rather than strafe the German columns, whilst at the same time being hampered by confusion as to which friendly formation was where. Little training had been carried out in low-level ground attack, and such attacks as were made were largely high-level bombing, which made little impact. To avoid anti-aircraft fire, bomb runs were made across rather than along the road, and only one or two vehicles at most would be hit by each pattern. When they followed up, the pursuers were astonished by the lack of damaged Axis vehicles on the road, although there were many abandoned for lack of fuel.

The problems were twofold. First, too many divisions had been committed to the pursuit, resulting in both confusion in command and control and a temporary supply problem. Kirkman was to say many years later that a single division, as long as it was highly mobile, could have done the job, suggesting that it could have been either 7 Armoured, the freshest of the lot, or 2 New Zealand, with its own brigades rested and restored to it, or 4 Indian Division, of which only one brigade had been involved in the battle and then only briefly in the closing stages. At the last of these the GOC, 'Gertie' Tuker, believing that his three brigades could be on the Egyptian frontier by the morning of 6 November, issued orders to them to be ready to move, with a flying column of all arms organized to lead the advance. To his dismay, the division was instead ordered to hand over its troop-carrying transport to the Greek Brigade and to begin work on clearing up the battlefield.

The second problem was that Lumsden appeared unable to exercise control over the *corps de chasse* and, worse still, failed to remain in close communication with Monty. Both to Monty and to those around the two commanders, this silence seemed to be intentional. Bill Mather, attached to Lumsden as a Liaison Officer, spent much of his time trying to persuade the X Corps commander to contact his superior. Whenever they stopped, Mather would begin the lengthy business of erecting the cumbersome Wyndham aerial necessary for his wireless to function, only to have Lumsden say, 'Whips out! We're off' – and he would have to dismantle the apparatus again.

Mather's brother Carol accompanied Monty for much of this period and was asked to navigate to a pre-agreed map reference in the desert for a meeting. There was no sign of Lumsden and Monty was predictably livid. In the end he summoned Lumsden to Main HQ, where a furious row ensued. Bill Williams, listening outside, communicated this to the Ops Room, where a board had been set up showing the odds on all the generals for future advancement. 'Sell Lumsdens' was Williams's advice and the price was duly marked down, only for Lumsden himself to come in, pull away the cloth hiding the board and leave without saying a word, but clearly seething with anger.

Main HQ had been very quick to move forward behind the advance; indeed, at one time it found itself ahead of Tac. With confusion reigning as to which formation was where and even where the front was, but in the belief that the Germans had withdrawn from Mersa Matruh, Mainwaring went forward to look for a new Main HQ site, taking with him Dick Carver, Monty's stepson, who was serving as a GSO2 (Ops). Belchem followed in a second jeep, accompanied by a puppy which he had recently adopted and which suddenly became carsick. Whilst he halted briefly to look after it, a German anti-tank round struck his jeep and he was forced to take cover in a ditch. Mainwaring and Carver drove on, only to be taken prisoner by a German unit forming part of the rearguard.[2]

Richardson was immediately made GSO1 (Ops). His replacement, together with Carver's as a GSO2, arrived shortly afterwards, both fresh from the Staff College at Haifa. Geoffrey Baker was a gunner who had served in 4 Indian Division in the East African campaign against the Italians, where he had been wounded and won the MC, before being posted to Haifa as an Instructor. Tall and fair, he had acquired the nickname of 'George the Swede' whilst a cadet at the Royal Military Academy, Woolwich, and was thereafter always called George. Harry Llewellyn, like Bill Mather, had arrived in the Middle East with 1 Cavalry Division, in his case with the Warwickshire Yeomanry, and had been a student at Haifa. Together with Andy Anderson of the Royal Signals, a fellow student who had been posted as an assistant to 'Slap' White, they paraded in front of Monty, who told them that if he liked them and they did a good job, they could stay; on the other hand, if they did not like him, they were free to go!

Llewellyn was immediately identified by Freddie for a role which he had not needed whilst Eighth Army was stationary behind the Alamein Line, but would become vital as it became highly mobile and Tac HQ moved out of regular physical contact. Together with Peter Paget, he was made a GSO2 (Liaison), carrying out a role akin to that which Carol Mather was performing at Tac HQ, but responsible directly to Freddie. The 'Freddie Boys', as the Main HQ LOs became known to differentiate them from the 'Monty Boys', were there, in Llewellyn's words, 'to see that Freddie did not get caught out by receiving information later than Monty did.'[3] When the distances between Main HQ and the leading formations lengthened so much that daily visits proved impractical, Freddie had his LOs located at the corps HQs, whence they would report back daily.

In early November another officer joined Tac HQ who would spend almost every day in Monty's company from then until well after the end of the war. Whilst John Poston had more than proved his worth as an ADC, Spooner was unfamiliar with the desert and had gone astray on occasion when taking Monty on visits.[4] Monty now asked Poston if he knew anyone who would suit the role and Poston immediately proposed Johnny Henderson, a lieutenant in an armoured car regiment, the 12th Lancers, whom he had known before the war. Monty consulted Henderson's CO, who told him that the young subaltern had a remarkable facility for navigating around the desert, having successfully crossed the Qattara Depression to see if it could be used by a large outflanking force.

Henderson was summoned to Tac, by then established near Mersa Matruh, where he had a brief interview with Monty. He was then invited to dine in

Monty's mess, where they were joined by Poston and also by Freddie and Williams, who were both visiting. During dinner he was subjected to an interrogation on his family, school and interests. Afterwards Poston gave him an invaluable piece of advice, which was that he should always tell Monty the truth, regardless of any potential consequences.

Ten days later, Henderson went to Monty to request a return to his regiment, where he might see some real action. Monty asked him to stay on until a replacement had been found and, shortly afterwards, the two men flew back to Cairo to attend the Thanksgiving Service for the victory at El Alamein. After the service Henderson was given the rest of the day and the evening off, during which he and a friend went to the zoo. Whilst there, the friend grabbed Henderson's military cap and offered it to an elephant, which duly began to eat it. With no chance of rescuing the item and no time to replace it, the improperly dressed Henderson was unable to attend the Guard of Honour at the airfield, as he had been instructed to do by Monty. Quizzed as to why his explicit order had not been obeyed, Henderson told the truth. Monty ordered him to board the aircraft and then spoke not a word on the return journey. However, he raised it at dinner and the amusement generated so softened his reaction that Henderson decided to stay on, as it turned out for nearly four years.

With the immediate opportunity to cut off the Germans now lost and Rommel conducting a skilful withdrawal, offering Monty no immediate opportunity to outflank him, the focus was turned fully on to the longstanding problem of desert warfare for both sides – how to sustain an advancing army which was moving rapidly away from its supply base. The distances were very quickly too great for the large dumps behind the Alamein Line to suffice alone, and mobility became of the essence. The options available were road, rail and sea, as air despatch was in its infancy at this stage of the war and there were in any event few suitable aircraft in the area. Although Eighth Army prided itself on its ability to move across open desert, the single metalled road would remain the main supply artery throughout the campaign, but it very quickly became cluttered with traffic of all descriptions and major jams built up, especially at the Halfaya Pass between Sollum and Bardia. The ports along the coast offered good possibilities, but other than Tobruk and Benghazi they were mostly small and it seemed certain that the Axis would block the channels and demolish port installations, causing inevitable delays to the landing of significant tonnages.

It was hardly surprising, therefore, that in the Eighth Army Administrative Instruction No. 140, issued shortly before the beginning of Operation LIGHTFOOT and setting out the policy for the Q branch in the event of a withdrawal by Rommel, Brian Robertson laid heavy emphasis on the third alternative, rail. In the aftermath of Operation CRUSADER, the Western Desert Railway had been extended from the railhead at Misheifa, first to Capuzzo on the Libyan frontier and then to Belhamed, about 20 miles south-east of Tobruk, where a railhead opened on 26 May 1942, the very day of Rommel's attack round the end of the Gazala line. In the subsequent retreat the railway played a major part in backloading stores, and only one locomotive was lost. During their occupation of the territory west of El Alamein, the Axis forces used the railway for their own supplies, but did nothing to increase its capacity. They did, however, extend the line from Belhamed to the harbour at Tobruk, which was to prove valuable to the Allies.

Robertson spelt out in his instruction where successive railheads would be opened and what supplies they would each cater for. The Movements and Transportation branch of the Q staff was responsible for ensuring that reconnaissance parties moved up immediately behind the forward troops to assess the damage caused by the retreating Germans and that repair material, railway construction units and labour companies would follow as required. A complete construction train was held ready at Alexandria and another two at Suez, ready to be called forward.

Q (Mov & Tn) was also responsible for coordinating joint military and naval parties to take control of the ports, with recce parties placed on stand-by to move in as soon as each was captured, in order to make an immediate assessment of the requirements and to define the docks area, the entrances to and exits from which were to be closely controlled. Arrangements were also made for the landing of limited quantities of supplies over beaches, to be used on the occasions when the forward troops could not be adequately maintained overland. At this stage of the campaign there were few specialized landing craft in the theatre, so cumbersome lighters had to be used.

Robertson set up 86 Sub Area to provide the necessary structure around the Army railheads and later the roadheads[5] as it moved forward. In addition to all the supply depots, the sub area included a Prisoner of War cage, a Transit Camp for reinforcements and a Main Traffic Control Post to manage the motor transport convoys. One of the main problems was the supply of POL, and Robertson directed that, in addition to the fuel tankers, every single vehicle proceeding westwards, from staff cars and jeeps to huge recovery vehicles, should carry more cans than it needed for its own purposes, to be offloaded as far forward as possible.

Another problem endemic to the desert was the supply of water. Kisch was made responsible for the development and repair of water points at suitable places in the line of communications, with 86 Sub Area taking responsibility for them as soon as they were ready. The ration was one gallon per man per day, including an allowance for vehicle radiators, with additional allowances for medical facilities and workshops and for certain vehicles which required large quantities of water, such as tank transporters.

In order to get supplies to the forward divisions, Robertson and Miles Graham created a new organization, the Field Maintenance Centre ('FMC'), which would provide the link between corps transport, which lifted supplies from the railheads, roadheads and ports, and divisional transport, which distributed them to the forward troops. In the desert, where space was not a problem, each FMC was laid out identically and became in essence a huge shopping centre. There were specified areas for POL, general supplies, water, engineering stores, ordnance stores and ammunition, together with a POW cage and a Field Post Office. Corps third line transport would approach from one direction to unload and divisional second line transport from the opposite direction to pick up, with clearly defined entrance and exit routes from each area. Each FMC held between one and two days stock of all commodities. Under the previous system, divisions had to notify their requirements three days in advance, but this was now not necessary, so switches in formations or units from one corps to another were no longer a logistical problem.

Every single item of supply, other than water, originated from Egypt, and Robertson thus had to rely on Middle East Command to provide Eighth Army with all its requirements. It was fortunate that the Chief Administrative Officer at GHQ was one of the most experienced in the business. Lieutenant General Sir Wilfred Lindsell had been a fellow instructor of Monty's at Camberley, where he had taught Q&A to Robertson among others. He had been Quartermaster-General of the BEF and then CAO of Home Forces before being posted to the Middle East. There was nothing he did not know about supply and he could be relied upon to deliver whatever was required.

Whilst Eighth Army retained responsibility for its immediate lines of communication, this became impracticable once the distances became too great. At such times GHQ took over the rear areas, so that Eighth Army could always focus on the task ahead. Once the Army had progressed as far as Benghazi, the responsibility for the LOC up to the frontier was devolved to British Troops in Egypt, whilst in due course Cyrenaica District and then Tripolitania District were set up as static organizations within Middle East Command.

After the setbacks at Fuka and Mersa Matruh, the advance gathered pace. Sidi Barrani was taken on 9 November, and the Libyan frontier crossed on 11 November. Tobruk fell on 13 November and the first ships were unloaded three days later. The railway was slower to reopen, but the railhead at Capuzzo, just across the frontier, received its first train on 20 November and the one at Tobruk on 1 December. Robertson had persuaded Monty to use fighting troops to provide the initial working parties at both ports and railheads, as bringing up Pioneer and Labour companies would use precious transportation resources.

That troops would be available for labour duties was an anticipated consequence of a fast advance, with divisions stalled for lack of supplies, even after the measures taken by Robertson. X Corps still controlled the leading formations, but only 1 and 7 Armoured Divisions remained in the field, and it was the latter which led the advance. Monty was cautious, excessively so in the eyes of a number of his critics, notably Tedder and Coningham. He refused initially to follow the example of O'Connor in 1940 by cutting across the desert to trap the enemy retreating from Benghazi, believing that he risked an upset that he could not afford. Instead, he sent only armoured cars on that route, whilst the bulk of 7 Armoured Division followed up methodically behind Rommel, reaching Benghazi on 19 November. A belated attempt by 22 Armoured Brigade, using tanks borrowed from 1 Armoured Division, failed to get behind Rommel at Agedabia, and the Germans established themselves on a well-prepared defensive line at El Agheila. The RAF was mollified to some extent by the capture intact of the key group of airfields around Martuba, in the bulge of Cyrenaica, just in time to provide cover to a vital convoy for Malta.

Monty had by now run out of patience with Lumsden. He was sent home to the UK, his place in command of X Corps assumed by Horrocks, who was ordered to take the corps into reserve and train it for future operations. Miles Dempsey, one of Monty's protégés, was summoned from the UK to relieve Horrocks at XIII Corps, which played no further part in the North African campaign. The front facing the Germans at El Agheila was taken over by Leese's XXX Corps, now comprising 7 Armoured, 2 New Zealand and 51 Highland Divisions.

Whilst Monty built up his supplies, there was a pause in operations, during which Main and Tac HQs were briefly co-located. A number of changes in key personnel took place, the most important of which was the Chief of Staff. Shortly after his own arrival in Benghazi, Freddie experienced acute stomach pains. Evacuated to Cairo, his chronic complaint of gallstones was diagnosed. The treatment was effective, but the subsequent Medical Board recommended three months leave, which he realized would mean the end of his time at Eighth Army. On Monty's return to Cairo for the Thanksgiving Service, he visited Freddie in hospital and heard the news. He asked his Chief of Staff how long he would need to recuperate and was told only three weeks. Monty immediately persuaded the doctors to change their minds and Freddie went off to Palestine to convalesce, getting married before his return! In the meantime, his place was taken temporarily by Bobby Erskine, who had been BGS at XIII Corps since Gott's time and was highly experienced, although he lacked Freddie's unique ability in handling Monty.

David Belchem was also taken ill, in his case with appendicitis, and his job as GSO1 (Staff Duties) was taken over by George Baker. Likewise evacuated to Cairo, after his recovery Belchem was initially posted as Brigade Major of 2 Armoured Brigade before being given command of 1st Royal Tank Regiment, which was serving with 7 Armoured Division. The posting came with the express approval of Monty, who was a strong believer in his staff having battlefield experience so that they could appreciate better what was happening on the front line. Other examples of this policy at much the same time were Carol and Bill Mather. Carol rejoined the SAS, having been persuaded to do so by David Stirling, who came on a visit to Tac HQ to discuss his plans with Monty; a month later he was captured during an operation and sent to a POW camp in Italy. Bill left on a posting as Brigade Major of 9 Armoured Brigade, which was reforming after the terrible losses incurred during Operation SUPERCHARGE.

Monty now wished to attack the German position at El Agheila with all speed. Both the attack and the subsequent drive on Tripoli required the efficient functioning of the port of Benghazi, but it had turned out to be in far worse shape than Tobruk. There were a number of ships sunk in the harbour and the Royal Navy were moving too slowly to remove them in time. This meant that the Army was still being supplied from the port and railhead at Tobruk, whilst the build-up of the RAF had also put huge demands on the whole logistic apparatus. Robertson's solution was to commandeer all the transport of X Corps and use it to move supplies up as quickly as possible, thereby enabling Monty's deadline to be met.

Monty moved Tac HQ up to XXX Corps on 5 December and the battle kicked off nine days later, when 7 Armoured and 51 Divisions began to advance through the minefields between Mersa Brega and El Agheila, the Highlanders in particular taking heavy casualties. Even before this, the New Zealanders had, on the night of 11 December, set off on a 200-mile left hook. By the evening of 15 December they were in sight of the sea and poised to cut off the Germans and Italians, but Rommel, plagued as always by lack of fuel, had already decided to withdraw. The New Zealanders were unable to close the net, and most of the enemy managed to break through the gaps. It was, nevertheless, a satisfying victory in terms of morale. O'Connor and Ritchie had both reached El Agheila, only to be thrown back again soon afterwards. The Army had come 760 miles and this time there was to be no reverse.

The next defensive position was at Buerat. Once again Monty was forced to pause for nearly a month for logistical reasons, not the least of which was the continued slow progress by the Royal Navy in clearing Benghazi harbour. Robertson was authorized by Monty to give the officer in command a rocket, after which the situation improved considerably, only for a major setback to occur when a violent storm hit the coast on 3–5 January, breaching the mole and causing a number of ships to come adrift from their moorings. X Corps transport was once again pressed into service to remedy the deficiency.

The attack on Buerat, launched on 15 January, was so successful that the Axis forces retreated in some confusion both along the coast road and into the more hilly country on the approach to Tripoli. There was a natural defensive line between Homs and Tarhuna, but Eighth Army was by then moving with such momentum that, to the surprise of both Monty and Leese, it bounced the line on the run and broke clear through towards Tripoli, which was entered on 23 January.

During the advance from Buerat to Tripoli, Tac HQ briefly became an operational headquarters. The left of XXX Corps, comprising 2 New Zealand Division and most of 7 Armoured Division and directed on Tarhuna, and the right, with 51 Highland Division and 22 Armoured Brigade moving along the coast road to Homs, were well separated. With Tac following closely behind 22 Armoured Brigade, Monty effectively became a corps commander, controlling the right-hand thrust directly and giving Douglas Wimberley, the Highlanders' GOC, a very hard time. He was quite evidently enjoying himself enormously, as was John Oswald, who had sometimes wondered if he had been doing a very useful job in charge of Tac. Clearly Tac lacked the full apparatus of a corps HQ, not least Ground/Air wireless tentacles, which inevitably limited cooperation with the RAF, but in the relatively short time – just over a week – that this situation existed, it hardly mattered. At Main HQ Freddie had by then returned, but for the first time Monty was so far ahead and so involved in day-to-day operations, that the COS found it difficult to keep fully in touch with what 'Master' was doing. This was to become a recurring problem.

Eighth Army's supply problems had become so severe that a temporary halt to major operations became a necessity, although 7 Armoured Division, now commanded by Bobby Erskine as John Harding had been seriously wounded in the final stages of the battle, pushed forward to the west. The port of Tripoli was initially unusable, the entrance blocked by sunken ships and the installations demolished. It was 3 February before the first ship could enter the harbour and three days later before a full convoy was able to unload. Serious restocking now needed to take place before the Army could take on the challenges ahead.

As Cairo was now over 1,000 miles away, it was decided to create a permanent base and lines of communication area in Tripoli. Robertson was given command, with promotion to major general, whilst Miles Graham stepped into his position as DA&QMG Eighth Army and was himself succeeded as AQMG by Rim Lymer, who now ran the Q activities at Rear HQ. Robertson was occasionally irked to be given orders by Graham, but took such firm control of the supply situation that it was not to be a problem for the remainder of the campaign. Graham, for his part, established a particularly close relationship with Freddie, which endured until the end of the war. He enjoyed many of the same interests, particularly gambling, and provided something of a safety valve for the Chief of Staff at moments of stress.

Main and Tac HQ were again briefly co-located, which was convenient for two significant events which took place in Tripoli. The first of these was the visit on 3 and 4 February of Churchill and Brooke. There was a minor hiccup in the arrangements when Monty's Humber car, which was to be used by the visitors, was stolen whilst Poston and Henderson were in nightclub on the evening before the victory parade. After a momentary panic, the situation was restored when the Military Police reclaimed it from a drunken soldier. The parade on the following day was led by the pipes and drums of the Highland Division, wearing their kilts, causing both the Prime Minister and the CIGS to become quite emotional. This was followed by a church parade at Main HQ, at which Padre Hughes gave an 'inspired sermon'.[6] Both parades were a propaganda gift for Geoffrey Keating, whose films received widespread distribution in both Britain and the Empire, and Warwick Charlton, who used them as a morale booster in his newspapers, which now included a new title, *The Tripoli Times*. Charlton was later to fall foul of Robertson, whose somewhat puritanical character disapproved of the newspaper's more risqué articles. He attempted to sack Charlton, which Monty refused to countenance.

The second event was a four-day conference from 14 to 17 February, presided over by Monty, during which he conveyed Eighth Army's experiences over the previous three months to an audience which arrived from Home Forces, Allied Forces (the name given to First Army and other formations now fighting in Tunisia and also based in Algeria and Morocco), Persia and Iraq Command and Middle East Command. The delegation from Home Forces was led by the C-in-C, Bernard Paget, and included a number of senior officers, including Henry Crerar from the Canadian Army and Gerald Templer, now GOC of a corps in the UK.[7] Air Marshal Sir Trafford Leigh-Mallory, AOC-in-C of Fighter Command, represented the RAF. Monty was less pleased by the lack of high-level representation from First Army in Tunisia: neither the Commander, Kenneth Anderson, nor any of his corps or divisional commanders attended, although Anderson sent a number of staff officers. On the other hand, there was one senior American General in the shape of George Patton.

The conference was held in a cinema in Tripoli and at some outdoor locations for physical demonstrations, which included a simulated attack by an armoured regiment. Monty opened with a two-hour exposition of the whole campaign to date and was followed by Freyberg and Wimberley on specific aspects. Richardson and McNeill, together with the Wing Commander (Ops), staged a very realistic presentation on Army/Air Cooperation and Kisch dealt with the problems of and solutions to mine clearance. Overall the staff worked hard to prepare and rehearse for the conference, an unusual activity for them in mid-campaign.

One of the staff officers to attend from First Army was Kit Dawnay, now the GSO1 (Intelligence) at Anderson's HQ. Seeing that he was present, Monty invited Dawnay to dinner in his mess and sat him next to himself:

Then occurred one of those appalling indiscretions to which Monty had always been prone, but usually not in front of so large a number of people. In a sudden lull in the conversation, he asked me a loud and highly rhetorical question: 'Who are you with now, Kit?'

'General Anderson, sir, 1st Army.'

'H'm – good plain cook.'

Observations such as this, gleefully repeated by his supporters, were calculated to make him more popular in some quarters than in others. To make matters worse, the more outrageous they were, the more he enjoyed them.[8]

Monty's aphorism soon spread round Eighth Army and reached First Army as well, doing little for the relationship between two formations which would have to cooperate before very long.

Chapter Twelve

The End in Africa

The presence of officers from First Army at Monty's Tripoli conference came as a result of Operation TORCH, which had been launched on 8 November 1942. Anglo–American troops landed at three locations in French North Africa, securing Algeria and Morocco for the Allies. Tunisia, however, was swiftly occupied by the Axis and Tunis itself remained out of reach, together with all the country which lay between the Dorsale Mountains and the sea, down as far as the border with Libya. Monty's hope that Rommel's army would be rolled up from the west came to naught, and Eighth Army was now committed to continue the campaign. Indeed, just as Monty was beginning his conference, two German panzer divisions, one of which had been on Monty's front, broke through the American positions on the Eastern Dorsale and attempted to do likewise in the passes of the Western Dorsale at Kasserine and Sbeitla, threatening the Allied rear areas. Only the rapid arrival of reinforcements from First Army saved a very serious situation.

At the same time, and arising from decisions taken at the Casablanca Conference in January, Alexander was appointed to command all Allied land forces in North Africa, taking up his position on 18 February at the newly created 18th Army Group, which comprised Eighth Army, First Army, II US Corps and XIX French Corps. He took McCreery with him as his Chief of Staff, together with many others from GHQ Middle East, responsibility for the latter falling on his successor, 'Jumbo' Wilson. For the time being, Eighth Army came operationally under 18th Army Group, whilst still being administratively linked to Middle East Command, which continued to provide both supplies and reinforcements via Robertson's new Tripolitania Base. Monty, deeply critical of the way events in Tunisia had been handled by Anderson and others and dubious about the Americans' fighting abilities, welcomed the appointment and was happy to continue with Alexander's light touch.

The overall plan was for First Army, the Americans and the French to continue to apply pressure from the west, whilst Monty drove up from the south, compressing the Germans and Italians into a small area around Tunis itself. The expectation was that, as Eighth Army advanced, opportunities would arise to cut off the Axis retreat.

By mid-February, the supply situation, with Robertson firmly in control, had improved to the extent that Eighth Army's offensive could resume. The main obstacle

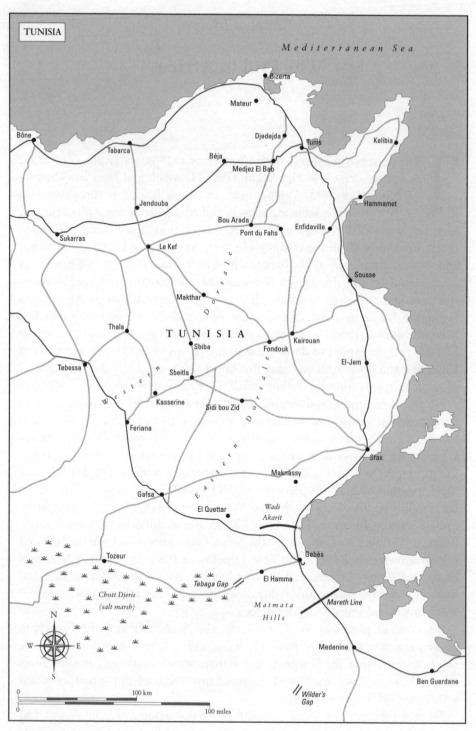

Map 3.

to the advance to Tunis was a formidable one, the Mareth Line, anchored to the east by the sea and to the west by the seemingly impenetrable Matmata Hills, with the deep Wadi Zigzaou running in between. In addition to these natural features, there was a system of fixed concrete bunkers. With a large part of Rommel's force engaged at Kasserine, Monty was able to move 7 Armoured and 51 Highland Divisions across the border into Tunisia and seize the area around Medenine. Rommel was taken by surprise but immediately reacted. The Western Dorsale passes were now closed to him, so he withdrew both 10 and 21 Panzer Divisions which, with 15 Panzer and 90 Light Divisions, now moved to attack Eighth Army.

For the first time since Alam Halfa, ULTRA was absolutely precise as to both the composition of the enemy forces and the timing of their attack, but it did not specify the direction. Monty had at last succeeded in getting Bill Williams promoted as his GSO1 (Intelligence),[1] but Williams was in hospital in Tripoli at the time the news was received and it was actually decrypted by Joe Ewart, who was deputising for him.[2] On hearing what was afoot, Williams had himself discharged from hospital and flew back to Main HQ. Monty now relied on him to a significant extent and required intelligence briefings every day.

Whilst Monty maintained, at the time and later, that all his battles except one had gone to plan,[3] in fact few did, but Medenine, like Alam Halfa, was certainly one of them. The key feature was a steep hill called Tadjera Khir, which became the pivot of Monty's line, from which he could face attacks either from the north or the west. This was just as well, as when Rommel attacked on the morning of 6 March, he did so in force from the west. XXX Corps still comprised 7 Armoured Division, now with 201 Guards Brigade under command, 2 New Zealand Division and 51 Highland Division, but it had been strengthened by exchanging worn-out tanks with fresh ones from 1 Armoured Division. In addition to the field artillery of the three divisions and the corps, Monty was able to deploy some 600 6-pounder anti-tank guns, and it was these which effectively won the battle. The head-on attacks by the panzer divisions failed to achieve any penetration. The Germans lost 52 tanks, a third of their strength, the British none; as at Alam Halfa, the British armour was strictly forbidden from undertaking any pursuit. Rommel was forced to withdraw and, his health shattered by his experiences over the last four months, went on sick leave to Germany, never to reappear in Africa.

If Medenine had gone exactly to plan, the Battle of Mareth equally emphatically did not. Right from the start Monty planned assaults from two directions, but in Richardson's words, 'We could never get Monty to come clean as to which was the main thrust, he was keeping both options open.'[4] Richardson himself thought that the frontal attack was Monty's preferred option, to be carried out initially by the newly arrived 50 Division, which had not been involved at all in the pursuit to Tripoli. The bridgehead established by 50 Division would then be exploited by 4 Indian, 7 Armoured and 51 Divisions.

As at El Agheila, 2 New Zealand Division, augmented on this occasion by 8 Armoured Brigade, some additional artillery, an armoured car regiment and a newly arrived Free French force under Major General Philippe Leclerc, was to undertake a wide left hook. The division concentrated near Medenine and then followed a route which crossed the Matmata Hills through Wilder's Gap, named after the Long Range Desert Group officer who had found it, then moved north along a route reconnoitred by the LRDG on the western side of the range. The whole formation was styled the New Zealand Corps and Freyberg was placed in overall command.

The frontal attack by 151 Brigade, which began on the night of 20/21 March, was a devastating failure, the British coming to grief in the Wadi Zigzaou, which turned out not only to have steep sides, but to be heavily mined and contain water from recent rains. A small but precarious bridgehead was established on the far side, but as Harry Llewellyn, who had gone right forward to get the best view, reported to Freddie, it had proved impossible to get any anti-tank guns over, leaving the infantry and the few Valentine tanks supporting them dangerously exposed to German counter-attacks. There was no option but to retreat, the first time this had happened since July 1942. Monty sent Henderson to 50 Division's HQ to find out what was happening and he, too, returned with a gloomy report. With no bridgehead, a further attempt was deemed impossible for the time being.

Very early on the morning of 23 March Richardson was phoned by Leese's BGS to be informed that there was a stalemate. For only the second time in the campaign, Freddie decided to wake Monty. A message was duly sent to Tac HQ, and Monty and Leese met at 02.00, following which Freddie was asked to go there immediately. He arrived at 07.00 to find a very different Monty from his usual confident self.[5] 'What shall I do, Freddie?' he asked. Balance, which Monty insisted on maintaining at all times when fighting his battles, had vanished with 50 Division's failure. Furthermore, the New Zealand Corps' existence was now known to the Germans through aerial reconnaissance. Monty was briefly nonplussed and, more than at any other time in their relationship, he badly needed Freddie's strong intellect and sound common sense. They discussed alternatives, with Freddie, who had never liked the frontal assault, strongly advising the reinforcement of Freyberg. He returned to Main HQ with instructions to effect this.

The revised plan was to send Horrocks, with X Corps HQ and 1 Armoured Division, to join Freyberg. This created some personal difficulty, as Freyberg and Horrocks were both lieutenant generals and both now corps commanders on a very narrow front. Freyberg, much older than and senior to Horrocks, was distinctly touchy and, when Horrocks arrived, he was given a chilly reception. Ever the diplomat, it was Freddie who helped to defuse the situation, writing a letter explaining what Monty wished to take place, addressing them jointly as 'My dear

Generals' and enclosing a bottle of brandy for them to enjoy together. As the New Zealanders were technically an independent entity, with Freyberg responsible to his own government, the situation required very careful handling. Richardson was later to say that the operation was portrayed as 'essentially a New Zealand enterprise but reinforced by General Horrocks's intellectual contribution'.[6]

Freddie's letter contained some news which was highly welcome, given that the force for Operation SUPERCHARGE (somewhat confusingly named only five months after the operation of the same name at El Alamein) was short of the artillery ammunition necessary to break through the narrow Tebaga Gap, where strong defences were now being prepared by the Germans. This was the conundrum most concerning Freddie, Richardson and the planners. Their solution was for the RAF to provide an entirely new kind of ground support, the first occasion on which a tactic was used which would transform the battlefield in the future.

At the end of January Coningham had been promoted to command the Allied Tactical Air Forces in North Africa, and his successor as AOC Desert Air Force was Harry Broadhurst. Broadhurst, who had become very close to Freddie as his opposite number,[7] had accepted the criticisms by the Army of the RAF's persistent failure to score hits on vehicles by virtue of its high-level bombing policy. He believed that it could do much better in future and asked Monty to supply a number of worn-out and captured vehicles on which his fighter squadrons could practise low-level attacks in the desert. The skills developed as a result by the pilots of the P-40 Kittyhawks, outclassed in their originally intended role as fighters by new models of the Messerschmitt Bf 109, but with good low-level characteristics, were first put to the test by harrying the German retreat from Medenine. Now they were to become a vital offensive instrument.

Broadhurst was effectively being asked to use his ground attack aircraft to replicate artillery during a major attack. These new tactics, which now incorporated the 'cab rank' system, whereby RAF officers in armoured cars close to the front line could call up air strikes very quickly, were initially unpopular both from above and below. Coningham stressed the inherent dangers to Broadhurst, sending his Senior Air Staff Officer to try to persuade him not to go ahead and to warn him of severe personal consequences if it all went wrong. At the more junior end, some of the Desert Air Force's pilots called him a 'murderer'. Broadhurst, to his great credit, stuck to his guns.

Having come up with the idea, Freddie sold it to Monty, as usual in a way which allowed him to adopt it as his own. The plans were then worked on in detail by Richardson and McNeill and were finally agreed with Broadhurst at an Army/Air conference on 24 March. Major Alex Wallace,[8] who now succeeded McNeill in command of 2/5 AASC, flew up to the joint New Zealand/X Corps HQ with his RAF colleagues to brief the forward air controllers.

The attack went in at 16.00 on 26 March, with 16 squadrons of 'Kittybombers' attacking out of the late afternoon sun. In spite of some difficulties caused by a dust storm over the airfields, it was outstandingly successful, only 13 out of 400 planes being lost and huge numbers of German guns and armoured and soft-skinned vehicles destroyed. By nightfall on the following evening, the enemy was in retreat, not only from the positions directly attacked, but also from the main Mareth Line, in order to avoid being cut off.

These new tactics were the foundation of those which were later used to great effect, not only by the Desert Air Force in the Italian campaign, but also by the Second Tactical Air Force in North-West Europe. Coningham was still highly sceptical, but Monty and Freddie were delighted, the pilots were convinced and the relationship with the Desert Air Force was significantly enhanced.

Mareth was arguably Freddie's finest hour in North Africa, when he pulled the chestnuts out of what had looked at one time like a disastrous fire. Monty himself recovered his poise very quickly, demonstrating as at El Alamein his willingness to change a plan which was not working.

The next defensive line was just north of El Hamma at Wadi Akarit. The wadi itself represented a very similar obstacle to Wadi Zigzaou, and there were two steep hill features inland with a narrow gap between them. In this case the door was unlocked by 4 Indian Division. Scarcely used at El Alamein, condemned to tidy up the battlefield thereafter and later assigned to stevedoring duties on the lines of communication, the division was seething with frustration by the time it arrived at Mareth. After the failure of the frontal assault Tuker persuaded Monty to allow him to carry out a short left hook through the Matmata Hills and, although it made little difference to the outcome, Monty was sufficiently impressed by the division's mountaineering skills to repeat the exercise at Wadi Akarit. The silent attack on the night of 5/6 April by two Indian brigades resulted in their taking the left hand hill feature, Jebel Fatnassa, turning the Axis flank and allowing 50 Division through the gap, whilst the Highland Division fought its way across the right hand hill feature and the wadi, albeit taking heavy casualties. Main HQ also suffered an important loss: Fred Kisch, up with the forward sappers as was his custom, stepped on a mine and was killed instantly, to be greatly missed by his colleagues. At the more junior level, Peter Paget, one of the 'Freddie Boys' acting as a Liaison Officer with X Corps, was another fatality.

Shortly afterwards the first American troops were encountered, and three days later the forward patrols of Eighth Army met those of First Army, closing the line around the Axis forces. There was little love lost between the two armies, Eighth being encouraged by Monty to play up their run of successes, First weary after a winter of disappointment in the mountains. Sfax was taken on 10 April, Sousse on 12 April and, two days later, Eighth Army arrived in front of the last defensive position on the Allies' right flank, at Enfidaville. A great opportunity to cut off the retreating Axis forces was missed when a joint British and American effort to penetrate through the Eastern Dorsale at Fondouk was foiled by a strong German defensive line, and the enemy withdrew in relatively good order.

The capture of Sfax was significant for Monty personally, as it enabled him to collect on a bet. During the pause at Tripoli he had been visited by Walter Bedell Smith, Eisenhower's Chief of Staff. Monty assured the American that he would be in Sfax by 15 April, which Bedell Smith doubted. Monty asked if he would care to bet on this, to be assured by Bedell Smith that if he reached the town before that date and ahead of First Army, the Supreme Commander would let him have anything he wanted. Monty said that, in that case, what he wanted was his own personal B-17 Flying Fortress. He now sent a signal to Eisenhower, calling in the bet. Eisenhower was not amused, but had to honour it: the aircraft, complete with a USAAF crew, arrived on the following day. As a heavy bomber, it was in many ways a completely inappropriate aircraft to be used for transport purposes, but Monty was inordinately proud of it and used it extensively until it came to grief some months later.

Monty's arrival at Sousse was notable for his being set up, unknown to him, by his high-spirited ADCs. The victorious liberator was invited to attend a ceremony at which the Mayor was to give a welcoming speech. A charming young lady was lined up to present the Eighth Army Commander with a bunch of flowers. Whilst making the arrangements, Poston and Henderson were asked what she should say and advised that the proper words would be 'Will you kiss me?' After much coaching the girl duly followed the script sufficiently clearly for Monty to understand the meaning and comply with the request. On being asked if she had accorded the same treatment to them, the ADCs assured Monty that the pleasure had been reserved for him alone!

Both 50 and 51 Divisions were now withdrawn from the front line as they had been earmarked for the invasion of Sicily. The commander of 50 Division, Major General J. S. 'Crasher' Nichols, was relieved of his command, Monty's scapegoat for the failure of the frontal attack at Mareth. His successor was Sydney Kirkman, who had transferred recently to 18th Army Group as Alexander's artillery adviser. Highly regarded as always by Monty, who some thought valued his advice less only than Freddie's, his reward was to command a division and later a corps in action, the only former member of Monty's staff to do so. The new BRA Eighth Army was Alan Hornby, formerly the CCRA of XIII Corps.

The mountains north of Enfidaville represented a formidable obstacle to Eighth Army. Two attacks were mounted on the Axis positions, the first by 2 New Zealand, 4 Indian and 7 Armoured Divisions on 19 April, which made very little ground, the second by the newly arrived 56 Division on the night of 28/29 April, which was repulsed with heavy losses. The division had only just arrived after a 3,200 mile journey from Iraq, and was not battle-worthy. Monty realized that there was little profit to be gained from hammering away on his front. On 18 April 1 Armoured Division had been sent to join First Army and, when Alexander and McCreery visited Monty at his HQ on 30 April, he proposed that 4 Indian Division, 7 Armoured Division and 201 Guards Brigade should follow them. McCreery had been suggesting this to Alexander for some time, but the C-in-C was reluctant to force such a move on his powerful subordinate. Now Monty was proposing just that: with Horrocks also going to First Army to replace the injured commander of IX Corps, he felt able to claim, without any real justification, much of the credit for the final victory in Tunisia.

By this time Monty had, in reality, lost interest in the North African campaign. Since late February he had been gradually drawn into the preparations for Operation HUSKY, the invasion and occupation of Sicily, and with no further role for him in action, his mind was now fully on that task. A planning team had been established in Cairo and Freddie, promoted to major general,[9] was sent there on 15 April to take over, with Richardson appointed as BGS in his place. David Belchem, who had recently won a DSO in command of 1st Royal Tank Regiment in 7 Armoured Division, was recalled to become involved in the planning, arriving in Cairo at the end of April. He was followed by Graham and members of the Q (Plans) staff, including Oliver Poole, who had left Eighth Army to join the LRDG on the day before Monty's arrival and now returned in a planning role. One by one, other key members of Eighth Army's staff were also drawn off to join the team in Cairo until, with the end of hostilities in North Africa on 9 May, HQ Eighth Army was effectively divided into two, one a much reduced establishment responsible for administering the remaining components of the Army from Sousse and later Tripoli, the other a growing planning staff in Cairo. Tac HQ was disbanded and John Oswald, a lieutenant colonel since late 1942, when it was discovered that there was a place on the establishment for a GSO1 (Training),[10] was put in charge of Main HQ at Sousse. Before very long he tired of the role and requested a return to regimental duty. As usual, Monty facilitated this and put his name in the little black book for future reference.

During the campaign, Monty had firmly established the command and control methodology which he would use for the rest of the war. For him it was above all vital to be closely in touch at all times with his corps and divisional commanders and, later in North-West Europe, with his army commanders. He could only do this by being physically close to them and by reposing complete confidence in his staff to put his outline plans into effect with the minimum of interference. The vital instrument of this methodology was the Tac HQ, which evolved considerably over time, although during the North African campaign it remained very small. After El Alamein all the operations, except Mareth, were undertaken by a single corps, so it was only necessary to be close to that corps' HQ, and in practice, other than between Buerat and Tripoli, Tac was usually sited within walking distance of it. As far as divisional commanders were concerned it was relatively easy for Monty either to make frequent visits to them himself or to use his ADCs or one of Oswald's GSO3s to do so, so there was no need to replace Carol Mather as a personal liaison officer. Freddie, on the other hand, needed Llewellyn and Paget to tell him what was happening at the front.

During and after the battle of Wadi Akarit, Eighth Army was visited by Brigadier Maurice Chilton, who had been instructed by the War Office to prepare a report on the functioning of its HQ. Chilton had been Monty's BGS at South-Eastern Command in 1942, so knew him well. He was shortly to go to Home Forces HQ as a BGS and the objective of his visit was to gain as much useful information as possible on the workings of an army in action. This would be especially useful when 21st Army Group was split off from Home Forces, as was to happen shortly.

Chilton was critical of the split between Main and Tac HQs. He observed that, during the planning for the attack on Wadi Akarit, Main had been 80 miles behind Tac and that, although the distance had been reduced to a mere 10 miles by 7 April, it had lengthened again to 100 miles as the Army galloped forward to Sfax and Sousse. During the period from 8 to 13 April, there was actually no telephone contact at all between the two HQs. Chilton believed that this placed a considerable strain on Freddie, Miles Graham and Bill Williams, all of whom were forced to make daily journeys to visit Monty. He also pointed out that Monty's advisers on armour, artillery, engineering and signals had to make a choice between remaining at Main HQ and out of touch with the Army Commander and the battle, locating at Tac HQ and out of touch with their own staff, and travelling between the two and out of touch with everybody for most of the time.[11]

As far as Rear HQ was concerned, housing as it did the majority of the staff from the Q and A branches, although the aim was to have it as close to Main HQ as possible, Chilton accepted that it had an even greater need to be adjacent to the roadheads or ports for which it was responsible. The distances between the two varied from three miles, during the pause at Tripoli, to 200 miles when the Army was advancing fast.

Chilton reported that the staff themselves considered that the use of a permanent Tac HQ made their lives very difficult. He blamed the situation partly on the requirement for Main HQ to be located alongside the RAF HQ, which itself insisted on being close to its airfields. He thought that an improvement in radio communications would improve this situation, allowing the RAF to move further forward, and that the great advances of hundreds of miles which had characterized the advance from El Alamein to Enfidaville were unlikely to be replicated in future campaigns. If these issues could be satisfactorily resolved, he queried the need for a Tac HQ at all.

Monty, of course, changed nothing.

Chapter Thirteen

Husky

The British delegation to the Casablanca Conference arrived much better prepared than their American counterparts and, as a result, came away with everything they wanted, including the invasion of Sicily. The Americans, who believed and would continue to believe that the only way to defeat Germany was by the shortest route to Berlin across the English Channel, were forced to accept that this would be impossible to execute in 1943. In order to demonstrate to the Soviet Union that the Western Allies were vigorously pursuing the land war, the only alternative was an operation across the Mediterranean. An invasion of Sardinia was promoted by the Americans, but in the end Sicily emerged as the most logical objective.

In the event, this made good strategic sense, albeit that it benefited Great Britain more than the USA. Control of Sicily would free up the passage through the Mediterranean from Gibraltar to Port Said, radically improving communications with India and releasing shipping for the Atlantic crossing. It would also be a grave setback for Italy and might go as far as persuading that country to seek peace. Furthermore, it would provide employment for the now significant Allied forces gathered in North Africa and the Middle East, who would otherwise be idle for the next year. The occupation of Sicily was, however, for the time being an end in itself, and no decisions were taken at Casablanca as to what to do thereafter.

Eisenhower was nominated as Supreme Commander for Operation HUSKY, with three British subordinate commanders-in-chief, Cunningham for the Western and Eastern Naval Task Forces, Alexander for Seventh US and Eighth Armies and Tedder for the various strategic and tactical air forces. At the end of January an inter-allied, inter-services planning HQ called Force 141 was set up in Algiers, with Charles Gairdner, formerly GOC of 8 Armoured Division and commander designate of the aborted Operation GRAPESHOT, as its chief of staff. Force 141 was established initially under the auspices of Allied Forces HQ, but effective responsibility passed in due course to Alexander. It began immediately to examine a plan which had been prepared by the British Joint Planning Staff in London.

David Belchem was later to say that he knew of nine plans for HUSKY. The planning process was certainly unsatisfactory for a number of reasons. First, the Joint Planners in London had little experience of active service and none

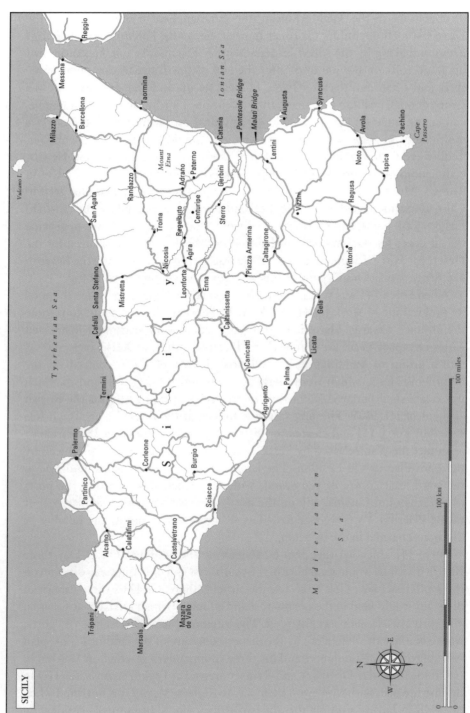

Map 4.

of operations in the Mediterranean; the same applied to some extent to the Force 141 staff, including Gairdner himself. Secondly, Force 141 was bereft of decision making by the Allied leaders. Neither Eisenhower nor Alexander had his mind fully on the job until after the end of the Tunisian campaign, some three and a half months after Force 141 was set up, and Gairdner was not in a strong enough position to demand their attention. Thirdly, there were numerous conflicting interests between land, sea and air. Last but not least, there was a multiplicity of HQs with an enormous geographical dispersal. Eisenhower, Tedder and Cunningham were in Algiers, as was Vice Admiral H. Kent Hewitt, commanding the (American) Western Task Force. Alexander was at Le Kef in Tunisia. Monty was on the move, but had set up his HUSKY planning staff in Cairo alongside Vice Admiral Sir Bertram Ramsay, commanding the (British) Eastern Task Force, and representatives from RAF Malta, which was to provide the air cover for the landings until airfields on Sicily had been secured for the Desert Air Force. Lieutenant General George Patton, commanding the Seventh US Army, was in Oran. None of this was beneficial to smooth planning.

When Force 141 was set up Monty had just taken Tripoli, and when it issued its programme of work for HUSKY on 17 February he was about to resume the advance towards Mareth. He thus had no time to spare and instructed Miles Dempsey to act for him in Cairo. Dempsey, GOC of XIII Corps, moved into a group of buildings in a residential district of Cairo centred on the Semiramis Hotel, which were thereafter codenamed GEORGE and in which was established Force 545,[1] the new inter-service planning HQ for the British element of HUSKY. The first task was to look at the revised plan which was issued by Force 141 and cleared for distribution by Alexander on 28 February.

In fact the plan released by Force 141 was very similar to that produced by the Joint Planners in London. The latter envisaged simultaneous landings on the south-east corner of the island, with the objective of securing the ports of Syracuse and Catania, and on the north-west corner, with a similar goal of taking Palermo. Ports were regarded as all important to supply the number of divisions engaged in the invasion.

Force 141 amended this plan by staggering the landings. On D-Day three British divisions would go ashore in the south-east and one American division on the south coast near Gela to secure the airfields there. On D+2 three American divisions would land in the north-west and a fourth British Division at Catania. The airborne element was enlarged. The intention, as well as to take the ports, was to confuse the defenders by the dispersed nature of the landings. This plan was approved by Eisenhower and his three commanders-in-chief on 13 March.

On the same day Dempsey and Ramsay arrived at Eighth Army's Tac HQ to discuss the plan with Monty on their way to Algiers. Monty was horrified when he saw it, believing strongly that the two armies should be mutually supporting and not dispersed. He sent immediate signals to both Eisenhower and Brooke, setting out his total disagreement with the proposals. Dempsey and Ramsay then flew on to Algiers for a meeting with Force 141 on 18 March at which, in the absence of Alexander, Gairdner had to bear the brunt of Monty's criticisms.

There followed a period of turmoil, during which various alternatives were proposed and rejected. Both Cunningham and Tedder had been in favour of the Force 141 plan, the former because dispersal offered better security to the fleet, the latter because the airfields inland from Gela were essential to the provision of air cover once the armies moved inland. Monty, in the meantime, became more and more frustrated, until by mid–April, with no rapid progress likely on his front in Tunisia, he decided to take charge himself. Freddie was sent to take over the army side of Force 545 on 15 April, whilst Monty himself met Eisenhower and Alexander in Algiers on 18 April to advance his own proposals. Not for the last time, he left a meeting believing that he had got his way, only to find out later that he had not. When he visited Cairo three days later, he found a state of extreme confusion. This was exacerbated when Freddie was injured in a plane crash on his way to Algiers on 28 April.

Monty's letter to his Freddie was evidence of his consideration for his Chief of Staff:

I am terribly sorry about your accident. I am sending Belchem to Cairo. You are to stay in your house and be completely quiet.

Belchem will do the whole thing and can come and see you if he wants advice on any point.

It is absolutely essential that you take it easy and get well.[2]

Belchem was at something of a disadvantage as a mere lieutenant colonel, with Ramsay, who was a vice admiral, and a senior RAF officer as his opposite numbers. Ramsay was most co-operative, but the RAF from Malta had no experience of working with Eighth Army. More difficult still were the representatives of GHQ Middle East, who were responsible for staging most of the Eighth Army formations from their area and for supplying them thereafter. Belchem fell foul of one of GHQ's senior administrative officers and it was only with the help of Lieutenant General James Steele, the Chief of Staff, that he was able to make a presentation which restored the equilibrium. With the support of a growing Eighth Army contingent, now including Miles Graham and Bill Williams, the Eighth Army plan was worked on and completed by the time Freddie returned to duty on 16 May.

In the meantime, Monty had been at work on the overall plan, which he recast to exclude the Palermo landings. In their stead he proposed to have the whole of Seventh US Army come ashore west of Eighth Army as far as Licata. His initial attempt to persuade the commanders-in-chief went awry when he became ill before a key conference on 29 April and, as Freddie was also out of action,

Leese was sent to represent him and failed to make the case. Monty persevered, however, and on 2 May he went to Algiers himself, this time accompanied by Richardson, who later described the journey:

> As I sat beside him in the aeroplane he explained that he was going to get agreement to the final plan for Husky. On his millboard he started writing in his schoolboy hand with soft pencil and an indiarubber within reach, and after some minutes he turned to me: 'Charles, read that. Is it clear? Is it clear?'
>
> Knowing my 'master' I knew that this was a formality: he never expected his staff, or indeed his ADCs, to agree to anything if they did not.
>
> I answered that it was quite clear. As usual he had summed up the strategic argument with great force and few words. However, knowing as I did something of the prejudices of Tedder and Cunningham who were going to be very disinclined to alter their arrangements to satisfy the 'egotistical' Monty, I felt his chances were small.
>
> But succeed he did. I was not present at the high powered conference, but on the return journey he was contented and relaxed.[3]

Monty's contentment came as a result of a coup which he had engineered in Algiers. This was to beard Bedell Smith, Eisenhower's Chief of Staff, in the lavatory during a break in the conference and convert him to the merits of the plan. Bedell Smith then sold it to Eisenhower. The inclusion of Gela and the airfields satisfied Tedder, but Cunningham remained unhappy. However, Monty had taken great care to come to the conference with Ramsay's explicit approval, so the naval C-in-C was forced to accept the new plan.

All now being agreed and the date of Operation HUSKY set for early July, Force 545 was disbanded and Main HQ was consolidated at Tripoli, with Rear HQ in Cairo, which remained the administrative hub for Eighth Army for the invasion itself. Richardson was sent to represent Monty at Force 141 as there remained a number of detailed but contentious issues to be resolved, particularly with Patton, although the substance of the plan remained the same. Gairdner, branded as 'useless' by Monty, was sacked,[4] to be replaced by his deputy, Alex Richardson, who became Alexander's Chief of Staff when 15th Army Group was formed to control the two Allied armies in Sicily.

Monty now felt sufficiently confident to take some leave. He left for the UK in his Flying Fortress on 16 May, accompanied only by Williams, Geoffrey Keating and his two ADCs. It was his first visit since August 1942 and he found himself the most famous person in the country. The papers had been full of Eighth Army's successes since the previous October, and *Desert Victory*, a film consisting entirely of footage from Keating's AFPU, had been showing in the cinemas. At a performance of *Arsenic and Old Lace* in the West End, the audience stood at the end to applaud not the cast, but the victor of El Alamein sitting in one of the boxes.

Poston and Henderson made the most of their trip. Staying with Monty at Claridge's, they chalked up significant personal expenses, which as they left they found had been added to Monty's bill and settled unknowingly by him. They decided to come clean, but Monty insisted on accepting the situation as it stood, saying that he had wanted them to have a good time. Having briefed the War Office on HUSKY, met the officers of 1 Canadian Division, which would be landing in Sicily directly from the UK, had tea at Buckingham Palace and satisfied himself that his son David was being well looked after, he left for Algiers on 2 June. There he met Brooke, who had recently arrived from the Trident Conference in Washington in order to meet Eisenhower. The latter was still seething over the Flying Fortress incident, which prompted Brooke to administer a dressing-down to Monty. Duly chastened, but unrepentant, Monty returned to Tripoli. The next few weeks were spent visiting all the formations in his command, when as usual he addressed all officers of the rank of lieutenant colonel and above, and attending some of the amphibious landing rehearsals.

On 1 July Main HQ opened in a subterranean cavern in Malta, in preparation for the invasion. Richardson had made all the necessary arrangements, Freddie arriving by sea with Graham and Belchem on the following day. Monty flew in on 3 July, staying for the next week at the Pavilion, a house just outside Valetta requisitioned by his resourceful ADCs. Having been much reduced in numbers after the end of the Tunisian campaign, the HQ was now being built up again and there were some new faces, two of whom were to last the course at Monty's HQs until the end of the war.

With Freddie now a major general, Richardson in the role of BGS and George Baker gone to command 127 Field Regiment RA in 51 Highland Division, there was room on the establishment for another GSO1 and this was filled by Gerry Duke. Duke was a sapper who had commanded a RE field squadron in 7 Armoured Division, taught at the Staff College at Haifa and then been Chief Instructor at the Combined Operations Training Centre in Palestine, this last role providing useful experience to an HQ which had never been involved in a seaborne landing.

At the more junior level another new arrival was Paul Odgers. Odgers was a civil servant at the London County Council who joined the Territorial Army before the war and was commissioned into the Oxfordshire & Buckinghamshire Light Infantry. After taking the Staff College course at Camberley he was posted as a staff officer to the Central Infantry Brigade in Malta, one of three charged with defending the island from invasion. That threat had been removed and there was no chance of immediate action, so he approached Harry Llewellyn, whom he had heard was looking for more liaison officers and who agreed to take him on. With two corps in action during the forthcoming campaign over a much wider front and in more inaccessible country than Eighth Army had been accustomed to, Freddie was determined to ensure that his information was at least as good as Monty's and built up his resources accordingly. With his approval, Llewellyn had about a dozen officers available to him, rather more than were provided for on the official establishment.

Freddie also set up a robust communications channel with Tac HQ. At one end was Duke, at the other Major Dick Vernon, a Regular officer from the King's Royal Rifle Corps, who had been a GSO3 on the Operations staff at Tac HQ from the outset at El Alamein and was now a GSO2 and in de facto command of Tac following Oswald's departure. He was charged with reporting at least daily to Duke at Main HQ, his signals becoming popularly known as 'Vernongrams'.

Another face familiar to Monty reappeared on his staff. As the Canadians were about to join his army, he requested that Trumbull Warren, who had returned from his Staff College course in Canada, should be assigned to him as a personal liaison officer for the duration of the Sicily campaign. Warren arrived shortly before the end of hostilities in Africa and was quickly integrated into the HQ. Several officers also returned who had been despatched to the UK by Monty to share their experience of active service with Home Forces, among them 'Slap' White. In his case he had done so at the School of Signals before being posted as Chief Signals Officer at Eastern Command. With a new campaign in the offing, he was summoned back, arriving at Main HQ just over a fortnight before the invasion.

The seaborne landings on 10 July went remarkably well, given the lack of previous amphibious experience. There was a great deal of confusion on the Eighth Army beaches and a number of formations and units went astray, but the whole army came ashore with very light casualties. This was largely because the Italian coastal divisions were taken by surprise and resistance was accordingly light, due not only to deception measures,[5] but also to the bad weather which had affected that part of the Mediterranean over the previous few days. XIII Corps, comprising 5 and 50 Divisions and 3 Commando, landed either side of the town of Avola, south of Syracuse. XXX Corps, consisting of 1 Canadian Division, now under Guy Simonds, who had impressed Monty so much as BGS of the Canadian Corps in early 1942,[6] 51 Highland Division, 231 Brigade and 40 and 41 Royal Marine Commandos, landed either side of Cape Passero. In the American sector, 1, 3 and 45 US Divisions all established beachheads.

The airborne landings, on the other hand, went badly awry. Most of 82 US Airborne Division's 505th Parachute Infantry Regiment dropped on the island, but the lack of experience of the pilots led to units being widely scattered over the countryside. It was only the initiative of the American paratroopers which enabled them to form small ad hoc groups and hit whatever targets they could find, causing significant disruption to the enemy.

The British airborne assault, conducted by 1 Airlanding Brigade in gliders, was little short of disastrous. The main objective was the Pontegrande Bridge on the main road to Syracuse, whose capture intact was integral to Monty's plan. A number of the glider tug pilots lost their way and turned back, whilst most of the others cast off the gliders too early. The majority landed in the sea, with a high level of fatalities from drowning. Only 12 of the 147 gliders arrived on target and a small party managed to capture the bridge before it could be demolished. It was then retaken by the Italians, but secured soon afterwards by troops from 5 Division, opening the way to Syracuse, whose port was found to be undamaged.

On the evening of D-Day Monty and Lord Louis Mountbatten, Chief of Combined Operations, accompanied only by their ADCs and a few liaison officers led by Llewellyn, boarded HMS *Antwerp*[7] and landed near Cape Passero at 07.00 on the following morning. Monty was expecting to be followed almost immediately by Tac HQ, but for once Freddie let him down by failing to ensure that Tac was loaded on to a ship ready to sail at a moment's notice. The delay infuriated Monty, who was forced to camp at one or other of his corps HQs for the next two days. 'I received the sharpest signal I think I ever got from him and I no doubt deserved it,' wrote the COS later. 'One thing I know, it never happened again!'[8] The fourteen officers and sixty-seven other ranks, with Monty's caravans and other vehicles, did not land until 13 July, joining Main HQ XIII Corps near Syracuse.

Freddie himself went over to Sicily with Miles Graham on the morning of 12 July. They failed to find Monty at XXX Corps near Pachino, so sailed up to Syracuse and motored on to XIII Corps, to discover that he had already left. They immediately returned by road to XXX Corps, where at last they met him. Fully briefed on the situation, the two officers arrived back in Malta on the evening of 13 July and made immediate arrangement for Main HQ to move to Sicily. The 'Step-up Party', which had been organized specifically to get the HQ operational in as short a time as possible, left on the same night, with the key officers, Belchem, White and the Deputy Director of Supply and Transport, travelling ahead by fast destroyer. Main HQ was eventually established just north of Syracuse on 15 July. It was only possible to include an advanced control section of the RAF, as the airfields in Malta were still being used and the full Air HQ was unable to relocate until the majority of its squadrons were based in Sicily.

Whilst Seventh US Army had to fight off a vigorous counter attack on 11 July by the Livorno and Hermann Goering Divisions, the latter the first German formation to be encountered by the Allies, the first 48 hours went well for Eighth Army, which took all its objectives, including the port of Augusta. The planning had focused on the landings themselves, with relatively little consideration given to what would happen thereafter, other than a general agreement that the goal was Messina at the north-east tip of the island. Monty envisaged a two-pronged advance by Eighth Army, with XIII Corps on the right up the main road from Syracuse to Catania and thence along the coast between Mount Etna and the sea, and XXX Corps on the left via Vizzini to Leonforte, a key road junction west of Mount Etna. As at Mareth the emphasis was on the right, and as at Mareth the right got stuck.

The main road to Catania ran over two key bridges. The Malati Bridge across the Lentini River was seized in an audacious operation by 3 Commando. To their surprise, the commandos found German paratroopers in the area, who had dropped in as the result of an urgent plea for reinforcements by the Axis commanders. There was a vicious battle and the bridge was initially lost, but was retaken by 50 Division before it could be destroyed. The second bridge was the Primasole, across the much wider Simeto River. To capture this, 1 Parachute Brigade was dropped on the night of 13/14 July and, as with the previous two airborne operations, few of the paratroopers landed on target, although the few that did so managed to create a bridgehead on the far side and remove the demolition charges from the bridge itself.

Bitter and confused fighting between the opposing groups of paratroopers took place all the next day, but the British were forced to give up their bridgehead. Only that evening did the advance guard of 50 Division and the first tanks of 4 Armoured Brigade appear on the scene. The following three days saw fierce fighting between 151 Brigade, with its three battalions of Durham Light Infantry, and the Germans. On 17 July the latter were at last forced to withdraw and the DLI established another bridgehead across the river, but the defences now erected by the Germans proved too strong to penetrate. As 5 Division upstream on the Simeto suffered the same fate, XIII Corps came to a halt.

XXX Corps started well, but 51 Division, 231 Brigade and 23 Armoured Brigade were held up for two days at Vizzini by a determined German defence. The Highlanders' axis of advance was then changed from moving alongside the Canadians on the far left to moving across country towards Paterno. Near the town of Sferro in the Plain of Catania they, too, were stopped by a vigorous defence. This had one particularly serious consequence: the group of airfields around Gerbini, badly needed by the Desert Air Force, remained under enemy control or hostile fire.

With the Germans now holding the Etna Line strongly, Monty was forced to put all his trust in a left hook by the Canadians. The intention was to split the two main German formations in the area, the Hermann Goering Division facing the British and 15 Panzergrenadier Division facing the Americans, and to get behind the former by advancing along the main road between Enna and Adrano, cutting off any retreat from the Plain of Catania west of Etna. Monty had already persuaded Alexander to give Eighth Army full use of the Vizzini to Enna road, which had hitherto been allocated to Seventh US Army, and this would be vital for the new plan.

Patton, already disenchanted by what he saw as a subservient role in which his army was expected merely to offer flank protection to the British, was not happy, and the commander of II US Corps, Omar Bradley, was furious. On 17 July Patton flew to Tunis to see Alexander with a request to be allowed to detach a significant part of his army for an advance on Palermo. This had never been anticipated in the original plan, but, to Patton's surprise, Alexander readily accepted the proposal. The US Provisional Corps made rapid progress against light resistance and was in Palermo by 22 July, the day on which the Germans were finally pushed out of Leonforte by the Canadians.

Monty had in the meantime brought in his reserve 78 Division, which he would have preferred not to use at all. It fitted into the line between 1 Canadian Division and 51 Division and made an immediate impact. The Canadians advanced along the road from Leonforte to Agira and Regalbuto, whilst 78 Division took the hilltop town of Centuripe on 3 August after heavy fighting. By 6 August Adrano was also in 78 Division's hands and any retreat to the west of Etna was now blocked. With the Americans taking Troina and then Randazzo and advancing along the north coast, both by road and by a series of seaborne landings, the Germans and Italians were forced to fall back to Messina, from where they crossed to the toe of Italy in good order. Seventh US Army entered Messina from the west on 17 August, Patton winning what in his mind was a race with Monty.

Although Sicily had been taken, the Allies had made heavy weather of doing so. This was partly because of Alexander's inability to provide any sort of clear direction or coordination to his two army commanders, who did much as they wanted without reference to each other. The first occasion on which Monty and Patton met was at Syracuse under the auspices of Alexander on 25 July, over two weeks after the invasion. Monty also flew to see Patton in Palermo three days later. This visit resulted in the demise of the Flying Fortress, as the runway turned out to be far too short and the pilot only stopped the aircraft by applying all the brakes on one side so that the aircraft slewed round, collapsing in the process. This was particularly alarming for Henderson, who always travelled in the bomb-aimer's position in the glass dome on the nose and saw buildings rushing up to meet him. As not only Monty but also Freddie and Broadhurst were aboard, the pilot's quick thinking averted a catastrophe to the British command. On his return to Tac, Monty sent an immediate signal to Eisenhower asking for a replacement and was allocated a C-47, a much more suitable aircraft.

The lack of communication between the two army commanders was not the only reason for turning into a hard slog what had, in the immediate aftermath of the landings, looked like a quick campaign. Monty had been unimaginative in the frontal approach to Catania, where the German defences were strong, but had little depth. A seaborne landing behind enemy lines, as carried out later by Patton on the north coast, might have unlocked the position. Although he once again showed his ability to move to an alternative plan, his two corps had lacked the ability to support each other. Richardson considered that the operations had been confused and wondered if he, as BGS (Ops), could have done more to overcome the muddles. In truth, both commander and staff had underestimated the difficulties of the terrain, which hampered progress and made it difficult to identify the enemy's location, whilst Freddie believed that 50 and 51 Divisions had not fully recovered from their long North African campaign.

The battles had been almost exclusively infantry affairs. There had been some use of tanks at Vizzini and in the Plain of Catania, but the terrain was for the most part against them. Realising that this might be the case, Monty had decided not to ask for either of the two armoured divisions then in North Africa, but to employ two independent armoured brigades, 4 and 23, with 1 Canadian Armoured Brigade in reserve. In late July he decided to give his own armoured adviser, Harry Arkwright, command of 23 Armoured Brigade, taking the incumbent commander, G. W. 'Ricky' Richards, formerly of the Royal Tank Regiment, in his place. Richards's first action was to point out to Monty the weaknesses of the British tanks relative to their German equivalents and particularly the inferiority of their guns. He was asked to write a short paper on the subject, which Monty immediately forwarded to the War Office.

As the campaign reached its conclusion there were some lighter moments, one of which was the liberation of Taormina. There were rival claims as to who arrived in the cliff-side resort first, but they were not the advanced patrols of XXX Corps. One of those who entered the town ahead of the fighting troops was Geoffrey Keating, in company with the war artist, Edward Ardizzone. Finding the road clear, the two made their way to a hotel, from where Keating summoned the local Italian commander and ordered him have his men pile their arms in the square before marching into captivity. A message was sent to Main HQ which found its way to Monty, who then contacted Leese asking him why his advance guard was not in the town. Leese was furious and banned Keating from visiting his HQ without express permission.

The other claimant was Llewellyn, acting on the instructions of Belchem to secure the best accommodation. He, too, accompanied only by his driver, arrived to find several hundred Italians still in the town and keen to surrender. By that evening Belchem himself was there and the two enjoyed a fine dinner in the best hotel, served by staff who had performed the same service for German and Italian officers twenty-four hours earlier.

For the first and only time in the campaign, Monty moved from his caravan, establishing himself in a luxurious house in Taormina, the Villa Florida, where some time later he was able to entertain Eisenhower, Patton and the American corps and divisional commanders. The villa came complete with an Alfa Romeo car, and Monty was given a peacock as a pet, which turned out to be noisy and troublesome and had to be quietly disposed of by Henderson. Tac HQ located to Taormina on 16 August for a brief period before Monty, believing that the environment was not conducive to a sufficiently workmanlike atmosphere, insisted on going back into caravans and tents at a site south of Messina as the next campaign approached. Main HQ remained in its rather uncomfortable and very hot location at Lentini, between Syracuse and Catania, before moving to a site some thirty miles west of Messina.

Chapter Fourteen

To the Sangro

E ven before it began, the Italian campaign was bedevilled by strategic disagreements between the Western Allies, which were to continue for the rest of the war. The Americans, whose spokesman was the US Army Chief of Staff, General George C. Marshall, were adamant that the main effort should be in North-West Europe. The British, led by Churchill with the acquiescence of Brooke, continued to advocate a Mediterranean strategy, the centrepiece of which was the invasion and conquest of Italy, followed by an advance into the Reich through the Ljubljana Gap to Vienna. The consequences of their differences were compromise and confusion.

With some reluctance the Americans accepted that it was impossible for the substantial forces in the theatre to remain idle for another nine months. There was silence, however, on the strategic and even the tactical objectives of the next move. As a result, Monty was thoroughly disenchanted. In his own words:

If the planning and conduct of the campaign in Sicily were bad, the preparations for the invasion of Italy, and the subsequent conduct of the campaign in that country, were worse still.[1]

His ire was directed at the higher command and specifically at Eisenhower and Alexander, not at Eighth Army's staff, who continued to perform to his exacting standards. Up until 17 August most of them were entirely concerned with continuing operations in Sicily, but the planners had been at work since mid-July on both Operation BUTTRESS, a landing by X Corps in the area of Gioia Tauro, some 30 miles north of Reggio di Calabria, and Operation BAYTOWN, another landing ten days later by XIII Corps near Reggio itself. Outline plans were issued by the end of that month. At a conference at Main HQ on 10 August, however, the staff were told that it had now been decided to scrap BUTTRESS in favour of landings by Fifth US Army under Mark Clark at Salerno – Operation AVALANCHE. This would now be the main event and BAYTOWN was seen as a diversionary measure. X Corps would be going to Fifth US Army.

To Monty this broke all the rules. Fifth US Army would be landing on its own, nearly three hundred miles away from Reggio and thus unsupported by Eighth Army, making the same mistake which he had succeeded in overturning

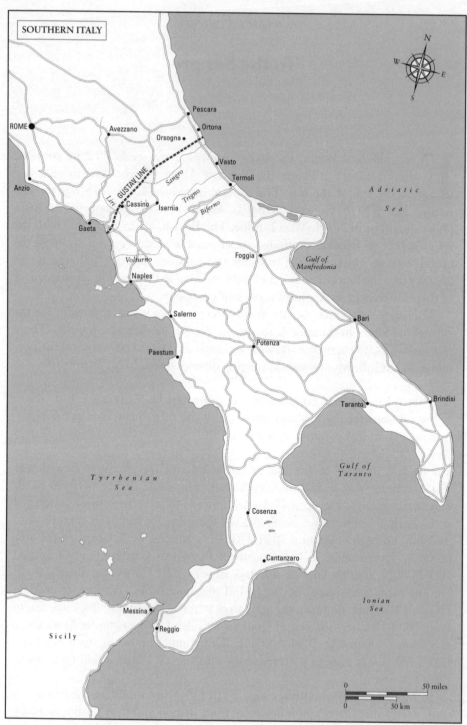

SOUTHERN ITALY

ROME
Avezzano
Pescara
Orsogna
Ortona
Anzio
Vasto
Termoli
GUSTAV LINE
Sangro
Trigno
Liri
Cassino
Isernia
Biferno
Gaeta
Volturno
Foggia
Naples
Gulf of
Manfredonia
Salerno
Bari
Potenza
Paestum
Brindisi
Taranto
Tyrrhenian
Sea
Gulf of
Taranto
Cosenza
Cantanzaro
Ionian
Sea
Messina
Reggio
Sicily

N
W
E
S

Adriatic
Sea

0   50 miles
0   50 km

Map 5.

for HUSKY. He was also far from confident in the abilities of Clark, who had had no experience in the field since the Great War. Asked to provide a senior staff officer for Fifth US Army, he nominated Charles Richardson, writing to him:

> You have been a member of my team for a long time and will be greatly missed. But when appealed to by the Americans we had to send our best; and you are very much wanted in that show. I do not altogether like the way things are shaping up in your 'party'!![2]

Richardson was appointed one of Clark's two Deputy Chiefs of Staff, with particular responsibility for liaison with X Corps, now commanded by Dick McCreery, whilst Belchem stepped up as BGS Eighth Army. Ordered by Alexander to get XIII Corps established on the toe of Italy to free up the Straits of Messina to Allied shipping, Monty remained in ignorance of any wider objective.

Following a massive bombardment by both Eighth Army and the Royal Navy, 5 Division and 1 Canadian Division landed north of Reggio on the morning of 3 September, immediately achieving Alexander's purpose. There was no resistance, the Germans having withdrawn some time beforehand. There was a warm welcome, on the other hand, from the inhabitants.

The actual landings proved to be the only easy part of the new campaign. As XIII Corps advanced, 5 Division on the left in the direction of Cosenza, 1 Canadian Division on the right towards Catanzaro, it became clear that the Germans were not going to make any serious stands. Instead, they destroyed all the bridges, blocked the passes and cuttings, laid mines and set booby traps, leaving a fighting rearguard to harry the advance at every opportunity before withdrawing in good order. A quick pursuit along the only two roads available proved to be impossible. The most important troops in Eighth Army became the engineers and the most vital piece of equipment the Bailey bridge.

Having given an interview to the BBC at 08.00 on D-Day, Monty boarded a DUKW and crossed to the landing beaches in the wake of the leading brigades. Freddie had learnt his lesson from the Sicily debacle, and the advanced party of Tac HQ was pre-loaded on to a LCT and ready to sail. Its composition provides some indication of the priorities in moving Tac: it consisted of Monty's staff car and jeep, three 15cwt trucks carrying signals stores and one for laying lines, one 3-ton lorry with general stores, a 15cwt truck for the Camp Commandant, responsible for setting up and running the camp itself, another jeep for a GSO3 (Ops) and a motorcycle for a liaison officer. Protection was provided by a Humber armoured car, a Daimler scout car and an infantry platoon in a truck and a lorry. On D+1 another LCT sailed with one of Monty's caravans, a lorry carrying all the equipment for his mess, the all-important map lorry, the cookhouse, the ACV, the remainder of the signals equipment and most of the Operations staff. A 10cwt BBC Dodge recording van was also scheduled to be aboard, but was delayed. The remainder of Tac, including Monty's other caravans and the balance of the protection troops, crossed on D+2. Main HQ, in the meantime, established itself just west of Messina.

On the morning of 9 September, Fifth US Army came ashore at Salerno. On the previous evening, the capitulation of Italy had been announced. Monty accorded little value to it militarily, believing that Italian troops would be more of a hindrance than a help and that German resolve would be strengthened. He proved to be quite correct. Clark met significant resistance at Salerno, and by 13/14 September the situation was so serious that he considered withdrawing. The stubborn resistance of X Corps, the reinforcement of VI US Corps by paratroopers from 82 US Airborne Division and the use of the Allied fleet to bombard German positions secured the beachhead permanently, but it had been a close run thing.

As a result of the crisis Monty was ordered by Alexander to drive towards Salerno as fast as possible, but the impediments remained and it was not until 17 September, by which time Clark had restored the situation at Salerno, that the advanced patrols of Eighth Army met those of Fifth US Army. This did not stop Monty from claiming the credit for saving the day.

On the same day as Operation AVALANCHE, 1 Airborne Division was landed by Royal Navy cruisers at Taranto in Operation SLAPSTICK. The paratroopers seized both the port and the town, but were held up outside, where their GOC was killed by a sniper. Nevertheless, with XIII Corps now approaching and Fifth US Army poised to break out from its bridgehead, the Germans withdrew and by the end of September were established along a line from the mouth of the Volturno in the west to that of the Biferno in the east. Meanwhile, 78 Division, with 4 Armoured Brigade under command, had landed at Taranto and Bari, following the Germans up the Adriatic coast and securing the key group of airfields around Foggia. The two British divisions, followed shortly by 8 Indian Division, came under the command of Lieutenant General Charles Allfrey's V Corps, which had fought throughout the campaign in Tunisia but had never served under Eighth Army. Monty paid his first visit to the corps on 22 September and Tac HQ moved to the Adriatic side of Italy shortly thereafter, whilst Main HQ set up on a site 15 miles west of Bari, concentrating there by 26 September. Major Bob Long, responsible for identifying sites for Main, had strongly advised locating it away from the coast, due to the heat, mosquitos and dirt, as well as congestion on the main road. A small C-in-C's camp was set up for Alexander nearby.

Monty had by now acquired a new ADC. Poston was still with him, but was due to leave for the Staff College course at Haifa before the end of the year, so he asked for Noel Chavasse, a subaltern in 51 Division's machine gun battalion, the 1st/7th Middlesex Regiment.[3] Monty had met Chavasse in January 1943 at the division's HQ, where he had been serving as a liaison officer, and learnt that he was the son of a friend, Christopher Chavasse, the Bishop of Rochester. The young officer came to his attention again at Wadi Akarit, where he won the Military Cross. In the knowledge that the division was due to return to the UK, he decided to bring Chavasse on to his personal staff.

Eighth Army was now restored to being a two-corps formation, employing five divisions[4] and two armoured brigades, the major thrust taking place under V Corps on the Adriatic coast whilst XIII Corps moved up the centre of the country in the foothills of the Apennines, with VI US Corps on its left on the other side of the watershed. The width of Eighth Army's front and the difficulty of communicating on poor roads meant that LOs were constantly on the move. Monty was still relying on his own ADCs to fulfil the role, but the 'Freddie Boys' had by this time adopted a well-practised routine, which was considerably better developed as a result of their experience of the Sicily campaign.

The G (L) section of Main HQ consisted of five GSO2s, including Llewellyn as the Senior LO, four GSO3s, four Staff Lieutenants, a corporal/mechanic responsible for vehicle maintenance and drivers for the LOs' jeeps. The Senior LO was based at Main HQ, but frequently found himself on the move, leaving one of the other GSO2s in charge. Two GSO2s were resident at each of the corps, from where they visited divisions, and one at Fifth US Army. Two of the GSO3s were based at Tac HQ, one acted in an admin role and one, who was specifically required to be staff-trained and battle-experienced, had a roving commission in a jeep with a W/T set and could be sent to any hot spot specified by the Ops staff. Two Staff Lieutenants acted as the Duty LOs at Main HQ, one from 08.30 to 18.00, the other from 18.00 to 08.30, the latter with a camp bed by a telephone next to the Watchkeeper's office: they were responsible for keeping the visitors' map up-to-date and ensuring that daily bulletins, situation reports and location statements were distributed appropriately. The other two carried out the visits to corps HQs.

At least one LO from Main HQ visited each corps HQ every day. Before leaving Main he was required to call first at Operations to be briefed by the GSO1, the Watchkeeper, the Map Room and the Ops 2 section which dealt with correspondence, records, and visitors. Whilst in the Map Room he would read and initial the report from the last LO visit to the corps in question, in order to preserve continuity. He then moved on for briefings by Intelligence, Staff Duties and the Signals Office. There was no need to see any of the other staff branches unless requested to do so by the Duty LO. On arrival at the corps HQ the LO would report to the resident GSO2 (L), before visiting all the Operations sections, including Air, and the Artillery, Engineer, Signals and A/Q branches. On returning to Main Army HQ, the LO was required to write out a report in triplicate and hand it in to the G (Ops) Duty Clerk, who would then disseminate it as necessary.

There was a considerable appetite at Main HQ for information from corps and divisions, and not just from Freddie himself. G (Ops) wished to know the locations of all corps, divisional and brigade HQs and all battalions, as well as patrol and defence lines, suitable sites for landing grounds and, most importantly of all, the commander's intentions as to future plans, the grouping of his subordinate divisions and the tasks allotted to them; the LOs had standing instructions to obtain vital extracts from the divisional operations orders. G (Air) was interested in the same, but wanted in addition information on proposed bomb lines, the effectiveness of ground support and enemy air activity. G (SD) needed advance warning of the movements of formations and units. G (I) wanted up-to-date reports on enemy dispositions, identification of enemy units and copies of any maps, documents or equipment which had been captured. The armoured and artillery advisers needed details of the suitability of the ground for the deployment respectively of armoured vehicles and guns and of any losses incurred. The engineers were concerned with the location of minefields, the extent of booby trapping, the conditions of river crossings and the progress of bridging, whilst the LOs were specifically required to carry and fill in road report forms. The signallers wanted to hear about any signal or cipher delays, and each LO was obliged to call at the corps signals office during his visit. The A/Q branches requested information over a wide range of issues, including traffic blocks, likely casualties from future operations and forecast ammunition, POL and general supply expenditure. Overall, the LOs made a very significant contribution to the store of knowledge at Main HQ, although they in no way substituted for direct communication between the staff officers there and their opposite numbers at the corps.

The major headache affecting Eighth Army was now administration, which caused serious problems for Freddie and Miles Graham. When Eighth Army came under the control of 18th Army Group in mid-February, it did so for operational purposes, but administratively the geography demanded that it was still maintained from Middle East Command, the organization of which was all the better for having Brian Robertson in command of the Tripoli Base. For the Sicily campaign, the same was only partially true, as GHQ Middle East was at the other end of just one of several supply chains. By this time 15th Army Group, with much the same staff as its predecessor in Tunisia, had taken full responsibility and it turned out to be seriously lacking in the necessary skills. Monty heaped most of the blame on Charles Miller, its Chief Administrative Officer, who had been the first DA&QMG of Eighth Army in 1941, but in his memoirs he characterized all the army group's administrative staff as having 'neither the knowledge themselves, nor the courage and good sense to put their trust in the information they received from the well-tried and veteran staff of the Eighth Army'.[5] The situation improved when Robertson was given command of Fortbase, the administrative HQ in Syracuse, but he was handicapped by a system which, in spite of all his efforts, was unable to deliver the right supplies and maintenance at the right time and in the right quantities, with large surpluses of some items and huge deficits in others.

The lines of communication in Sicily were relatively short, which helped to ameliorate the problem, but this was not true of Italy. As with operations, the uncertainties of timing and objectives right up to the last moment blighted the administrative planning. Robertson, who continued to be the lynchpin in the administrative chain, remained uninformed about 15th Army Group's plans right up to the last moment. Thus, when XIII Corps landed, it had almost immediately to be placed on reduced rations, whilst both the tenuous lines of communication and the urgency with which the army was ordered to relieve the Salerno beachhead resulted in it running out of some essential supplies.

The problem was exacerbated when the axis of advance was changed so that the supply ports became Taranto, Brindisi and Bari; 15th Army Group proved to be completely unprepared for this and ships arrived with their cargoes poorly loaded, requiring much work on sorting them out, thereby causing serious delay before they could be carried on by road. The situation was not helped by the requirements of the tactical and strategic air forces, which demanded both large quantities of construction equipment to convert the Foggia airfields to all-weather operations and the POL and bombs to carry them out. Eighth Army nearly ran out of fuel, whilst its ammunition supplies also reached perilously low levels. On the A side it found that arrangements had not been made to evacuate the sick and wounded from casualty clearing stations and field hospitals.

Monty's solution was to replace Miller with Robertson, and he found an influential ally in Humphrey Gale, the Chief Administrative Officer at AFHQ. The intermediate step was to have Robertson appointed as Deputy Chief Administrative Officer, AFHQ, Italy, on 12 October, with his HQ in Naples and the clear understanding that he would act as Alexander's administrative adviser on all A and Q matters, thus effectively supplanting Miller. However, it was not until February 1944 that he became CAO of Allied Armies in Italy, as Fifteenth Army Group was renamed. In the meantime, the administrative situation improved markedly.

In mid-September Alexander wrote to Monty and Clark setting out how he saw the campaign developing, with the objective of reaching a line from Lucca to Ravenna by the end of November. He was to be swiftly disillusioned. In the immediate future, however, the campaign seemed to be going well, as X Corps liberated Naples on 1 October. Just as encouragingly, the line along the Biferno River was outflanked by the commandos of 1 Special Service Brigade, who landed north of Termoli just before dawn on 3 October, seizing the town and the port and enabling a brigade from 78 Division to disembark there. The crossing of the Biferno to relieve the force at Termoli, now under counter-attack, proved to be difficult and costly, but by the morning of 6 October the position was secure and the advance could continue. However, Eighth Army was by now aware of the single most difficult aspect of its campaign on the Adriatic side of Italy, the need to cross what seemed like endless rivers, all of which would shortly be swelling with the rains of autumn.

Monty paused to regroup before attempting the next water obstacle, the Trigno. It proved to be less of a problem than expected and both 78 Division near the mouth and 8 Indian Division upstream crossed without difficulty. By 5 November V Corps had taken Vasto and XIII Corps Isernia, an important communications centre up in the Apennines. Monty, heartened by his progress, produced a plan to drive straight through the Gustav Line and then turn west to approach Rome via Avezzano. By the end of the month, 78 Division had crossed the Sangro and established a bridgehead, but the weather deteriorated sharply and it became clear that Monty's plan was unlikely to be achieved in the near future. A much more modest plan was put in place, to establish a firm foothold north of the Sangro.

One of the immediate consequences of the Italian surrender was that large numbers of POWs were released from or broke out of the prison camps in Northern Italy, whence they made their way south towards the Allied armies. Many were recaptured by the Germans, but a good number, assisted by friendly civilians, managed to evade the enemy patrols and walk across the mountains, often in circumstances of great hardship. They included some senior officers, including Monty's friend and the victor of the first campaign in the Western Desert, Dick O'Connor, but there were also some familiar faces from Eighth Army HQ.

One of the first to appear was Hugh Mainwaring, dressed as an Italian peasant, in a truck from XIII Corps. Monty initially failed to recognize him when he walked up the steps to his caravan to announce himself, but gave him a warm welcome and insisted on holding a dinner party in his honour with twenty old friends, which turned out to be a highly enjoyable reunion. Monty was away when Carol Mather turned up, but Johnny Henderson looked after him and his travelling companion, the latter being accorded the honour of a night in Monty's bed. Monty took the trouble to get an immediate message to his parents. Perhaps the most important arrival from his personal perspective was his stepson, Richard Carver, who did not reach safety until early December and was somewhat taken aback to be greeted with the words, 'Where the hell have you been?' Like the others, he was sent back to the UK to recuperate.

The last month of 1943 was deeply frustrating for Monty. On 4 December heavy rains caused the Sangro to rise to the extent that all Eighth Army's bridges were washed away or under water and the bridgehead was temporarily cut off. The sector was reinforced by 5 Division and 1 Canadian Division, but the Germans also poured in reinforcements and little headway could be made. Orsogna and Ortona were taken, but any further advance was impossible as the battlefield, difficult already for its topography, became a sea of mud. All thoughts of Rome vanished.

Monty was generally exasperated. Unlike the most senior British leaders, he had never really shared in the enthusiasm for the campaign and he disliked the way in which it had evolved into a major commitment. He continued to hold a low professional opinion of Alexander, from whom he derived little in the way of constructive guidance, and felt that he was in competition with Clark. It was a far cry from the days when he could operate with considerable freedom in the desert. Alan Brooke, who visited Eighth Army on 14 and 15 December, wrote in his diary, 'Monty is tired out and Alex fails to grip the show!!',[6] later comparing Eighth Army unfavourably with McCreery's X Corps.

Freddie was equally tired. The strain of seventeen months of planning and fighting, with breaks only for sickness or injury, had left its mark. He continued to work very long hours, but suffered also from insomnia. His visits to Tac HQ became less frequent and Monty took to transmitting orders to him, always verbally, through relatively junior officers. One of these was Bill Mather, who was now running Tac following a request by Vernon to return to his regiment and who used to call in at Monty's caravan before breakfast to receive the instructions for Freddie. As always, Monty never wrote anything down and, although the messages were models of simplicity and clarity, it was extraordinary that something so important should have been conveyed in this way.

Mather had just been made second-in-command of the 3rd Hussars in Syria when his new posting arrived and he had to go by sea to Salerno and then hitch a ride from there to Vasto. Asked on arrival why he had taken so long, his answer demonstrated to Monty that, outside Eighth Army, his wishes no longer commanded the sort of priority that he had been used to in North Africa.

There had been conjecture for some time about the command structure for Operation OVERLORD, the invasion of France, which was now known to be agreed for the summer of 1944. The news that Eisenhower would be the Supreme Commander in North-West Europe was conveyed to Churchill and Brooke on 4 December and Eisenhower was told personally by President Roosevelt three days later. The major question now was who would command the ground forces, a role reserved for a British officer. When Brooke met Eisenhower in Tunis on 11 December, he was told that the Supreme Commander Designate favoured 'Jumbo' Wilson as his successor in the Mediterranean, Alexander for the OVERLORD position and Monty to take over from Alexander.

Once the news of Eisenhower's appointment went public, speculation grew about the identity of his ground forces subordinate. Bill Cunningham and Rupert Clarke, Alexander's Military Assistant and ADC, decided to play a trick on their opposite numbers at Eighth Army, sending a signal asking if Monty would like to have their C-in-C's caravans, with the clear implication that it was he who would be leaving. The recipients fell for the ruse and showed the signal to Monty, who immediately sent Freddie to see Alec Richardson, Alexander's COS, who declared his complete ignorance of the matter. Only forty-eight hours later, on 23 December, Monty received a signal from Brooke that he was required for the command of 21st Army Group. The CIGS had always been dubious about Alexander's military abilities and considered that only Monty possessed all the skills and experience necessary to take on such a vital role.

On 30 December the staff of Main HQ, the corps, divisional, brigade and battalion commanders of Eighth Army and senior representatives of the Desert Air Force gathered in the opera house at Vasto, where Monty delivered an emotional farewell[7] to the formation which he had led to successive victories over the last sixteen months. Oliver Leese, who had flown out from England to replace him, was seriously delayed at Naples by the weather. Monty, insistent as always on dining and retiring to bed at the usual times, postponed the start of dinner until 20.30, and Leese arrived ten minutes later. Monty told him that he would be going to bed at precisely 22.15 and that the handover would have to take place before then. Leese later wrote to his wife that he and Monty had gossiped well into the night, so Monty must for once have broken his golden rule.

Leese came via the Main HQ at Vasto, where his Chief of Staff, George Walsh, stayed on for a rather fuller briefing by Freddie, who left to stay the night at Tac HQ immediately afterwards.

At first light on the next day, the last of 1943, Monty, Freddie and a number of others flew out from the airstrip at Tac, bound for England.

Chapter Fifteen

Prelude to Overlord

Monty's C-47 flew him to Marrakesh via Algiers. Freddie and the others, with the exception of Henderson, travelled on to the UK in another aircraft, whilst Monty stayed behind at the invitation of the Prime Minister, who was in Morocco convalescing from pneumonia. Churchill had been joined by his wife and Lord Beaverbrook and, on the afternoon of Monty's arrival, by Eisenhower.

Monty found Churchill reading the plan for Operation OVERLORD, the invasion of North-West Europe, and was immediately given a copy and asked for his comments. Monty had met Eisenhower in Algiers a few days earlier, from which encounter he already understood that the newly appointed Supreme Commander was unhappy with the plan. He was now asked to evaluate it in time for Eisenhower's arrival in London in mid-January. After a New Year's Eve dinner with the Prime Minister and his entourage, to which Henderson was also invited, against Monty's wishes but on the insistence of Mrs Churchill, he requested permission to retire to bed early, as always, and began to study the plan.

By the end of 1943 OVERLORD had already had a long gestation. In strategic terms this went back to the entry of the United States into the war over two years earlier. The British and Americans had immediately agreed a 'Germany First' policy, whereby the European theatre would take precedence over the Pacific; but from the very start the Americans had totally unrealistic expectations of what might be achieved there. Three operations were proposed very quickly. The first of these was BOLERO, the build-up of United States forces in the UK prior to an invasion. The easiest element of BOLERO to achieve was that relating to the air force, which began to be implemented in the late spring of 1942 with the transfer of a number of Bomb, Fighter and Troop Carrier Groups, although some of these were later diverted to North Africa. The quick transfer of sizeable ground forces proved far more problematic, both because the US Army was still relatively small at the end of 1941, with the vast majority of its troops only recently drafted and still requiring basic training, and because there was only limited shipping available.

This had a significant impact on the other two strategic plans presented to the British by General Marshall and Harry Hopkins, President Roosevelt's personal adviser, in April 1942. The most ambitious of these was ROUNDUP, a full-scale invasion in the spring of 1943. It soon became clear that, with only a very limited American contribution, the Allies would have insufficient troops to counter the 25 to 30 divisions which the German were thought to have available in Western Europe, whilst the necessary landing craft were also unavailable. The same argument applied in some measure to SLEDGEHAMMER, a plan to land an expeditionary force to capture the ports of Brest or Cherbourg in the event of a collapse of either Germany or the Soviet Union in the autumn of 1942. The disastrous Dieppe Raid in August 1942 showed what would happen if a well-defended port was attacked from the sea and effectively put paid to SLEDGEHAMMER, whilst the Americans were eventually persuaded that ROUNDUP was impractical and agreed to go forward instead with Operation TORCH in North Africa.

At the tactical level the British were hard at work from early in 1942, when General Sir Bernard Paget, C-in-C Home Forces, Admiral Sir Charles Little, C-in-C Portsmouth, and Air Chief Marshal Sir Sholto Douglas, C-in-C Fighter Command, who were together known as the Combined Commanders, with Lord Louis Mountbatten, Chief of Combined Operations, were instructed to prepare the detailed plan for ROUNDUP. When this was shelved in mid-1942, at least by the British,[1] it was decided that the Combined Commanders would continue to work on an invasion plan for an undetermined date in the future. This was called Operation SKYSCRAPER.

The SKYSCRAPER planners laboured under a serious disadvantage, in that they had no idea of what resources would be available, not only as to troops, but also as to air and naval assets and particularly landing craft. They were, however, able to obtain a very considerable amount of information on the topography, tides, harbours and defences along the coast of Europe from Jutland to the French-Spanish border, from which they determined that the most suitable place for an invasion was the Bay of the Seine, and specifically from just east of the mouth of the River Orne to rather less than a third of the way up the east coast of the Cotentin Peninsula. This was exactly the area eventually chosen in due course for Operation OVERLORD. Moreover, the eventual number of beaches, assault divisions, airborne divisions and follow-up divisions for OVERLORD were almost identical to those in the SKYSCRAPER plan. However, when the plan was presented to the British Chiefs of Staff in April 1943, it was summarily rejected as being both far too general, as well as impractical in terms of the resources required.

In the same month there was a significant development, which arose from the decision taken at Casablanca that the invasion would be mounted as early as possible in 1944. The Western Allies delegated the planning to an officer with the title of Chief of Staff to the Supreme Allied Commander (Designate) or COSSAC;[2] the identity of the Commander himself was unknown at the time and would remain so until the end of the year. The man chosen for the job was

Lieutenant General Frederick Morgan, a gunner who had served in exceptionally frustrating circumstances as commander of 1 Armoured Division's Support Group in France in 1940, before going on to divisional and corps commands in Home Forces. Alan Brooke, still something of a sceptic on the invasion, outlined the task to him, finishing with the words: 'Well, there it is. It won't work, but you must bloody well make it.'[3]

Morgan immediately assembled a joint services and inter-allied staff, with Major General Ray Barker of the US Army as his Deputy. He was given three objectives, of which the full invasion plan was the third, albeit the most important. The other two were a deception plan (STARKEY), largely for the benefit of the Soviet Union, to persuade the Germans to expect an invasion in 1943 and thus to keep as many as possible of their divisions in Western Europe, and a plan for a return to Europe (RANKIN) in the event of any German disintegration, in some ways an extension of SLEDGEHAMMER. Both of these fell away as 1943 unfolded, leaving Operation OVERLORD and Operation NEPTUNE, its assault phase, as the priorities.

Morgan and his staff were faced with three questions – where, how and when? The answer to the last of these had already been partially provided, but the precise timing depended on the weather, which tended to rule out the earliest months of the year, the accumulation of the necessary resources and, within a particular window, the tides and the moon. A decision was made relatively early on to go for the first week of May 1944, but this was later moved back by a month at Eisenhower's request. As far as the location was concerned, the COSSAC planners had the benefit of all the work carried out on SKYSCRAPER. As Morgan readily conceded, they were 'heirs to a considerable fortune'[4] in this respect and, perhaps unsurprisingly, they came to the same conclusion on location as the Combined Commanders, notwithstanding the competing claims of the Pas-de-Calais.

All the real difficulties emerged in the resolution of 'How?' Here COSSAC was in entirely the opposite situation to the Combined Commanders, in that its planners were not obliged to estimate the available resources but were told exactly what they would be. The major problem was the availability of all types of landing craft: there were demands on their production, largely by the campaign in the Central Pacific which was due to kick off in the autumn, and a need to retain existing craft in the Mediterranean for Operation ANVIL, an invasion of the South of France being planned to take place simultaneously with OVERLORD. As COSSAC saw the capture of Caen as critical, the shortage of landing craft rendered impossible any landings on the Cotentin Peninsula, so the western end of the assault area was pulled back to the east bank of the mouth of the River Vire. COSSAC was forced to reduce the number of both landing beaches and assault divisions from the five proposed in SKYSCRAPER to three.

The lack of any beachhead on the Cotentin ruled out the early capture of Cherbourg and made it vital that some sort of alternative should be produced to total reliance on landing over open beaches. Commodore John Hughes-Hallett, a member of Morgan's naval staff, made the suggestion that if the invaders were not able to capture a port they should take one with them, and from this the 'MULBERRY' harbours were conceived. A further proposal was developed, codenamed PLUTO, to construct a flexible pipeline across the English Channel to carry bulk POL. In addition, COSSAC did a tremendous amount of valuable work on the detail of the landings and solved a number of problems which had seemed intractable at first. In an astonishingly short space of time the outline plan was conceived and submitted to the British Chiefs of Staff in July 1943. They gave it their approval and, at the end of the month, Morgan and his Chief Administrative Officer, Major General Nevil Brownjohn, travelled to the United States to present it to President Roosevelt and the Joint Chiefs of Staff. It was discussed in detail at the Quebec Conference in August and final approval was given subject to the agreement of the Supreme Commander, once he had been appointed. Their job done, the COSSAC planners were reorganized on the American staff system, in the knowledge that the Supreme Commander would be an American, and awaited his arrival as the nucleus of the Supreme Headquarters Allied Expeditionary Force ('SHAEF').

In July 1943 Bernard Paget was ordered to form 21st Army Group, which would be the superior ground forces formation for the invasion and continue to control Second Army and First Canadian Army after the Americans had split off their own army group following the breakout from the invasion beachhead. Paget had been C-in-C Home Forces since December 1941, when he had succeeded Brooke on the latter's appointment as CIGS. He had previously acted as Brooke's Chief of Staff, before becoming Monty's predecessor at South-Eastern Command. In contrast to Monty's own disparagement of him as a trainer of troops, it was generally recognized that he had done an outstanding job in preparing the divisions in the UK for war; indeed, many of his contemporaries considered that he was the best trainer in the Army since Sir John Moore in the early nineteenth century. A significant number of these divisions had departed during 1942, either for the Mediterranean or for the Far East, and he was now instructed to transfer most of those that remained into 21st Army Group, leaving Home Forces as a considerably truncated organization, whose remaining divisions would train reinforcements for active service.

GHQ Home Forces had originally been based in Whitehall and other locations in West London, but in 1940 it moved to St Paul's School in Hammersmith. The buildings there were hit during the Blitz of 1940/41 and one particularly valuable communication cable was severed, so GHQ relocated to Wentworth Golf Club, where it occupied the clubhouse and a number of surrounding properties. The HQ of 21st Army Group initially inherited Wentworth, but in September 1943, with the bombing threat much diminished, it returned to St Paul's.[5] There it was much closer both to the War Office and to SHAEF in Norfolk House, St James's Square, which had earlier housed not only COSSAC, but also the planners for the Combined Commanders. Most of the General Staff had offices in the main school buildings alongside the Q staff and RAF and Royal Navy liaison officers, but Air and part of Intelligence were in the High Master's house. The A, B and C Messes, for officers down to the rank of lieutenant colonel, were located in Latymer Court on the other side of Hammersmith Road. All the other staff branches and departments were situated in the area between the school and North End Road or on the other side of Talgarth Road down as far as Queen's Club Gardens.

Paget brought much of the GHQ Home Forces Staff with him, including Lieutenant General William 'Monkey' Morgan, the CGS, and Brigadier Charles Loewen, the BGS (Ops), who was leading the planning for OVERLORD. Loewen left in November, to be succeeded by Brigadier Brian Kimmins, who, like Morgan, had seen no active service since 1940. Most of the other staff members were also longstanding Home Forces officers and few had any recent operational experience.

By the time that 21st Army Group moved to St Paul's, the decision to replace Paget had already been taken by Brooke and Churchill, although some debate remained to be had on the various merits or otherwise of Monty and Alexander. It was not until 13 December that Paget was told, but even this was ten days earlier than Monty himself. Paget had seen it coming for some time and was disappointed but understanding.[6] What he might not have expected was that a very large part of his senior staff would suffer the same fate.

Chapter Sixteen

The Monty Men Take Charge

Monty subsequently recorded his return to England in his diary:[1]

1. I left Eighth Army in my C/47 from the SANGRO strip at 0715 hours on 3 December. Oliver LEESE had arrived the night before and I had been able to have a good talk with him.

2. I took with me the following:

Major-General de GUINGAND	My Chief of Staff
Brigadier GRAHAM	My head administrative officer
Brigadier RICHARDS	My head R.A.C. officer
Lt.-Col. WILLIAMS	My head Intelligence staff officer
Capt. J.R. HENDERSON	My A.D.Cs
Capt. N.W. CHAVASSE	
Lt.-Col. T. WARREN	My LO for Canadian forces
My Mess Sergeant	(Sgt. SHIP)
My car driver	(Sgt. EDWARDS)
My jeep driver	(Pte. BURFORD)
My batman	(Cpl. ENGLISH)

The Sgt-Major Clerk to the Chief of Staff (Sgt-Major HARWOOD)

All the above would be wanted by me to get the show going in 21 Army Group in England. It was fairly certain that I would want others as well, and I was particularly anxious to get home the following:

WHITE	My Chief Signal Officer
LYMER	My Q (Maintenance)
HUGHES	My head Padre
BELCHEM	My BGS (Ops)
DUKE	My GSO1 (Ops)
McNEILL	My GSO1 (Air)

The wholesale removal of staff from an HQ by a commander on his transfer to another appointment was not common practice in the British Army, as Monty himself had discovered in his moves to corps and army commands in the UK in 1940 and 1941 and his appointment to Eighth Army in 1942. That he was now able to do this was a measure both of his status as Great Britain's pre-eminent field commander and of the effectiveness of his contention to Brooke and the War Office that he would be unable to do what was necessary to mount a highly complex invasion in a very short time without men behind him who had the requisite experience and whom he trusted implicitly. When he left Italy he had no idea of the quality of the staff of 21st Army Group, but he was not prepared to take any chances.

The moves came as a surprise at Eighth Army HQ, even to those who had been chosen. Bill Mather recalled that a book had been made on who might accompany Monty, showing his batman and cook at evens and all the others at odds against, including Freddie at 2-1. Monty discovered that the book existed and demanded to see it. He was particularly amused to find Graham with heavy odds of 16-1 against, remarking, 'Miles, you must have been found out!' In fact Monty did not have War Office approval to take Graham, unlike the others on the plane, but he did so anyway, certain that he could argue the toss successfully, as indeed turned out to be the case.

All those who left in the first wave moved into predictable positions, Freddie taking over as Chief of Staff from 'Monkey' Morgan,[2] who he later said could not have been more helpful. Kimmins stayed on as DCGS until he, too, was found to be surplus to requirements.[3] Graham, now fully approved, was promoted as Major General Administration, whilst Richards took over from Willoughby Norrie, who had an uneasy relationship with Monty and was expecting to go. Williams was promoted to brigadier and placed in full control of Intelligence.

The 'reserve list' was secured by Monty very rapidly. Belchem had only been left behind to provide assistance to Leese's Chief of Staff for the first week. After a difficult journey, on which he had to hitchhike on numerous aircraft, he arrived in London on 14 January to report to Monty, who allowed him a scant 24 hours leave before taking up an interim job as BGS of the Special Planning Section, later assuming the key role of BGS (Ops). White, like Graham and Richards promoted to major general, took on the role of Signals Officer-in-Chief, whilst Lymer became Brigadier Q (Maintenance). Hughes was initially rejected by the War Office as Deputy Chaplain General, but Monty persisted and in due course got his way. McNeill was too junior to lead the Air section of the General Staff, but agreed to serve under the BGS (Air), Claud Oxborrow; in due course he was attached as the principal liaison officer to Second Tactical Air Force, where his experience in ground/air operations could best be utilized. Duke moved from the General Staff to the Q Staff as a brigadier, responsible for representing 21st Army Group in the Back-Up Control Organization

('BUCO'), the joint tri-service/civilian body responsible for ensuring that the flow of men and materials continued unabated after D-Day.

It did not stop there. Harry Llewellyn had been sent back to the UK with top secret documents for the War Office and was about to return after a brief leave, only to receive a signal from Freddie ordering him to remain where he was. He later discovered that the trip to England was a ruse of Freddie's to have him on the spot when he arrived, ready to take up a temporary position as Freddie's Personal Assistant. At his request he was promised a return to the role of GSO1 (Liaison) in due course, whereupon he was succeeded by Bill Bovill, who had once served at Eighth Army HQ, albeit not under Monty or Freddie. Oliver Poole and Joe Ewart came back to find that they were now full colonels, the former in charge of Q (Plans), the latter as Williams's deputy and the principal guardian of ULTRA. Two officers bolstered the Staff Duties branch as GOS1s, George Baker, recalled from commanding his regiment, and Frank Byers, who had done the job in Eighth Army after Baker left.

Last, but far from least as far as the old Eighth Army team was concerned, in March 1944 Charles Richardson was summoned from his position as a Deputy Chief of Staff at Fifth US Army to become BGS (Plans). He was by then too late to have any input into the main OVERLORD and NEPTUNE plans, but began to work on alternative scenarios following a successful lodgement on the Continent.

Other favourites of Monty's were pulled in from elsewhere. He was unhappy about the MGRA, Otto Lund, who was one of the most influential artillerymen in terms of the development of the arm, but had no operational experience. There was, however, an outstanding and battle-experienced gunner already in England in the shape of Meade Dennis, the longstanding CCRA of XXX Corps, who had been responsible for the main part of the barrage at El Alamein and a tower of strength thereafter until the corps returned to the UK. He was very highly regarded by Monty and made an immediate impact, bringing with him as his GSO1 a member of his own staff from XXX Corps, John Gibbon.

Perhaps the most important recruit from a personal perspective was Kit Dawnay, whom Monty managed to detach from a job as GSO1 in the Military Operations branch of the War Office, to which he had been recruited by 'Simbo' Simpson. Dawnay was now to lead Monty's personal staff as his Military Assistant for the rest of the war. Trumbull Warren, whom Monty had extracted from the Canadian Corps just before leaving Italy and then brought home with him, was to support Dawnay as Monty's Personal Assistant, with particular responsibility for dealing with First Canadian Army. In addition to his two existing ADCs, Monty decided that he should have an American, as for the first part of the campaign he would have First US Army under his command. Two officers, Ray BonDurant, a former mining engineer who had served under Patton in Sicily and been wounded there, and Edwin 'Bill' Culver, were produced by

Eisenhower for him to choose between. They both seemed so good that Monty found the decision very difficult, but in the end took the former, who would in future accompany him on most of his visits to American commanders and troops, whilst securing the latter for Freddie, with Eisenhower's agreement.

A number of officers at brigadier level and above survived the cull. Some of them, such as the BGS Publicity and Psychological Warfare, the Director of Survey and the Director of Civil Engineering (Airfields), were in functions which had not existed in Eighth Army and in which the Monty Men had no experience. Others were immediately acceptable to Monty, notably the DQMG (Maintenance & Army Equipment), who was Gerry Feilden, Monty's former AQMG at V Corps. Some thought that Graham himself lacked flair, but that both Feilden and Poole were very able and provided the necessary backing. Graham's other two immediate subordinates, the DQMG (Movements & Transportation), Brigadier I. L. H. McKillop, and the DAG, Brigadier Cyril Lloyd,[4] were unknown quantities, but were already well entrenched.

The most senior member of the General Staff to retain his position was Brigadier Otway Herbert, the BGS (Staff Duties). Unlike most of his colleagues when 21st Army Group was formed, he had a great deal of operational experience, as a staff officer at GHQ BEF and as the CO of a field regiment in Tunisia, having won the DSO and bar in the process. He was thought to be doing his job well and, possibly because he had already built up a detailed knowledge of the formations and units in the army group and had good relations with the Q and A branches, both integral to Staff Duties, was retained, with Baker acting as his deputy. Monty himself was later to write that he was a 'tower of strength ... a terrific worker'.[5]

The only member of the A (major generals) mess to survive the purge was Drummond Inglis as Chief Engineer. He might have been thought a surprising choice, having fallen foul of Monty in Sicily. He had arrived in Malta with a number of others from the UK to pick up first-hand experience of the campaign, only to be confronted by an order from Monty that no one was to land without his express permission. Intending to circumvent this, Inglis hitched a ride in a landing craft, but news of his presence leaked out and he was confronted with a message that he would be placed under immediate arrest if he set foot on the island.[6] He may have owed his retention to his friendship with Freddie, although by early 1944 his familiarity with the engineering problems of OVERLORD would have been highly valuable.

Perhaps the most unlikely of all the officers to keep their jobs was the Deputy Military Secretary, Colonel Jack Gannon. On the face of it, Gannon represented everything that Monty disliked about certain officers. For a start, he was from the Indian and not the British Army, and that organization was one for which Monty frequently expressed scorn. This may have been because of his failure at Sandhurst to pass out high enough to gain a commission in it, but was amplified by the time he had spent in India and his experience of senior officers such as Auchinleck. Secondly, Gannon was a cavalryman and Monty had a generally low opinion of the cavalry and some of their officers, such as Lumsden, Gairdner and Norrie. Much of this was because he considered that they had spent far too much time on sport in the inter-war years and not enough on mastering their profession. Gannon was the archetypal cavalry officer when it came to sport and particularly anything to do with horses: an outstanding high-handicap polo player who had run the sport at the 1936 Olympic Games, he had been the Master successively of the Quetta Hunt and the Lahore Hunt before the Great War and a formidable pig-sticker. By 1944, moreover, he was 62, probably the oldest officer on the staff and five years older than Monty. He had retired as long ago as 1932, becoming the Manager and Secretary of the Hurlingham Club.

Gannon rejoined the Army in 1939, becoming Assistant Military Secretary at Home Forces, possibly on the strength of his having served as Military Secretary to Lord Rawlinson, C-in-C India from 1920 to 1925. In July 1943, when 21st Army Group was set up, he was appointed Deputy Military Secretary. By early 1944 he had an encyclopaedic knowledge of the senior and middle-ranking officers of the army group which, in all probability, could not be quickly replicated by anyone else. When an officer was sought to take up a vacant appointment, he would immediately produce the most suitable candidate. In a situation where there was likely to be considerable attrition, especially amongst infantry COs, this ability would be vital. Thus he was retained and actually became indispensable to Monty, Freddie later describing him as a 'wise old bird',[7] although 'Shrimp' Coghill was brought back from Eighth Army as Assistant Military Secretary to ensure that Monty's way of doing things would be adhered to. Gannon was a regular and popular visitor to Tac. Johnny Henderson thought he was 'gentle, old-fashioned and wholly delightful',[8] whilst Monty took pleasure in ribbing him about cavalry officers' priorities in life.

Monty himself arrived back in England on the morning of 2 January 1944, 24 hours after Freddie and the main party and 12 hours after Henderson, who had been sent on to make the accommodation arrangements. The flat being prepared for the new C-in-C at Latymer Court was not yet ready, so Henderson had to find an alternative. As he was later to write: 'The decision was not difficult. We had stayed at Claridge's for three nights after reaching Tunis and enjoyed ourselves immensely. We had six glorious weeks there until the flat was ready.'[9] He and Chavasse shared a room in the suite.

As instructed by Churchill and Eisenhower, Monty had read the OVERLORD plan in Marrakesh. He was horrified by what he saw. In his opinion, the plan offered no hope of success, landing too few troops on too narrowly contained a beachhead. The former would lack the strength to beat off the inevitable German counter-attacks, whilst the latter would restrict the landing of supplies and reinforcements, causing severe congestion. The quick capture of Cherbourg would be rendered near impossible by the need to cross the marshy ground and inundations inland from the estuary of the Vire.

Monty convened the first of three consecutive days of conferences with COSSAC at St Paul's for 09.00 on the morning after his arrival. In addition to Freddie and members of his own staff, Bedell Smith was there representing Eisenhower, whilst Admiral Ramsay, Air Chief Marshal Leigh-Mallory and members of their staffs also attended. Morgan and Barker were there for COSSAC, but the presentations were made by the chief planners, Major General Charles West and Brigadier Kenneth McLean. After they had spoken, Monty stood up and brutally demolished the plan, calling for a much wider beachhead to be established. He asked the planners to consider not only the east side of the Cotentin Peninsula, but also the west side, Brittany and the Normandy coast as far as Dieppe. On the next day, the west of the Cotentin and Brittany were ruled out, largely because of Ramsay's concern about the threat posed by German batteries on the Channel Islands. Monty continued to insist on both a five-division force and a landing on the east side of the Cotentin, and by the end of the third day it was agreed to extend the beachhead to include the future Utah Beach. Any less than this and Monty said that he would not be prepared to continue in command. He was supported by Bedell Smith, himself only too conscious of Eisenhower's unhappiness with the original proposals. The major constraint remained the availability of landing craft, but it was now quite clear that, without an adequate supply of these, the invasion could not be mounted.

Eisenhower did not arrive in the UK until 15 January, and it was not until 21 January that a conference was held at Norfolk House to brief him on both the original COSSAC plan and the revised plan demanded by Monty. Monty proposed that First US Army should focus on securing the Cotentin and capturing Cherbourg, subsequently breaking out towards the Loire and Brittany, whilst Second Army held firm on the eastern flank of the army group against German counter-attacks. Eisenhower agreed to proceed with Monty's plan, although it would be some weeks before formal approval was received from the Combined Chiefs of Staff.

At this point the coordination of planning for the ground forces devolved on 21st Army Group, whilst the COSSAC team was integrated into SHAEF, with Morgan appointed as one of several Deputy Chiefs of Staff. As was his wont, Monty left all the detail to Freddie. He now embarked on a series of visits around the country to get to know those whom he would be commanding in battle.

Chapter Seventeen

G, Q & A

In order to understand the contribution of the staff, it is necessary to have some idea of their organization and duties.* An army group HQ was an enormous undertaking, particularly one which was preparing to launch the largest amphibious operation in history and then conduct a complex and potentially fast-moving campaign, whose course was far from predictable.

The HQ was divided into three parts. Monty himself, as had been his custom since El Alamein, operated from a small Tactical HQ, which is described in a separate chapter. Freddie was located in Main HQ, which housed a substantial majority of the General or G staff, for which he was directly responsible, together with the staff of the Major General RA, the Major General RAC, the Chief Engineer and the Signals Officer-in-Chief. The Quartermaster General's or Q staff was largely located at the even larger Rear HQ, other than Q (Plans), which needed to be close to G (Plans), and Q (Maintenance), which was responsible for sustaining those doing the fighting, both of which were at Main HQ. The Adjutant General's or A staff was almost entirely located at Rear HQ, although the DAG had an office and small team at Main HQ. Most of the Q and A Services, such as RASC, RAOC, REME, RAMC and RAChD were also based at Rear HQ, as were sundry departments such as Finance. Miles Graham was in command of Rear HQ, but in practice he spent most of his time at Main HQ, so Feilden was designated as the principal staff officer there.

The largest individual component of Main HQ was 21st Army Group Signals: shortly before D-Day this comprised no fewer than 718 personnel out of a total of 2563, the latter number including 297 temporarily attached US Army personnel. GHQ Liaison Regiment – 'Phantom' – also had its headquarters there, so communications were exceptionally good. A Defence Company provided protection, whilst there was also a Provost Company and a Field Security Section. Warrant officers, NCOs and other ranks were largely represented by signallers, clerks, drivers, mechanics, storemen, cooks and mess staff. There was a Camp Commandant in charge of the administration of each of the three HQs.

---

* See also Appendices II, III & IV.

Tac HQ moved very frequently, but Main HQ was to move only four times from its initial location at St Paul's and spent most of the campaign in buildings. It was, nevertheless, organized on a mobile basis. For this purpose it was divided into seven groups – Chief of Staff's, Operations, Intelligence, Staff Duties and Advisers, Administration, Camp and Signals – each of which was further divided into two echelons, one of which would move first and establish the new HQ, upon which the old HQ would close and the second echelon follow. This meant that the problem identified in North Africa, that Eighth Army's Main HQ could be out of contact when on the move, would not happen again. The groups also reflected the layout of Main HQ, with messes allocated accordingly and a Visitors' Mess and Sergeants' Mess run by the Camp Commandant, whilst the other ranks were fed directly from their respective cookhouses.

When not housed in buildings, Main HQ was largely accommodated in tents, although there was a collapsible hut for the Operations Room, a large marquee (known as 'the Big Top') for the Information Room and specially designed 3-ton lorries for a number of the offices. Freddie and David Belchem rated both a Class I and a Class II caravan, whilst the major generals, brigadiers and Deputy Military Secretary were allocated Class II caravans, which doubled as a personal office and sleeping accommodation, of which there were also three for visitors. Everyone else was housed in the ubiquitous 160lb tent, one each for colonels, two per tent for lieutenant colonels, four for majors and junior officers, six for warrant officers and sergeants and eight for the rest. When Main HQ was housed in buildings and there was a lack of suitable rooms on the site itself, the officers slept in hotels or were billeted out, whilst the men were in barracks.

Whilst every staff branch was important to the whole, the General Staff might be called the sharp end of HQ 21st Army Group, and G (Ops) was at its heart, so much so that Freddie nominated Belchem as his deputy whenever he was away. Its functions were as follows:

- To keep the Chief of Staff and through him the C-in-C informed as to the progress of current operations
- To maintain close liaison with Intelligence and with the Operations branch of the Second Tactical Air Force, keeping them informed of the progress of operations
- To provide up-to-date situation maps for the Chief of Staff, the Operations Room and the Information Room
- To deal with G (Ops) matters concerning higher and lower formations
- To issue orders, instructions and directives to lower formations

G (Ops) was itself divided into two parts, each led by a full colonel. G (Ops) A comprised the Watchkeepers, who were on duty round the clock in the Operations Room and responsible for recording all the information received and initiating appropriate actions, and the staff of the Map Room, where the maps showing the situation of the Allied ground forces were constantly updated. It was also in charge of G (L), the Liaison sub-section, which in addition to its other duties ran the Information Room, which was open to all the staff officers at Main HQ and also to visitors. G (Ops) B ran the correspondence section, kept the war diary, was responsible for matters related to training and lessons from combat, had overall responsibility for Main HQ moves and dealt with all visitors.

As well as running the Information Room, G (L) provided liaison officers for regular visits to both 21st Army Group and Allied formations. In addition to the GSO1, Harry Llewellyn, the 'Freddie Boys' had an establishment of six GSO 2s and six staff lieutenants, whilst four American officers were also attached for the early stages of the campaign. G (L) was operated in a very similar manner to that which had been developed in Italy and obtained exactly the same information.

G (Air) also came under the control of G (Ops). The creation of this sub-branch had taken place after the end of the North African campaign, upon which it effectively subsumed the Army Air Support Controls at army level, although it continued to function in much the same way. It was regarded as co-equal to G (Ops) A, the former dealing with ground warfare whilst the latter dealt with the air equivalent. To reflect its status it was later called G (Ops) Air, and a report produced immediately after the war recommended that the BGS should be downgraded to a Colonel GS.

G (Ops) Air was located at the heart of the Operations area alongside representatives of RAF (Ops). In addition it sent its own representatives to the HQ of the Allied Expeditionary Air Force at Stanmore during the planning and preparation phase of the invasion, although this increment was disbanded once Main HQ had moved to the Continent and been co-located with HQ Second Tactical Air Force. There was unfortunately some reluctance among senior RAF commanders to accept G (Ops) Air as an authority on operational matters, although relationships at a more junior level were good. Once in the field, other than a brief hiccup sorted out by Charles Richardson, the tactical cooperation worked well, both at the various ground forces HQs and with the Air Liaison Officers at RAF Groups and Wings; but there were considerable difficulties at the strategic level, not helped by the conflicting personalities of Monty and the RAF chiefs. Oxborrow remained in charge, with McNeill returning from Second Tactical Air Force once Main HQ was in the field, where he was responsible as GSO1 for day-to-day operational routines.

G (Plans) was also located in the Operations area, and worked closely with G (Ops), but its purpose was to deal with the future, not the present. In Richardson's words:

In our appreciation of the development of operations, we strove to anticipate and influence the course of future events beyond the prevision of our Commander-in-Chief, knowing that he, having set the immediate pattern, would necessarily have to concentrate on its vigorous implementation. From our long association with him, Freddie and I knew that he would not engage himself, even if he had the time, in hypothetical speculation; yet long-term anticipation was essential if the vast resources at his command were to be marshalled in such a way as to meet likely developments. This was our purpose.[1]

Compared with the other General Staff departments, Richardson had a very small officer team of one GSO1, two GSO2s and a GSO3, but it was all that was needed to fulfil the role. By the time he arrived on 1 April, all of the outline and much of the detailed planning of the landings had taken place under Belchem, who now reverted to his main role as BGS (Ops). G (Plans) thereafter devoted itself to a study of what might happen next, working closely with the Colonel Q (Plans), Oliver Poole.

The Intelligence staff under Bill Williams, known as GSI, were located adjacent to the Operations area. GSI worked very closely with G (Ops) and was responsible for recording the enemy's dispositions on the maps in the Operations and Information Rooms. It was a large body, with a number of sections, some of which were responsible for processing the various sources of intelligence, such as the Y Service and photo-reconnaissance, whilst others were specialists, for instance in technical issues and engineering. There was also an interrogation section for prisoners of war. The establishment included 46 officers, plus another 12 in the Special Liaison Unit, which was located in a separate area for decrypting and disseminating ULTRA.

Also located in the Intelligence area was G (R), which was responsible for deception. It was led by Lieutenant Colonel David Strangeways, who had been selected by the War Office in the autumn of 1942 to deliver the plans for Operation TORCH to the Governors of Gibraltar and Malta and then to Alexander in Cairo. Alexander passed him on to Dudley Clarke, the officer responsible for deception at GHQ Middle East, who placed him in 'A' Force. Although he was too late for El Alamein, Strangeways was involved in most of the subsequent deception operations in North Africa, Sicily and Italy and became well known to the Eighth Army Staff.

Even the R in G (R) was a deception. It originally stood for Research but in fact had no such role. Strangeways was unique among the General Staff officers in that he was simultaneously a field commander. R Force, which was responsible to Main HQ but usually distant from it, was specially formed to carry out deception activities in support of the army group. It consisted of No. 5 Wireless Group, No. 3 Light Scout Car Company, whose vehicles carried a sonic apparatus which could reproduce the noise of tanks and other vehicles, and a number of RE field companies, specially trained in camouflage and the construction of decoy vehicles and installations.

Loosely associated with GSI was one of the most obscure departments at Main HQ, Publicity and Psychological Warfare, headed by Brigadier A. G. Neville, formerly Deputy Director of Information and Propaganda at the War Office. There is little evidence that either Monty or Freddie took much interest in it, probably because it was largely irrelevant to the army group's operations. It was, in fact, a creation of the Americans, and it was Eisenhower who had initially established a Psychological Warfare Branch at Allied Forces in the Mediterranean and subsequently at SHAEF. It did, however, have the enthusiastic support of the British Political Warfare Executive, which was effectively its co-sponsor with the US Office of War Information. G (P&PW) was concerned mainly with the production and dropping of leaflets, produced with the objective of demoralising the Germans.

Last but far from least, Staff Duties was the one of the most important General Staff departments. G (SD) was not physically located in the Operations area, but with the Advisers on Armour, Artillery, Engineering and Signals, whilst Bert Herbert and his officers messed with the Q and A staff at Main HQ. Although the Staff Duties department was responsible in the British Army for staff training, officer education and standards of staff work, in a field formation these took a back seat and the focus was on organization and particularly the creation, deployment and disbanding of formations and units. As such it had to work closely with G (Ops), which would specify the requirements for each phase of the campaign, with the Q branch, which would have to move and supply the formations and units concerned, and with the A branch, which was specifically responsible for manning and reinforcements. It also had a particularly close relationship with the Staff Duties department at the War Office.

Herbert, who had the onerous responsibility of ensuring that all the loose ends were brought together, was later to say that his job was to keep any of the detail from landing on Monty.[2] He sent all his plans, proposals and recommendations to Freddie, who passed them on to Monty if appropriate. Only on very few occasions were they not accepted – yet another example of Monty's trust in his subordinates.

The Q branch was divided into two, each under a DQMG, one dealing with Maintenance and Army Equipment, the other with Movements and Transportation. Q (Maintenance) was responsible for the overall system of maintenance of the army group, estimating its requirements and establishing the scale of reserves to be held forward at Field Maintenance Centres and Army Roadheads. The FMCs, created in the desert by Robertson and Graham, had now become an established feature of operations as the most effective way to ensure that a fast-moving army could be constantly supplied. They were, however, operated at army and corps level and the army group staff had no direct involvement with them. Q (Maintenance) did, however, have to adjudicate on priorities, which was not always straightforward. Rather depending on the situation at the time, the requirements for ammunition, fuel, bridging, airfield construction and ordnance stores might vary considerably. It was the responsibility of the Q (Maintenance) staff to make sure the C-in-C's intentions and plans would not be upset by too much of some and too little of others, as had happened in Sicily and Italy.

A number of Q Services came within the ambit of Q (Maintenance), including Supply and Transport, which was responsible for many of the activities of the Royal Army Service Corps. The Director of Works, whose responsibilities included road repairs and the allocation of engineering equipment, was the Engineer Adviser to the Q Branch in much the same way that the Chief Engineer was the Engineer Adviser to the G branch. Other services included Claims and Hirings, which dealt with quartering and the acquisition of land and buildings for use by the army group, Labour, which allocated Pioneer Units wherever they were necessary, and Postal.

Q (Army Equipment) dealt with the provision of weapons, ammunition and vehicles, including spare parts. For that reason it had a close relationship with two Q Services, the Royal Army Ordnance Corps, which dealt with ordnance stores, and the Royal Electrical and Mechanical Engineers, which was responsible for the recovery, repair and maintenance of vehicles.

Q (Movements & Transportation), under the second DQMG, had three functions, one being the rehabilitation and then the operation of ports, railways, inland waterways and administrative airfields. This was often an exceptionally difficult task, not only because many of these facilities were found to be seriously damaged by both Allied bombing and enemy demolitions, but because the competing demands of military and civil traffic meant that few of their users could ever be fully satisfied. This was the part of the HQ which needed to maintain the closest cooperation with 21st Army Group Lines of Communications, an entirely separate body under Major General Robert Naylor, formerly Vice QMG at the War Office, whose function was to ensure the smooth flow of men and materials along its network of LOC Areas and Sub-Areas. There was also a requirement for Q (Movements & Transportation) to liaise very closely with national governments and the civilian operators of the various facilities; these bodies would often want to use them for their own purposes, which usually had very little regard for the effective functioning of the army group.

Q (Movements & Transportation) was also responsible for overall movement planning. In the initial stages it had to work very closely with the Build Up Control Organization ('BUCO'), which controlled the movement of troops and equipment into the concentration and embarkation areas both for the invasion itself and then in the build-up phase, the Movement Control Organization ('MOVCO') based in Portsmouth, which planned the movements across the English Channel and allocated the shipping, and the Turn Round Control Organization ('TURCO'), a substantially naval body which controlled the day-to-day shipping movements in and out of the Channel ports. In addition to staff from 21st Army Group, led by Gerry Duke, BUCO comprised representatives of Second Army, First Canadian Army, the Allied Naval Commander Expeditionary Force, the Allied Expeditionary Air Forces, Second Tactical Air Force, the War Office and the Ministry of War Transport. There were also liaison officers from the Americans, who controlled their own concentration and movements.

Finally, Q (Movements & Transportation) was directly in charge of the Transportation Service, which controlled all Transportation troops on the ground.

The last of the three main branches of the staff was the A branch under the DAG, which dealt with all personnel matters. A staff work was unpopular in the army, possibly because its success or failure was difficult to measure and it was not an obvious route to advancement, but also because it was difficult to teach. In the army in general, A dealt with every step of a soldier's career from recruitment to discharge, covering promotion – except for officers, which was handled by the Military Secretary's department – pay, education, discipline, health, religion, welfare and morale. It was also responsible for prisoners of war and war graves.

The major impact of the A branch came in the shape of reinforcements, which were to be absolutely vital to the smooth running of the army group. In this respect the staff were handicapped by a factor which would affect the whole campaign, namely that Great Britain's manpower resources had reached their peak and would begin to decline immediately after the invasion. In essence, only those who reached conscription age from then until the end of the war would add to the stock of human resources, although it might be possible to release men who were serving in units which were less important than formerly. This would not compensate for casualties, and the deficiency would prove to be particularly problematic in the infantry, where the rates of attrition were higher than anticipated.

Grouped together with the A staff were the A Services, notably the Royal Army Medical Corps, the Royal Army Chaplain's Department and the staffs of the Paymaster-in Chief, the Provost Marshal and the Judge Advocate General.

Finally, there was the Civil Affairs staff which, at least in the planning phase and the early part of the campaign, seemed to be the poor relation of the other branches and departments. It was not fully accepted into the military hierarchy, largely because its officers tended to be older than their equivalents elsewhere, had often been rejected from active service and were frequently somewhat eccentric. Rather like G (P&PW), they were taken more seriously at SHAEF than at 21st Army Group, but this was because Eisenhower had a much more overtly political role than Monty.

Civil Affairs was responsible for relationships with friendly governments of the countries through which the army group would pass, but these were dissimilar in many respects. There were recognized governments-in-exile in respect of both Belgium and the Netherlands, but the status of the government of France on the liberation of the country was uncertain, the Vichy regime being regarded as collaborationist whilst De Gaulle's Free French had not yet received a seal of approval from the Americans. It was generally accepted that the top field commanders, Monty in the case of 21st Army Group, would act as Military Governors of the liberated territories until such time as a transfer of power was agreed. In this role the Deputy Chief Civil Affairs Officer, Brigadier Tom Robbins, would be his adviser, for which purpose he had an office at Main HQ. However, he maintained a full staff elsewhere, divided into six divisions – HQ Staff, Finance, Legal, Public Safety, Economic and Technical.

On its incorporation at the end of 1943, Civil Affairs had 248 staff, of which 84 were officers, and it would grow significantly through the campaign. Its complexion would change when the army group reached Germany, at which point it would form the nucleus of the Military Government, which would operate on a quite different basis from that appropriate to friendly regimes. It had already been decided not to go down the route taken in Italy, where a separate organization called the Allied Military Government of Occupied Territories took over as quickly as possible behind the fighting troops, but to retain the responsibility for running the defeated country in the hands of the army group commanders.

All this, however, was many months ahead.

Chapter Eighteen

Preparing for D-Day

Following the conference on 21 January Monty spent a minimal amount of time on planning, content to leave the detail to his staff. There were still some fundamental issues to be resolved, notably the US insistence on Operation ANVIL. After considerable debate, it proved impossible for Churchill, Brooke, Monty and others to change the Americans' minds, but at least it was delayed until mid-August under the new name of Operation DRAGOON, allowing sufficient landing craft to be available for the NEPTUNE phase of OVERLORD. In the meantime D-Day for OVERLORD was also put back by a month from early May to 5 June.

Eisenhower and Monty held regular weekly conferences at Norfolk House and St Paul's, but Monty otherwise spent much of his time travelling the country to meet not only the formations and units of Second Army and First Canadian Army, but also those of First US Army, which would come under his command until the land forces were divided between 12th US and 21st Army Groups. Just as importantly for the purposes of morale, he also took the time to address the workers in the factories, ports and dockyards whose contribution was vital to the invasion. For these journeys he had the use of a train, formerly allocated to Paget. 'Rapier' comprised four carriages, refurbished as offices, meeting rooms, sleeping accommodation and mess facilities, together with a covered flat car for Monty's Rolls Royce or one of his other vehicles. Other than the locomotive crew, it was staffed entirely by the military, with the management under a formidable ATS NCO, Sergeant Gouk, to whom Monty warmed immediately. He was usually accompanied only by members of his personal staff, taking Warren and BonDurant with him when visiting, respectively, the Canadians and the Americans. On one occasion he was joined by his son David, who wore his school OTC uniform as the train was off-limits to civilians.

On the whole, Monty's visits were very well received by both servicemen and workers, but there were occasions when his approach to the former, which was to get up on the bonnet of a jeep, gather the assembled troops around him and then tell them very plainly what their role would be, did not go entirely to plan. This was particularly true of some of the formations and units withdrawn from the Mediterranean, who were most unhappy that they were being asked to take the brunt of the action yet again. The Americans were generally more sceptical about the message than the British and often foxed by Monty's accent, but were nevertheless amazed that someone so senior should come to meet them.

Monty decided that he should use some of the time he necessarily spent in London having his portrait painted, and Dawnay, who knew the artist Augustus John, arranged for sittings to take place. Monty did not hit it off with John, disapproving of his personal habits and his very evident attachment to the fairer sex, and he insisted that Dawnay attend all the sittings. These were at least enlivened on one occasion by the presence of George Bernard Shaw, with whom Monty formed an instant rapport. On the other hand, when the portrait was completed, he disliked it intensely and refused to accept it. John was delighted and sold it for much more than the sitter's fee commanded!

Dawnay was also asked to provide a number of interesting guests for the C-in-C's mess, so that Monty could take his mind off purely military matters. He managed to invite an eclectic selection, which included Ernest Bevin, Minister of Labour in the Coalition Government, with whom Monty got on famously, and Dr Hewlett Johnson, the 'Red Dean' of Canterbury, who was vociferously supportive of the Soviet Union and the Red Army, only to be silenced by an interjection from Mrs Churchill, another of the guests. One of Monty's favourites was his old friend, A. P. Herbert, the independent MP for Oxford University. Herbert was seemingly as unlike Monty as it was possible to be, a humorist who contributed regularly to *Punch*, a columnist for the *Sunday Mirror*, a novelist and a playwright, but he was highly entertaining, responding gleefully to Monty's provocations. He had served in the Royal Navy during the Great War and had rejoined in 1940 as a Petty Officer, whose uniform he invariably wore. He was to appear not only at St Paul's but on a number of occasions at Tac HQ in the field.

Freddie was in control at St Paul's during Monty's absences, chairing a full scale staff conference at the beginning of each day, whose attendees included not only the heads of branches, but also more junior officers. He was the ultimate arbiter on all decisions and would give out his orders at the end of each conference: as always, most of these were verbal to cut out any unnecessary paperwork. He also attended inter-service staff meetings, which were chaired in turn by him and his Royal Navy and RAF opposite numbers, Rear Admiral George Creasy and Air Vice Marshal Philip Wigglesworth. He had a particularly close association with the former, both Creasy and Admiral Ramsay sleeping and messing at Latymer Court whenever they were in London.

As had been the case in the closing stages of his time in Italy, Freddie was overworking and occasionally showed sign of stress. Monty was concerned and asked Llewellyn to report to him if the Chief of Staff became too sick to carry out his duties. This was never necessary, but there were a number of occasions on which the blue light outside his office was switched on, signifying that entry was not permitted, usually because Freddie was catching up on some much needed sleep.

In terms of planning, Freddie, Belchem and the staff were responsible for thoroughly evaluating the work carried out by COSSAC, amending it where necessary and then ensuring the detailed implementation of the resulting plan by the formations in 21st Army Group. The order of battle for both the landings and the follow-up had to be decided and then communicated to BUCO, the allocation of landing craft and targets for shore bombardment agreed with the Royal and US Navies, and both ground/air support and the airborne operations coordinated with the RAF and USAAF. Other issues included the optimum use of the specialized armoured vehicles operated by 79 Armoured Division and the eventual deployment of the MULBERRY harbours and the PLUTO pipeline. There were numerous engineering problems, including the handling of the obstacles expected on the beaches. The involvement of Inglis, who had been considering many of these from the inception of 21st Army Group, now proved invaluable.

Nearly 300 American officers and other ranks were attached to Main HQ, spread over all the staff branches, and they included a team of planners led by Colonel Charles 'Tic' Bonesteel, who had been involved in invasion planning from as early as 1942. One of Bonesteel's specific tasks was to study the topography of Normandy, and he drew attention particularly to the 'bocage' country to the south of the invasion beaches, characterized by small fields, each of which was enclosed by high banks and hedgerows. He pointed out that this country was ideal for defence, particularly against tanks. This was picked up by Richardson and his planners in their appreciations of how the campaign might develop and subsequently proved to be a serious factor, impacting adversely on both the British and the Americans.

During the planning process an event took place which seemed at first to represent a disastrous lapse of security. At Main HQ there was only one map showing all the invasion beaches and the forces designated to land on them. It was kept in Belchem's office, could only be taken out against the signature of a senior officer and was locked away at night. One day it went missing and there was no signature to indicate where it might be. Colonel Leo Russell, Belchem's British deputy, went through Main HQ with a toothcomb, whilst Belchem himself did the same thing at Norfolk House, but to no avail. It seemed all too possible that OVERLORD had been gravely compromised. After twenty-four hours Freddie told Belchem that he would have to call in Scotland Yard if it was not found quickly, but soon afterwards there was a call from Russell to say that it had been located in the draughtsman's cupboard, to Belchem's huge relief.

Whilst most of the planning staff were considering the problems associated with getting ashore in Normandy and establishing a strong beachhead, Williams and his staff were hard at work estimating the strength of the opposition, their estimate proving in due course to be remarkably accurate. It was well known by then that Rommel, once again Monty's opponent, had been busy strengthening the defences of the Atlantic Wall, and Monty's initial feeling was that he would hold back his reserves for a counter-attack until he was clear about where the main effort of the Allies was directed. Williams was not so sure, believing that the German commander was likely to attack vigorously at the first opportunity to drive the invaders into the sea, an assessment to which Monty rapidly subscribed. He and his team also, not long before D-Day, identified the German Army's 352 Division moving into position opposite Omaha Beach, but somehow this intelligence never reached First US Army.

If the Allied Intelligence services were devoting most of their time to establishing who would oppose them when they landed, the Germans were even more desperate to know who would be coming and where. In order to throw them off the scent, a multi-faceted deception operation was put in place. Operation FORTITUDE was one of the most complex of its kind during the war, and one of the most successful. Its objective was to lead the Germans to believe that the main invasion would not take place in Normandy, but in the Pas-de-Calais, and would be accompanied by a secondary landing in Norway. FORTITUDE SOUTH created a fictitious formation, 1st US Army Group or FUSAG, commanded by Patton and located in the South-East of England, the threat of which would hopefully hold the German Fifteenth Army in the Pas-de-Calais area for as long as possible. FORTITUDE NORTH was designed to deter the Germans from sending reinforcements from Norway to France.

The overall coordination of FORTITUDE was in the hands of a secret organization, the London Controlling Section. The LCS used double agents[1] to feed snippets of intelligence to the Germans which were trifling in themselves and not connected with each other, but which taken all together built up into a convincing story. It also leaked information through neutral diplomatic channels which it knew would find its way back to Berlin and which would corroborate the story. FORTITUDE SOUTH was designed to support this, and a major element, codenamed QUICKSILVER, was placed under the control of SHAEF, which passed it on to 21st Army Group. As no one else in the UK had the requisite experience of deception, Monty put Strangeways in charge, with orders to mobilize all the resources of G (R) and R Force. Strangeways now devoted most of his time to this, not only at Main HQ, but also on trips around South-East England and East Anglia.

There were several strands to QUICKSILVER. One was the creation and location of dummy installations, vehicles, aircraft and landing craft. The last, codenamed BIGBOBS, were the most important, flotillas of them being assembled in harbours and river mouths north and south of the Thames Estuary. By this time the Air Defence of Great Britain was so successful that few Luftwaffe reconnaissance aircraft overflew the South of England, but the

Germans were able to take oblique photos from about fifteen miles from the coast, which were sufficient to show any vessels in harbour. Strangeways made the point that it would be all very well to let them see the BIGBOBS, but they would not be fooled unless these were moored close to hards from which troops and vehicles could board, so these now had to be constructed.

Even more critical to success was the radio traffic created by R Force's No. 5 Wireless Group, supported by 3103 US Signals Service Battalion. The former had the use of a device whereby one transmitter could replicate six others, so that the signals of a division and all its brigades could be sent from a single truck. The latter had the capacity to replicate the signals of an army group HQ, an army, three corps and nine divisions. A programme was devised to simulate the wireless traffic of FUSAG and all its supposed formations and units.

Another strand of QUICKSILVER was the air plan. Strangeways insisted that there should be two reconnaissance flights over the Pas-de-Calais for every one over Normandy and that much of the bombing, carried out in accordance with the Allied Air Forces' Transportation Plan to destroy the German transport network in France, should also be focused on the former.

Monty was personally involved in another deception exercise, although it failed to have the same impact as FORTITUDE. Operation COPPERHEAD was an attempt to persuade the Germans that he was out of the country only a week or so before D-Day and that the invasion was thus still some way off. An officer in MI5 had noticed a similarity between Monty and Lieutenant M. E. Clifton James, an actor some twelve years younger than Monty who was serving in the Royal Army Pay Corps. A plan was hatched to send him to the Mediterranean in the hope that this might suggest that an invasion of Southern France was imminent. Clifton James was allowed to tail Monty for a few days in early May to pick up his speech and mannerisms and then to spend some time alone with him on Rapier. On 26 May, ten days before D-Day was due, he landed in Gibraltar and was very visibly seen with the Governor. He then flew on to Algiers where he met Jumbo Wilson but unfortunately allowed his alcoholic intake to get the better of him, and the operation was closed down. There is evidence that the Germans were alerted, but none that it made any difference to their dispositions.

At the time of the meeting with Clifton James, Monty was in Scotland, about to take a short holiday. He had spent much of the previous month observing a series of exercises undertaken by 21st Army Group formations around the British Isles and had led one of his own, Exercise THUNDERCLAP, at St Paul's on 7 April. The members of the Chief of Staffs' Committee attended, as did Eisenhower, whilst Churchill appeared after tea to give an uninspiring talk. Monty opened the conference with an impressive hour and a half's introduction, followed by Ramsay, Leigh-Mallory, Bradley, who would be commanding First US Army for the invasion before moving up to 12th Army

Group, Dempsey, who had been chosen by Monty to command Second Army, and their respective corps commanders. Apart from Churchill's contribution, Brooke thought that it was 'a wonderful day'.[2]

To illustrate his own presentation, Monty produced a map which he would live to regret. On it were drawn phase lines showing how the campaign was expected to develop over the first 90 days, by which time the Allied armies were expected to be on the Seine to the north and the Loire to the south. Belchem later attributed the requirement for these to the Americans, at the specific request of his American deputy, Colonel Mudgett, but in fact they were drawn for Monty by Dawnay, who subsequently explained:

> The first line I wrote covered the beachheads and showed them linked up together. The final line covered the Seine, Paris and the Loire. I then asked Monty how I should draw the lines in between. 'It doesn't matter,' he said. 'Shall I draw them equally then?' I said. 'Yes, that will do,' said Monty.[3]

The lines would be used in due course by Monty's detractors as evidence of his plan failing. In the meantime, far from insisting on phase lines, Bradley wanted them removed, at least in the American sector, as he had not been consulted in advance. Monty himself put little value on them at the time or later, and Richardson and others regarded them as an illustration rather than a commitment.

Monty's Scottish holiday from 9 to 13 May provided his only extended spell of relaxation during the five months in the UK before D-Day. Rapier remained in a siding next to the distillery at Dalwhinnie, which was where Monty met Clifton-James. Other than Henderson, who organized daily excursions, he was accompanied only by his stepson, Dick Carver, who was about to command an RE field company for the invasion, Freddie, who Monty felt also deserved a break, and Dawnay. Gerry Feilden had a house nearby and joined them on occasion for picnics, but Monty's main relaxation was fly-fishing, not a sport for which he had had much time in the past. He was totally unsuccessful, failing to land a single salmon, but enjoyed the experience nevertheless.

On 14 May Monty arrived back in London and on the following day the King, the Prime Minister, the Supreme Commander and all the other military leaders involved in OVERLORD gathered at St Paul's for the final presentation of the plans. Eisenhower presided over the proceedings, but Monty was the first main speaker, giving yet another impressive address, outlining his own intentions, the expected dispositions and reactions of the Germans and the likely development of the battle in the first weeks. He was very clear that the British and Canadians would hold the left of the Allied line, attracting on to their front the enemy armoured divisions, which would be determined to prevent an advance to the Seine. The Americans, having fought their way through the bocage, would then break out towards the Loire and Brittany before wheeling round towards the Seine and Paris. If he left his listeners with one impression, it was of complete confidence in the Allies' ultimate success.

By this time St Paul's housed only Rear HQ, both Main and Tac having moved at the end of April to join the Naval HQ at Southwick House, just outside Portsmouth. There they were joined by the Advanced Command Post of SHAEF, Southwick becoming the nerve centre for the invasion. HQ Allied Expeditionary Air Force, however, remained at Stanmore. There had been numerous difficulties with the Air Forces during the planning. 'Bomber' Harris and his American counterpart, Carl Spaatz, had argued unsuccessfully that their bombers should not be diverted from the strategic bombing campaign in order to implement the Transportation Plan, whilst Leigh-Mallory became very nervous about the possibility of heavy casualties in the American airborne assault and had to be overruled by Eisenhower when he proposed to cancel it. To ensure that nothing more would go wrong, Monty sent Richardson to Stanmore to act as a personal liaison officer to Leigh-Mallory during the opening stages of the campaign.

Two days before 5 June 1944, which was still expected to be D-Day, Monty set out some thoughts on the previous five months in his diary. At the end he wrote this of his staff:

> My own team at 21 Army Group is quite first-class.
>
>   I can say definitely that if I had not brought my own team of senior officers back with me from ITALY, I could never have done the business and got ready for the OVERLORD operation. It was essential to have practical knowledge on the job, with officers who know the battle end of the business; those that Paget had collected round him in ENGLAND were pure theorists and were mostly useless anyway. I like PAGET very much and he is a very old friend; but he is not a good judge as to what constitutes a high-class officer.[4]

That Monty was now backed by 'high-class officers' would be amply demonstrated by the events of the next eleven months.

Freddie and Auchinleck, shortly after the former's appointment as BGS Eighth Army.

Brian Robertson, DA&QMG Eighth Army.

Fred Kisch, Chief Engineer Eighth Army.

Sydney Kirkman, BRA Eighth Army.

Cecil 'Slap' White, CSO Eighth Army, later SO-in-C 21st Army Group. *(Reproduced by permission of the Provost and Fellows of Eton College)*

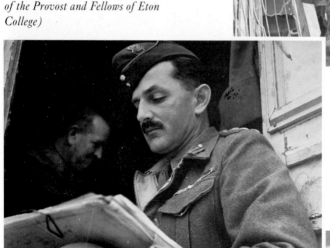

Freddie with Geoffrey Keating, the Head of the Army Film & Photo Unit in Eighth Army.

David Belchem, GSO1 Staff Duties, later BGS Ops Eighth Army & 21st Army Group. *(Drawing by S. Morse-Brown, owned by the author)*

Charles Richardson, GSO1 Plans, then Operations, Eighth Army, BGS Plans 21st Army Group.

Bill Williams, GSO1 Intelligence Eighth Army, BGS Intelligence 21st Army Group.

Monty out on the battlefield with John Poston (the officer on the left is Bill Cunningham, ADC to Alexander).

Poston with Johnny Henderson.

Monty's Flying Fortress, complete with American crew.

Monty with his senior staff officers in Malta shortly before Husky. Freddie sits on his right, Miles Graham on his left, Charles Richardson behind his right shoulder.

The underground office in Malta prior to HUSKY – (L to R) Gerry Duke, Sergeant Major Harwood, Dick Vernon & Harry Llewellyn.

Dick Vernon, who ran Tac HQ in Sicily & Italy. *(Reproduced by permission of the Provost and Fellows of Eton College)*

Geoffrey Keating & the artist Edward Ardizzone, shortly after 'liberating' Taormina.

Monty's villa in Taormina, with his Alfa Romeo.

Henderson unpacks a picnic in Messina for Monty, Eisenhower & Commander Harry Butcher, Eisenhower's Naval Aide.

Corporal English, Monty's batman, makes his bed.

Sergeant Edwards, Monty's driver, polishes his Packard before loading it onto Rapier.

Monty on Rapier with Sergeant Gouk, the ATS train manager.

Monty picnicking in Scotland with (L to R) Dick Carver, his step-son, Gerry Feilden, DQMG 21st Army Group, and Kit Dawnay, his Military Assistant.

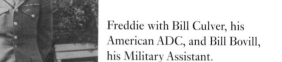

Freddie with Bill Culver, his American ADC, and Bill Bovill, his Military Assistant.

Llewellyn Hughes, Assistant Chaplain General, Eighth Army, Deputy Chaplain General, 21st Army Group.

De Gaulle's visit to Monty at Creully – Fuzzy Sanderson can be seen in the distance between the two men.

Monty in Normandy with Noel Chavasse.

Churchill at Tac HQ admiring 'Rommel'.

Monty and his personal pilot, Flight Lieutenant Martin, next to the Miles Messenger. *(Reproduced by permission of the Provost and Fellows of Eton College)*

Trumbull Warren escorts Eisenhower to meet Monty. Air Marshal 'Mary' Coningham can be seen behind Eisenhower's left shoulder

The subject of the 'Pig Incident'.

James Gunn's 'conversation piece'. Monty at table in the mess with (clockwise from the left) Dawnay, Ray BonDurant, Henderson, Warren and Chavasse. *(Royal Collections Trust / All Rights reserved)*

Freddie in his office in Brussels.

John Poston, Joe Ewart and Carol Mather at Main HQ in Brussels during Monty's temporary location there. *(Reproduced by permission of the Provost and Fellows of Eton College)*

Above: The King with Monty and his personal staff at Eindhoven in October 1944. (Standing L to R) Dawnay, Sir Piers Legh (Master of the Household), Henderson, Chavasse, Warren, Sir Alan Lascelles (Private Secretary), BonDurant. *(Reproduced by permission of the Provost and Fellows of Eton College)*

Above: A welcome visitor to Tac HQ – A.P. Herbert with Monty, Evelyn Barker of VIII Corps and Neil Ritchie of XII Corps.

Right: Another welcome visitor to Tac – Sir James Grigg, Secretary of State for War, with Monty and Brian Horrocks of XXX Corps.

Above: The Tac Liaison Officers during the Battle of the Bulge – (L to R) Carol Mather, Eddie Prisk, Charles Sweeny, Maurice Frary, Dudley Bourhill, Dick Harden and John Poston.

Right: Padre Tindal greets Churchill & Brooke after the church parade held at the time of the Rhine crossings.

Schloss Ostenwalde, Monty's favourite Tac site and his personal HQ after the War.

The Tac Liaison Officers in mid-April 1945 – Back row (L to R) John Sharp, Poston, Frary, Tom Howarth – Front row (L to R) Harden, Prisk, Monty, Sweeny, Peter Earle.

Tac on the move towards the end of the War. Henderson and Terry Coverdale are standing 2nd and 3rd from the left. *(Reproduced by permission of the Provost and Fellows of Eton College)*

The surrender. Ewart, in his role as interpreter, stands behind Monty's right shoulder.

The celebration dinner after the surrender. Bill Woodward, Tac HQ Camp Commandant, Frary, Henderson & Toby Wake.

John Whiteley (left), Freddie's predecessor at Eighth Army and later a senior officer at SHAEF, meets Charles Richardson shortly after VE-Day.

Ostenwalde after the war. Henderson, Coverdale & Chavasse stand behind Dawnay, with his dachshund Max.

Monty's team in 1960. Back row (L to R) Harry Llewellyn, Oliver Poole, David Belchem, Sydney Kirkman, Brian Horrocks, Geoffrey Keating, Sandy Galloway, Gerald Templer, Johnny Henderson, Bill Williams, Charles Richardson. Front row (L to R) Oliver Leese, Bobby Erskine, Monty, Harry Broadhurst, Freddie, Slap White, Brian Robertson.

Monty's 80th birthday in 1967, including some post-war subordinates. Back row (L to R) Kit Dawnay, Hugh Mainwaring, Simbo Simpson, Johnny Henderson, Bill Williams, Charles Richardson, Llewellyn Wansborough-Jones, Dixie Redman, George Cole, Richard Sharples. Front row (L to R) Freddie, Monty, Brian Robertson, Miles Graham, John Harding, Oliver Leese.

Chapter Nineteen

Tac Goes to War

In Monty's eyes, his Tac HQs in North Africa, Sicily and Italy had been a great success, allowing him to run his battles from close to the front, where he could be in constant touch with his formation commanders. That this was far from satisfactory to the staff at Main HQ was, if understood at all by Monty, of insufficient concern to cause him to change the arrangements. On the contrary, whereas Tac had been run on a fairly informal basis in the Mediterranean, it now became institutionalized.

One of the last and most junior officers to be summoned back from Italy was Paul Odgers[1] at the end of March. When he reported at St Paul's he was told that he had been selected to form and train Tac, which was already planned to be much larger than its Eighth Army predecessors. Odgers had worked in G (Ops) and had had relatively modest experience of Tac and little personal contact with Monty, but he had evidently caught Freddie's eye as a capable organizer. He now found himself given all the backing he needed to meet Monty's requirements.

The role of Tac was, for the first time, given expression in writing in its operational instructions:

2. The primary role of Tac HQ 21 Army Group is to keep the Commander-in-Chief fully informed both as regards the progress of the battle being fought by the forward troops and as regards the general operational picture as seen by Main HQ 21 Army Group.

3. Tac HQ is not executive; that is to say it will not issue orders to Armies. Any verbal instructions given by the Commander-in-Chief will be transmitted to Main HQ where the appropriate branch will be responsible for detailed action and the issue of executive orders as required.

4. By virtue of its primary role Tac HQ will often be in a position to serve as a forward information and liaison centre for Main HQ. All information received by Tac HQ, which is unlikely to reach Main HQ by other channels, will be passed back to Main HQ by W/T or Liaison Officer, or by telephone when available.[2]

Tac's major concern was with operations and thus G (Ops), with its G (Liaison) section, was the only staff branch initially represented.[3] This would change

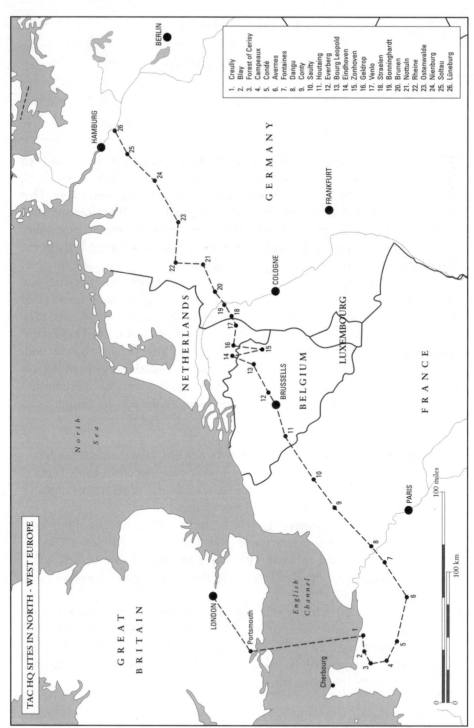

1. Creully
2. Blay
3. Forest of Cerisy
4. Campeaux
5. Condé
6. Avernes
7. Fontaines
8. Dangu
9. Conty
10. Saulty
11. Houtaing
12. Everberg
13. Bourg Leopold
14. Eindhoven
15. Zonhoven
16. Geldrop
17. Venlo
18. Straelen
19. Bonninghardt
20. Brunen
21. Nottuln
22. Rheine
23. Ostenwalde
24. Nienburg
25. Soltau
26. Lüneburg

Map 6.

during the campaign, when there was a significant influx of GSI staff. The other major element of Tac was communications, represented by both Royal Signals and a small Phantom detachment. The balance was made up of Camp and Transport personnel, an infantry platoon and an armoured car troop for defence and a Field Security (later called Counter Intelligence) section. Immediately before D-Day, the numbers of officers* and men in each group were as follows:

	Officers	Warrant Officers & NCOs	Other ranks	Total
C-I-C's party	6	8	28	42
G (Ops) & G (L)	14	7	0	21
Camp	1	19	27	47
Signals & Phantom	5	24	44	73
Defence Troops	2	9	44	55
Transport	2	8	36	4 6
Field Security	0	10	3	13
Total	30	85	182	297

This was a not inconsiderable number of men and required a great deal of organization from the start. Moreover, as the campaign developed, the numbers increased, not only by the addition of GSI staff, but also through significant growth in signals personnel, the defence troops, whose numbers proved to be inadequate early in the campaign, the Field Security section, which was enlarged in preparation for entering Germany, and engineers, who had to clear mines in hostile territory. The transport personnel grew commensurately. On the other hand, the numbers at the end of May 1944 included 26 Americans, most of whom departed elsewhere at the end of August.

Tac was designed to be highly mobile. This placed a heavy burden on both Odgers, who was responsible for training it before deployment to France and became its de facto chief organizer for most of the campaign thereafter, and Bill Woodward, the Camp Commandant, who had to set up and manage new sites with great frequency. The former devised the standing orders for moving to a new site. Following the selection of the general area, a relatively small 'recce party' of about forty, with representatives from all the Tac HQ groups, including at least one of Monty's ADCs, and fuel and supplies for three days, would set

---

* See Appendix V.

off in advance to choose the specific location. Woodward would then supervise the marking out of the perimeter, the entrances, the internal tracks and the position of every group, with its messes, latrines, water points and vehicle park. Only when this task was complete would a signal be sent for the main party to move. Once it arrived, the camp could be set up in 45 minutes.

The layout of the camp was subject to local geography but remained broadly the same wherever it was located, other than in buildings. The C-in-C's camp was situated about 100 yards from G (Ops) and had its own entrance. The Signals Office was on the main track axis, midway between the main entrance and G (Ops), with the Cipher Office and W/T vehicles nearby. The Camp Office was next to the main entrance, with the Transport Office and main vehicle park adjoining it. The defence troops were based in the same area, but deployed as appropriate.

Accommodation was provided on the same basis as Main HQ, with a mixture of caravans and tents for sleeping and caravans, specialized vehicles and tents for offices. There were two officers' messes, one for Monty and the five members of his personal staff, to which certain visiting personnel from Main HQ belonged in an honorary capacity, notably Freddie, Graham, Belchem and Williams, and to which the most distinguished visitors were also invited. The B mess, for all other officers and most visitors, was located in the G (Ops) area and the sergeants' mess in the Camp area.

Of the seven caravans at Tac, two were reserved for senior members of Main HQ and distinguished visitors, one was occupied by Dawnay and one by the Colonel GS. The remaining three were for Monty.[4] The longest serving of these was the one he had inherited from Auchinleck when he arrived at Eighth Army. It was of Italian manufacture and had originally belonged to General Bergonzoli, nicknamed 'Electric Whiskers' for his luxuriant beard, who had been captured in Operation COMPASS in early 1941. It had served as Monty's home from Egypt to Tunisia and was now used as his office. In it he kept a signed photo of Rommel and photos of Field Marshals Von Runstedt, Model and Kesselring, his opponents in North-West Europe, which he would study in an attempt to understand what sort of men they were.

The second caravan was also of Italian manufacture and had been captured at the end of the North African campaign, when Monty moved very smartly to secure it against the rival claim of Freyberg. It had been occupied immediately beforehand by Marshal Messe, the Axis commander in Tunisia, but Monty was assured by him that it had previously been used by Rommel. Luxuriously appointed and including a bath, it became his bedroom. He would give it up only to the King or the Prime Minister.

Monty's third caravan was used as his map room. He had felt the need for one in the earlier campaigns, but had never satisfied it. On arrival back in England, his personal staff approached the British Trailer Company, which agreed to manufacture a caravan to their specifications before presenting it to Monty as a gift. It contained a large map on the wall on which was marked the latest information on both the 21st Army Group and enemy positions. It was here that he received the reports of his liaison officers every night on their return from the front.

Other than Dawnay, Warren and Lieutenant Colonel Miller, the Senior US LO, the officers at Tac were all of relatively junior rank, majors and below. Monty would have been quite happy to leave it this way, but Freddie was insistent that there should be a more senior officer in overall command. He selected Colonel Leo Russell, who had been Belchem's British deputy during the planning phase and was now spare. Freddie, as always, was concerned that he should know everything that was going on at Tac; this had worked reasonably well with John Oswald, Dick Vernon and Bill Mather, but with a much larger Tac and one which was expected to be at times even further away from Main than in the Eighth Army days, he wanted his own man on the spot.

Russell was not a regular soldier but a Territorial, whose background was in newspaper publishing. He had held a number of staff appointments in Home Forces, but had no operational experience. Odgers liked him, but others, particularly the livelier liaison officers and ADCs, thought him rather officious. His somewhat abrasive personality, combined with a lack of battlefield know-how, meant that he found it difficult to earn their respect.

Planning for Tac was completed on 20 April, and on 26 April it moved to Southwick, where it established itself in a corner of the park close to Broomfield House, where Monty, Freddie and their aides slept and messed. Odgers, who was just back from honeymoon, now organized a series of movement exercises, first on the South Downs at nearby Horndean and then further afield at Crawley and Petworth. These were full-scale operations involving the whole of Tac in closing down, moving and setting up on a new site, followed by the whole procedure in reverse, and they proved invaluable in identifying the problems involved.

'In the midst of these activities,' wrote Odgers later, 'the Liaison Staff began to arrive. Few will forget the sense of a great wind blowing and the place suddenly jammed with Jeeps, trailers, 2½ ton trucks and steel helmeted Americans.'[5] No longer would Monty's personal LOs be few in number and frequently supplemented by his ADCs. The nine officers would all have no other responsibilities but to keep 'Master' fully informed as to what was going on in his command on a daily basis.

There were some familiar faces among the newly arrived 'Monty Boys', for old Eighth Army hands at least. John Poston returned after his course at the Middle East Staff College, whilst Carol Mather, fully recovered from his incarceration and escape, was summoned by Monty to Claridge's to be told that, if he took the job, his chances of survival were not good, an approach guaranteed to persuade him to join. The LO with the longest connection to

Monty, however, was 'Fuzzy' Sanderson, his ADC at the outbreak of war. Back with his regiment, the King's Own Scottish Borderers, Sanderson had seen action in 78 Division in Sicily and Italy, during which he had been awarded the MC. He had been on the same course as Poston in Haifa when both received invitations to join Monty, Sanderson as the result of a letter he had written enquiring about possible opportunities in 21st Army Group. They returned to the UK together, but not before enjoying a riotous few days in Cairo. Sanderson was hopeful of leave, but was told by Monty that he had to stay for one of Odgers's exercises first.

The other new arrivals were Dick Harden, a contemporary of Sanderson's at Sandhurst who had served as a tank officer in the desert, Dudley Bourhill and four Americans, of whom only two were to remain with Monty after 12th Army Group was created. They were Maurice Frary and Eddie Prisk, both of whom lasted to the end of the war. They were notable for wearing their helmets at all times, unlike their British confrères, who very rarely bothered. This was a strict American regulation, and Frary nearly got caught out when Patton made a surprise visit to Tac, disappearing with some alacrity to get properly dressed.

The primary task of the LOs before D-Day was to establish contacts with the armies, corps and divisions with which they would be liaising during the campaign. These would include not only the various staff officers, but also the GOCs, as Monty had made it quite clear that his LOs should have access to them at all times and that they were to provide answers to any questions that were asked, regardless of the differences in rank. This required a hectic bout of activity across Southern England. It also, in the run-up to the end of May, provided cover for a plan devised by Poston, who was already becoming something of a leader among the 'Monty Boys', partly because of his attractive character and partly because he knew exactly how far it was possible to go with the C-in-C. Poston proposed a last lightning tour of all the formations, which received official blessing, but was in fact a ploy to allow the LOs to make final pre-invasion visits to their families and sweethearts. It was agreed that on the last day they should rendezvous at Liphook before going on to Brighton for a night out. All went to plan, except that Mather's jeep was stolen during dinner. It contained all Poston's kit, but whilst he was not at all worried by that, he was mortified by the loss of all the letters from his girlfriend.

Monty had one other Personal Liaison Officer, but he was not based at Tac HQ, although he was a frequent visitor. Tom Bigland was a gunner who had served as a battery commander and second-in-command of an anti-tank regiment in the desert, winning a DSO, before going to the staff college at Haifa, where he was a contemporary of Dick Harden. He had subsequently been an instructor at the Junior Staff School at Sarafand, before being selected for a course at the US Command and General Staff School at Fort Leavenworth, Kansas. On his arrival back in the UK, he was initially appointed a Liaison

Officer for 21st Army Group with Second Army, before being sent as Monty's LO with Bradley, probably on the strength of his recently acquired knowledge of the very different American staff system. Administratively he was subordinate to Llewellyn at Main HQ and all his reports went there as well as to Tac, but he was regarded as a 'Monty Boy'. He would fulfil his role with Bradley for the rest of the war in circumstances which would become increasingly difficult and require great skills of diplomacy.

On 2 June Monty gathered all the officers of Main and Tac HQs on the lawn at Southwick House. He spoke about the war in general, how it had developed to that point and what the task of the Allied armies was now to be. As usual, it was a model of clarity. Mather later described the end of his address:

> For a moment, after he had finished speaking, time stood still as minds dwelt on the enormity of the task, whilst Monty intoned the words of Montrose.

> He either fears his fate too much,
> Or his deserts are small,
> That will not put it to the touch,
> To win or lose it all.[6]

> Then everyone burst out cheering and we knew we were going to win.[7]

There was to be no repeat of Operation HUSKY, for which Tac had not been pre-loaded and arrived late in Sicily, or even BAYTOWN, when it crossed to Italy over three days. Under cover of yet another movement exercise, substantially the whole of Tac moved to a marshalling area on the morning of 3 June and began to load on to three Landings Ships at Gosport the next morning. That afternoon the little flotilla sailed out into the Solent to await the signal to cross to France. Like the other tens of thousands of men on ships all around, their expectation had been that the invasion would take place on 5 June, but the weather was terrible, and it was delayed until the following day and only occurred then after a courageous decision by Eisenhower, strongly supported by Monty.

Tac had been split for the crossing. The element in LST 377, under Russell, was operationally independent, whilst those in LSTs 378 and 379, respectively under Odgers and Warren, were supposed to operate together. The plan was for all the ships to transfer vehicles and men on to Rhino ferries some way out from Juno beach, but attempts to do so failed initially and it was not until the afternoon of D+1 that LST 377 managed to unload in this way. LST 379 succeeded that evening, but LST 378 became stuck on a sandbank and had to wait for the tide to carry it in early on D+2. The disruption caused by the separation of the two interdependent groups proved to be only temporary and the personnel all came ashore safely, but there was one disaster when the lorry carrying the contents of the officers' and sergeants' messes, including the supply of Scotch whisky, slid off its ship into the sea!

At the head of the first group ashore, Russell set up camp on what turned out to be a highly unsuitable site at St Croix-sur-Mer, exposed to enemy shellfire and so close to the beaches that it was surrounded by the chaos of troops trying to move inland. Warren, in the meantime, had been on the lookout for a better location and had found just the place in the grounds of the Chateau de Creullet, near the village of Creully. It was actually closer to the front line, but was not a particular target for enemy artillery and was satisfactory in most other ways. Madame de Douval, the wife of the owner, 'a dubious ex-cavalry aristocrat' according to Odgers, seemed pleased to see them, her previous guests, some German officers, having departed in haste very recently! A number of German soldiers[8] were discovered in the outbuildings and taken prisoner by Warren, Mather and Sanderson at pistol point, but once the grounds were pronounced clear, preparations began for Monty's arrival.

Monty stayed at Broomfield during the daylight hours of D-Day, but was sufficiently satisfied by the news of progress on and beyond the beaches to sail as planned for France that night. Leaving Dawnay behind with a small rear party to ensure that communications with Main HQ were satisfactory and taking Henderson and BonDurant with him, he embarked on the destroyer HMS *Faulknor*, which weighed anchor at 22.00. At first light the next morning Henderson went up to the bridge, only to be told by the captain that they were lost. Monty remained sanguine and, having taken directions from a passing American battleship, the destroyer came back on course. Henderson was sent across to Bradley's command ship to invite the US commander to meet Monty. The American had satisfactory news about Utah Beach, but reported serious problems on Omaha, where huge casualties had been incurred and the beachhead was much smaller than planned. Monty decided to attach BonDurant to him as a temporary liaison officer until the situation improved. There was an encouraging report from Dempsey, who also came on board, and later in the day Monty himself went to see Eisenhower and Ramsay on the latter's flagship, by that time expressing confidence that all was well, following a signal from Bradley that his troops were at last making good progress inland from Omaha.

Early on the morning of 8 June, the destroyer moved towards shore, going aground as she did so, but Monty and Henderson were picked up by Chavasse in a DUKW. Taken initially to Russell's first choice of Tac HQ site at St Croix, Monty immediately pronounced it unsuitable, but the alternative at Creully was now available and Tac was fully located there during the day. Second Army and Broadhurst's 83 Group RAF both subsequently established their HQs nearby.

By this time the LOs had already been in action for 24 hours. Sanderson had been given the furthest British formation to visit, 6 Airborne Division on the left flank beyond Pegasus Bridge. The Sword beachhead had not joined up with those of Gold and Juno and he experienced a strange feeling of emptiness over part of the route, which turned out to be exactly where 21 Panzer Division was attempting to drive a wedge towards the sea. His visit to the divisional HQ was rudely interrupted when it had to withdraw at short notice to avoid being overrun, and on the return journey he experienced the same sensation that he had earlier, but encountered no Germans.

The LOs quickly settled into a routine which would continue until the end of the campaign. Some departed very early for their chosen divisions or corps, from where they would send a signal to Tac on the previous night's operations, which would be marked up on in the map in Monty's map caravan by the Duty Operations Officer, ready to brief him at 07.30. Others remained behind for the briefing and specific orders before leaving, whilst one always remained at Tac on a roster for duty in the map room. Those travelling by road carried special passes giving them priority of movement through traffic. The LOs would spend the day covering the chosen formations, which always included each Allied army, corps and division in action and occasionally those due to go into action, calling on the senior staff and the formation commander. They would return in the evening and report verbally to Odgers for the map to be marked up again, following which they would each be debriefed in turn by Monty in the map caravan. A short handwritten report was also completed. Save for a period immediately after the landings when the some of the LOs had to use motorcycles, they travelled mostly in jeeps, with a driver and a signaller with a No. 19 wireless set, and they carried chinagraph boards on which they could write cryptic notes and draw rough maps and which could be wiped very quickly in an emergency. Otherwise everything remained in the LOs' heads and no papers were involved, a contrast to the LOs sent out by American formations, who carried documents in sealed envelopes.

The LOs were instructed to deal directly with corps and divisional commanders and, in their absence, with their senior general staff officer. Most commanders understood that they came with the express authority of Monty and seldom stood on the significant difference in rank between the LOs and themselves, although some LOs encountered irritation or even mild hostility. The American LOs had the most difficult time as the US system, with orders being conveyed in writing down through a relatively rigid, albeit effective, chain of command, did not always adapt well to Monty's requirements.

Monty himself was out visiting formations and units on most days, always returning to Tac by 17.00. Accompanied by one of his personal staff, he would normally use his Humber Tourer staff car, a four-seater open vehicle with a soft top for wet weather. If he wanted to impress he would be driven in one of his two Rolls Royce Wraiths, whilst for journeys deemed to be dangerous he had a converted Staghound armoured car. On most trips to active formations he was accompanied by another armoured car from the Tac HQ troop.

Monty had to remain in camp for VIP visits, which began very quickly at Creully. The first of these was by Churchill, Brooke and Field Marshal Smuts on 12 June, which went off without a hitch as did those by the King and Sir James Grigg, the Secretary of State for War, four and six days later respectively. General de Gaulle, who proved to be a much more awkward proposition, arrived on 14 June. Sanderson was released from LO duties to escort him, with strict instructions that the French leader should be accompanied by no more than three other officers, should have no ceremonial welcome and no flags and should leave again by 16.00. De Gaulle arrived late and with a large retinue. He was dismayed by the transport, consisting only of Sanderson's jeep, and insisted on displaying the French flag, for which a makeshift piece of driftwood was tied to the windscreen. Three other jeeps had to be requisitioned for the rest of the party.

Matters then got worse. In Sanderson's words, 'The meeting between Monty and de Gaulle could hardly have been more frigid.'⁹ There was no guard of honour at Tac, as expected by de Gaulle, and Monty, already displeased at being kept waiting, ordered him to extinguish his cigarette. The meeting itself was brief and the lunch frugal. As part of the itinerary, de Gaulle went on to Bayeux, where he made a speech to the bemused residents. Sanderson was subsequently dismissive of de Gaulle's appeal to the crowd, describing it as lacking fervour, but Lieutenant Colonel Lewthwaite, GSO1 (Ops) at Main HQ, who was also present on a visit to the front, reported that there was no doubt about the general's popularity, although attempts to accompany the Marseillaise on a gramophone had proved ludicrous! Anxious to have him back on the beach according to the agreed schedule, Sanderson was dismayed to be ordered instead to proceed to Isigny, some way to the west in the American sector, where de Gaulle made another speech. At last he agreed to return to the beach, where Sanderson was told that Monty had been asking where he was. He returned to Tac HQ to tell the whole story; Monty was furious, but not with his LO.

The day before Churchill's visit a lone German soldier had been discovered hiding in the grounds of the chateau, frightened and hungry. This, together with fears expressed by Freddie to Russell about the possibility of an airborne raid by German paratroopers, and the absolute disregard by Monty himself for his own safety, led to the defence troops being significantly increased, largely by Commandos. The security at Creully had also been compromised by some injudicious reporting of the King's visit in the British press, and it may not have been a coincidence that Tac was shelled not long afterwards, albeit with no casualties; Monty himself rejected completely a suggestion by Henderson that he should take shelter in a slit trench. The location now looked less than optimal, both for this reason and because the expansion of the American bridgehead into the Cotentin Peninsula had shifted the centre of gravity to the west. It was therefore decided to move it to Blay, a village well away from the front, west of Bayeux and north of the Forest of Cerisy, but more importantly on the boundary between the Americans and British armies. The move took place on 23 June.

Tac was now working exactly as Monty wanted, the arrival of Dawnay and the rear party, together with his Roll-Royces, having completed the establishment. The C-in-C had legitimate grounds for satisfaction. The lodgement in Normandy had gone well, with the Allied armies now consolidated ashore with a continuous front and unlikely to be thrust back into the sea. To the surprise of all, Operation FORTITUDE was continuing to hold major German forces in the Pas-de-Calais. Reinforcements and supplies had been seriously disrupted by a major storm in the English Channel, but were expected to come back on schedule shortly. Cherbourg was about to fall.

There was, however, one rather large fly in the ointment. Caen, which the planners had anticipated would fall on D-Day itself, was still firmly in the hands of the Germans.

Chapter Twenty

The Hinge

The airborne assault which opened D-Day did not go entirely to plan. The first Allied troops to land in Normandy carried out one of the outstanding airborne operations of the war, when a glider-borne company of the Oxfordshire and Buckinghamshire Light Infantry took the bridges over the Caen Canal and the Orne between Benouville and Ranville in an audacious pinpoint *coup de main*. The subsequent parachute and glider landings by the rest of 6 Airborne Division, on the other hand, were distinguished by their inaccuracy, which resulted in troops being scattered over a wide swathe of country. In spite of this, the objectives were largely taken, securing very quickly the Allies' left flank, which would be held until the eventual 'break-out' in mid-August.

If the British paratroopers found themselves widely dispersed and often separated from their units, this was even more the case with the Americans. The order to 82 US Airborne Division was to capture Sainte-Mère-Eglise, a town in the Cotentin Peninsula astride one of the main roads to Cherbourg, while 101 US Airborne Division was to seize and control the routes leading inland from Utah Beach. In the event, the paratroopers were dropped across a huge area, rather than concentrated as intended. That they managed to achieve their missions was due to the same resourcefulness that the Americans had displayed in Sicily, with small groups, often comprising men from both divisions, coming together to launch vigorous attacks on German positions. Casualties were high, but there was no disaster of the sort predicted by Leigh-Mallory, who was man enough to write to Eisenhower to admit it.

The landings by 4 US Division on Utah Beach were successful, in spite of the current depositing the troops from their landing craft some 2,000 yards south of their intended destination. The achievements of the paratroopers made the passage through the marshy ground behind the beaches much easier and, although there was no clear perimeter, the Americans here were well established by the end of D-Day.

The contrast with Omaha Beach could not have been greater. Unlike at Utah, where the DD tanks had almost all swum ashore safely and provided excellent support for the infantry, off Omaha these mostly foundered, having been launched too far out in difficult seas. The bombing of the coastal defences had been inaccurate, causing little damage, and the reinforcement of a static coastal

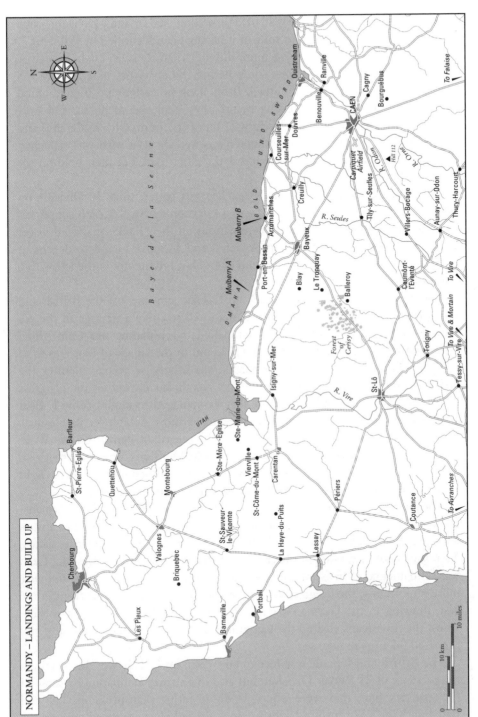

Map 7.

division by an experienced German field formation, 352 Infantry Division, came as a surprise to the invaders, in spite of it having been identified by Williams.

The beaches themselves were more difficult than those at Utah, casualties were very high and it was some time before the survivors of 1 and 29 US Divisions had the strength to attack from their precarious positions behind the sea wall. It was mid-morning before they managed to do so, and only then through a combination of weight of numbers, impressive leadership and heroic effort. By nightfall, the perimeter was well short of what was expected. The attackers had managed to get across the coast road, but their hold on the beachhead was still tenuous.

The situation on Second Army's beaches was better, since 50 Division on Gold, 3 Canadian Division on Juno and 3 Division on Sword, each supported by an armoured brigade and with commandos on their flanks, managed to get ashore with fewer casualties than expected and to move inland to depths of between five and eight miles by the end of D-Day, linking up on the left with 6 Airborne Division.

The only organized counter-attack on D-Day came against the British and Canadians, when 21 Panzer Division attempted to drive a passage to the sea between Juno and Sword. This was repelled by enfilading fire from Allied tanks and artillery, although a garrison held out in the village of Douvres until 17 June. The response by the Germans was otherwise feeble. Neither the Kriegsmarine nor the Luftwaffe made any significant impact on the progress of the Allied armada and, whilst the former managed to mount some E-Boat attacks subsequently, the latter continued to be more notable by its absence. Most importantly, Hitler did not sanction the release of Panzer Group West, with its powerful 12 SS Panzer and Panzer Lehr Divisions, until the afternoon of D-Day. By that time, with Allied air superiority making movement in daylight very dangerous, it was too late to make any impression on the landings.

The lodgements were consolidated over the next few days, notably at Omaha, and by 10 June there was a continuous Allied front. Caen, however, the capture of which had been a D-Day objective, remained firmly in German hands. Monty was not interested in the capture of 'trophy' towns and cities, but Caen was fundamental to his strategy. It was a key communications centre, but also, more importantly, the hinge around which he planned to build his front in the east, drawing in the German armoured divisions and destroying them there whilst the Americans cleared the Cotentin Peninsula, captured Cherbourg and prepared for a break-out.

The British and Canadian failure to take Caen on D-Day was due partly to the presence of 21 Panzer Division, but also to a strong inclination by some of the attackers, once they were ashore, to dig in rather than press on. The 2nd Battalion King's Shropshire Light Infantry nevertheless advanced towards the city, but its armoured support failed to materialize. It came tantalisingly close, but had to withdraw after sustaining heavy losses. Further attacks were mounted on 7 and 8 June but were repulsed, and it became clear that the Germans on the direct approach were too strong.

Monty now adopted the alternative tactic of envelopment, using two of his old Eighth Army formations, 7 Armoured and 51 Highland Divisions. He wanted to incorporate into the operation an airborne assault by 1 Airborne Division south of Caen, but to his fury this was vetoed by Leigh-Mallory. On 12 June, however, it seemed that 7 Armoured Division had found a hole in the German line. Undertaking a wide right hook from north of Tilly-sur-Seulles, it approached the town of Villers-Bocage from the west. Villers-Bocage was well behind the German front line and commanded one of the main roads leading south-west from Caen, which would have been seriously threatened by its capture. The division was, however, on its own: 50 Division, the third of Monty's desert formations, was intended to attack in support, but found its way blocked by the Panzer Lehr Division and made no progress.

Entering Villers-Bocage in the lead, the County of London Yeomanry had the misfortune to encounter a detachment led by Hauptmann Michael Wittman, whose Tiger tanks rampaged along their column, wreaking enormous damage. The detachment destroyed up to 14 tanks, most of which were accounted for by Wittman himself, a similar number of carriers and half-tracks and two anti-tank guns. The attack ground to a halt in confusion and, lacking support, 7 Armoured Division was forced to beat an undignified retreat with significant further losses. Carol Mather, who was the unlucky LO sent to the division at the time, described Villers-Bocage as 'a death trap', and it was certainly the scene of a major setback. The Germans rapidly closed the gap in their line and also easily repulsed a left hook mounted by 51 Division from 6 Airborne Division's area. Until further reinforcements arrived, Monty lacked the resources for another initiative.

The separation of Main HQ from Tac and the fighting troops began to make an immediate impact. Freddie was in daily touch with Monty by scrambler phone, but his responsibilities included not only controlling the work of Main itself, now at full stretch in all branches, but also acting as 21st Army Group's principal contact with Eisenhower, Ramsay and Leigh-Mallory. It was usually important that he remained at Southwick, close to SHAEF and the Allied Naval HQ, rather than being absent on visits across the Channel. For his visits to Tac, however, he was much helped by being allocated his own C-47 by Eisenhower. On these occasions he greatly enlivened the discussions in Monty's mess, so much so that when he was not there the personal staff were ordered to talk more.

Freddie's inability to spend much time in the battle area meant that it was vital that his own liaison officers should function extremely effectively. There were resident LOs at each army, Bigland at First US Army, Major H. T. N.

Batchelor, another Eighth Army 'old boy', at Second Army and Major W. A. Fife at First Canadian Army, as soon as it had landed in July. In addition to these, Llewellyn had up to a dozen other officers, both British and American, available to make trips to armies in the field and to man the Information Room at Main. These appointments tended to be temporary, often officers resting from or preparing to return to the front, but all of them battle-experienced. If he had time, Llewellyn would induct them himself, going across to Normandy on a number of occasions. He also ran a small number of staff lieutenants as couriers of 'Officers only' despatches.

It was clearly important that the fighting formations should not be swamped by LOs, so those from Main HQ were not usually allowed to visit subordinate HQs directly, but instead required to obtain their information from three sources. Two of these were at the Army HQs, the first of which was the Resident LO, to whom they were obliged to report and by whom they were briefed. In his absence their first point of contact was the GSO3 (Ops), followed by other branches as appropriate. The second source of information was the respective Army's own liaison officers, on their return from corps and divisions. The third was Tac itself, in its capacity as a forward information and liaison centre for Main, each LO being obliged to include it in his itinerary. The information sought was essentially the same as that requested by Eighth Army in Italy, but the priorities were explicitly spelt out. These were the army commander's intentions and future plans, the line of the forward troops, the enemy reaction on land, the enemy reaction in the air and the situation of the supporting arms. In addition, each LO was required to return with a trace of the Army Operations Room map.

The organization of Main HQ LO visits to the operational area was made more difficult by their having to cross the Channel each time. A Naval Despatch Boat shuttle service was set up immediately between Whale Island, Portsmouth, and Gold Beach, leaving and arriving five times in each 24 hours, but taking seven hours for the crossing. At least one LO returned for each of the twice daily situation reports at Main at 08.00 and 20.00. The time spent on travel was highly unsatisfactory, but matters improved as soon as the opening of airfields permitted a good air service. Now LOs could leave Main daily at 17.30, arriving at Tac at 19.30, spend the next day on their visits and catch a return flight at 10.00 on the following day, arriving back at Main at 12.30. Each one produced a handwritten report, but urgent information could be communicated from the relevant Army HQ by scrambler phone or in cipher by W/T.

Llewellyn's other function, which he carried out for the remainder of the campaign, was to identify and requisition suitable sites for Main and Rear HQs in the field. His first visit to France began on the evening of D-Day itself, when he travelled over to Normandy in an MTB with Colonel Jones, the Main HQ Camp Commandant, Wing Commander Spencer from Second Tactical Air

Force and three others. They arrived at dawn on the following morning, making them the first officers of any of 21st Army Group's HQs to set foot in France. They spent several days looking for sites, by which time the beachhead had expanded significantly, and eventually settled on one at Le Tronquay, south-west of Bayeux. Llewellyn had been instructed by Freddie to obtain Monty's approval and duly went to Tac to obtain it. Monty queried whether the site might be within range of enemy artillery and suggested two alternatives, both of which, as Llewellyn reminded him, had been allocated for other functions. In the end, Monty grudgingly conceded, but on his return to Main, Llewellyn was told by Freddie that he had been banned from visiting Tac in the future. He asked Gannon if he could obtain a transfer, but was told that he was too valuable to move.

The restrictions on travel under which Freddie laboured did not apply with quite the same force to other senior officers at Main. Belchem and Williams flew over to see Monty almost every day and Williams sometimes stayed on for several days. He was impressed by how well informed Monty was on operations through the reports of his LOs, but felt he should have better access to intelligence. After a few weeks he and Monty decided that Tac HQ should have its own ULTRA reading capability, and Joe Ewart was attached to it for this purpose for the rest of the campaign. Others were summoned at need, including Graham to discuss administrative issues and White to resolve communications problems. Gannon travelled by MTB to consult with Monty in person on 14 and 15 June. He had been hard at work since D-Day providing new unit commanding officers and formation commanders. On one single day, for instance, Monty required replacements for eight COs and two brigade commanders who had been killed or wounded. Whilst the attrition did not continue at this pace every day, the demand remained heavy throughout the Normandy campaign, especially for infantry officers. On 24 June Gannon was asked to provide a new GOC for 3 Division as Tom Rennie had been wounded. Monty asked for Lashmer Whistler, a brigade commander who had already been earmarked for another job; his posting was rapidly changed.

In the first weeks of the campaign Charles Richardson doubled up as both BGS (Plans), which required him to issue a series of appreciations on the current position and the options to be entertained for the future, and 21st Army Group's Liaison Officer to the Allied Expeditionary Air Force. It was the latter job which consumed most of his time, and he had his own caravan parked in the grounds of Bentley Priory at Stanmore. He thus took part in a series of conferences at which all the 'air barons' were present, including not only Leigh-Mallory, who was supposed to coordinate their activities, but also Tedder, in his capacity as Deputy Supreme Commander with specific responsibility for air matters, Coningham, the AOC-in-C of Second Tactical Air Force, the AOC-in-Cs of Bomber and Coastal Commands and the Commanding Generals of the US Strategic, Eighth and Ninth Air Forces. Few of these men rated Leigh-Mallory very highly, partly because his background was in fighters, whereas most of them were experts in either bombing or tactical support, and partly because his stance was perceived as too close to that of the army. Richardson described them as 'this incomparable collection of prima donnas',[1] who could be relied on to air their own prejudices in any context.

Leigh-Mallory was genuinely disposed to be helpful to 21st Army Group, although his refusal to countenance landings by 1 Airborne Division in support of Monty's plan to encircle Caen[2] resulted in a temporary rupture in the relationship, partially repaired a few days later when, on a visit to Tac, he offered to support the army with medium bombers. On the other hand, both Tedder and Coningham were beginning to complain about the inability of 21st Army Group to secure the key German airfields around Caen, notably at Carpiquet. This demonstrated a failure to understand that, if Monty was successful at Caen, the airfields would follow, and that in the meantime their full cooperation was required. It also downplayed the fact that army engineers and specialist RAF units were building and commissioning airfields all over the British sector, with ten delivered by the end of June and a further seven by the end of July.

At Second Army HQ some of these disagreements began to affect army/air cooperation, largely because Coningham was inclined to impose his own views. Relations between Dempsey and Harry Broadhurst, now commanding 83 Group RAF in support of Second Army, had been difficult in Sicily but were now cordial. On the other hand, the lack of operational experience at the HQ resulted in a less than optimal performance and Richardson was seconded to Dempsey for a week to sort it out. Within that time he managed to arrange matters so that the high levels of mutual understanding considered normal at Eighth Army were now also inculcated into Second Army, resulting in a much improved level of ground support.

Broadhurst, for his part, never thought that the lack of airfields was a major problem and neither did his American counterpart, Major General Pete Quesada. Broadhurst's relationship with Coningham was as frosty as it had been in North Africa, so it was fortunate for him that Coningham refused to relocate to Normandy on the grounds that most of his forces were compelled to remain in England. Moreover, Coningham's jealousy of Monty, which had developed in the Middle East, where in his opinion Eighth Army received all the credit and the air forces very little, was affecting his judgement. In these circumstances it was easy for Monty to justify dealing with the RAF primarily through Broadhurst, leaving Freddie to act as the main channel of communication with Coningham.

Although the great majority of those in Main and Rear HQs remained in England, a number of officers and men moved over to Normandy in small parties early in the campaign, an example being a detachment to work with Second

Army's Chief Engineer on Works Services. Monty's senior advisers on the various arms, Dennis, Inglis and Richards, also had to be on the ground as much as possible. Richards flew over a few days after the landings and established his own small HQ in the area selected by Llewellyn. Thereafter he spent his days visiting both formation HQs and individual units and assessing the performance of the latter and their equipment, reporting back to Main, but seeing Monty on a number of occasions. The issues about the overall inferiority of the Allied tanks relative to their German opponents were much as they had been in Sicily, except that, and partly as a result of Richards's representations to Monty at that time, all armoured regiments now had a troop in each squadron of Sherman Firefly or Challenger tanks, with their excellent 17-pounder guns.[3] The specialized AFVs in 79 Division, led by Monty's brother-in-law Percy Hobart, had performed extremely effectively, and Richards was especially pleased with the performance of the amphibious DD tanks. Like many others, however, he was concerned about the inability of any of the tanks to tackle the bocage country with its seemingly impenetrable banked-up hedgerows. The problem was in due course at least partly resolved by welding on a device at the front of a number of tanks, then known as 'Rhinos', which enabled them to drive gaps through the banks.

Administratively, the work done in preparation for the invasion proved to have been well planned. In the initial stages three beach areas were formed, one under XXX Corps and two under I Corps. So that the two corps did not have to look over their shoulders, No. 11 Lines of Communication Area, including an advanced HQ of 21st Army Group Q (Movements & Transportation), assumed the direction of these on D+5 under the command of Second Army. The original intention was for 21st Army Group Lines of Communication to take over on D+18, but the lack of progress in expanding the beachhead meant that this was delayed until D+37. In the meantime, BUCO, MOVCO and TURCO all functioned smoothly and supplies and reinforcements arrived on schedule over the first two weeks. As soon as they were firmly established the two corps immediately formed their own Field Maintenance Centres, augmented by those of other corps as they arrived. Two Army Roadheads were established, one for Second Army, the other for First Canadian Army once it had moved to France. These were later folded into the Rear Maintenance Area for the British sector, which was laid out in a huge area along the roads radiating from Bayeux and operated under the direct control of 21st Army Group.

The capture of Port-en-Bessin on D+1 provided a welcome surprise. The little port was both substantially undamaged and found to have a greater capacity than expected. It was capable of taking tankers with a draught of 14 feet, making it ideal for bulk petrol discharge and storage as well as mixed cargo. The first mixed cargo was unloaded on D+5 and the first bulk petrol on D+19. In the meantime, work began on the construction of pipelines into both the British and American sectors.

By D+4 the first of the concrete caissons for MULBERRY B, the artificial harbour in the British sector, had been dropped into position, and on the following day there were sufficient in place for craft to discharge on to the beach in sheltered water. They were followed by blockships to complete the artificial breakwaters. Preliminary work began on the two prefabricated piers, which were towed across the English Channel. One was for the discharge of stores from conventional ships, the other for the unloading of LSTs. On 19 June, however, before they could be fully commissioned, disaster struck. The worst Channel storm ever recorded blew up and lasted for three full days. A large number of ships were driven on to the shore and MULBERRY B was badly damaged, whilst MULBERRY A in the American sector was effectively destroyed. However, it was immediately cannibalized to repair MULBERRY B, which began to take stores ships on 23 June, but could not accept LSTs until as late as 17 July. First US Army was compelled to land all its requirements over open beaches until Cherbourg could be made available. It did this so effectively that it actually produced better results than the British MULBERRY/beach combination.

The storm had a considerable impact on operations. Unloading was severely disrupted and, whilst a good reserve of POL had been built up, there was already a shortage of field artillery ammunition by the time it began, and it was only by changing the priority away from tank and AA ammunition, both of which had seen far less usage than expected, that the stocks could be restored. This was vital, as Monty was poised to launch a major operation which would require significant artillery support.

Operation EPSOM, launched on 25 June, was similar to the attack on Villers-Bocage in that it involved a right hook from the western side of the British front. However, it did not have the same primary objective, to envelop Caen. Whilst this might be achieved if success allowed its exploitation, Monty's main purpose was to continue to draw the German panzer divisions on to the British front. With Cherbourg about to fall, he considered that this would allow Bradley to push south more readily from the base of the Cotentin Peninsula.

EPSOM was carried out largely by Dick O'Connor's VIII Corps, comprising 11 Armoured, 15 Scottish and 43 Wessex Divisions, all of which were untested in action. The corps' arrival had been delayed for 48 hours by the Channel storm and it was not until 25 June that all the divisions were in position. On that day an attack was mounted by 49 Division in the neighbouring XXX Corps, with the objective of pushing back the Panzer Lehr Division and creating a buffer on the right of VIII Corps. On the following day VIII Corps itself advanced, led by 15 Division. The Scots made good progress at first, but even with the support of 11 Armoured Division, they were unable to reach their immediate objective, the River Odon at Tourville. On the following day, however, whilst 43 Division moved up on the left, 15 Division managed to capture one of the bridges over the river, allowing 11 Armoured Division to create a small bridgehead on 29 June and to seize the strategically important Hill 112, which not only dominated the Odon Valley but also overlooked the Orne Valley to its east. A furious counter-attack by II Panzer Corps ensued, and Dempsey, fearful of another and even stronger attack on one of the flanks, ordered withdrawal, which was in hindsight a great mistake as no such attack was planned and valuable ground was lost unnecessarily. Monty called an end to the operation on 30 June.

In one way EPSOM succeeded in its objective, as Second Army had attracted no fewer than seven panzer divisions on to its front west of Caen. However, First US Army had not been able to take advantage of their absence to begin its thrust southwards, so the only immediate result was a new salient. Caen itself had not been seriously threatened, but if nothing else the operation had demonstrated that the former Home Forces Divisions were, for all their lack of experience, more effective than their ex-Eighth Army counterparts.

Although Monty himself believed that his strategy was bringing results, he could no longer completely ignore the criticism which it was attracting. This came from a number of quarters, led by senior officers at SHAEF, notably Tedder and Freddie Morgan, the former COSSAC, but also in the US Army, although Bradley himself remained conspicuously loyal. There was also unease both in Downing Street and at the War Office. Monty realized that there was no alternative to a frontal attack on Caen, but he wished this to be accomplished with the minimum of casualties, as it was by now clear that the attrition of manpower in Second Army could not be afforded at the rate experienced over the previous four weeks. The last three British divisions, Guards Armoured, 53 Welsh and 59 Staffordshire, had now arrived and, subject only to room being found for them in the severely crowded beachhead, 2 Canadian, 4 Canadian Armoured and the Polish Armoured Divisions were due to follow. After that, the barrel would have to be scraped for reinforcements.

The need to conserve manpower if at all possible meant that any attack on Caen would have to rely heavily on bombarding the defenders, using artillery, naval guns and, if at all possible, air power. Richardson was sent to Stanmore to plead the case for the last of these, receiving initially no commitment at all from the 'air barons'. Appealing to Tedder, he was advised to see 'Bomber' Harris at his HQ at High Wycombe. Having discovered why Richardson was there, Harris sent for Air Vice Marshal Bennettt of the Pathfinder Force to ask whether he thought it possible. Bennett confirmed that his men could do it and he and Richardson immediately produced an outline plan. To Richardson's astonishment, Harris then suggested that he should have a good dinner in London before crossing to France and lent him his Bentley for the evening.

Operation CHARNWOOD opened on the night of 7 July, when 467 bombers dropped 2,560 tons of bombs on the northern suburbs of Caen. On the following morning, John Crocker's 1 Corps began its advance into the city, with

59 Division in the centre, 3 Division on the left and 3 Canadian Division on the right. Over two days' hard fighting the Germans were pushed back across the Orne, where they remained entrenched. The northern half of the city had been taken, but only by wreaking devastation, the victims of which were largely the remaining citizens. Richardson, who visited shortly afterwards, found the impact of the bombing disappointing, and this was confirmed by a RAF survey conducted in the immediate aftermath. The morale of the troops had been lifted, but the fighting had been just as intense as ever; indeed, the ruined buildings were ideal for defenders. Rather more important was the capture of the large airfield at Carpiquet, which Tedder and Coningham had been calling for so volubly since D-Day. Its possession, however, was not about to silence them or Monty's many other critics.

Chapter Twenty-One

The Phase Lines

Paul Odgers thought that the site at Blay was one of the best which Tac HQ occupied, a sentiment echoed by others. This was just as well, as Tac spent more time there, just under six weeks, than in any site other than the winter quarters in Belgium. It was situated in a number of fields on a slope overlooking a valley and was much more spacious than the rather cramped situation at Creully.

Tac was now able to settle down to a regular rhythm of activity. With the front extending from beyond the mouth of River Orne to the other side of the Cotentin Peninsula and traffic in the beachhead still very congested, it became impossible for some of the LOs to get to and from their allotted formations within a day. Accordingly, a small flight was formed, initially of only three Austers crewed by bomber pilots resting from operations, which flew the LOs out each morning and returned them in time for their evening reports. Sanderson, responsible for 51 Division on the far left, used to leave his signaller there every night with orders to pick him up in a jeep from the local airstrip on the following morning. Monty had his own mode of air transport, a Miles Messenger. This was one of only twenty-one of the type built during the war by Miles Aircraft and, in addition to its versatile take-off and landing characteristics, was roomier than the Auster, with three seats instead of two. It was flown by his own personal RAF pilot, Flight Lieutenant Trevor Martin, and Monty was to use it extensively for the rest of the war.

Monty's American LOs were just as busy as their British counterparts, although some found it difficult to get out of the habit of carrying sealed envelopes everywhere and rely instead only on chinagraph boards and their memories. The initial decision by the Americans not to accept the British offer of Phantom patrols denied their formations a valuable communication medium, but not long after D-Day Lieutenant General Joe Collins of VII US Corps, one of the best American commanders and a favourite of Monty's, saw the light and asked to be sent one. Captain Mackintosh-Reid, commanding the Phantom detachment at Tac, was ordered to assemble a patrol and despatched with Maurice Frary to provide the service; more soon followed to other American formations. Ray BonDurant was also occasionally used in a liaison capacity by Monty. He was sent on a mission to Cherbourg shortly after its capture, where he succeeded in liberating five cases of Hennessy brandy, much to the joy of Monty's personal staff.

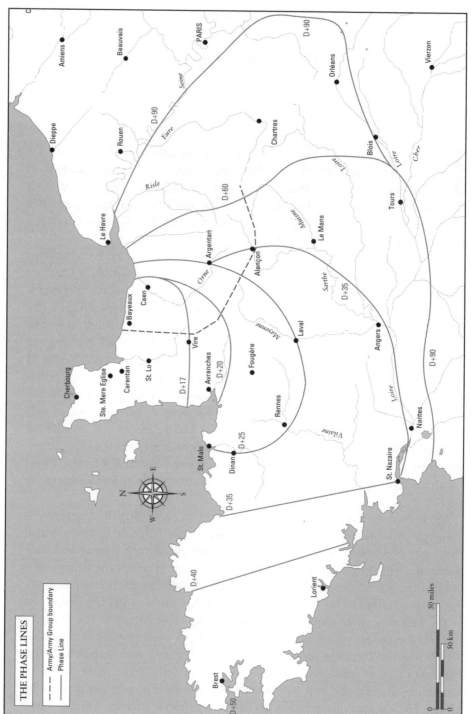

THE PHASE LINES

--- Army/Army Group boundary

— Phase Line

Amiens

Beauvais

PARIS

Orléans

Vierzon

Dieppe

Rouen

Seine

Eure

Chartres

Blois

D+90

Loire

Cher

Le Havre

Risle

D+60

Tours

Argentan

Mayenne

Le Mans

D+35

Bayeaux

Caen

Orne

Alençon

Sarthe

Cherbourg

Ste. Mere Eglise

Carentan

St. Lo

Vire

Avranches

D+20

Fougère

Laval

Mayenne

Angers

D+90

D+17

Rennes

Vilaine

Nantes

St. Malo

Dinan

D+25

St. Nazaire

D+35

N
E
W
S

Brest

D+50

D+40

Lorient

0   50 km

0   50 miles

Map 8.

One of the key figures at Tac was Sergeant Norman Kirby, who was in charge of the Field Security detachment. Throughout the campaign he provided the principal connection with the local population in the immediate area around each site, partly because it was his job to assess the security risks inherent among them and partly because of his linguistic ability.[1] In Blay one of his main contacts was the local curé, through whom he was able to arrange for services to take place in the Roman Catholic church, in accordance with Monty's insistence that church parades should be held every Sunday. The first such service there was conducted by Llewellyn Hughes, but this raised a furore amongst the Army Roman Catholic chaplains, who were aggrieved that one of their churches had been used by the Church of England. They even appealed to the Bishop of Bayeux, but ecumenism prevailed. The Sunday church parade was usually followed by a football match between the officers' team, captained by John Poston, and the NCOs and other ranks.

Monty, as always, derived a great deal of satisfaction from regular interaction with his personal staff at dinner each evening. He felt the need, however, for an additional feature in his domestic life and decided that this should be a dog. At lunch one day he proposed that Dawnay, who was due to visit Main, and Mather, who was about to return to England to recuperate from a serious bout of asthma, should obtain one whilst they were there. Monty suggested that Frank Gillard of the BBC might mention this in his programme, thus attracting offers of potential pets by listeners, and Dawnay was instructed to see him. In the end Monty received two dogs, a cocker spaniel through Dawnay's own efforts and a Jack Russell terrier presented by Gillard. The first was named 'Rommel' and the second 'Hitler', and they provided Monty with much amusement over the coming months.

Whenever Monty was away the dogs were looked after by a recent arrival at Tac and one of its least busy officers, Bob Hunter, a major in the Royal Army Medical Corps. Monty's disregard for personal danger and more general concerns about his health, dating back to the episode in Palestine in 1939, had spurred 21st Army Group's Chief Surgeon, Arthur Porritt, into insisting that Tac should have its own Medical Officer. Hunter was chosen for his quiet approach on medical matters, which Porritt thought would suit Monty. Another newcomer was Padre William Tindal, who looked after Tac's spiritual needs, although Hughes continued to visit regularly in his dual capacities as Deputy Chaplain General and friend of and confidant to Monty.

Amidst the general harmony at Tac, there was one discordant note, the position of Leo Russell. Russell's attempts to exercise authority over the LOs were frustrated by their insistence on taking orders only from Monty, a practice which the C-in-C did nothing to discourage. His lack of battle experience was only too evident, and they made it abundantly clear that he had nothing to offer on how they should carry out their jobs. Although Dawnay tried to keep Russell informed about what was happening, Monty himself never confided in him, thereby nullifying Freddie's objective, which was to ascertain what was going on in 'Master's' mind in a way which was impossible to achieve through the brief daily phone calls. Matters eventually came to a head, however, over an incident which had nothing to do with either Russell's role or the LOs' duties.

At the centre of the affair was a pig, which was discovered running apparently wild, captured and butchered for the C-in-C's mess. The owner, a local farmer, then appeared at the camp gates to lodge a protest and present a demand for compensation. The finger of suspicion for the abduction pointed at Chavasse, and he and Henderson were placed under arrest by Russell on a charge of looting. Wider enquiries established that a number of other animals were being kept at Tac for fresh meat and that Poston was also implicated. The farmer was recompensed, but Russell now called for the suspects to face a court martial. Monty was informed and, notwithstanding his own strong position on the iniquities of looting, dismissed the allegations. Russell, bravely but foolishly sticking to his principles, refused to back down, causing Monty to demand that he be removed from Tac immediately. Freddie flew over to try to make Russell see reason over what Monty regarded as a trivial matter, but Russell maintained his stance and was duly removed, following which he wrote a detailed report, among other things accusing Monty of condoning looting. This was sent to the VCIGS, Lieutenant General Nye, who ensured that the matter went no further.[2]

This episode might seem to be comic in retrospect, but its implications were far more serious. It was clear that Russell had been sidelined by Monty, who believed him to be more in the nature of a spy in the camp than a part of the team. The same applied to his successor, Lieutenant Colonel Kirke, who was dismissed by Monty in September after making an issue of Poston arriving for the morning briefing in his pyjamas. Much to the relief of the LOs, Dawnay then effectively assumed command of Tac, which thenceforward tended to tie him to the spot, his job being among other things to know where Monty was at all times and to answer the telephone on his behalf, whilst Odgers ran Operations. All this might not have mattered if Monty had been a good communicator, but he was relying on Freddie to do this for him and Freddie did not always have the full story.

Monty was excellent at keeping in touch with his subordinate commanders, but very poor at doing so with his superiors. This had certainly been the case in Home Forces with Auchinleck and to some extent in the Mediterranean with Alexander, of whose military skills he was scornful. The one exception was Brooke, whom Monty had always held in the highest regard. A ridiculous situation now developed in which Monty sent daily signals to the CIGS, who had no command role in the campaign, but left Freddie to deal with his immediate superior, the Supreme Commander, whom Monty regarded as a capable manager but no soldier. As a result, Monty's apparent failures to meet expectations were not always adequately explained. Serious and potentially damaging criticism began to be heard from two main sources, SHAEF itself and the RAF.

The problem began with the phase line map, which had been produced for the conferences at St Paul's on both 7 April and 15 May. The lines had been drawn by Dawnay and lacked the authority of the planners. Whilst his staff understood clearly that they were only illustrative of what might happen, and Monty himself placed little emphasis on them, no such caveats were given at the time. Merely because they were produced at the conferences, however, a number of those present took them to be commitments.

The criticisms began to be heard early in the campaign with the failure to take Caen, an objective for D-Day which was not achieved until a month later and even then not completely. This failure was exacerbated, at least as far as senior officers in the RAF were concerned, by the Germans continuing to hold Carpiquet and other airfields around Caen. Monty's contention that everything was going to plan was not helped by the general lack of forward momentum in the British sector, Operation EPSOM having been seen as yet another failure by the critics. The next major Second Army operation was now to add grist to their mill.

Monty was confident that his strategy was working well, keeping the German panzer divisions on the British front to prevent any quick advance to the Seine, whilst allowing the Americans to build up for a break-out into Maine and Brittany, but he was not devoid of problems. One of the most serious was the attrition to the British infantry divisions, especially after General Sir Ronald Adam, the Adjutant-General, visited Monty and Dempsey to tell them that he would run out of reinforcements by the end of July. This would be a significant factor in his future thinking.

On 7 July, Richardson issued an appreciation by G (Plans) of the situation at D+30. The key paragraph read:

> To sum up, our superiority in infantry is of the order of two to one, which is sufficient to justify offensive operations, but is not sufficient by itself to sustain a rapid advance through 'bocage' country. Our artillery and air superiority is immense; our tank superiority is sufficient to enable us to take big risks provided a plan can be formulated to use this tank superiority on ground of our own choosing. Our initial superiority in fighting efficiency will lessen as our casualties increase and as the enemy's supply position improves, as it is likely to do from now onwards.

The appreciation went on to say:

> A thrust towards FALAISE provides an opportunity to use tanks in mass and hence to assert our great superiority in numbers. The enemy is fully

alive to this but unless we are prepared to fight him with our tanks it seems that no further progress on the British sector is available for many weeks to come.

Extraordinarily in the light of this, three days later Monty issued a directive to his army commanders which called for an advance southwards by the British infantry divisions from the west of their sector, the objective being the line Thury-Harcourt – Mont Pincon – Le-Bény-Bocage, whilst the Americans were not only to move towards Avranches, but also to pivot south-east towards a line Le-Bény-Bocage – Vire – Mortain. This would take both armies through the worst of the bocage. The bridgehead east of Caen would not be expanded, although an armoured corps would be held there in reserve to await Monty's orders pending favourable developments.

When he read this, Bonesteel was horrified and immediately lobbied Belchem, Richardson and Williams to have it changed. They immediately saw the point and, as a result of their persuasion, a new directive was issued to Second Army three days later which bore no resemblance to its predecessor and which also utilized the relatively unscathed armoured formations, whilst conserving the vulnerable infantry. Operation GOODWOOD called for an advance by all three of the army's armoured divisions through the good tank country south-east of Caen towards Falaise.

GOODWOOD was to become the subject of further controversy, as once again Monty managed to raise expectations which were not fulfilled. His own objective was quite limited, to take the important Bourguébus Ridge lying across the route to Falaise, thus ensuring that no German panzer divisions were diverted from the British front to oppose First US Army's Operation COBRA, the break-out into open country to the south and west planned for the same time. That this was the case was specifically spelt out in a letter which Monty sent to Brooke and which Dawnay delivered by hand to Simpson, now DMO at the War Office, on 14 July. On the same day Freddie was sent to Eisenhower to explain Monty's intentions, in terms which were equally clear.

Two other important parties were, however, deceived as to Monty's intentions. The first of these was the RAF. In order to obtain from Tedder and Harris the necessary support by heavy bombers in advance of the attack, Freddie exaggerated the objective of the operation, telling them that it would be a turning point in the campaign. The second was the press, summoned to a briefing by Monty as the operation began. The correspondents were told that GOODWOOD would be decisive and interpreted this as a break-out on the British front. When the limited nature of the gains became apparent, this was seen as a failure and reported as such. Dawnay felt that if Freddie had been there he would have counselled a more cautious approach, but Freddie was fully occupied at Main. Even Monty was later to concede that he had been 'too exultant'.[3]

GOODWOOD kicked off on the morning of 18 July. The preparations were no secret to the Germans, who had observers in the towers of the steelworks in the south-western Caen suburb of Colombelles. The tanks of VIII Corps' 11 Armoured Division, followed by those of Guards and 7 Armoured Divisions, made slow progress on to the battlefield due to limited access across the Orne and through the minefields. The bombing, however, had made a significant impact on the defenders, and initial progress was good. Some of the anti-tank defences were nevertheless untouched, particularly at Cagny, from where German 88s raked the passing tanks, destroying large numbers. O'Connor had wanted to send carrier-borne infantry in support of the tanks, but was stopped by Dempsey because of the traffic constrictions, so none were available to clear the German strongpoints. Progress was much slower than planned, with 7 Armoured Division barely entering the battlefield on the first day. Furthermore, the German defences on the rear slope of Bourguébus Ridge turned out to be in greater depth than anticipated.

Fighting continued on 19 July, with significant progress also being made by 2 and 3 Canadian Divisions, who between them not only took the rest of Caen, but also pushed the front forward considerably to the south and south-west of the city. On 20 July, however, it became clear that no further advance was possible, and Monty closed down the operation. He had not advanced as far as even he expected, but he had succeeded in what was, in his own mind at least, the primary purpose of the operation, to hold the German panzer divisions on his front.

The perceived 'failure' of GOODWOOD had serious consequences, both at SHAEF and within RAF circles. Led by Coningham, who had watched the operation from VIII Corps Tac HQ, where his frustration was all too evident, a number of senior officers began conspiring to remove Monty. In addition to Coningham and Tedder, these included Freddie Morgan, the former COSSAC, and Lieutenant General Sir Humphrey Gale, Morgan's fellow Deputy Chief of Staff at SHAEF, where he was responsible for administration. There is some evidence that both Eisenhower and Bedell Smith were drawn into the discussions about Monty's future, although Freddie later wrote of the former, 'Never to my knowledge did he criticise Montgomery's tactics during this phase.'[4] However, Eisenhower was clearly unhappy with the outcome of GOODWOOD and angry at the deceptions which had been employed, which had caused him to use his personal influence to add weight to Monty's demand for bomber support.

The conspirators did not by themselves have the power to sack an Allied C-in-C, and even Eisenhower could not do so without reference to the Combined Chiefs of Staff. There was one man, however, who could and that was Churchill. Moreover, Churchill was currently very angry with Monty, not because of GOODWOOD, but because he had been prevented from visiting the front. That this move had been initiated by Eisenhower to prevent Monty from being diverted during GOODWOOD did not deflect the Prime Minister's anger. He summoned Brooke on the morning of 19 July and loosed off a volley of criticism aimed at Monty. Brooke was in any event about to leave for a visit to Normandy, providing him with a timely opportunity to convey the extent of the Prime Minister's ire and also to warn Monty that the views of Tedder and Coningham might be having some influence. The CIGS suggested that he should immediately write a letter to Churchill saying that he was unaware of his wish to visit and inviting him to come over as soon as he liked. The letter was delivered personally to 10 Downing Street by Brooke that evening.

In the meantime, Monty had also requested that Eisenhower should visit him, stipulating that he should come without Tedder or any other airmen. Eisenhower arrived on the afternoon of 20 July, just as GOODWOOD was being closed down. The conversation was not recorded, but the Supreme Commander arrived a worried man and left, if not completely convinced, at least comforted. He wrote on the following day in very firm language – although Tedder did not think it was strong enough – to urge that Second Army should keep pressing forward, but whatever thoughts he might have entertained of dismissing Monty were put aside.

Churchill turned up on the following morning, still very grumpy. It was commonly believed at Tac that a dismissal letter was sitting in his pocket, although in retrospect that seems unlikely. In any event, as with Eisenhower, the Prime Minister's mood was transformed by Monty's remarkable ability to explain his plans with absolute clarity and with the certain conviction that they would bring the required results. Monty was once again secure in his position, for the time being at least.

COBRA was launched on 25 July, the ground operations preceded by a huge blitz of the German defences by the USAAF. Although this shattered the defenders, a significant weight of bombs fell short, causing a large number of casualties among the troops waiting to attack.[5] The Americans nevertheless made considerable progress. By 28 July they had broken through the crust of the defence all along their line, two days later Bradley had his armoured divisions in Avranches and on 1 August Third US Army was activated under Patton, just in time to round the corner into Brittany. At the same time 12th US Army Group was created, with Bradley in command and Courtney Hodges relieving him at First US Army. It was agreed that the new army group would come under Monty, but only until 31 August.

Monty and Bradley had worked in harmony since the beginning of the campaign. Monty very sensibly confined himself to agreeing outline plans with Bradley and coordinating the movements of the two armies, otherwise letting him take all the key decisions. This differed significantly from his approach to Dempsey, whom he tended to treat more as a corps than an army commander. The relationship with Bradley, however, would gradually change for the worse as the American began to demonstrate both his independence and his equal status.

A sizeable number of American officers who had been working at Main HQ 21st Army Group now left to form the kernel of Bradley's staff, although Llewellyn hung on to a few LOs and Monty insisted on retaining Frary and Prisk at Tac. Bigland reported to Monty to discuss his own future. He was asked if Bradley would want to retain him and replied that he thought he would. This was speedily confirmed, and Bigland moved to be Resident LO at 12th Army Group, where he continued to operate in much the same way as before.

On 30 July, as the Americans approached Avranches, Second Army began its next significant offensive, Operation BLUECOAT. This was a joint operation, with VIII Corps on the right directed at Vire whilst XXX Corps on the left advanced towards the commanding height of Mont Pinçon. The former made excellent progress, the latter stalled and Monty lost patience with its commander, Gerry Bucknall, and with the GOC of 7 Armoured Division, Bobby Erskine. Both were his protégés, Bucknall having been brought out to Sicily to experience divisional command there and in Italy, whilst Erskine had relieved Freddie in North Africa during his absences on sick leave. Both were now sacked.

Monty had been deeply disappointed by the performance of all three of his desert divisions. In due course, 50 Division found its feet, but 7 Armoured and 51 Highland Divisions both continued to underperform, one at Villers-Bocage and in GOODWOOD, the other on the left flank. A fortnight before the sacking of Bucknall and Erskine, Charles Bullen-Smith had also been fired. He had served on Monty's staff in 3 Division and, like Bucknall, had been brought out from England to assume command of 51 Division whilst it was still in Sicily. The Highlanders deeply resented the replacement of Douglas Wimberley, especially by an officer from a Lowland regiment. They would not fight for Bullen-Smith and their performance was only restored when Tom Rennie, who had served in the division for many years, was brought back, having recovered from wounds suffered whilst leading 3 Division early in the campaign.

With the territory controlled by the Allies much enlarged, it was time for both Main and Rear HQs to move to Normandy. Llewellyn had carried out another reconnaissance from 4 to 7 July, visiting much of the British and American sectors. This confirmed Le Tronquay as the most suitable site, just off the main road from Bayeux to St Lo and about five miles from Tac at Blay. A site was also found for Rear HQ at Vaucelles, just west of Bayeux and well situated in the middle of the Rear Maintenance Area, which was now created out of the former Army Roadheads. Main began its move in the second half of July and was substantially in place by the end of the month, whilst Rear opened on 11 August. On 3 August Tac moved forward a few miles to the Forest of Cerisy, where it was the closest to Main that it would ever be. Moreover, four days later Eisenhower established the Advanced Command Post of SHAEF, codenamed 'Shellburst', at Tournières, much the same distance away as Main, but to the north-west. Never again would physical communications be so good.

In launching BLUECOAT Monty had complied with Eisenhower's demand for Second Army to keep pressing forward. By the end of the first week of August the British had taken Mont Pinçon and held a line running north-east from Vire, which marked the boundary with the Americans, to the Bourguébus Ridge. Second Army, with VIII, XII and XX Corps under command, continued its advance, but it was now time for the newly formed First Canadian Army to take the field. It was commanded by Henry Crerar, an officer whom Monty had under his command in England in 1942 and in Italy in 1943, and whom he did not rate highly. However, Crerar was responsible to the Canadian Government and Monty did not have the power to replace him. More happily, II Canadian Corps was under Guy Simonds, with whom Monty had always enjoyed an excellent relationship and who had performed admirably for him in Sicily and Italy.

On 7 August Operation TOTALIZE was launched, an attack by First Canadian Army down the main road from Caen to Falaise, with Simonds on the right and John Crocker's I Corps on the left. It made good progress at first, but the German defence was tenacious and it ground to a halt three days later on the River Laizon, seven miles north of Falaise. At the same time, the Germans, in response to a direct order from Hitler, launched their last serious counter-attack against the Americans at Mortain, with the objective of driving through to the sea north of Avranches and cutting Patton's lines of communication. The remnants of a number of panzer divisions were committed, but Bradley rushed in reinforcements, whilst RAF Typhoons attacked the German panzer formations around the clock. By 12 August the Germans were in retreat.

Events were developing faster than at any time in the campaign and there was confusion about how best to exploit them. Third US Army had raced into Brittany and was on the Loire by 10 August. More importantly, Patton had turned one of his corps east and it reached Le Mans on 8 August. The question now became one of how to trap the German forces south of the Seine. Should the Allies conduct a long envelopment, consisting of a drive directly to the river from Le Mans, seizing the crossings and cutting off the retreat there, or a short one, with the Americans advancing round tightly behind the German front line whilst the British and Canadians maintained the pressure from the north? Both Bradley and Montgomery preferred the former in the first instance.

De Guingand, Belchem and Bonesteel had started looking at the practicalities of a long envelopment only two weeks into the campaign, and as late as 7 August Richardson's planners were assuming that this was what would happen. The very tenaciousness of the Germans' defence, their move away from the Seine towards Mortain and their reluctance, in accordance with orders from OKW[6] to make a strategic withdrawal, now opened up the possibility of a short envelopment instead. Bradley now supported this and Patton was ordered to send his XV US Corps north from Le Mans to Argentan, which was reached on 13 August, whilst Hodges began to execute a right hook to create the south side of what would shortly become known as the Falaise Pocket. To the north, Simonds launched Operation TRACTABLE, a renewed drive on Falaise itself, on 14 August.

There has been considerable controversy about the failure of the Allies, and specifically of Monty, to close the neck of Falaise Pocket, or 'Falaise Gap', before a significant number of Germans escaped. The Canadians and the Polish Armoured Division continued to make hard work of their advance and Monty, overestimating their capabilities, failed to reinforce them with one or more divisions from Second Army, which he certainly had the resources to do. He also refused to countenance a proposal, conceived by Bonesteel and enthusiastically supported by Belchem and Richardson, to drop in two airborne divisions. Bradley, however, was equally to blame. XV US Corps was under strict orders to remain at Argentan, ostensibly to avoid 'friendly fire' between the Allies, when it could readily have pushed north. Patton's attention was instead focused by Bradley on the race to the Seine and the liberation of Paris. It was only on 17 August that 90 US Division, now under V US Corps in First US Army, was ordered to attack to close the Gap and 19 August before it met the Poles at Chambois. The Gap was finally sealed two days later. An estimated 40,000 Germans escaped, but 10,000 died in the carnage wreaked in the Pocket and 50,000 were taken prisoner.

The battle for Normandy was now at an end and the pursuit was about to begin. The victory had been conclusive, albeit short of the total destruction of the German armies which should have been possible at Falaise. Monty later reflected on the past two and a half months:

> I never once had cause or reason to alter my master plan. Of course we did not keep to the times and phase lines we had envisaged for the benefit of administrative planning, and of course, too, we didn't hesitate to adjust our plans and dispositions to the tactical situation as it developed – as in all battles. Of course we didn't. I never imagined we would. But the fundamental design remained unchanged; it was to that that I pinned my hopes and clung so resolutely, despite increasing opposition from the fainter-hearted.[7]

On the evidence of the results, it may seem difficult to argue with this assessment, but in fact Monty was being disingenuous. The plan and the execution differed considerably and, if Monty is to be admired, once again it is for his ability to adapt to changing circumstances. Any expectation of consistent progress as illustrated in the phase lines never came to fruition against the best army in the world, which was not going to give ground lightly. It was a blessing for the Allies that, even after Patton's presence in France became known, Operation FORTITUDE kept the Germans believing in a landing in the Pas-de-Calais, limiting the reinforcements sent to Normandy.

The staff work of 21st Army Group had, for the most part, been brilliant. The General Staff at Main HQ were provided with very accurate and up to date information on current operations through the liaison officers. As Monty's directive of 10 July had shown, however, they were not always fully in touch with the C-in-C's intentions. On the administrative side the enormously complex plan for D-Day itself had been near faultless and the build-up had only been disrupted by the Channel storm in late June. The constricted nature of the beachhead delayed the transfer of administrative responsibilities on the ground from Second Army to 21st Army Group, but on the other hand the very lack of a long line of communication enabled both POL and other stores to be accumulated in large quantities. This was about to change as the armies moved very rapidly away from their base.

The major problem, which would be an enduring one, was the relationship between Monty and SHAEF, and particularly Eisenhower himself. The Supreme Commander was an infrequent visitor to Tac HQ, whilst Monty, in accordance with his principles that field commanders should go forward to see their subordinates and not vice-versa, never went to SHAEF. Relying on Freddie to convey his intentions to Eisenhower was a second class option. Eisenhower, and particularly Bedell Smith, accordingly never really recognized that Monty measured success in Normandy not by the seizure of territory, but by the destruction of the enemy. Bradley, on the other hand, understood it completely.

The last phase line had always been the only one which mattered to Monty. The Germans' efforts to keep the cork in the bottle had led to such enormous pressure being built up that the ensuing explosion proved irresistible. There was some resistance to the British and Canadian advance, but there were no resources to create a defence line on the Seine. The first American units crossed the river on 19 August and the four Allied armies were arrayed along it from the mouth to Paris and beyond by 25 August. It was D+80 and Monty was on the last phase line ten days ahead of schedule.

Chapter Twenty-Two

The Great Leap Forward

On the morning of 14 August, as the Germans were being pushed back on three fronts into the Falaise Pocket, Tac HQ left the Forest of Cerisy. The site, which was naturally camouflaged, had been an excellent one for making the necessary preparations to go on to a fully mobile basis. This proved to have been time well spent, as over the next 25 days Tac moved nine times covering a distance of over 300 miles.

The new site was at Campeaux, a few miles east of Le-Bény-Bocage, where Dempsey had his Tac HQ, and still close to the boundary between the two army groups. Bradley's main command post, with his two armies spreading out over a much greater area than the British and Canadians, was located at Coutances, well behind his front, but he had decided to form his own advanced command post, named Eagle Tac, which would perform much the same function as Monty's. It already numbered some 65 officers and twice as many enlisted men and would grow considerably as the campaign developed.

On 19 August Tac moved again, this time only a short distance to Proussy, north-east of Condé-sur-Noireau, where it was at last out of the bocage and into open country. The Falaise Gap was about to be closed and, for the first time, those at Tac were able to see the carnage wrought by the Second Tactical Air Force and Quesada's Ninth US Tactical Air Force. Broadhurst flew Freddie low over the Pocket and the latter was physically sick. Although an immediate survey showed that the claims of the airmen regarding the destruction of tanks had been greatly exaggerated, there was no doubt about the impact on soft-skinned vehicles and on the enemy troops. The techniques of ground/air support had reached their zenith at Falaise, using the same 'cab rank' principle conceived by Broadhurst and his RAF and Army colleagues at Mareth.

At a staff meeting at 'Shellburst' on 20 August, Eisenhower confirmed that he would assume control of the two army groups on 1 September and decided that 12th Army Group should be directed towards Metz and the Saar. Freddie, who was present, recommended consulting Monty before any orders were issued and was despatched to Tac to do so. Monty had already given considerable thought to the future prosecution of the campaign. The fact that the advance had not been steady since D-Day, but had been sudden and explosive more than two months later, if anything added strength to the proposals he now put forward to Eisenhower. These came in the form of notes, delivered by Freddie to the Supreme Commander on 22 August, which read as follows:

1. The quickest way to win this war is for the great mass of the Allied armies to advance northwards, clear the coast as far as Antwerp, establish a powerful air force in Belgium, and advance into the Ruhr.
2. The force must operate as one whole, with great cohesion, and be so strong that it can do the job quickly.
3. Single control and direction of the land operations is vital for success. This is a WHOLE TIME job for one man.
4. The great victory in N.W. France has been won by personal command. Only in this way will further victories be won. If staff control of operations is allowed to creep in, then quick success becomes endangered.
5. To change the system of control now, after having won a great victory, would be to prolong the war.[1]

These notes, and Eisenhower's response, became the basis for major differences in opinion between the two men which were to bedevil most of the rest of the campaign and in due course to come close to rupturing their relationship.

There were two fundamental points of disagreement. The first lay with strategy. Monty was strongly advocating what became known as the 'Northern Thrust', which would involve the whole of 21st Army Group and at least one, if not two, of the armies in 12th US Army Group. Patton's Third US Army, together with 6th US Army Group, which had been formed following the landings in the South of France (Operation DRAGOON) exactly a week earlier, would threaten Germany from North-East France, but would not be supplied or reinforced in such a way as to permit a major offensive. Eisenhower, on the other hand, envisaged a 'Broad Front' along which all the Allied armies would advance steadily side by side on a front stretching from the Channel to Switzerland.

The second point of disagreement was on leadership. Monty was quite clear that the campaign would only succeed if there was a single ground forces commander. By implication this would not be Eisenhower, who in Monty's opinion lacked the necessary experience and, moreover, had other responsibilities, both military and political, which were inconsistent with command in the field. Because the preponderance of troops in the Northern Thrust would initially be British and Canadian, it was clear that Monty had this role in mind for himself. He was also advocating his own philosophy, namely that the commander should be in direct and constant touch with his subordinates and should not attempt to control operations from the rear, where he would be unduly influenced by the staff.

Montgomery had seen Bradley at Eagle Tac near Fougères on 17 August and obtained his agreement to the notes sent to Eisenhower. He flew to see him again, this time at Laval, on 23 August and was astounded to hear that he had changed his mind and was now backing Eisenhower. Eisenhower himself appeared at Tac later on the same day, accompanied by Gale and Bedell Smith, whom Monty had not seen since D-Day. Monty insisted on meeting the Supreme Commander alone and tried to convince him of the merit of his proposals, even agreeing to serve under Bradley if the American contribution to the Northern Thrust merited such a decision to satisfy public opinion in the USA. The result was compromise. The advance of 21st Army Group was accorded some sort of priority, but the Broad Front would remain the official policy.

Monty's refusal to relinquish his position on either strategy or command meant that the debate would rumble on for months. Whilst far from alone in his view – he was strongly supported by Brooke and by Sir James Grigg, the Secretary of State for War – there were those among his advisers who disagreed with his stance, the most prominent of whom was Freddie. 'It is only fair to say', he wrote later, 'that throughout the war, this was the only major issue over which I did not agree with my Chief.'[2] Freddie's reasoning was more objective than Eisenhower's, the latter swayed to a considerable extent by Marshall, Bradley, Patton and American public opinion. Freddie doubted that the administrative situation would permit sustaining such an immense effort on a narrow front whilst the ports remained closed, saw the problems involved with crossing the Rhine, considered that the flanks of the salient which would have to be created would be especially vulnerable to counter-attack and recognized that Eisenhower would have to utilize the forces now being built up to the east. In public, however, he remained entirely loyal to Monty and did his bidding, even if he disagreed with him.

Williams, as always, took a balanced view, agreeing with Monty on the importance of the Ruhr, but accepting immediately that he would lose the command argument. Freddie, who was unable to press the point himself, sent him to see Monty, knowing that the C-in-C respected Williams's judgement and that, as a 'hostilities only' soldier with a career to return to, he could say plainly what would be very difficult for a regular like himself. Williams told Monty that even if the Americans considered him to be the best possible commander in the world, which they did not, it would be quite unacceptable for him to command a force which would in due course be dominated by the Americans. He said subsequently[3] that he was not even sure that Monty had understood the argument. Instead, the C-in-C was baffled that Eisenhower was unable to see the right way to win the war and astonished that American public opinion had anything to do with a purely military matter.

Two days after Monty's meeting with Eisenhower, Tac moved again, this time to Avernes-sous-Exmes, between Argentan and Gacé, close to the most direct road to the Seine. Whilst it was there Monty was visited by Brooke. The weather was too bad to use the small landing strip, so Brooke was driven there and back from Main HQ by Freddie, experiencing the shambles of the Falaise Gap at first hand on the way. Brooke had been in Italy when the debate had taken place with Eisenhower, but although he was strongly in Monty's camp, believing that Eisenhower's strategy would add three to six months to the war, it is highly improbable that he would have been able to counter what was effectively an American-inspired fait accompli.

On the previous day another visitor had arrived at Tac, one who was to remain there for the next two and a half weeks. This was the artist James Gunn, who had been commissioned to paint a portrait of Monty. Gunn was a highly fashionable portraitist, numbering members of the Royal Family and senior politicians such as Chamberlain among his subjects, and it flattered Monty's ego that he should now paint him as well. They had met in February when Gunn visited Augustus John's studio on the same day as Bernard Shaw and sketched a 'conversation piece' of the three men which he presented to Monty. Although others were not so impressed by the new arrival, notably Trumbull Warren, who thought him very conceited, he was made an honorary member of Monty's mess for the duration of his stay and was well looked after by the personal staff. He also kept a diary, which provides a detailed impression of Tac during its most mobile period. Like many others, he was particularly taken with the relaxed atmosphere in the mess and the constant banter between the C-in-C and his aides.

On 26 August XXX Corps crossed the Seine at Vernon, and XII Corps followed near Louviers two days later. Dempsey grounded VIII Corps and used its transport to reinforce his double thrust towards the Belgian border. There was a strong sense of exhilaration within Second Army as it now raced forward, meeting very little opposition. On the left, First Canadian Army had a more difficult task. I Corps was ordered to swing west to take Le Havre, whilst II Canadian Corps advanced up the coast to capture the other Channel ports of Dieppe, Boulogne and Calais.

The pace of the advance was astonishing and Tac, trying to keep in touch with Dempsey, spent no more than two nights on any site from 30 August, when it left Avernes-sous-Exmes en route for Fontaines-sous-Jouy, until 8 September. At Fontaines, on the escarpment overlooking the Eure Valley, the reconnaissance party made one of its few errors, becoming bogged down in the chosen site after two days of heavy rain. The main body was diverted to a local chateau, which had until recently been the local Luftwaffe HQ and which yielded a number of trophies, notably skull-and-crossbone flags which rapidly adorned Tac's 3-ton lorries, but little in the cellar. On 1 September Tac was off again, crossing the Seine by the large Class 40 Bailey bridge at Vernon, and arriving that evening at the Chateau de Dangu, south-west of Gisors. Monty had at least one reason to be very pleased as he crossed the river, standing up in the front foot-well of his Humber. Shortly before midnight some completely unexpected news had arrived. He had been promoted to field marshal on the recommendation of Churchill, who, in Brooke's words, 'felt that such a move would mark the approval of the

British people for the *British* effort that had led to the defeat of the Germans in France through the medium of Montgomery's leadership.'[4] It was, indeed, some recompense for having lost the overall command of the Allied ground forces on the same day. Chavasse was sent off to London to pick up the new badges of rank.

The Rolls-Royce probably did not look martial enough for the photo opportunity presented by the Seine crossing, which was just as well, as it had been commandeered by Dawnay, BonDurant and Gunn for a trip to Paris. Monty had turned down Eisenhower's invitation to attend the liberation ceremonies in the city, on the grounds that he was far too busy, but he was happy to extend its pleasures to his staff. The three men did some sightseeing, looked up friends and tried to avoid the members of the Resistance, who were taking their revenge on known collaborators, especially women who had slept with the Germans.

Dangu, the seat of a curious aristocrat of Corsican origin, the Duc de Pozzo di Borgo, whose relations with the Germans had been far from unfriendly, at least provided somewhere other than a tent for Gunn to paint the new field marshal. He had decided to start on two portraits, the first a relatively informal one of Monty seated in a chair, wearing the grey sweater which had become his everyday apparel, with one single medal ribbon, that of the American Legion of Merit.[5] The second was of Monty standing up and wearing battledress with a full set of medal ribbons. Whilst at Dangu, Gunn also started work on a third painting, this one described, like the drawing in Augustus John's studio, as a 'conversation piece', which became the only depiction of Monty at table in his mess with his five personal staff officers. Gunn's attempt to paint Henderson alone, however, was quashed by Monty, who made it clear that he had been invited for a single purpose, which did not include portraits of others.

On 3 September Tac moved again, this time to a location which served only as an overnight harbour, at Conty, just short of Amiens. The recce party had already gone on ahead to Saulty, near Arras, where once again Tac was found a site in the grounds of the local chateau, which Odgers thought had something of the 'damp melancholy' of Creullet and was similarly cramped.

It was en route to Conty that the news arrived that XXX Corps had entered Brussels to the accompaniment of wild celebrations by the populace. Right up with the advanced units of the Guards Armoured Division was Harry Llewellyn, who had once again been despatched with Colonel Jones and Wing Commander Spencer to find suitable accommodation for Main HQ. The small party had only just established itself in the best hotel in Amiens when a signal arrived from Belchem, ordering it on to Brussels. There Llewellyn claimed the Residence Palace,[6] a complex of buildings which had been hurriedly vacated by the German Military Government. Llewellyn had to forestall a move by the Belgian authorities to take it over, successfully invoking the names of both Eisenhower and Montgomery and immediately putting a stop to looting by the locals. He also commandeered a nearby house for himself and his LOs, which he renamed the 'Maison Liaison'. This was staffed by three efficient Russians who had been working for the German Todt Organization and were nicknamed Omsk, Tomsk and Minsk!

Monty was strongly opposed to any of his HQs being housed in buildings and this had been the rule in Eighth Army, with the modest exception of Taormina, and in Normandy. However, this caused significant problems for 'Slap' White, who as SO-in-C was responsible not only for the general direction of the Royal Signals arm in 21st Army Group, but also more practically for the communication systems of the army group's HQs. Although these had not been a problem at Southwick Park, they were not very efficient in Normandy, where fixed lines were limited and where wireless, with delays inevitably imposed by the coding and decoding of messages, was relatively slow. Thereafter the advance had been so rapid that the signallers had not been able to lay the usual lines. In buildings in a big city, however, good communications could be established via telephone and telegraph with the War Office and other key establishments in the UK and with SHAEF in France, whilst internal telephones facilitated contact between all the staff branches. The arguments were put to Monty, who reluctantly agreed that this was the only way to operate efficiently.

Both Llewellyn's 'Freddie Boys' and the 'Monty Boys' were finding their jobs extremely demanding as the armies surged forward. For the former, the instructions to call in at Tac became impossible for those visiting First Canadian Army, although visitors to Second Army usually found it nearby. The roles of Majors Fife and Batchelor as Resident LOs at the two armies became even more important as their HQs moved, whilst Bigland continued to submit daily reports from Eagle Tac, now vanishing into the distance in a north-easterly direction. The use of aeroplanes became a daily occurrence for most of the LOs. The army group's HQs now enjoyed the use of the Tactical Air Force Communications Squadron, which by the autumn of 1944 would deploy two Dakotas, fifteen Avro Ansons, which were commonly used for visits to the UK, twenty-nine Austers and fifteen sundry other aircraft, including Monty's Messenger and three Spitfires for close protection.

The allocation of responsibilities at the beginning of September took Sanderson to I Corps, Mather to II Canadian Corps, Bourhill to XII Corps and Harden to XXX Corps, whilst Frary handled XIX US Corps and Prisk V US Corps, Second Army's closest neighbours on its right. For Sanderson and Mather this posed serious problems, as they had to travel both across and against the axis of Second Army's advance, which was taking place on two well defined routes from the Seine to Brussels and Antwerp.[7] This meant leaving Tac at between 03.00 and 04.00 each day. The use of an Auster might have been thought desirable and it did indeed remain the conveyance of choice, but in practice, with all Divisional HQs on the move so frequently, it was often impossible to locate their new sites from the air, whilst at least on the ground the Military Police were providing excellent signposting. Over the few weeks from the break–out towards and across the Seine until the armies came to a halt, this sometimes meant up to 14 hours driving in a day. Furthermore, the LOs could never be quite sure that the country they were crossing was in Allied hands, as the swift advance had left isolated German units to be rounded up, not all of which were disposed to surrender without a fight. Moreover, mines had not been cleared on the side roads and Sanderson experienced a nerve-racking situation when he was forced to lift four anti-tank mines obstructing his route by himself.

In spite of these difficulties and the fact that wireless communication was often difficult and the use of fixed line telephones usually impossible, the LOs invariably appeared back at Tac, by then often a long way from where they had set out that morning, on time and carrying all the information required by Monty. At Tac itself both Phantom and the signals unit were working at full stretch to keep in touch with the two armies.

The stay at Saulty was as brief as the others, only distinguished by the replacement of the commandos who had reinforced the defence platoon in the early days with another platoon from 21st Army Group Defence Company. Encouraged by the enthusiastic reports of Brussels from those LOs who had been there, Tac set off for Belgium on 6 September, making a two–night stop in the grounds of the Chateau de Houtaing, near Ath, south-west of Brussels. The chateau itself was full of evacuee children, who lined up and sang It's a Long Way to Tipperary in French and Flemish by way of a welcome. On 8 September Tac moved again, coming to a halt at a location east of the Belgian capital, the Chateau of Everberg, seat of the Prince de Merode, who had been imprisoned for three years in Germany and was accordingly most welcoming. Odgers was impressed by the way in which every branch of Tac had proceeded smoothly to its location on its arrival, which he ascribed to good Provost work, but which was just as much the result of his training exercises on the South Downs ahead of D-Day.

Monty had in one way come full circle. The chateau was only a few miles from Louvain, where he had sited the HQ of 3 Division following the advance into Belgium by the BEF in May 1940.[8] Tac was to stay there for nearly two weeks, giving it much needed time for reorganization. With Germany now not far away, the two defence platoons were enlarged to a full company and the Field Security/Counter Intelligence detachment strengthened, whilst a Light Aid Detachment was added in order to cope with the repair and servicing requirements of the growing number of vehicles.

The unexpectedly rapid movement into Belgium took everyone, including the Q Branch, by surprise. The main problem for 21st Army Group until early August had been the constricted nature of the beachhead, with the necessity to fit all the functions into a very small space. Now the opposite became true and plans to support the advance had to be hastily rewritten. The Rear Maintenance Area had built up fourteen days of working margins plus fourteen days reserves, but supplies now had to be transported over much longer distances than expected. The answer was to use every available vehicle bar the bare minimum required for clearing ports and beaches. All L of C units were temporarily grounded, with their transport diverted to support the advance in addition to that of VIII Corps.

The priority became POL, as enormous amounts were consumed by both armoured and transport vehicles. The rule that the consumption of ammunition was always in inverse proportion to that of fuel held firm, releasing some capacity, but by the end of August no pipe heads were available nearer than Billy, south-east of Caen, whence all supplies had to be carried forward in road tankers or in containers loaded on to lorries. The engineers worked tirelessly to extend the pipeline to beyond Rouen by mid–September, by which time Second Army was 200 miles away on the Netherlands frontier, although First Canadian Army was much closer. It would be late October before the PLUTO line from Dungeness to Boulogne was opened, which, with a new network of pipelines across Belgium and the Netherlands, allowed POL to be brought significantly closer to the consumers. In the meantime, the supply situation remained critical.

As far as general supplies were concerned, at the end of August the whole tonnage was still being unloaded through MULBERRY B or over open beaches. The rapid advance and the use of transport for other purposes led to a big dip in imports in early September, whilst the army group lived off its reserves. It was vital, however, to build up again as quickly as possible, for which ports were needed much closer to the armies. Some progress was made. The clearing of the country as far as the Seine allowed the small port of Ouistreham, which had hitherto been subject to artillery fire from German batteries along the coast, to be opened, along with the inland port at Caen itself, to which it was connected by canal. To the surprise of all, Dieppe, which was captured on 1 September, was found to be substantially undamaged and was opened to shipping within a week. Ostend was taken on 9 September and opened by the end of that month, but Boulogne and Calais required far more work and Dunkirk was held by the Germans until the end of the war. Le Havre, stormed at great cost by 1 Corps and captured on 12 September, was handed over to the Americans.

The great prize, however, was Antwerp, unquestionably the most important port between Cherbourg and Rotterdam and vital to any further large-scale movement forward. The city was liberated by 11 Armoured Division on 4 September and the port installations were captured almost intact, thanks in great measure to the actions of the Belgian resistance movement. Miles Graham, visiting Tac on the same day, told James Gunn that his last excuse for problems with the supply chain was gone. He was wrong: the port was inaccessible to shipping. Lying more than 50 miles from the sea up the Scheldt estuary, whose waters were heavily mined and both sides of which were strongly held by the Germans, it remained tantalisingly unavailable.

Chapter Twenty-Three

Arnhem and Antwerp

O n 8 September Guards Armoured Division crossed the Albert Canal and two days later established a bridgehead on the north side of the Meuse-Escaut Canal,[1] west of Neerpelt. German resistance, however, was growing as those formations and units which had withdrawn in disarray from Normandy and the Pas-de-Calais reformed and turned to face the Allies. With supply now becoming a serious concern, the offensive ran temporarily out of steam, both on the XXX Corps front along the canal line and further west, where XII Corps had made no progress beyond Antwerp. A sizeable and well-defended pocket had also been created by the Germans south of the Scheldt estuary.

On the day that the Guards crossed the Meuse-Escaut Canal, Monty held two vitally important meetings. The first was with Dempsey and Lieutenant General 'Boy' Browning, the commander of I Airborne Corps. Monty now recognized that if he was to continue to press the merits of the Northern Thrust he could not afford to lose momentum. The lack of transport and shortages of fuel meant that he was having difficulty in bringing all his divisions forward from Normandy, whilst losses during the battles meant that he would shortly have to break up 59 Division and use it to provide reinforcements to the others. The only reserve available was I Airborne Corps, which was at the disposal of SHAEF.

It had been a frustrating three months for I Airborne Corps. Numerous operations had been planned and cancelled. These included not only the landings vetoed by Leigh-Mallory, but the even more ambitious plans to seize the Brittany ports, to drop into and hold the Paris-Orleans Gap, to capture Boulogne, to cut off the Germans retreating through Tournai and to control the Aachen–Maastricht Gap. Most had been aborted because of the unexpectedly rapid advance, in which the proposed landing zones were overrun by the Allies before the airborne forces could set off from the UK.

The most recent plan was Operation COMET. On 3 September, with the Guards Armoured Division passing through Brussels and optimism high, Monty sent a signal to Freddie: 'require airborne operation of one British Division and Poles on evening 6 Sep or morning 7 Sep to secure bridges over RHINE between WESEL and ARNHEM'. The impetus which had developed over the previous week had persuaded him that an opportunity had opened to

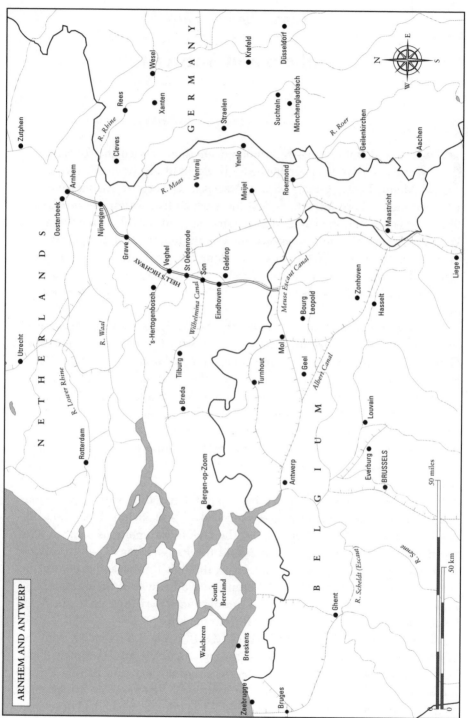

Map 9.

bounce the Rhine itself and the various rivers and canals in between, creating a corridor up which he could pass 21st Army Group into the North German Plain and around the Ruhr. D-Day for the operation was delayed until 10 September, by which time the situation had perceptibly changed. Resistance was increasing behind the canal line, lack of transport was delaying reinforcements and the supply situation was deteriorating by the day. Monty cancelled the operation on the evening of 9 September and ordered Dempsey and Browning to meet him in Brussels on the following day.

The new operation was far more ambitious. COMET had called for only 1 Airborne Division and the Polish Parachute Brigade, with 52 Lowland Division, organized on an air portable basis, flown in as soon as an airfield was secured. Operation MARKET was to involve the whole of I Airborne Corps, which also included 82 and 101 US Airborne Divisions. The ground element, Operation GARDEN, would bring in XXX Corps to pass up a corridor created by the airborne troops, whilst VIII and XII Corps expanded its shoulders on either side.

The furthest and most important objective, crucial to penetrating Germany itself, was the bridge over the Lower Rhine at Arnhem. Arnhem had been chosen in preference to Wesel on the advice of Browning, who advanced two reasons. The RAF considered that Wesel was too close to the major flak defences of the Ruhr, whilst a successful thrust towards Arnhem would cut off the V2 rocket sites in the Netherlands, now the main menace to England itself following the destruction of the V1 sites in the Pas-de-Calais. Dempsey, on the other hand, would have preferred to hold the canal line, whilst advancing with a strong force alongside the Americans towards Cologne. If an airborne operation was mounted, his choice of objective would have been Wesel, as it involved crossing fewer water obstacles and was much closer to the Ruhr.

Richardson's planners had for some time consistently advocated driving through the Aachen Gap, but if an airborne operation was to be mounted they, too, recommended Wesel as the objective. Richardson proposed this to Freddie on 3 September, although a welter of planning memos and instructions over the next week showed that every possible option was being explored. The staff, however, was not directly involved with the planning of MARKET, which was carried out at First Allied Airborne Army, the superior formation for the airborne forces, and by Browning's own staff at I Airborne Corps. Monty accordingly came down firmly in favour of Arnhem.

The combined MARKET GARDEN plan was extremely ambitious: 101 Airborne Division was to land north of Eindhoven and take the bridges over the Wilhelmina Canal at Son, the Zuid-Wilhelmsvaart Canal at Veghel and some lesser waterways; 82 Airborne Division was ordered to seize the longest bridge in Europe, over the River Maas at Grave, and the bridges over the Maas-Waal Canal. More controversially, its other primary objective was to take and hold the Groesbeek Heights, dominating the approaches to Nijmegen from the south, and only then to capture the bridge over the River Waal north of the town, while 1 Airborne Division was given the road, rail and pontoon bridges over the Lower Rhine at Arnhem. It would be reinforced by the Polish Parachute Brigade on D+2 and by 52 Division once the airfield at Deelen, north of Arnhem, had been captured.

XXX Corps would break out of its bridgehead on the Meuse-Escaut Canal, take Eindhoven, pass up the corridor created by the three airborne divisions and then exploit north of Arnhem to Apeldoorn and Nunspeet, before turning east to cross the River Ijssel into the North German Plain. XII Corps would advance to the left of the corridor towards Tilburg and 's-Hertogenbosch and VIII Corps to the right towards Helmond.

This mammoth undertaking required considerable logistical support for Second Army and, whilst Graham himself thought that the resources would be adequate, some strong reservations began to be expressed within the Q branch. Although an army roadhead was established near Brussels on 6 September, and whilst Dieppe, with a capacity of 6,000 tons per day, was just beginning to make a difference, the army was still living on its reserves. Monty felt that he needed more and any increment could only come from SHAEF. For this reason, as well as to ensure the availability of I Airborne Corps, the second meeting he held on 10 September, with Eisenhower at Brussels airport, was as important as the first. It also provided Monty with a further opportunity to advance the rationale for the Northern Thrust.

Eisenhower had now relocated SHAEF Forward to Granville, on the sea north of Avranches and about as far from his two army group commanders as it was possible to be. He flew up to Brussels in a C-47 and remained on the aircraft, as he had injured his leg and was finding it difficult to walk. This was the first time Monty had seen the Supreme Commander for over two weeks and he launched immediately into a litany of complaints about the lack of supplies and Eisenhower's failure to grasp what was clearly the only sensible strategy. 'Steady, Monty, you can't speak to me like that. I'm your boss,' replied Eisenhower. Monty apologized, but continued to advance his cause. Eisenhower maintained the stance which he had adopted since the meeting on 23 August, refusing to give full priority to 21st Army Group or to scale down Patton's advance towards the Saar. He did, however, authorize the use of I Airborne Corps for MARKET GARDEN.

With supplies needing to be built up, Monty sent off a signal on the next day advising Eisenhower that he would have to delay the operation until 23 September. The response was immediate. On 12 September, Bedell Smith arrived in Brussels to tell Monty that Eisenhower had now agreed to divert the transport of three American divisions to supporting the new operation, to halt the Saar thrust, to give priority within 12th US Army Group to Hodges's

First US Army on Monty's right flank and to allow Monty to deal directly with Hodges, rather than through Bradley. It seemed that the Northern Thrust was now becoming a reality and an exultant Monty advanced D-Day for MARKET GARDEN to 17 September.

It all proved to be an illusion. Bradley, who visited Monty on 13 September and heard all about the proposals, then lobbied Eisenhower, with the result than none of the promised support materialized. With Monty, Dempsey and Browning all completely unaware of this, preparations for the operation continued. Concerns, however, were now growing at Main HQ. It probably did not help that it was in the throes of moving, first to Amiens during the week ending 9 September and then to Brussels in the following week, with the full HQ not finally installed in the Residence Palace until 23 September. It certainly did not help that Freddie was away in England. Monty had become concerned that his Chief of Staff was overworking and potentially heading for a breakdown, so had him sent back for a rest and medical treatment on 9 September. Freddie did not return until D-Day itself.

The Operations staff at Main were worried about two significant elements of 1 Airborne Division's plan. The first was that the nearest landing site was six miles from the bridge, whilst others were even further away. The RAF refused to countenance anything closer, due to flak concentrations being reported south of the town itself and around Deelen airfield. This, together with a belief that the country south of the bridge was unsuitable for gliders, also ruled out a *coup de main* of the type carried out so successfully at Pegasus Bridge. As a result of this decision only one parachute brigade would be available on D-Day to capture the bridge, and it would have to march there. The airlanding brigade would have to remain behind to defend the landing and drop zones due to the second flaw, which was that only one lift of the three needed was planned for the first day. This meant that half the division, including the second parachute brigade, would arrive on D+1, and the Polish Parachute Brigade not until D+2. On this issue the RAF was amenable to a second lift on D-Day, but was overruled by the commander of IX US Troop Carrier Command, which provided the transport for the paratroops, who ruled that the returning aircraft would need to be serviced and that their crews would require a rest.

The Intelligence staff were more concerned with messages intercepted by ULTRA, which suggested that 9 and 10 SS Panzer Divisions were refitting near Arnhem following their escape from Normandy. In fact, both divisions had been reduced to about 3,000 men, a small fraction of the normal establishment, and they had sent most of the surviving tanks back to Germany for repair and servicing. However, the remaining troops were seasoned soldiers, most with experience on the Eastern Front, and they still had other armoured vehicles available. As early as 10 September, Williams tried to persuade Monty not to go ahead and he and Oliver Poole, who was particularly worried about the supply situation, spent much time trying to think of ways of stopping him. Joe Ewart at Tac told Williams that he had briefed Monty fully about the panzer divisions, but that Monty was determined to proceed. Belchem, deputising for Freddie, gave Monty a full briefing on the flaws of the plan and he and Richardson together recommended a postponement to provide time to correct them. Monty did agree to send Belchem to England to ask Lieutenant General Lewis Brereton, Commanding General of First Allied Airborne Army, to allow two drops on the first day; but Brereton, an airman himself, was obdurate, and Monty was unable to contest the primacy of the air arm when it came to such decisions. Finally, Freddie was persuaded to ring Monty from his hospital bed, warning him that stiffening resistance, the logistical situation, the weather and the vulnerability of the corridor all combined to put the success of the operation in serious doubt.

Monty, physically isolated at Tac from his most senior staff, ignored all their advice to delay or cancel the operation.

MARKET GARDEN nevertheless started well. The Germans were taken by surprise and the parachute drops and glider landings were initially uncontested. Moreover, in the first ever major daylight airborne operation, the troops arrived substantially on target, unlike in Sicily or Normandy. While 101 US Airborne Division took most of its objectives, a *coup de main* by 82 US Airborne Division secured the Grave bridge. The latter division also captured a key bridge over the Maas-Waal Canal and seized and held the Groesbeek Heights. The 2nd Parachute Battalion managed to reach the Arnhem road bridge and to hold its northern end. In the south, Guards Armoured Division broke out of its bridgehead.

Problems, however, were already emerging. The bridge over the Wihelmina Canal at Son was blown up by the Germans. The Guards were held up at Valkenswaard and then, on D+1, delayed by huge crowds on their progress through Eindhoven. The result was that the bridging equipment could only be brought up that evening and, by the time it was in place, the timetable was slipping badly. It was not until the morning of 19 November that the Guards reached Nijmegen, to find that 82 US Airborne Division, with its glider regiment delayed by bad weather in England, had lacked the strength to take the Nijmegen bridge. In the meantime, the Germans had reacted fast under the energetic leadership of Field Marshal Model and were attacking the narrow corridor, the Groesbeek Heights and, most alarmingly, the paratroopers at Arnhem. Most of the D+1 lift had arrived, but now the Poles were also grounded by the weather. In the south, XII Corps was making very slow progress, whilst VIII Corps had started two days late, due to one of its divisions being delayed on the way from Normandy.

On the afternoon of 20 September, all other attempts to take the Nijmegen road bridge having failed, an audacious attack in small boats across the Waal was carried out by 82 Airborne Division, seizing the north end of the bridge, which the Germans were unable to destroy. A few tanks of the Guards Armoured Division managed to cross the bridge in daylight, but were unable to advance further, due to the lack of infantry support.

The situation went from bad to worse. On several occasions the Germans cut the airborne corridor, although each time they were eventually repulsed. The 2nd Parachute Battalion was overwhelmed on the morning of 21 September, whilst the remainder of 1 Airborne Division, whose GOC had been cut off for 48 hours and had only just reappeared, was penned into a defensive perimeter at Oosterbeek, west of Arnhem. The Poles were diverted to the opposite bank of the river at Driel, where they made a heroic attempt, together with a battalion from 43 Division, to cross the Lower Rhine, but were repulsed with great losses. On 25 September Browning and Horrocks, having consulted Monty and Dempsey, agreed to cut their losses, and the survivors were brought back across the river, including 1,741 men from 1 Airborne Division out of the 8,969 who had flown in.

Monty, who remained MARKET GARDEN's 'unrepentant advocate',[2] claimed afterwards that it had been 90 per cent successful. He was wrong. It totally failed to achieve its strategic objective and destroyed 1 Airborne Division as a fighting formation for the remainder of the war. The two men most to blame were Monty and Browning, the chief architects of the operation, although many others contributed, notably the airmen for their decisions on the lifts and the drop and landing zones. Monty himself maintained that the operation would have succeeded completely if it had received the support he had been promised, placing this above other reasons, of which he singled out the weather in England delaying the arrival of reinforcements and the presence of the German panzer divisions north of Arnhem. The simple fact, however, was that it had been executed on the back of a bad plan, whose deficiencies had been clearly identified by Monty's own staff. Other factors contributed, including the failure of 1 Airborne Division's signals, which resulted in both its internal communications and those to the outside world being poor to non-existent throughout the battle,[3] the brushing aside of intelligence on the presence of the panzer divisions and an irrational over-confidence about the collapse of the Germans. As it turned out, the Germans responded vigorously and proved to be highly effective against an operation whose tolerances were so tight.

The operation was atypical of Monty. He was generally meticulous in his preparation, refusing to move until he was absolutely ready, with the odds stacked in his favour. On this occasion, blinded by his determination to seize the opportunity to pursue his Northern Thrust strategy, for the first and only time he accepted a plan which had not been endorsed by his staff, but was firmly in the hands of others. His dispositions also lacked the balance which had always enabled him to change a plan very quickly if the situation so demanded. In this case I Airborne Division and the whole of XXX Corps were so far out on a limb that no such change could take place. He also seemed to lack the day-to-day grip on operations for which he was justly renowned and which alone justified the use of a Tac HQ. Apart from the decision to withdraw across the Lower Rhine, Monty made very little impact on events.

This may have been in part because his Liaison Officers were having an even more difficult time than usual. A single road between Eindhoven and Nijmegen, aptly named 'Hell's Highway', was the only route to I Airborne Corps and XXX Corps. This lay across open country, above which it was occasionally raised, and was itself narrow and congested with traffic of all descriptions. The road was frequently subjected to German counter-attacks, some of which succeeded in cutting it for hours or even days. This vulnerability resulted in some of the LOs being issued with Daimler scout cars, which were at least impervious to small arms fire, in place of their jeeps. Those using Austers were not immune, one of the aircraft being shot up north of Eindhoven, although it managed to land safely.

Confusion often reigned supreme. On one occasion Sanderson thought that he was the object of an enemy attack and quickly abandoned his vehicle, only to find out that he had inadvertently strayed into crossfire. On 21 September, Mather found himself in the middle of a German counter-attack at Veghel and at one moment he was only yards from a Tiger tank, which was luckily facing in the other direction. He and his driver were forced to shelter for the night with another LO on hard benches in a rough Dutch hostelry, the only occasion on which he failed to report to Monty the same evening. On the next day, although the road remained cut, he managed to find a way through and bring news of the situation on the ground. On the day he set out, Tac had moved from Everberg to Bourg Leopold, which at least meant a shorter return journey.

Llewellyn was not devoid of problems with his own LOs, but in addition to the usual resident at Second Army, he arranged for Major Ben Hutchings to be embedded with XXX Corps, improving the reliability of his information. Others from Main HQ were also on the road. Immediately after the operation was launched, Richardson and Poole set off for Nijmegen. 'We realized that there was little we could do about the forward battle,' wrote Richardson later, 'but by short-circuiting the long complex chain of command we might make ourselves useful over any logistic emergency that might have arisen.'[4] Like others, they were repeatedly held up by German incursions and they became very worried about the slow progress of the follow-up. Arriving in due course in Nijmegen, they reported to Horrocks, who seemed to Richardson to be less decisive than usual, and also met Browning. Although their services were not required, they had at least been able to see for themselves the situation on the ground. Like Mather, they were cut off on their return and had to spend an uncomfortable night in a Dutch cellar.

The failure of MARKET GARDEN spelt the end of the Northern Thrust, after a very brief period when it seemed that Monty might get his way. On 21 September, even as it was becoming apparent that the operation was in trouble, albeit not at that point hopeless, Monty urged Eisenhower to put First US Army under his command for a concerted advance to the Ruhr. Eisenhower, who had recently relocated SHAEF Forward from Granville to Versailles, convened a conference with his senior commanders on the next day. Monty, disliking such events and believing that field commanders should never have to go back to see their superiors, particularly in the middle of a major operation, declined to attend and sent Freddie in his place, accompanied by 'Simbo' Simpson, who was on a visit from the War Office and could represent Brooke's views. Simpson had been briefed by Monty to complain to Eisenhower and to Bedell Smith, with whom he was on friendly terms, about the lack of the supplies Monty had been promised.

Bradley arrived at the conference with an alternative proposal, which was not only to use First US Army and Ninth US Army, the latter about to deploy for the first time, for a thrust to the Ruhr via Aachen, but to swing Third US Army left in support. The implication was that the move would be firmly under the control of 12th US Army Group. To his surprise, Eisenhower came down in Monty's favour, even to the extent that Patton's advance would be stopped. Bradley was ordered to see Monty on the following day to make the necessary arrangements.

Monty's triumph, however, was short-lived. Not only was MARKET GARDEN stuttering to a close, leaving 21st Army Group in a cul-de-sac, but the logistics situation at 12th Army Group had become dire, causing Bradley to transfer one corps to 6th Army Group, where at least it could be maintained through Marseilles. The impetus for thrust in any direction had been lost, for the immediate future at least. The priority now was to open Antwerp, without which the armies would be unable to sustain any major move forward.

Monty had no great enthusiasm for the ensuing operation to clear the Scheldt. It diverted him from what really captured his interest, driving into Germany as quickly as possible; and even as late as the second week in October, he was examining the possibilities of crossing the Maas into the Rhineland. However, the majority of the army group's supplies were still being transported from Normandy by road, as the rail network was substantially under repair following the highly successful Allied bombing campaign, and the first railway bridge over the Seine was not rebuilt until 22 September. The opening of Ostend on 26 September and Boulogne on 14 October made a difference, but their combined capacity was insufficient to enable him to mount a major offensive. There was no alternative to Antwerp.

By the end of September the French Channel ports had all been captured, other than Dunkirk, which was invested by the Czech Brigade. This freed First

Canadian Army to take on the Scheldt operation, beginning with an advance northwards from Antwerp by 2 Canadian Division on 1 October to seal off the neck of the Beveland Peninsula. The division made good progress at first, but was then held up by very strong defences, which were not reduced until the middle of the month. While 3 Canadian Division was given the task of eliminating the Breskens Pocket, 4 Canadian Armoured Division and the Polish Armoured Division completed the clearance of the south bank of the Scheldt immediately west of Antwerp. It was late October before the pocket was cleared and it became possible to mount both an amphibious assault across the estuary to South Beveland and an advance overland along the neck of the peninsula. At the beginning of November another amphibious assault by commandos took place on to the now flooded Walcheren Island, whilst the Canadians and 52 Lowland Division crossed from South Beveland. The defenders held out until 8 November, but four days before that minesweepers began the clearance of the estuary. The first coasters docked at Antwerp on 26 November and the first ocean-going cargo ships two days later and 85 days after the port had been captured.

On 27 September, following the end of MARKET GARDEN, Tac moved to Eindhoven, where it occupied a site close to the perimeter of the public park. Eindhoven was a good location for access to formations whose immediate priority was to close up to the Maas to the north and to the east. Good communications were at the centre of Tac's operations, and the signals detachment was growing fast and would eventually be three times the size of its original establishment. Part of this was due to the numbers of men required to operate what became one of the most important pieces of equipment in the campaign, the Wireless Set No. 10. This was a technological masterpiece, a highly reliable radio station contained in a 2-ton trailer, providing eight telephone circuits. It required a clear 'line of sight' to the next relay station, which was usually about 20 but could be up to 50 miles away, so although either permanent structures such as the Phillips factory in Eindhoven or pre-fabricated 60-foot towers could be used to provide the necessary height, future Tac sites ideally had to be raised above the surrounding country. The set used a very narrow beam, which meant that it delivered the security of a telephone line. Monty, who called it his 'number 10 thingy', could now talk to Main HQ, SHAEF, the War Office or 10 Downing Street with complete clarity and the assurance that the conversation could not be overheard.

The most notable event which took place in Eindhoven was a visit by the King, who arrived on 11 October for six days, staying the nights in a caravan at Tac and travelling each day around 21st Army Group and to First US Army, where he met Eisenhower. On 15 October, the day before leaving, he held an Investiture at Tac. Sergeant Kirby had, as was his practice, developed a number of connections in the local community, which he used to great effect when asked by Henderson to provide a footstool and cushion. The former was donated by the local church, the latter by friends, one of whom cut up a red-wine coloured evening dress for the cushion, and they were duly produced after church parade on the day.

On 18 June Monty had written to the Military Secretary putting forward the names of some of his closest senior officers for awards 'in recognition of the great and outstanding services that they have rendered'. These had been duly accepted and gazetted, but the recipients had inevitably been unable to attend an Investiture at Buckingham Palace. Dempsey and Freddie were awarded the KBE, Graham the CB and Belchem and Williams the CBE, the first two dubbed by the King whilst kneeling on the stool and cushion. A number of others also received awards made over the last year or more, with MCs, or bars if they had them already, for Harden, Mather, Poston and Sanderson and an MBE for Henderson.

The award of a knighthood to a major general was unusual, if by no means unprecedented. Freddie had unquestionably deserved it and Monty was by that time in such a strong position that the Military Secretary would have thought twice before challenging it. It did confirm to the outside world what the staff already knew, that Monty put a high price on Freddie and was deeply appreciative of the load which had been taken off him by his Chief of Staff.

The site in Eindhoven, unlike any of the others, was in the middle of a large town and the Tac officers made the best of it on the occasions when they were allowed to relax. A dance was organized, with the female sex represented by some local girls and by nurses from the Military General Hospital set up nearby. Monty was invited, but unsurprisingly declined to attend. On the next day, however, he was keen to establish what had transpired. Sanderson, as the only married officer among the LOs, was assumed to have played only a small part in the proceedings, so was invited for tea and pumped for information. As a result, Harden, always one of Monty's favourites, probably for his outspokenness, was charged with being drunk and, when he denied it, was told that it was good for him from time to time. Poston was accused of monopolizing the same woman all evening and even sleeping with her. When he protested his innocence, Monty replied, 'In that case, John, you must be slipping. It's not like you to miss such a golden opportunity!' These encounters were a good illustration of the nature of the relationship between the C-in-C and his LOs and personal staff.

Such light-hearted moments were far from rare at Tac, but there was much serious work still to be done as winter approached.

Chapter Twenty-Four

The Bulge

If an opportunity had ever existed to end the war in 1944, it was now clear that it had evaporated. The evidence of the Germans' recovery was comprehensively demonstrated by their growing resistance on all fronts and confirmed by the intelligence analysed by Williams and his officers. Monty was now resigned to pursuing the campaign though the winter, in recognition of which he sent Dawnay back to England to pick up his warm clothes.

In late October, whilst II Canadian Corps was fighting on South Beveland and Walcheren, First Canadian Army's other subordinate formation, I Corps, reinforced by 104 US Division, was edging its way north to the Maas. At the same time XII Corps of Second Army continued to expand the left hand shoulder of the corridor to Nijmegen towards Tilburg and 's-Hertogenbosch. Both found the going slow and difficult, their progress impeded not only by enemy resistance, but also by the nature of the country, flat but often waterlogged. By 5 November, however, the last Germans had withdrawn over the Maas and 21st Army Group had closed up to the river from its southern mouth to Nijmegen.

Monty's intention was also to clear all the country west of the Maas where the river runs from south to north. This task was allocated to VIII Corps, which by the end of September had penetrated as far as Meijel on the road to Venlo. If the terrain to the north was difficult, that of the Peel Marshes country, lying between the Eindhoven to Nijmegen road and the river, was far worse. Boggy after the slightest rain and criss-crossed by dykes and ditches, it had always been considered by the Dutch to be impassable to invaders. It was certainly extremely difficult for armoured vehicles, and the fighting became largely an infantry affair. VIII Corps managed to penetrate as far as Venraij in the north of their sector, but Meijel was lost to a counter-attack on 27 October.

Although the Northern Thrust via Arnhem was dead and buried, Monty did not immediately give up on his other hobby-horse, the command structure, and on 10 October he sent some notes on the subject to Eisenhower, expressing his dissatisfaction with the current organization. He proposed that either he or Bradley should be named as the land forces commander, with one serving under the other. In his reply of 13 October Eisenhower flatly rejected it, telling Monty that if he felt that his conceptions and directives were endangering the success of operations, the matter should be referred to a higher authority. As Monty had held a less than satisfactory meeting with General Marshall on 8 October, it was

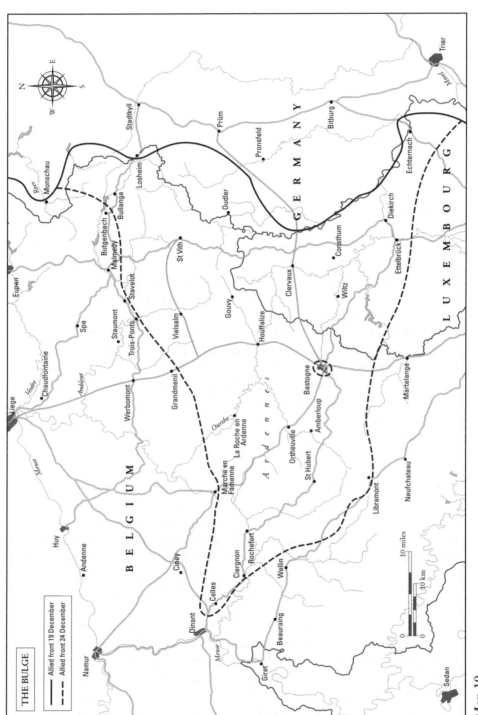

Map 10.

clear which way any decision would go. He wrote back to Eisenhower assuring him that he would hear no more on the subject, and there it rested, albeit not for long.

On 22 October Monty did something he had never done before during active operations, relocating to Main HQ. The reason was that Brussels was far closer than Eindhoven to the First Canadian Army, whose activities had temporarily assumed the greatest importance. He took up residence with his personal staff in a handsome mansion in the suburbs of the city, whither the LOs still reported to him daily, although all the other Tac officers remained in Eindhoven.

Brussels was subject to attack from V-1 flying bombs, and a soldier was stationed on the roof of the mansion to provide a warning if any of them looked like landing nearby. In the case of such an event, he was ordered to press a button, which rang a bell in Monty's office. On the one occasion when a V-1 actually appeared he forgot, in his excitement, to do so, and the bomb exploded in the back garden, shattering all the windows on that side, including Monty's. Henderson rushed to see if Monty was all right, only to find him draped in a net curtain, which had prevented the shards of glass from injuring him. As usual, he was totally unperturbed.

Main HQ had by then settled down into a well-ordered existence. This even allowed Freddie to take a day off to mount a small private expedition of his own. He had become concerned over the fate of the French resort of Le Touquet, to which he had become much attached before the war for its golfing facilities and, perhaps more enticingly, for its Casino. He had taken care, during the bombing campaign of the Pas-de-Calais as part of Operation FORTITUDE, to try to select targets away from the residential area, although this became progressively more difficult. Now, with Boulogne and the surrounding country liberated and in response to enquiries he had received from a number of friends, he resolved to see for himself what had happened.

A reconnaissance party, led by Llewellyn and including some sappers, was sent off in jeeps to locate a suitable landing strip and clear any mines on it before notifying Freddie of the map reference. This was duly done and a small party of Le Touquet enthusiasts, including Graham, Belchem and Freddie's MA Bill Bovill and ADC Bill Culver, took off in a C-47, enjoying alcoholic refreshments en route. The landing site was less than ideal, but the plane made it down safely and the party transferred to the jeeps. The town appeared to be deserted and the villas were largely badly damaged and deserted. However, an old lady emerged who welcomed them into what remained of her café, where she insisted on cooking an omelette for them, washed down with a bottle of Scotch which she had hidden away for well over four years. It was a sad reminder of what civilians had suffered, not just in the occupation, but also during the liberation.

As usual, Llewellyn's main job other than running the 'Freddie Boys' was to seek alternative sites for Main HQ and, with the front still advancing, it was felt that it might be necessary to move further forward than Brussels. Over three days at the end of September, therefore, he looked at a number of alternative sites. With communication by secure landlines being the most important criterion, only two of them were seriously considered. Nijmegen was rejected as it remained far too close to the front. Turnhout, about 30 miles north-east of Antwerp, was the other possibility on the grounds that it lay at the end of an underground cable, after which lines were carried overhead. The circuit capacity, however, proved inadequate to support the signals requirements of both Main and the Second TAF HQ, so it was rejected by White. To the relief of all, Main stayed in Brussels.

Tac did move, however, on 12 November to the small town of Zonhoven, lying back in Belgium about five miles north of Hasselt. The park in Eindhoven had become increasingly cold and damp and Monty now accepted that Tac should go into buildings for the winter. Zonhoven was that much nearer to what was then believed to be the likely focus of activity during the winter months, the push into the Rhineland by both 12th US and 21st Army Groups.

For once the move did not go entirely to plan, the column becoming hopelessly lost. This was largely because it took place at night as part of a deception scheme, which also involved the site in Eindhoven remaining apparently occupied, whilst the No. 10 set there continued to be operated remotely from Zonhoven. The relocation into a number of schools and houses in the town proved to be not entirely welcome to the local population and Zonhoven turned out be a rather unhappy place, which was unfortunate as Tac was to be there for nearly three months, its longest ever stay. The buildings were drab and lacked much comfort, fuel was severely rationed during what turned out to be a very harsh winter, there was little to do by way of entertainment and the surrounding countryside was exceptionally dreary. Worst of all, a four-year-old boy was run over and killed by one of the Tac vehicles, as was Monty's beloved spaniel Rommel some weeks later.

Monty returned to Tac from Brussels soon after its arrival in Zonhoven. He had taken the opportunity of a slight lull in operations to go back to England from 6 to 10 November, his first visit since leaving for Normandy in June. Apart from seeing his son David in Winchester, his stay was not entirely satisfactory. There was a very brief interview with Churchill, whose mind was on other things. Brooke, whom Monty met twice, was sympathetic on the command issue and subsequently took it up with Eisenhower, but he was much more realistic than Monty about the prospect for change, given the fast growing number of Americans in the theatre, at a time when the British and Canadians could look for little further in the way of reinforcements. Indeed, only a month later, another of Monty's formations, the veteran 50 Division, had to be broken up to strengthen the remainder.

There were some changes in personnel at Tac during the autumn. Sanderson had been suffering from recurrent bouts of malaria, which on three occasions had resulted in a week's hospitalization. After the third, Monty decided that he should be examined by Bob Hunter, who concluded that he was not fit enough to carry out a Liaison Officer's job. Reluctant to lose Sanderson, Monty then referred him to the Chief Physician at Main HQ, who confirmed Hunter's advice, and Sanderson was invalided back to the UK. Considerate as always for the well-being of those close to him, Monty wrote to Charles Bullen-Smith, now DDMT at the War Office, to recommend Sanderson for a senior training job once he had recuperated: he was in due course appointed Commandant of an OCTU, with promotion to lieutenant colonel. He was replaced, just as in early 1940, by Charles Sweeny, who was serving in the theatre and had visited Tac whilst it was at Everberg. Another of Monty's former ADCs, Ken Spooner, who had been working with Odgers in Operations since the formation of Tac, was also invalided home.

During the autumn fighting continued all along the front as 21st Army Group renewed its efforts to close up to the Maas in the east. In mid-November, both VIII and XII Corps launched attacks, respectively from north-west and south-west of the German pocket, and, after very heavy fighting, succeeded in clearing the west bank of the river. At the same time an attack was mounted on the German town of Geilenkirchen by 43 Division and 84 US Division, both under the command of XXX Corps. The town was taken, but German reinforcements were rushed to the area and Monty decided to move on to the defensive. Little progress was also being made by the Americans to the south, where First US Army suffered a serious setback in the Hürtgen Forest during its efforts to take the Roer dams, which controlled the water downstream into the country between the Maas and the Rhine. Much further south, Patton had ground to a halt in front of Metz, which he was unable to take until mid-November. His progress thereafter remained slow.

On 8 December Eisenhower convened a conference at the command post at Maastricht of Lieutenant General Bill Simpson's newly arrived Ninth US Army. It was attended by both Monty and Bradley, who arrived with widely differing proposals. Monty reverted to a variant of the Northern Thrust, with substantially the whole of 12th and 21st Army Groups, including Patton's Third US Army, combining in an offensive north of the Ardennes towards the Ruhr, under unified command. Bradley on the other hand, favoured a two-pronged attack, in which he gave equal weight to the southern push through the Saar and the Palatinate to Frankfurt and then on to Kassel. He had already sold his plan to SHAEF. Believing that Monty was advancing his own proposal with the intention of taking overall command of the ground forces, he told Eisenhower that in such circumstances he would resign, as he would have been deemed to have failed as an army group commander. Monty, always concerned with balance, believed Bradley's strategy to be the antithesis of good military practice, but he was overruled by Eisenhower, who could not afford to lose his top American field commander.

Bradley's plan required his forces to be concentrated to the north and the south of his front. In the hilly and forested Ardennes sector in between an 80-mile line was held by five divisions, mostly newly arrived or recovering from operations elsewhere. Bradley had evidently forgotten or disregarded the lessons of the invasion of France in 1940, when the Germans had followed precisely that route, likewise thinly held by the French, with devastating effect. Now they were to use exactly the same tactics, stripping their other fronts to create three strong armies with a substantial armoured element. Codenamed WACHT AM RHEIN (Watch on the Rhine),[1] the operation was designed to break through the thin crust immediately opposite, cross the Meuse between Namur and Liège and then drive hard for Antwerp, splitting the Allied armies in two and destroying their main line of communications.

For once ULTRA and other forms of Intelligence were not as forthcoming as usual. The Germans had placed a blanket ban on all wireless communication, assisted by their ability to use the excellent fixed line telephone system within their own country. All troop movements were made at night and no one with knowledge of the plan was allowed to fly west of the Rhine, lest they be forced down in Allied territory. Although Ewart at Tac believed that he had identified another panzer army being formed in the Reich, its location was unknown and it was thought to be a strong reserve. He did, however, receive from Bletchley one signal to the Luftwaffe instructing it not to destroy certain bridges on the Meuse. Williams and Monty were informed, and the latter put on hold an imminent move north by XXX Corps, which was resting from operations east of Brussels. In the meantime, Llewellyn at Main HQ went to Belchem on 15 December to point out that little information had been forthcoming from the Ardennes area. He wrote later that 'our experience had often shown that "no news was bad news"'.[2] With Belchem's agreement he sent one of his US LOs, Major Tommy Bullitt, to Bastogne to find out what, if anything, was happening.

On the following day the Germans launched their attack. By way of confirmation Bullitt telephoned from Marche on the morning of 17 December to say that he had been confronted by a Tiger tank, which had destroyed his jeep, and that he had only escaped by walking seventeen miles. Freddie was due back from a conference and two days' leave in England, but was temporarily fog-bound. In his absence Belchem and Llewellyn reacted fast. Every available Main HQ LO was diverted from his other duties, allotted a bridge over the Meuse and sent off with a SAS jeep patrol to report on the position. By the following morning all had confirmed that the bridges were intact. With Monty's agreement 29 Armoured Brigade, resting from operations, was instantly mobilized. Brigadier Roscoe Harvey, who was on a woodcock shoot, was hastily recalled and told to grab back the tanks he had just handed over for servicing and repair and proceed with all despatch to Dinant. The remainder of XXX Corps was put on immediate notice to move south.

One other unit, responsible directly to Main, was also available. R Force, which by then numbered about 2,000 men, was carrying out its usual deception role when the attack began. Most of its establishment had been so engaged since D–Day, although No. 5 Wireless Group remained in South-East England in its Operation FORTITUDE role until the end of August. Now No. 3 Light Scout Car Company was deployed along the Meuse between Dinant and Namur, whilst Strangeways despatched officers to make contact with the nearest US commanders. Unfortunately, in the febrile mood which had developed in First US Army, many of them were arrested as German spies, although they were quickly released. In the meantime, R Force's RE field companies prepared the bridges for demolition.

On the morning of 18 December Bigland set out from Bradley's Eagle Tac to visit Tac at Zonhoven, accompanied by an American LO. On the way he dropped in at First US Army's command post at Spa, where everything seemed to be under control. At Tac Bigland found Monty deeply concerned by the situation and was ordered to return to Spa, taking with him Mather and Harden, who could bring information back to Monty and elsewhere if appropriate, whilst he returned to Bradley in Luxembourg.

Early on the following morning the three LOs set off for Spa. In Mather's words:

We arrive at First Army HQ, located in a hotel, and find it abandoned. A hurried evacuation has evidently taken place. We walk in. The tables in the dining room are laid for Christmas festivities. The offices are deserted. Papers are lying about. Telephones are still in place. It is as though we had come across the *Marie Celeste* floating abandoned upon an open sea. The truth begins to dawn. The German attack is more serious than we had thought, for the evacuation of the headquarters shows every sign of a panic move.[3]

The LOs then drove to the First US Army Rear HQ at Chaudfontaine, near Liège, where they found Hodges and his chief of staff. The former was seriously shaken and unable to provide a coherent explanation of what was happening. Communications with 12th Army Group had been broken. Whilst Bigland made his way to Eagle Tac to report to Bradley, Mather and Harden returned to Zonhoven. Mather was instructed by Monty to go back to Chaudfontaine immediately to tell Hodges that he must block the Meuse bridges, using all means at his disposal, and to inform him of the steps already taken by 21st Army Group, including the deployment of XXX Corps to stand between the Germans and Antwerp. He left at midnight and made slow progress through the numerous checkpoints which had just been erected. Hodges was asleep when he arrived, but was woken by his staff. The situation was described as extremely fluid, but more worryingly, neither Hodges nor his chief of staff seemed to be fully aware of the urgency of the situation.

Having arranged a meeting between Monty, Hodges and Simpson for later in the day, Mather was back at Tac by 06.00 on the morning of 20 December to find the C-in-C awake. Monty now diverted all his own LOs, regardless of nationality, to the American corps and divisions of First US Army, ordering them to report to him at Chaudfontaine in order to let him know exactly what was happening before his meeting with the two American army commanders.

Meanwhile, there had been significant developments at SHAEF. On 19 December Eisenhower held a conference at Verdun for his senior commanders, attended by his own staff and by Bradley, Patton and General Devers of 6th US Army Group. Monty was invited, but declined due to what he believed was more pressing business and was represented by Freddie. It was agreed that Patton should break off his operations in the Saar, turn to attack the German salient from the south and relieve Bastogne, where 101 US Airborne Division was surrounded. The north, which had attracted the brunt of the German offensive, was more problematical: neither Hodges nor Simpson was present for obvious reasons and intelligence from that front was poor. The only option for them was to hold and attack when ready.

Back in Versailles that night, Major Generals Kenneth Strong, SHAEF's British Head of Intelligence, and Jock Whiteley, acting Head of Operations, became increasingly concerned by news of German advances. In the early hours of 20 December they woke Bedell Smith to tell him that, in their view, the forces north of the Bulge, as the salient began to be called, needed a unified command and that Bradley, separated from his two armies there, was in no position to assume it. The only alternative was Monty. Smith phoned Bradley, who doubted that such a change was necessary and queried its effect on American public opinion. Smith then told the two British officers that their suggestion was partisan and that, in the light of this, they would no longer be acceptable as staff officers at SHAEF. They nevertheless appeared at the staff conference on the next morning, to be told by Smith that he had changed his mind and would put their proposal to Eisenhower as his own, as it could only succeed if it was seen to come from an American. Eisenhower informed a dismayed Bradley that he concurred with the proposal and, at 10.30 on the morning of 20 December, rang Monty to inform him of his new role.

This was in time for the conference with Hodges and Simpson. Having briefed Dempsey and Crerar at Zonhoven, Monty set off for Chaudfontaine in his Rolls Royce with eight motorcycle outriders, accompanied by Belchem, Williams and BonDurant and flying the largest Union Jack available. His first task there, however, was to debrief his LOs, using a map spread out on the bonnet of one of their jeeps. By the time he had finished with them he had a much better idea of what was happening than either of the American commanders and was able to issue confident orders accordingly. Those present recalled later that both the Americans seemed to be greatly relieved that someone had taken firm control of the situation. In the coming weeks, Monty was to meet them almost daily to confirm their orders and boost their morale and was also to make a number of visits at divisional level and below, seeing as many of the American troops as possible.

As was his custom, Monty began by tidying up what he saw as muddle. Simpson was given command north of Monschau, with Hodges responsible for holding the front along the north of the Bulge against the Germans and, when Monty was ready, mounting a vigorous response. Freddie was now back from England after a difficult journey and found 'Master' enjoying himself hugely. They agreed the necessary dispositions, which primarily involved VII US Corps, under the command of one of few American generals Monty admired, 'Lightning Joe' Collins, being held in reserve for the counter-attack. XXX Corps, apart from 29 Armoured Brigade and a few additional armoured units, was kept behind the Meuse, so that this should be seen to be an entirely American affair. Freddie, however, in order to be able to exercise some degree of control from Main, ordered Llewellyn to install resident LOs at both First and Ninth US Armies, whilst the two armies sent reciprocal officers to Brussels.

With Patton having executed a remarkable change of direction and already attacking from the south towards Bastogne, Monty now began to attract criticism for his caution, including from Collins, who was desperate to begin the counter-attack. Monty's information on his new command, however, was much more accurate than anyone else's by virtue of the constant reports from his LOs and he was determined not to go on to the offensive until he was certain of success. He was helped by a change in the weather, which had been foggy, snowing or at best overcast with low clouds since beginning of the German offensive. On Christmas Eve the skies cleared and the Allied air forces, hitherto grounded, began to attack the Germans with devastating results. The Germans also took to the air, sending the strongest concentration of aircraft ever seen on the western front to hit Allied airfields in Belgium, France and the Netherlands on New Year's Day 1945, causing considerable damage to planes on the ground, including those of the Second TAF Communications Squadron at Brussels. The Allied losses were easily replaced, however, whereas the Germans, their factories subjected to constant bombing attacks, were much less able to produce new aircraft. In the Ardennes they were becoming short of fuel, having relied on overrunning American dumps, which they failed to do. Moreover, ULTRA was now producing results and Ewart, in particular, was able to determine the line of their advances from Luftwaffe signals agreeing ground support.

The German offensive had run out of steam, but the Bulge still needed to be eliminated. It was 3 January 1945 before Monty felt sufficiently confident to launch his counter-attack from the northern edge, which proved highly successful in spite of a fresh snowfall. VII US Corps led the advance as planned, whilst XVIII US Airborne Corps, under another of Monty's favourites, Matthew Ridgway, also made considerable progress on its left. In the meantime, the tip of the salient, which had reached a point only four miles from the Meuse, was pinched out by XXX Corps. It was not until 16 January that First and Third US Armies fully restored the front, but by then the outcome had been in no doubt for some time. The Germans had wagered and lost, and the result was to prejudice their defence of the Rhine in due course.

Monty, in the meantime, had been in serious trouble with Eisenhower, due to his renewed attempts to obtain the Supreme Commander's agreement on the single thrust to the Ruhr and the overall command. On 28 December, he met Eisenhower at Hasselt. The Supreme Commander, concerned about the possibility of assassination,[4] arrived on a heavily protected train in which the meeting was held. He was not accompanied on this occasion by Bedell Smith, and Monty refused to allow Freddie or Williams, both of whom were there, to attend. Thus there were no witnesses to the discussion, but as had happened on earlier occasions, Monty may have taken silence as acceptance. In any event, that evening he reported to Brooke that he believed that Eisenhower had conceded on two conditions, without which Monty had told him that he would fail:

FIRST. All available power must be allotted to the northern front.

SECOND. One man must have powers of operation and coordination of the whole northern thrust which would be from about PRUM northwards.[5]

On the following day he wrote a letter to Eisenhower, which was delivered by Freddie, who flew to Versailles on 30 December primarily to explain why the First US Army counter-attack would take place on 3 January and not two days earlier, as had been previously agreed. In the letter Monty reiterated his two conditions and proposed that the Supreme Commander should now issue a directive to enact them.

Eisenhower was not prepared to do any such thing. Not only were the senior members of his own staff unanimously against Monty's proposals, but at just that time he received a signal from Marshall telling him to make no concessions on the ground forces commander. Thoroughly exasperated, he drafted a signal to the Combined Chiefs of Staff, effectively inviting them to choose between him and Monty. Freddie, warned of what was happening by Bedell Smith and appalled by the potential implications, saw Eisenhower immediately and, having read the draft signal, begged him to delay sending it for 24 hours, to allow him time to deal with Monty.

Freddie flew back to Belgium on New Year's Eve, landing at the strip closest to Zonhoven. Monty was having tea in his small house when he arrived, but sensed that something was wrong and asked Freddie to join him in his office. Freddie laid out the situation, giving his opinion that, in a choice between Eisenhower and Monty, the CCS would certainly back the former, and that Alexander was to be the likely replacement at 21st Army Group. He wrote later:

> I felt terribly sorry for my Chief, for he now looked completely nonplussed – I don't think I have ever seen him look so deflated. It was as if a cloak of loneliness had descended. His reply was, 'What shall I do now, Freddie?'[6]

Freddie had already prepared a draft of a signal to send to Eisenhower which read:

> Dear Ike
> I have seen Freddie and understand you are greatly worried by many considerations in these very difficult days. I have given you my frank views because I have felt you like this. I am sure there are many factors which have a bearing beyond anything I can realise. Whatever your decision may be you can rely on me one hundred per cent to make it work, and I know Brad will do the same. Very distressed that my letter may have upset you and I would ask you to tear it up.
> Your very devoted subordinate
Monty[7]

It was agreed by Monty and sent off immediately.

This was, by any standard, a monumental climb-down by Monty. It spelt the end of his demands for an overall ground forces commander and for concentrating the Allied strength north of the Ruhr. Further debate would take place over Monty's continuing command of the two American armies, but it was now clear that he, Bradley and Devers would have equal status under Eisenhower for the rest of the campaign and that Bradley had won the argument for a double-pronged advance by 12th Army Group.

It was also the greatest service which Freddie could have provided, almost certainly saving Monty's career. It is fruitless to speculate on what might have happened if Eisenhower's appeal to the CCS had been sent, but the damage to the Western Alliance would probably have been considerable. With no part to play in the ultimate victory, it must also be doubtful whether Monty could have gone on to the illustrious post-war positions he was to hold.

In the event, much as he resented the rejection of what he saw as the only sensible way forward from a purely military perspective, his climb-down actually made him more secure in the position he occupied, enjoying the full support not only of Churchill and Brooke, but now also of Eisenhower, who was too great a man to crow over his triumph. This was in spite of a serious faux pas which Monty committed soon afterwards.

The battle won, he decided to hold a press conference. By way of preparation he signalled Churchill to explain what he hoped to achieve, which was to demonstrate Allied solidarity and teamwork and his own friendship with Eisenhower. Churchill, naturally, expressed his support.

Much of the ensuing trouble was not the result of the conference itself, but of an announcement by SHAEF on 6 January, the previous day, that control of First and Ninth US Armies had passed from Bradley to Monty, a fact which had hitherto not been disclosed. This was immediately played up by the British press, whilst even the American Forces newspaper, *Stars and Stripes*, referred to the Americans north of the Bulge as 'Monty's troops'. This caused great distress to Bradley, his staff and his supporters such as Patton.

What then happened at Monty's own press conference served to pour oil on the fire. Unusually, he chose to speak from a script rather than extempore, as was his normal practice. He explained how he had initially reacted to the German attack and how he had come to be placed in command of all the Allied forces north of the Bulge. He then went on to talk about how he had approached the battle and the steps he had taken to 'see off' the enemy. He attached great emphasis to the 'good fighting qualities of the American soldier' and the teamwork of the Allies. He emphasized that the captain of the team was Eisenhower, to whom he was devoted, and said that it grieved him to read uncomplimentary articles about the Supreme Commander in the British press. On the face of it, all this was good for Allied harmony. It was not, however, what he said, but how he said it and what he did not say which caused the problem.

This time Freddie, the one man Monty might have listened to, was not available to provide sound advice. Once again he was ill and was about to go into hospital in Cambridge. Some on the staff, such as Warren, found it difficult to understand why the words should have caused offence. Others saw considerable problems with the text right from the start, notably Ewart, who tried hard to get Monty to alter it, and Williams, who sensed that the emphasis on him being asked to help out would not go down at all well with the Americans. Part of it – 'The battle has been most interesting; I think possibly one of the most interesting and tricky battles I have ever handled, with great issues at stake' – bordered on the condescending, whilst although the American soldier was lauded, there was no mention of his commanders. Odgers, who was also present, feared immediately that it would not do the job which Monty intended, indeed that it would do more harm than good, although he accepted that Monty was genuinely trying to do his best for the relationship with the Americans.

That relationship was, in the event, seriously damaged, particularly as it affected Bradley. The subsequent reports in the British press were laudatory of the field marshal to the exclusion of any other commanders. The fire was further stoked by 'Mary of Arnhem', the announcer at an English-speaking German radio station, which operated on a waveband very close to the BBC and broadcast news at the same times, to which were added subtle twists to drive a wedge between the Allies. Poor Bigland, who brought the text of Monty's talk back to Eagle Tac, was advised by one of his American colleagues to make himself scarce, as even his friends would find it difficult to be polite. Having taken notes for Bradley and found Monty's approach intolerably patronizing, he completely understood their viewpoint. Frantic attempts were made to put things right, including by Churchill in Parliament, but it was too late.

It was an unfortunate start to 1945.

Chapter Twenty-Five

The Rhine

In spite of the demands imposed by the Battle of the Bulge, the overall logistics situation for the Allies improved towards the end of 1944. This was very largely due to the opening of Antwerp, which, because of its capacity and its accessibility to ships sailing directly from the USA, became a joint British and American port, operated by a combined staff set up by Q (Movements) of 21st Army Group in accordance with a document called 'The Charter of Antwerp'. Ostend handled bulk POL and the arrival of both reinforcements and replacement vehicles for the British and Canadians, whilst Calais became the main port for troops going on and returning from leave. Neither Dieppe nor Boulogne was needed any longer, and MULBERRY B was dismantled.

This meant that 21st Army Group's Lines of Communication could be shortened significantly. Apart from a small area around Caen and Bayeux and the extreme north-western corner of the country from just south of the Somme to the Belgian border, the liberated areas in France were transferred to the French Provisional Government for civil affairs and to the US Communications Zone for military logistics purposes. Another significant development was the construction of the PLUTO pipeline from Dungeness to Boulogne, where a terminus was opened on 28 October, allowing oil to be pumped directly to the Continent from tankers discharging in Liverpool. Overland pipelines were now constructed forward into Belgium, also connecting with the bulk storage facilities in Ostend.

All of these factors meant that it was now necessary to close the Rear Maintenance Area in Normandy and to create a new Advance Base in the Brussels/Antwerp area. Although the quantity of supplies arriving in Belgium was satisfactory, their movement thereafter was not always efficient, and this also applied to the transfer of stocks from the RMA. The railways were still not operating satisfactorily, many road and rail bridges had been destroyed in the German retreat and some of the canals also needed repairing. Problems emerged frequently and the finger of blame was directed at the DQMG (Movements & Transportation), Brigadier McKillop. Graham and other senior members of the Q staff demanded change, and McKillop was replaced by Major General Charles Napier, who had been Chief of Movements and Transportation at SHAEF and was widely considered to have done a good job in the early stages of the campaign.

The high demand for supplies came as a result not only of the need to stockpile for operations on both sides of the Rhine, but also to sustain the civil population, which involved the Civil Affairs branch. Civil Affairs had only been able to operate on a very small scale in Normandy, due to the size of the beachhead. De Gaulle moved fast to appoint both a Regional Commissioner and a Prefect for the Calvados Department, and they and their staffs collaborated very effectively with the Civil Affairs detachments, particularly in Caen, where the problems caused by the near destruction of the city were immense. The dash across Northern France from the Seine allowed little time for Civil Affairs to do more than brief the local mayors as to what was happening on their way through. In these areas, as in Normandy, the Provisional Government rapidly assumed control.

In Belgium and the Netherlands the governments-in-exile now returned but, especially in the case of the former, were not universally popular with those who had remained behind, particularly the resistance movements. Whilst civil administration was largely in the hands of these governments, supported by SHAEF missions, a serious shortage of food and fuel, notably coal, in both countries meant that the allocation of stocks and the means to transport them became a matter for agreement between the Q and Civil Affairs branches of 21st Army Group. Happily, common sense prevailed and, once the transportation problems were solved, an acceptable balance between the needs of the army group and the civil population was established, as least as far as the liberated areas were concerned. The occupied part of the Netherlands continued to cause great concern, as it seemed that famine might be imminent, but no solution was possible, as Monty had decided that its liberation was not a military priority.

As in Q (Movements & Transportation), there was a change at the top of the A branch, but in this case the incumbent DAG, Brigadier Lloyd, was wanted by the War Office to take up an appointment as Director of Army Education. He left warmly recommended by Monty and was replaced by Brigadier Maurice Chilton, the very man who had written the somewhat critical report on Eighth Army's HQ towards the end of the North African campaign. Chilton had, however, subsequently done an excellent job as Dempsey's chief of staff and was well regarded in 21st Army Group. Monty had initially been offered Brigadier Kenneth McLean, who had been one of the chief planners at COSSAC. However, he was perceived to be in the anti-Monty camp at SHAEF and his appointment was firmly vetoed.

The major problem with which Chilton would have to deal was reinforcements. The level of casualties which had been experienced in Normandy had diminished, but the problem remained that there were still not enough men reaching conscription age to make up the losses. This was particularly true of the infantry, where by October 1944 the deficiency amounted to 970 officers and 11,900 other ranks. The disbanding of 50 Division addressed the requirement for other ranks by the end of the year, but 520 officers were still required. The artillery regiments which had formed part of 50 Division were therefore broken up and their officers returned to the UK for infantry training and redeployment as soon as possible, to which were added officers from a number of RASC and Pioneer units. There was also a move to replace young and fit officers on the staffs of 21st Army Group formations with those whose age or health prevented them from undertaking front-line duties. This was, however, strongly resisted by their commanders, who were determined to hold on to staff-trained officers with experience of active service.

In addition to McKillop and Lloyd, there were a number of other departures from Main HQ, mostly in one direction, towards the Far East. In November 1944 Oliver Leese left Eighth Army in Italy to become C-in-C Allied Land Forces South East Asia. During his briefing by Brooke he was handed a letter from Mountbatten, now Supreme Commander in the theatre and thus Leese's immediate superior. In it Mountbatten, who had visited Monty in Normandy in mid-August, wrote that the Q side of the ALFSEA staff was notoriously weak and that Monty thought he might persuade Graham to release Feilden, who had been Leese's AA&QMG in Guards Armoured Division in 1942. As it turned out, Feilden stayed in 21st Army Group, probably because he was the real brains behind the Q branch and thus irreplaceable, but a number of others went in response to a series of requests by Leese. Monty needed little persuading provided that he kept a core of experienced officers; indeed, he was pleased that his staff were in demand and did what he could to choose good people. Amongst those posted to ALFSEA was Jock McNeill, one of Monty's original Eighth Army staff, who went out to India with promotion to Colonel (Air). In the meantime, both Feilden and Chilton were promoted to major general to recognize their growing responsibilities.

At the end of January 1945 Monty went on another visit to the UK. He had originally hoped to be there for Christmas, but his plans had been rudely interrupted by the Germans. In spite of his capitulation to Eisenhower, he used his meeting with Brooke to air all his old concerns, but the CIGS was not optimistic about any change. Churchill was no more encouraging, instead telling him off for getting on the wrong side of the Americans. Somewhat depressed by his reception, he left London to spend a few days quietly at Hindhead with David's guardians, the Reynolds. His spirits were lifted, however, by a pleasant lunch à deux with the King shortly before his return to the Continent on 3 February.

The Battle of the Bulge forced a month's delay to Monty's next major operation, the clearing of the near bank of the Rhine between Nijmegen and Düsseldorf. This was to take the form of a pincer movement from two directions, by First Canadian Army driving from the north through the Reichswald and the flat country along the Rhine in Operation VERITABLE, and by Ninth US Army, which remained for the time being part of 21st Army Group, attacking across the Roer from the south through Mönchengladbach and Krefeld in Operation GRENADE. Second Army HQ was withdrawn in the meantime to plan the Rhine crossing.

The launching of the two operations very nearly foundered, as far as Monty was concerned, at a SHAEF conference at Versailles on 31 January, which as usual he had not attended. Bradley had been pressing for Ninth US Army to be returned to him, as First US Army had been in mid-January, but it was clear that 21st Army Group did not have the strength to mount a coordinated offensive without it. Bradley wanted to continue advancing through the Ardennes towards Cologne, for which he needed as much manpower as possible, leaving Ninth US Army short of its full complement of divisions. He pressed his case strongly, but for once the staff at SHAEF were more favourably disposed to Monty's plan and Bradley was overruled. The divisions which Simpson needed for GRENADE were duly despatched.

In preparation for VERITABLE and GRENADE, and to the relief of all, Tac relocated on 7 February from Zonhoven to Geldrop, just outside Eindhoven, where it was much better placed for Monty to control both operations. It was still winter and accommodation was in houses and empty factories, but the local population was far more friendly and Eindhoven was nearby for those off-duty.

First Canadian Army's attack began on 8 February on a very narrow front through the Reichswald, south-east of Nijmegen. Although controlled from above by the Canadians, the majority of the divisions were British and tactical command was initially exercised by Horrocks in XXX Corps. The attack was kicked off by 2 Canadian Division and 15, 51 and 53 Divisions, with 3 Canadian Division joining on the left flank later in the day. The defences had been strongly constructed and, once they had been penetrated, both the forest and the flat ground to the north, which had been flooded by the Germans, proved exceptionally difficult, but by midnight all the initial objectives had been taken. Further progress was made the next day and 43 Division was inserted into the battle as the front expanded.

The Tac LOs covering the operation all had to fly from Geldrop to Nijmegen, where their jeeps waited to take them forward to their allotted divisions. This necessitated flying extremely close to German-held areas where, although there was overall air superiority, incursions by the Luftwaffe were frequent. On 9 February, Harden and Mather were on their way to Nijmegen in an Auster when it was attacked by a FW 190 at 1,000 feet over Grave. The pilot, Flight Lieutenant McQueen, a quiet but exceptionally popular figure at Tac, was killed instantly, whilst Mather was seriously wounded. Harden, sitting next to McQueen, had no experience of flying a plane, but managed to grab the controls and brought the plane miraculously down in a crash landing, coming to rest in a shallow swamp. He was cut on the head and badly shaken, but otherwise unscathed. Mather was still capable of walking and the two of them managed to flag down a jeep, which took them to the nearest casualty clearing station. Harden got away with a few stitches, but Mather required major surgery by Arthur Porritt to remove the bullets and a kidney and to repair a badly damaged arm. He wrote subsequently:

> A few days later, at a hospital near Eindhoven, Monty was standing by my bedside and quizzing the army doctor in a bracing sort of way, 'Tell me doctor,' he demanded, 'how many holes in him?' and the doctor's reply, 'Counting the shrapnel – thirteen.' 'Thirteen, thirteen! Excellent, excellent!' was my Master's response and he disappeared again.[1]

Monty was much more concerned than he appeared. He had already written to Mather's mother, telling her precisely what had happened, expressing his sadness at the loss of his longest-standing LO and telling her how well he had done. It was accepted that Mather was in for a longish convalescence and it was, as it turned out, the end of his war. Harden returned to duty and Mather was replaced by Tom Howarth, who was serving in 3 Division, in which he was a brigade major and which was just going into action in the Reichswald.

As VERITABLE progressed, not only 3 Division, but also 52, Guards Armoured, 11 Armoured and 4 Canadian Armoured Divisions were fed into the battle, and it became necessary for II Canadian Corps to take control of the north-eastern sector of the front. The fighting was brutal and, on much of the battlefield, conducted in country which was under water. It was not until 8 March, a month to the day after the operation began, that the First Canadian Army took Xanten, effectively completing its part of the offensive.

Ninth US Army was unable to begin its attack as originally planned due to the Germans releasing the pent-up water behind the Roer dams, which flooded all the country downstream. It was only on 23 February that the inundations subsided sufficiently for XII and XIX US Corps to attack across the Roer, breaking through the enemy defences four days later and then advancing fast to take Mönchengladbach and Krefeld. XVI US Corps then moved up the east bank of the Maas to liberate Roermond and Venlo and to make contact with 53 Division on March 3. Howarth later recalled the confusion caused by the two armies' convergence, prompting Monty to take immediate action to resolve it as a direct result of Howarth's report. By 10 March the last German rearguards had withdrawn across the Rhine, but they left behind large numbers of dead, wounded and prisoners. Hitler's determination to fight every battle to the bitter end, rather than to conduct a tactical retreat, severely depleted the numbers available to defend the Rhine itself.

Churchill, accompanied by his own Chief of Staff, 'Pug' Ismay, and by Brooke, arrived on 2 March for a four-day visit, the last day of which was spent at SHAEF, which had now relocated to Rheims. Eisenhower put his train at the Prime Minister's disposal and for the first three days it was parked in a siding at Geldrop. On the first evening the Prime Minister and the CIGS met many of the Tac staff and attended the daily debriefing of the LOs, which Brooke found both interesting and impressive. They then spent a day each with Ninth US Army and First Canadian Army, both of which were still in action in the Rhineland. Churchill was even allowed to fire an 8-inch heavy field gun, much to his pleasure.

On their last evening at Geldrop the visitors dined with Monty and Freddie on the train. Monty, as usual, asked to be excused so that he could observe his custom of retiring to bed at 21.30, but Freddie was required to stay on. Churchill then made it clear that, when the Rhine crossing took place, he expected to be there to watch it, insisting that he should have a close-up view and possibly even cross the river himself. Freddie, knowing Monty's dislike of visitors during the critical phases of active operations, stalled for time, but said that he would talk to Monty about it later.

Brooke recognized the warning signs:

> De Guingand, not knowing the P.M., unfortunately adopted quite the wrong attitude with him and I at one time was afraid that we might have trouble. Winston was in deadly earnest in his desire to come out for the crossing of the Rhine and to be well forward in this operation. I knew we should have difficulties in providing for his security, but I was even more certain that de Guingand's rather grand-motherly arguments against Winston's wishes would ultimately lead to an explosion.[2]

The matter did not end with Freddie's departure from the dinner table at 01.30 on the following morning. Later that day he put the Prime Minister's request to Monty, whose initial reaction was, 'Certainly not! Never!'[3] Monty, however, then received a letter from Brooke, saying that Churchill should be humoured and, realising even at this stage of the war that the Prime Minister's support remained vital, he relented, although he told Freddie that Churchill would have to be kept under control. A short time afterwards Freddie was attending a meeting in London at the War Office when a message arrived that the Prime Minister wanted to see him immediately. At No. 10 Downing Street he found Churchill sitting in an armchair, wreathed in cigar smoke and demanding to know what arrangements had been made. Freddie was able to tell him that a tank, stripped of its turret, would be made available to him, from which he could watch the operation in relative safety. As he was to write later: 'He didn't appear to think much of this, but more or less gave his approval.'[4]

On 9 March, even as the last remaining Germans west of the Rhine were being mopped up, Monty held his first army commanders' conference for

Operations PLUNDER and VARSITY, respectively the crossing of the river north of the Ruhr and the supporting airborne operation. His original concept was that PLUNDER should be carried out entirely by Second Army, but that Dempsey would have to borrow a corps from Ninth US Army to provide the necessary strength. Bill Simpson objected strongly. He was entirely loyal to Monty, but he knew that he would have problems with his American colleagues if Ninth US Army was not to be involved in this major undertaking. Monty, who did not want the issue referred to Eisenhower, conceded without further argument.

The river was the most significant obstacle encountered since the D-Day landings, and the preparations for crossing it absorbed an enormous amount of the planners' time. A significant amount of the preparation work devolved on the engineers and pioneers and was coordinated by Inglis. Most of this involved bridging and, in order to get both troops and equipment into the concentration areas, it was necessary to construct eleven bridges across the Maas. For the Rhine itself sixteen floating bridges, with an aggregate length of 19,000 feet, were brought forward to erect immediately after the crossings. In addition, the road network between the Rhine and the Maas had to be dramatically improved to carry 130,000 tons of stores into the area as well as the ordinary daily maintenance requirements. For the crossings themselves, large numbers of landing craft, manned by the Royal Navy, and other amphibious vehicles, such as DUKWs and 'Buffalo' infantry carriers, were transported from the Channel ports.

On 11 March, shortly after Monty's initial planning conference, Tac moved to a site on heathland above Venlo, where accommodation and offices reverted to tents and caravans. The demands of the No. 10 set, together with the construction of good Auster strips, meant that in future two days would be required for site preparation. The recce teams were accordingly despatched that much earlier than had been the practice. On 17 March, as D-Day for PLUNDER drew near, Tac moved once again, crossing the Maas at Venlo and setting up on its first site in Germany, in the grounds of a riding school south of Straelen, where the scaffolding tower for the No. 10 set had to be erected for the first time. Here the emphasis of the Counter Intelligence detachment changed noticeably. No longer concerned about collaborators, it was now alert to the possibilities of infiltration or ambush by well-trained soldiers left behind in the retreat. On the whole, however, all they encountered were deserters, anxious to surrender. Monty's menagerie, which by this time included budgerigars and tropical fish, was augmented by a cow called Mabel, who was to provide fresh milk!

There was considerable debate at SHAEF and elsewhere about what forces should cross the Rhine and how they should be disposed thereafter. Monty, inevitably, argued initially in favour of the major thrust taking place north of the Ruhr, and this had indeed been agreed by the Combined Chiefs of Staff at Malta in February. On 7 March, however, First US Army had unexpectedly captured intact the Ludendorff Bridge over the Rhine at Remagen and quickly established a bridgehead. Moreover, a lightning advance by Third US Army through the Palatinate put Patton, too, in a good position to cross the Rhine, which he succeeded in doing in two places south of Mainz on 22 March. These successes strengthened the hand of Bradley and others pressing for the Ruhr to be enveloped from both the north and the south. Eisenhower was in any event unwilling to offend public opinion in either Great Britain or the United States by imposing a single ground forces commander from the other country, as would have been necessary for a new Northern Thrust, and engineered a release from the CCS directive. The die was thus now cast for the Broad Front to continue across Germany.

Operation PLUNDER opened at 21.00 on 23 March when 51 Division[5] began crossing the Rhine at Rees. At 22.00 1 Commando Brigade crossed near Wesel, followed in the early hours by 15 Division immediately downstream and 30 and 79 US Divisions upstream. By the morning of 24 March, small but solid bridgeheads had been established. Now 6 Airborne Division and 17 US Airborne Division, in Operation VARSITY, began landing by parachute and glider to seize the bridges over the next obstacle, the River Issel. Casualties were heavy, albeit no more than anticipated, but in this case, unlike at Arnhem, the airborne troops received immediate artillery and air support and the ground troops made contact by the end of the first day.

More divisions were now introduced into the battle and, by the evening of 28 March, a single large bridgehead had been formed. The assault formations had operated under XII Corps, XXX Corps, XVI US Corps and XVIII US Airborne Corps. Now VIII Corps, II Canadian Corps and XIII US Corps were also activated to exploit the breakout.

On the afternoon of 23 March, Churchill and Brooke arrived at Straelen where, after an early dinner, they were given a full briefing on the operation by Monty. They retired to bed at 22.00, an exceptionally early hour for the Prime Minister, as they were to watch the airborne fly-in on the following day from a vantage point some way away. From there they set off in two separate armoured cars – the turretless tank was not used – for the Rhine itself, where they toured a number of the corps HQs. Later that day, Brooke was taken up in Monty's plane to have a look at the ground over which VERITABLE had been fought. In the evening he and Churchill once again heard the reports from the LOs, all of which were encouraging.

On 25 March, following a church parade, the CIGS and the Prime Minister accompanied Monty to the Ninth US Army sector to meet Eisenhower, Bradley and Simpson. After lunch they were taken forward to a house from which a good view of the other bank was possible. Having spotted a small landing craft, Churchill suggested to Monty that they should cross to the other side and, to his surprise, the answer came in the affirmative. Accompanied by a number of Americans, they reached the far shore, where they spent 30 minutes. Back on the near bank, they drove to Wesel, where Monty's instruction that Churchill should be kept under control failed when he escaped his minders and was found clambering up the side of a destroyed railway bridge, exposed to both shell fire and snipers. He was speedily brought down again!

The two men left on 26 March, but not before crossing the Rhine again, this time by the new Class 40 bridge at Bislich, returning in a Buffalo. Just before lunch that day, Brooke was amused to see the Prime Minister relieving himself in the river!

Churchill had had his wishes fulfilled but, much more importantly, 21st Army Group was now across the greatest obstacle in its path and driving hard into Northern Germany.

Chapter Twenty-Six

Triumph and Tragedy

Monty's primary objective was the Elbe. He directed Second Army and Ninth US Army towards, respectively, the stretches of the river from Hamburg to Wittenberge and Wittenberge to Magdeburg. Second Canadian Army was bolstered by the arrival from Italy of I Canadian Corps of two divisions, to which was added 49 Division. As they had been ever since the breakout from Normandy, the Canadians were responsible for the left flank, which for this phase meant clearing the north-east of the Netherlands and the North Sea coast and its hinterland from the Zuider Zee to the estuary of the Elbe.

Good progress was made by 21st Army Group, although Second Army encountered pockets of stubborn resistance along the Dortmund–Ems Canal. Ninth US Army was particularly successful, pushing forward towards Hanover and making contact on its right on 1 April with First US Army at Lippstadt, thereby completing the encirclement of the Ruhr.

Monty was already thinking beyond the Elbe, as a signal to Eisenhower and Brooke on 27 March indicated:

> My Tactical Headquarters moves to an area 1033 Northwest of Bonninghardt on Thursday 29th March. Thereafter the axis on which my Tactical Headquarters will move will be WESSEL – MUNSTER – WIEDENBRUCK – HERFORD – HANNOVER – thence via the Autobahn to Berlin I hope.[1]

It was not to be. In a series of extraordinary decisions, which had implications not only for the advance itself but also for the post-war history of Europe, the whole emphasis of the campaign moved in a different direction. Eisenhower decided to reduce the Ruhr, which Monty felt should be masked but otherwise ignored, to send 6th US Army Group to tackle the 'National Redoubt' in the Alps, which turned out to be totally fictitious, and to direct the bulk of 12th US Army Group on Leipzig. Without informing the Combined Chiefs of Staff, he signalled his intentions to Stalin, making it quite clear to the Soviet leader that he was leaving Berlin to the Russians. Although it had already been decided that the German capital would be in the Russian Sector after the war, any chance of using its possession to strengthen the Western Allies' hand had now been lost.

In order to achieve his strategy, Eisenhower removed Ninth US Army from 21st Army Group on 4 April and placed it once more under Bradley, who had been lobbying intensively for its return since mid-January. Monty, who was informed of the decision on 28 March, was predictably furious. Simpson had done very well under his command and Monty was relying on him to provide the necessary weight for 21st Army Group to get to the Elbe. As usual, Freddie was deployed to put the case for retaining Ninth US Army to SHAEF, using his close relationship with Bedell Smith. His efforts were in vain, although it was agreed that Simpson should protect Monty's flank.

Freddie was now exhausted by the constant struggle to advance Monty's arguments in the face of determined opposition, whilst at the same time retaining Allied harmony. His staff had for some time been deeply worried by his state of health. His memory was not always accurate and his Military Assistant, Bill Bovill, was instructed by Freddie's senior subordinates to act as a 'remembrancer', keeping track of his decisions and instructions. Brigadier Bulmer, a specialist on the medical staff, reported his concerns to Monty, who summoned Freddie to see him. Freddie agreed that he was badly in need of a rest, but argued that, at this late stage of the war, it was vital for him to stay on. After much discussion, it was agreed that he should remain, but that he should be treated with drugs to help him to sleep and should take a complete rest in Brussels every two to three weeks, where he would be completely sedated. If the war did not end within three months, he would be relieved of his appointment. Whilst the drugs worked reasonably satisfactorily, the enforced rest in Brussels did not. Freddie carried on much as before, with Bovill keeping a very close eye on him.

One issue which had been taking up a significant amount of Freddie's time was North-West Holland, which Monty, for sound reasons, had decided was not a military objective. Ever since MARKET GARDEN, when the Dutch unions came out on strike, temporarily paralysing transportation in the country, there had been a severe shortage of food supplies and this had translated into famine over the winter. Civil Affairs and the Q branch had done what they could to prepare for liberation, but were constantly distracted by other issues. Graham suggested that a District Headquarters, responsible to 21st Army Group and acting in conjunction with the Dutch Government and the SHAEF Mission, should be set up to handle the situation, a proposal to which the War Office agreed. Sandy Galloway, who had been the first BGS of Eighth Army, was appointed to command the new Netherlands District, relieving Main HQ of the direct responsibility for stockpiling food, fuel and other essential supplies and assembling the transport – road, rail, canal, sea and air – which would be required to distribute them as soon as circumstances permitted.

It probably did not help Freddie that Main was temporarily disrupted by its first move since arriving in Brussels in the previous September. Now that

21st Army Group was advancing increasingly rapidly, the Belgian capital became too distant for driving to and from Tac to be a practical proposition, and it was vital to get closer. The relocation was first considered in early February, with the intention of being installed in the new site by the date of the Rhine crossing, in order to avoid moving during a mobile battle. Eindhoven was initially chosen, but Llewellyn's recce party reported that, whilst physically possible, it would require widespread dispersion, with 100 per cent billeting. It would also be necessary to clear several entire streets of more than 1,000 inhabitants, which it was felt might cause repercussions with the Dutch. Moreover, it was thought to be very difficult to accommodate both Main and the HQ of Second Tactical Air Force. The proposal was shelved and a new site was sought.

Further reconnaissance identified a location in the Ninth US Army sector between the Maas and the Rhine. This was the Johannistaler Institution, a lunatic asylum at Suchteln, north-west of Mönchengladbach, whose fifty or so buildings were spread over a wide area, but were able to accommodate both Main and Second TAF. There were as many as 6,000 staff and inmates to rehouse, which caused strong but unsuccessful representations to be made by the local Burgermeister, and the whole site needed to be disinfected, but it otherwise satisfied the criteria. The necessary work was carried out in time for the advanced party to move on 29 March, followed by the first echelon on 4 April and the second echelon on 6 April. It was much further forward than Eindhoven, let alone Brussels, but by this time Tac was already about 100 miles away.

Whilst most branches of Main HQ continued to work as before in the new location, this was no longer true of Civil Affairs and Military Government. Monty himself had been thinking about Military Government since the previous September, when it seemed for a brief period that 21st Army Group might be in Germany within weeks or even days. He was horrified to hear at that time of a proposal by the War Office to create a new organization, separate from the Military Government, to be called the Wehrkreis Control Mission,[2] which would be responsible for disarming and disbanding the German armed forces. He understood that it would have a large staff and would be commanded by Major General Charles West, a former COSSAC planner and subsequently a staff officer at SHAEF, where he was thought to be in the anti-Monty camp. Monty wrote a strong letter to Grigg, disparaging West and proposing that the tasks should instead be carried out under the control of 21st Army Group through the normal chain of command.

In the event the Wehrkreis Control Mission was never formed, as it was decided that the administration of the British Zone after the defeat of Germany, including dealing with its armed forces, should be exercised entirely through static Corps Districts, under the control of a Zone HQ which would itself replace the Army Group HQ. The German civil administrative units

– *Provinzen, Länder, Regierungsbezirke* and *Kreise* – would be retained and military government detachments would appoint and supervise local officials and run the country through them. Corps District boundaries would follow the administrative boundaries of one or more of the larger units. Until the end of hostilities, however, I Corps, which was not needed for active service after the end of 1944, was to establish the first such Corps District in the areas of Germany which progressively came under British control, reporting to 21st Army Group Main HQ. Civil Affairs was now delegated to the SHAEF Missions in the liberated countries, and the focus was shifted entirely to Military Government.

This in turn led to a change of leadership. Brigadier Robbins, the Deputy Chief Civil Affairs Officer, was succeeded on 17 March by Gerald Templer, a long-time favourite of Monty's, who was designated Director of Civil Affairs and Military Government, the first part of the title being dropped before very long. The appointment was upgraded to the rank of major general, which put it on a par with the heads of other branches.

Templer had been a student of Monty's at Staff College and had always been marked out by him for advancement. He served in 1940/41 as commander of an independent brigade in V Corps, of which he became BGS in succession to Simpson when Monty left. He was then swiftly promoted to divisional and corps command in Home Forces, before asking for demotion in order to be able to go on active service. Having led 56 Division in the early part of the Italian campaign, he was transferred to 6 Armoured Division, in command of which he was badly wounded. After convalescence in England, he was given a highly frustrating job in SOE before being summoned by Monty, who had characteristically followed his wartime career very closely.

Monty's insistence on Templer's appointment did not go down well with the War Office, who believed that Robbins had done an excellent job. Both Grigg and the Permanent Secretary, Sir Frederick Bovenschen, suspected that his relief was due to the animosity of Feilden, which may have been the case, given the often conflicting requirements of Civil Affairs and the Q Branch. One argument against his retention, however, was that Robbins was not a regular soldier, and the demand for one in the very different environment of administering a hostile territory in the aftermath of a war was compelling.

Templer, renowned for his incisiveness, was just the man for the job. Unlike Robbins he could speak to the corps commanders as an equal. 'Bubbles' Barker, who succeeded O'Connor at VIII Corps, had been a fellow student at Staff College, Horrocks had been his neighbouring brigadier in Home Forces and Kirkman, Monty's onetime BRA in Eighth Army, who now relieved Crocker at I Corps, had been his corps commander in Italy. Templer immediately set about weeding out the weaker officers in his branch and replacing them with more suitable material, including George Baker, released from Staff Duties to take on a senior administrative role.[3] This was just in time, as the front was moving forward fast and more and more areas were coming under British control.

Another consequence of the speed of the advance was that Tac found itself in the same situation that it had experienced in August and September 1944, when it scarcely had time to pause for breath at each new location. On 29 March it moved to a ridge near Bonninghardt, still some way back from the Rhine at Wesel, on ground which had been fought over in VERITABLE and GRENADE and was heavily mined. For these and other reasons, its ranks had been swollen by a detachment of engineers, who were to be employed in future to make sites safe. On the last day of March Tac crossed the Rhine by one of the great floating bridges and passed through Wesel to an escarpment above the village of Brunen, close to where Operation VARSITY had taken place. On 3 April it moved towards Münster and camped in an uncomfortable site north of Nottuln, a quarry which was flooded in parts but whose choice was dictated by the presence of a large tower on which to fix the No. 10 set's transmitter.

There were now some changes to the Liaison staff. One of the originals, Dudley Bourhill, left and was replaced by Peter Earle. Earle, a regular officer in the King's Royal Rifle Corps, had caught Monty's eye as Military Assistant to Archie Nye, the VCIGS. He had visited Monty in Normandy, both with Nye and as his emissary, and had also met him on his visits to the War Office. He was anxious for a more active role and Monty duly obliged. Monty also added to the number of LOs, which had been stuck at seven since some of the Americans had left in August. It was now increased to eight with the addition of John Sharp. Another regular, this time a gunner, Sharp had served in the BEF and with a field regiment in North Africa, where he had won the MC and bar. He had subsequently attended the wartime staff college course at Quetta.

As Ninth US Army was no longer under command, on 27 March Monty shifted Tac's line of advance away from the axis proposed to Brooke and Eisenhower onto a more northerly course, so to be as close as possible to Dempsey's Tac HQ. The next stop on 6 April was thus at Rheine, where the site was a recently evacuated and heavily bombed Luftwaffe camp. Bigland, still diligently maintaining contact between Monty and Bradley, now found that he was having to travel hundreds of miles by car and plane between Tac and Eagle Tac, which had relocated at Namur for the Rhine crossings, before moving back to Luxembourg and then on first to Wiesbaden and next to Bad Wildungen, near Kassel.

The advance continued inexorably. On the right of Second Army, VIII Corps experienced the least difficulty with the Dortmund–Ems Canal and made good progress past Osnabrück, crossing the River Weser at Minden and Stolzenau on 5 April and taking Celle and a bridgehead over the River Aller on 10 April. In spite of stiffening resistance it reached the Elbe on 19 April and cleared the bank along its sector over the next five days. XII Corps in the centre experienced some fierce fighting around Rheine, but its Weser crossing near Nienburg was almost unopposed. It took Soltau on 18 April and Harburg, on the Elbe opposite Hamburg, on 23 April. On the left, XXX Corps had been held up for the longest on the Dortmund–Ems Canal and continued to experience strong resistance as it approached Bremen. It was only on 26 April that the city was fully taken and the corps could advance towards Cuxhaven at the mouth of the Elbe.

In the meantime, First Canadian Army was also making good progress. II Canadian Corps, which had crossed the Rhine under Second Army, now reverted to its original parent, forcing its way up the east bank of the River Ijssel, thereby blocking the way to any German forces attempting to escape from the Netherlands between the Zuider Zee and the Lower Rhine. It was in Groningen by 16 April from where it moved towards the Weser at Oldenburg. With XXX Corps now past Bremen, it focused on capturing the ports of Emden and Wilhelmshaven. In the meantime, the newly arrived I Canadian Corps made an assault crossing of the Lower Rhine upstream from Arnhem, taking the town on 14 April, almost seven months after the beginning of the ill-fated Operation MARKET GARDEN. It reached the Zuider Zee on 18 April.

From the barracks at Rheine, one of its least appealing sites, Tac moved on 10 April nearly due east to one of the very best, Schloss Ostenwalde, between Osnabrück and Lübbecke. This attractive and comfortable seventeenth century country house was the home of Baron von Vincke, a cousin of Prince Bernhard of the Netherlands, who was rapidly ejected to the local Gasthof. Unusually for a location when Tac was on the move, the building was used in preference to tents for the messes, and Monty himself was so enchanted by it that he decided then and there to have it as his HQ after the war had been won. It seemed to many to be an oasis in the middle of war, but it was only for four days, after which Tac was on the move again, to a site just west of the Weser at Nienburg. There it paused for a whole week near a water tower which did service simultaneously to host the No. 10 set transmitter dish and to supply the besieged inhabitants of Bremen with water. On 21 April Tac set off again, this time to settle around some farm buildings among cornfields north-west of Soltau.

One result of the swift advance was that a large number of German units found themselves isolated behind Allied lines. Many surrendered, but a few fought on. This was to have tragic consequences for Tac, which now found itself, in its urgency to get as far forward as possible, in the middle of a battle zone. The LOs were as busy as ever, with many having to travel by Auster to reach ever further flung formations, particularly in First Canadian Army. Peter Earle, who was responsible for VIII Corps, which was situated near Lüneburg, had been in an Auster which was written off landing at the corps airstrip on 19 April. Two days later he was to visit the corps again and this time elected to go by jeep. The safest route was to travel along the corps axis, which ran from Uelzen north to Lüneburg, but this meant first driving east from Soltau to Uelzen, nearly doubling the distance and making it very difficult for Earle to return in time to brief Monty. He therefore resolved to take a more direct, albeit also more risky route.

Just as he was about to leave, Earle was approached for a lift by John Poston, who had been allotted 11 Armoured Division. As the division was known to be resting, both men thought this a waste of time, but Earle suggested that they both go to VIII Corps HQ, where information on the division's future employment should be readily available. Leaving Earle's driver behind, they made the outward journey without serious incident.

At VIII Corps Earle met Barker, who explained his plans and also advised that another route, somewhat further south, was likely to be more satisfactory for the LOs' return journey. At about 18.30 they were making good progress towards Soltau across some open heathland when shots were fired at them and they saw Germans ahead on both sides of the road. They both fired their Sten guns until they ran out of bullets, whereupon Earle, who was driving, was wounded in the arm. He aimed the jeep at the greatest threat, a machine gun on the right, but the vehicle overturned and both men were thrown out. Poston, lying on the ground with his hands above his head, was bayoneted to death and Earle was captured, but not before he had substantially erased his chinagraph board. He was taken to a German dressing station, from which he was rescued by British troops the following day. It was only then that he was able to send a signal to Dawnay reporting Poston's death. Transferred to the casualty clearing station at Soltau, he was visited first by Ewart and Sweeny, telling them what had happened, and then by Monty, who pinned the ribbon of the Military Cross on his pyjama jacket.

Poston was the longest serving of all Monty's junior staff, first as one of his two ADCs from Egypt to Italy and then as a LO. He was the unofficial leader of the LOs, the one who knew just how far to play Monty, and a swashbuckling character in his own right, even 'liberating' a German caravan, in which he lived with his pet dachshund. He was the Master of Ceremonies in the B Mess, which he kept well supplied with liquor and where he was a keen exponent of chemin de fer, and he worked just as hard as he played, being thought fearless by his fellow officers.

Monty was distraught. He remained in his caravan and hardly spoke for two days, refusing to see visitors. Sweeny and Bob Hunter recovered Poston's body from a shallow grave at the ambush site and brought it back to Tac. The funeral at Soltau, at which Padre Tindal gave a moving address and Monty wept openly, was attended by a number of senior officers who flew up from Main HQ. Poston was buried with full military honours, including a guard of honour from his regiment, the 11th Hussars, which was serving nearby. The Prime Minister, who greatly admired Monty's LOs, sent his condolences and Monty himself wrote an obituary in *The Times*, concluding with the words: 'I was completely devoted to him and I feel very sad: something has definitely gone out of my life.'[4]

The German soldiers who had killed Poston and wounded Earle were part of a substantial regimental group, some 4,000 strong, which had been bypassed in the advance. Sergeant Kirby, billeted in a house some distance from Tac, was rung one night by the Officer Commanding the Defence Company and urged to get back within the perimeter immediately. The Defence Company and armoured cars formed a screen and all other personnel were armed and on full alert. An uneasy night was passed, during which tanks were heard passing nearby, but they failed to spot the camp and were wiped out by a brigade of 53 Division on the following day.

Three new officers replaced Poston and Earle. The first was Terry Coverdale, a major in the King's Own Scottish Borderers who had served in Monty's old 3 Division throughout the campaign and who joined whilst Tac was still at Soltau. On 28 April, however, Tac moved to its last wartime location, a windswept site on Lüneburg Heath, situated on a bluff with a magnificent view to the south, whose elevation was as usual dictated by the demands of the No. 10 set. It was there that the last two wartime LOs reported for duty.

Toby Wake, unlike the other new arrivals, already knew Monty and also had personal connections at Tac, as Dawnay was his brother-in-law and Henderson an old school friend, whilst he had been Carol Mather's best man. He had served in the 9th Battalion of his regiment, the King's Royal Rifle Corps, at Gazala, and in the 1st Battalion from El Alamein to Tunis, winning the MC before being wounded a few days before the Axis surrender and repatriated to England.[5] Shortly before the Battle of Mareth, he and his brother Peter, serving in the same battalion, were invited to join Monty and Henderson for a picnic lunch on a hill not far from the front line, where Monty explained graphically and, as it turned out, mistakenly, how he expected the battle to go. After his recovery, Wake attended both the Senior Officer's School in Oxford and the wartime Staff College course at Camberley, before joining the 2nd Battalion of the KRRC as a reinforcement in Normandy, seeing a great deal of action there and in Holland and the Reichswald. He was then posted to Pip Roberts, GOC of 11 Armoured Division, as a GSO2 before being ordered to join Monty.

Richard O'Brien had been summoned before either Coverdale or Wake, but only arrived at Lüneburg after a long journey. He had come from Italy, where he was serving very happily with the Leicestershire Regiment when the call arrived, prior to which he had had a busy war in the Middle East, winning the DSO and MC. He later found out that he had been warmly recommended to Monty by Sandy Galloway, who had been impressed by O'Brien as his ADC when in command of 1 Armoured Division in 1943.

It was now vital for 21st Army to cross the Elbe and advance to the Baltic, both to cut off the remaining German forces in North-West Germany and to prevent a westward advance towards Denmark by the rapidly approaching Russians. For this operation Monty was reinforced by Ridgway's XVIII US Airborne Corps of three divisions. VIII Corps forced a crossing on the night of 28/29 April and was followed to its right by the Americans on 30 April. Opposition was light in both sectors. While 11 Armoured Division entered Lübeck on the afternoon of 2 May, 6 Airborne Division had arrived in Wismar, some 40 miles to the east, that morning, only hours before the first Russian patrols were encountered. The Russians were permitted to enter the town in small parties, but prevented from advancing any further to the west. In the meantime, Hamburg was invested by XII Corps and the garrison commander surrendered the city on 3 May.

On the same day Dawnay received a phone call from 'Spud' Murphy, Bill Williams's predecessor at Eighth Army and now the senior intelligence officer at Second Army, to say that a high-level German delegation from Field Marshal Busch, C-in-C North-West, had arrived at Dempsey's HQ. He was instructed to send them on to Tac. Monty ordered a Union Jack to be erected on a flagpole and, when the party arrived, instructed that its members should stand at attention underneath it until he made his appearance. He immediately demanded to know who they were and what they wanted. They turned out to be Admiral von Friedeburg, the recently appointed C-in-C of the Kriegsmarine, Rear Admiral Wagner, his flag officer, Major General Kinsel, Busch's Chief of Staff, and a Major Friedl.

With Ewart acting as interpreter, von Friedeburg explained that he had come to offer the surrender of all German forces in the North, including those facing the Russians in Mecklenberg. Monty replied that he had no authority to treat in respect of any force opposing the Russians, but would take the unconditional surrender of those in Holland, the Friesian Islands, Heligoland, Schleswig Holstein, Denmark and those parts of Germany west of the Elbe still under German control. If this did not happen, he would be happy to continue fighting and, rubbing home the point, he showed the Germans his dispositions on the map. Upon seeing the hopelessness of their situation, von Friedeburg broke down. He said that he was not empowered to agree on that basis, but that he and Friedl would return to Flensburg, the capital of Germany following Hitler's death and the appointment of Grand Admiral Dönitz in his place, where he would recommend its acceptance to Dönitz and Field Marshal Keitel, Chief of Staff of the OKW.

Whilst Wagner and Kinsel remained at Tac, Warren and Ewart accompanied von Friedeburg and Friedl back to the German lines through Hamburg. On the following day, 4 May, Warren returned to the same spot to pick up the two officers, now accompanied by a third, Colonel Poleck, who had brought with him the German army, navy and air force ciphers. They were driven back to Tac, where Monty insisted on seeing von Friedeburg alone to satisfy himself that the Germans were complying fully with his demands. They then moved over to the tent to sign the surrender document, which would take effect at 05.00 on the following morning. The event, with Monty sitting on one side of the table, the Germans on the other, and Ewart standing behind Monty's shoulder, was immaculately stage managed, although the initial surrender document produced failed to include the German naval forces in the area and had to be re-typed. The audience consisted of Tac staff, war correspondents and photographers, with two BBC microphones on the table. Neither Freddie nor any other member of the staff at Main was invited. Monty read out the surrender document, the Germans signed and then he, too, signed on behalf of Eisenhower. After almost eleven months, 21st Army Group's campaign was at an end.

The war, however, was not quite over. On 5 May von Friedeburg was flown to SHAEF at Rheims, from where he signalled Keitel asking for permission to sign the instrument of unconditional surrender. The response was that this was to be carried out by Colonel General Jodl, Chief of Operations of the OKW, who was duly flown by Freddie from Tac to Rheims on the following day, which at least enabled Freddie to be present at the celebrations after the signing early on the morning of 7 May. The detailed terms of the surrender were communicated to Tac by SHAEF, with a request that they should be delivered by hand to Keitel, who was due to go to Berlin to sign once again for the benefit of the Russians on 8 May. They were taken to Flensburg and handed over personally by O'Brien, accompanied by the war correspondent Chester Wilmot, with Sergeant Kirby acting as interpreter.

Prior to that, Freddie had been handling the negotiations for the relief of the population of Holland. The Germans, led by Seyss-Inquart, the *Reischskommissar* of the Netherlands, and Colonel General Blaskowitz, the C-in-C, proved very difficult, but on 30 April, with Freddie and Galloway now joined by Bedell Smith and Prince Bernhard, agreement was reached, and on the following day Galloway's trucks, trains and barges began to move into the occupied territory, whilst RAF and USAAF planes dropped in food.

By the end of the war Tac had more than doubled in size from its beginnings at Southwick Park and now numbered some 50 officers and 600 other ranks. It had 200 vehicles, a dozen dedicated aircraft and had travelled 1,100 miles since landing in Normandy. It now became a temporary centre of communications and the channel through which orders were transmitted to the German forces in the British sector, for which purpose a small German staff was set up in its own camp under Kinsel, who proved to be highly efficient. Freddie held a meeting of the senior staff there on 5 May before leaving for Rheims, to deal with the liberation of Denmark, the immediate policy for the fighting formations of 21st Army Group, the disarming of the Germans and the provision of food and medical supplies. Of those present, Belchem, Richardson, Williams and White had all been at Eighth Army's Advanced HQ when Monty arrived.

Emotions at Tac ranged from relief to jubilation to utter weariness, but amidst the general celebration of victory there was one more tragedy to come. On 10 May, escorting a German admiral in a jeep to Kiel, Charles Sweeny was fatally injured in an accident. What made it worse was that he had very recently married, and his new wife wrote to Monty to ask if she could attend the funeral. In what Monty later called one of the hardest decisions of his life he refused to allow her to come, as it would set a precedent which he could not allow. As he had done for John Poston he wrote a moving tribute in *The Times*, which included these words:

> It is with a heavy heart that I record the death of another member of my team of liaison officers, who was also a former A.D.C. – Charles Sweeny of the Royal Ulster Rifles ... The loss of Charles is hard to bear ... He became my A.D.C early in 1940 and was with me at Dunkirk. Charles was an orphan and possibly it was that fact that drew us close together; he knew the depth of my devotion to him because I had told him of it; he knew that he could call on anything from me, as if I was his father ... He had a very strong character and was utterly incapable of any mean or underhand action; his sense of duty was highly developed, and his personal bravery was very great ...
>
> I loved this Irish boy and his memory will remain with me for all time.[6]

Chapter Twenty-Seven

Post War

In the immediate aftermath of the surrender, little seemed to change at Tac. A grand celebration dinner was held in B Mess, which Monty attended, even sipping an unaccustomed glass of champagne, and a rest camp was established by a lake near Lübeck, but the pressure of work remained considerable. The American LOs left very quickly, but the British remained, carrying out their duties as before with daily visits to field formations.

The major problem was not so much the disarming of the Germans, who were highly disciplined and gave little trouble, but the arrangements for some two and a half million displaced persons who were now roaming the country. These were both German civilians who had fled in front of the Russians, and former prisoners of war and forced labourers from previously occupied countries. Those heading for France, Belgium and the Netherlands were passed through as quickly as possible, but the citizens of countries to the east were much more difficult to handle, notably those who had fought for the Germans; these were understandably highly reluctant to be handed over to the Soviet Union. It had been agreed at the Yalta Conference, however, that full repatriation would be carried out, and the Russians made it clear that Allied POWs in their own zone would be not be released until they saw this happening.

There was also an urgent requirement to deal with the survivors of the concentration and labour camps, four of which – Belsen, Fallingbostel, Neuengamme and Sandbostel – were liberated by 21st Army Group. By VE Day there were 9,000 hospital cases, putting serious additional strain on medical facilities. Special general hospitals were set up and field hygiene units and a mobile bacteriology laboratory were deployed.

The LOs, accustomed in the past to focusing on military operations, were now Monty's eyes and ears on what was happening to resolve these problems in each of the corps districts. Carol Mather, who returned to duty in July, was responsible for liaison with VIII Corps and got into serious trouble with Barker for his criticism of the conditions in a camp holding SS POWs at Neuengamme. Monty ordered the camp to be shut down immediately and Barker was furious, banning Mather from his district. Wake reported an issue common to all the districts, which was that many officers and men were now being posted to the Far East, others were already being demobilized, formations and units were being disbanded and it was not known from one day to the next who would be available to carry out the work.

The job did have its compensations, however. A number of LOs were sent off on missions outside the British Zone. Mather and Wake travelled to Copenhagen and Prague together and were warmly welcomed in both places, whilst Mather also enjoyed three trips to Switzerland, where for the first time he was able to enjoy the comforts of a country which had not been exposed to war. One of his missions was to retrieve Monty's skiing boots from a hotel in Lenk, where they were prominently displayed in a glass case in the hotel in which they had been left before the war.

Some LOs also occasionally accompanied Monty on his visits, as Howarth did when Monty received the Grand Cross of the Legion of Honour from de Gaulle in Paris. As Henderson was away, John Sharp was detailed to act alongside Chavasse as a temporary ADC to Monty on a visit to Marshal Rokossovsky. The Russians were highly hospitable, and either Sharp took advantage of this to compensate for 'Master's' abstinence or, as he maintained afterwards, his drink was spiked. In any event, he had to be bundled on to the plane by Chavasse and locked in the lavatory in time for Monty's return to Tac. As the plane taxied down the runway, the Russians fired a 21-gun salute, which was matched shot for shot by Sharp, who loosed off his revolver in a *feu de joie* through the window of the lavatory until he ran out of bullets, whereupon he had to resort to clicks. Monty inevitably demanded to know what was going on and, once Sharp had sobered up two days later, summoned him for an interview. He told the young officer that he could not afford to have someone on his staff who behaved in such a way and that he was demoting him to captain and returning him immediately to his regiment. He went on to say, however, that no official report would be made and that he would tell Sharp's commanding officer that he was to be given command of a battery as soon as possible, thus restoring him to the rank of major.

On 3 June Tac closed down on Lüneburg Heath and moved to Schloss Ostenwalde, the attractive site which Monty had decided should be his personal HQ during his brief sojourn there in April. Wake was despatched to Berlin to collect six mallard ducks from the zoo to swim on the pond. The establishment was significantly reduced, to the extent that it could be substantially accommodated in the castle and adjoining buildings. There was no further need for the engineers or Phantom, and the defence troops and signals element were cut back. The Counter Intelligence Detachment was also thinned out, but the need for security remained and Kirby was to stay on in charge until early 1946. The Operations and Intelligence staff were largely redeployed, but not before there was yet another tragedy among the latter a month after the move, when the brilliant Joe Ewart was killed in a car crash. Aged only 28, he had been a major contributor to the victory through his handling of ULTRA and was at Monty's side on a number of key occasions, notably at the final surrender.

Main HQ moved at the same time as Tac, the first echelon two days earlier and the second a day later, so that there should be no disruption. Its destination was Bad Oeynhausen, a rather unexciting town south-west of Minden, which on 25 August was to become the HQ of 21st Army Group's successor, the British Army of the Rhine.[1] It was not the original choice, which was Bückeburg, some 17 miles away, together with the nearby spa town of Bad Eilsen, where the hotels and recreational facilities were good. They proved to be too small, so were allocated to the RAF, which also used the large airfield nearby. Even Bad Oeynhausen was only big enough for Main itself, so Rear HQ and the HQ troops were located in Herford, Bielefeld and as far afield as Detmold.

Partly as a result of running down the numbers commensurate with its changing status and partly because of posting and demobilization, there were a number of departures from Main HQ. One of the first to go was Freddie himself, a few days before the move. He badly needed a complete rest and, in line with what had previously been agreed, was sent home to recuperate. This was in spite of a proposal by none other than Churchill that he should be appointed Deputy Military Governor, which was vetoed by the War Office. Harry Llewellyn, who was about to be demobilized, wrote afterwards:

I went home on the aeroplane that followed Freddie; but not before he had called in a small group of about a dozen officers who had been in his team in the desert and north-west Europe, to say goodbye – and, at the end, a barely audible 'Thank you, gentlemen.' Such was our respect, admiration and affection for our boss that not one of us could say a word as we left.[2]

Monty put his own thoughts in writing on 31 May:

My dear Freddie

I feel I would like to send you a short note of personal thanks for all you have done for me during the time we served together. No commander can ever have had, or will have, a better Chief of Staff than you were; you never spared yourself, in fact you wore yourself out completely for the good of the show.

Together we achieved much; and together we saw the thing through to the end. You must now have a good rest, and then later on, together we will conquer fresh fields.

Thank you very much.

Yrs ever

B.L.Montgomery[3]

Freddie replied on 2 June, writing among other things:

It is no good my trying to say all I feel, or to thank you adequately for all you have done for me. Being Chief of Staff to you was not difficult for two main reasons. First, you gave us such clear direction and secondly you showed me your confidence by letting me get on with the Business without petty interference. For these two Blessings I thank you most deeply.[4]

Freddie was relieved by Sandy Galloway. Others stayed on for weeks or months, but by the end of the year both the complexion and the duties of HQ BAOR had significantly changed. Tac HQ was no longer styled as such, but was still Monty's personal domain. In line with the practice he had adopted during the war, he was an infrequent visitor to Bad Oeynhausen. His personal staff changed, with Dawnay and Warren leaving to be replaced by Coverdale as Military Assistant and O'Brien as Personal Assistant. BonDurant went back to the USA, but Henderson and Chavasse both remained until after Monty left Germany. The requirement for LOs also diminished. Howarth moved on briefly to the Control Commission for Germany before leaving the Army, and Earle, recovered from his wounds, Harden, Mather and Wake had all either returned to their regiments or been posted elsewhere by early in 1946. One new arrival at Ostenwalde was Belchem, who was summoned by Monty to draft the history of his campaigns in both Eighth Army and 21st Army Group. *El Alamein to the Sangro* and *Normandy to the Baltic* were published in 1946, both under Monty's name. Neither acknowledged Belchem's contribution! They were, however, uncontroversial, containing in particular no reference to the disagreements with Eisenhower in the last year of the war.

On 3 September the Military Government branch of BAOR ceased to exist, its staff transferred to the British element of the Control Commission for Germany. BAOR itself continued to be responsible for all military matters. Templer became Deputy Chief of Staff (Execution) at the CCG, but his job remained the same and it was largely due to him that the German people in the British sector managed to survive the forthcoming winter without starvation or extreme fuel shortages. He was responsible to Monty's Deputy, initially Lieutenant General Sir Ronald Weeks, who had been DCIGS for the last three years of the war, and then, following Weeks's illness, to Brian Robertson, who had served as Alexander's CAO ever since Monty had engineered that appointment. A number of other senior officers went to the CCG, including Richardson, who became Weeks's Military Assistant before becoming Chief of the British Military Division of the Control Commission in Berlin.

As early as July 1945 it was known that Monty was likely to become the next CIGS in succession to Brooke. Brooke himself preferred Alexander, but Alex was persuaded by Churchill to become the Governor-General of Canada, and as the other pre-eminent British soldier, Monty was the only serious alternative.

However, Churchill's own successor, Clement Attlee, persuaded Brooke to stay on until the end of June 1946.

It was apparent from Monty's letter to Freddie of 31 May 1945 that he was expecting his former Chief of Staff to serve under him again. In the autumn of 1945 both clearly construed this as Freddie becoming VCIGS in succession to Archie Nye. In order that he should obtain experience of the War Office, of which he had none other than as Military Assistant to Hore-Belisha in 1939/40, Monty persuaded Brooke to appoint Freddie as DMI as soon as he completed his sick leave. The appointment did not suit him. Although Freddie had been DMI at Middle East Command for a relatively brief period in 1942, the new job was completely different, strategic rather than tactical in nature, and he struggled with it. Moreover, he had still not completely recovered his health. The upshot was that, when Nye was selected in early January 1946 to become Governor of Madras, Brooke, who was to remain in office for another six months, refused to accept Freddie for the job. His preference was Dick McCreery, at the time the British C-in-C and High Commissioner in Austria. Monty vetoed McCreery, with whom he had had a difficult relationship in the latter's capacity as Alexander's Chief of Staff. The compromise was 'Simbo' Simpson, who was wholly acceptable to both as he had performed very capably as, successively, DDMO, DMO and ACIGS at the War Office, whilst simultaneously acting, next only to Brooke, as Monty's main contact in Whitehall.

Freddie, who was informed in person of this turn of events by Monty himself, was devastated. He already had some cause for complaint about his treatment in the recent past. He had been increasingly marginalized on the important operational decisions during the latter stages of the campaign in North-West Europe, whilst at the same time exhausting himself in his efforts to keep the peace between Monty and Eisenhower. He had not been promoted to the rank of lieutenant general, which was appropriate to his role and had been held by his predecessor at 21st Army Group, William Morgan. When, in September 1945, he was compelled for lack of a suitable appointment at that time to revert to his substantive rank of colonel, his appeals to Monty to have the decision reversed fell on deaf ears, and it was only after representations by Eisenhower that his acting rank as major general was restored. He now wrote a letter to Monty expressing his disappointment, only to receive a brusque reply telling him not to bellyache. Four months later, after another period of sick leave, he resigned his commission.

On a colonel's pension[5] and with no other means, Freddie knew that he would have to find a job. His inclination, for health and other reasons, was to look outside the United Kingdom and he eventually decided on Southern Rhodesia. He had fallen in love with Africa during his secondment to the King's African Rifles from 1926 to 1931 and he was encouraged in his decision by Bob Long, who had served in Eighth Army Main HQ, where he had particular responsibility for reconnoitring new sites following the Mainwaring debacle. David Stirling, who in his capacity as the commander of the SAS had been a frequent visitor to Freddie in North Africa, asked Freddie to chair a local company and, although this was not a success, it led him on to a number of other boards in Southern Rhodesia and South Africa, in both of which countries he had a number of wartime friends. Before very long he became a prominent member of the business community and financially secure.

Monty duly became CIGS on 26 June 1946. He was not a success. He had never served at the War Office and had little idea of what the role entailed. He was inclined to treat it as being Commander-in-Chief of the British Army, a position which had been abolished in 1904. One of his great strengths, the ability to simplify, would not always work with the complex issues with which he was now faced. He disliked dealing with politicians and civil servants, something from which Alexander and Brooke had always sheltered him. Most damagingly of all, he failed to establish good relations with his colleagues on the Chief of Staffs' Committee.

From the appointment of Brooke as CIGS in December 1941, the Chiefs of Staff had been a happy and united group. They did disagree on a number of issues, but Brooke, Dudley Pound, succeeded as First Sea Lord following his death in October 1943 by Andrew Cunningham, and Charles Portal, the Chief of the Air Staff, always took a united line when it really mattered and they became good friends. Cunningham's successor was John Cunningham, for whom Monty conceived a dislike which became mutual. Portal was followed by Tedder and he and Monty loathed one other. Tedder had been jealous of Monty ever since they had served together in North Africa. For his part Monty ascribed to Tedder much of the difficulty he had experienced with SHAEF in the last year of the war. If he knew Tedder was to attend a COS meeting, Monty would send Simpson in his place, and later Templer, Simpson's successor as VCIGS. The relationship was not helped by the publication in 1946 of the diaries of Commander Harry Butcher, Eisenhower's Naval Aide,[6] which revealed Tedder's role in the plot to remove Monty. The result was that little useful could be achieved.

It was therefore a relief to all parties when, two years later, Monty was offered and accepted the position of Chairman of the Western Union Commanders-in-Chief Committee. Before leaving he attempted to have John Crocker appointed as his successor. Clement Attlee, who as Prime Minister had the job in his gift, felt that Crocker carried insufficient weight and brought back Bill Slim from retirement, the first and only Indian Army appointee to the position of CIGS.

The Western Union, which was formed in early 1948, was a military alliance between Great Britain, France, Belgium, the Netherlands and Luxembourg. Monty's term was dominated by his long-running feud with General Jean de Lattre de Tassigny, who had commanded the First French Army in the last year of the war and who was now the C-in-C Land Forces of the Western Union. Both claimed supremacy. Monty believed that, in the event of hostilities with the Soviet Union, which seemed more likely with the beginning of the Berlin blockade, he would be become Supreme Commander of the Western European forces. De Lattre considered that Monty, as the mere chairman of a committee, had no powers over planning, or for that matter very much else. Neither would give in, and the relationship became poisonous.

David Belchem, a French speaker, was appointed as Monty's Chief of Staff, with promotion to major general. He set up the HQ in the chateau at Fontainebleau, where he established a multinational staff. In spite of the antagonism between the two main players, the staff members of the various countries were on friendly terms and their work enabled some good progress to be made on bringing together the disparate armed forces of the member states. Nevertheless, and even though Monty and de Lattre became reconciled late in the day, the folding of the Western Union into NATO in 1951 was widely welcomed.

Monty spent the next seven years as Deputy Supreme Allied Commander Europe, initially under Eisenhower, and then under Generals Ridgway, Gruenther and Norstad. He retired from active service on 18 September 1958 after a career of 50 years to the day, a record which is unlikely ever to be surpassed.

Other than the two volumes on his campaigns ghosted by Belchem, Monty had refrained from publishing anything until his *Memoirs* came out shortly after his retirement. It was clear from the quote from the Book of Job on the very first page after the title – 'Yet man is born unto trouble, as the sparks fly upwards'[7] – that he expected to book to be controversial, and this was indeed the case. The last paragraph of the Foreword read:

> I have tried to explain what seems to me important and to confine the story to matters about which my knowledge is first-hand. Whatever the book may lack in literary style, it will therefore have, it is my hope, the merit of truth.[8]

Truth is a tricky concept and in this case it was seen entirely through one man's prism. It was not always recognized as such by others; indeed, the book created something of a furore. This was largely because of Monty's adverse comments about Auchinleck and particularly the latter's apparent readiness, in Monty's opinion at least, to retreat from the El Alamein line. Auchinleck threatened legal action. Freddie, an admirer of Auchinleck, offered to mediate, but was warned off by Monty. In the end it was Bill Williams who brokered a compromise, drafting a note to be inserted by the publishers in the front of future copies of the book, in which Monty grudgingly acknowledged his gratitude to Auchinleck for stabilizing the British front and noted the latter's intention to launch a new offensive when Eighth Army had rested and regrouped.

Freddie's attempted intervention was not his first foray into what might be called 'The War of the Memoirs', which went back over a decade. In fact his own memoirs, *Operation Victory*, had been published in 1948. The book was controversial only in one respect, that it introduced for the first time the information that Freddie had disagreed with Monty on the Northern Thrust. Monty wrote to Freddie, congratulating him on a 'first-class' work, but saying that he could not remember either the disagreement itself or that the issue had ever been argued. This was later confirmed by Johnny Henderson, who wrote: 'There were often discussions at dinner when we were alone with Monty and Freddie about the need for the Northern Thrust and I never heard Freddie say anything other than supporting Monty on the issue.'[9] The conclusion must be that Freddie, in spite of his misgivings, loyally supported Monty's views to Eisenhower.

Eisenhower himself went into print with *Crusade in Europe* in the same year. This brought to public notice for the first time the disagreement between himself and Monty over the unified ground forces command from 1 September 1944 onwards. Eisenhower presented a picture of the difficulty of dealing with Monty:

> He consistently refused to deal with a staff officer from any headquarters other than his own, and, in argument, was persistent up to the point of decision.[10]

He contrasted this with Freddie:

> [He] lived the code of the Allies and his capacity, ability, and energy were devoted to the coordination of plan and detail that was absolutely essential to victory.[11]

Eisenhower's book received a great deal of adverse publicity in the British press, seen as it was, quite accurately, as the American version of the war in contrast to the British. Freddie wrote a review in the *Sunday Graphic*, which was favourable in general, but which drew attention to the author's deprecation of Monty's eccentricities and the difficulty of dealing with him and which claimed that the solution to the command issues would have been the appointment of an overall land force commander. Eisenhower replied, defending his portrait of Monty on the grounds that concealing it would have raised charges of bias from many quarters, and setting out the arguments against a single ground commander.

Eisenhower's views were supported by Bradley's publication of his own wartime memoirs, *A Soldier's Story*, in 1951, which revealed for the first time the deep hurt inflicted on the author by Monty during the Battle of the Bulge and particularly in the subsequent press conference. Although his assessment of the Normandy campaign, in which Bradley had been one of the few senior Americans who appreciated what Monty was out to achieve, was entirely fair, the book elicited two sharp letters from Monty expressing his great disappointment. It did not help that Bradley was, at the time, Chairman of the NATO Military Defence Committee and thus technically Monty's boss.

Freddie, barred by Monty from dealing with the Auchinleck problem, weighed in privately with Eisenhower regarding the *Memoirs*, in which Monty applauded the former Supreme Commander's character as an Allied leader, but disparaged his military skills. His mediation failed when Eisenhower drew a line under the affair, preferring to keep silent in public. In private he was furious and it marked the end of his friendship with Monty.

In 1964 Freddie returned to the fray with his last book, *Generals at War*, whose title had an obvious double meaning. His depictions of Wavell, Auchinleck, Eisenhower and Monty were all sympathetic, but if he had expected to heal any breaches, he was unsuccessful. On the other hand, his relationship with Monty himself had recovered markedly after the disappointment of being passed over as VCIGS. The two men met quite frequently, both in the UK and Southern Africa, and it was clear that Monty still valued his Chief of Staff's opinion. However, there was another disappointment yet to come. In 1967, Monty visited Egypt to see the battlefield of El Alamein on the 25th anniversary of his victory. Freddie expected to be included, but was told that the party was to be a 'closed shop', the only former member of his staff to be included being Hugh Mainwaring. His letter expressing his distress at this decision led to another sanction, exclusion from Monty's eightieth birthday party later that year. Both Dempsey and Leese threatened to boycott the event if he was not included, and Monty relented. Afterwards it was Brian Robertson who told both men to stop behaving like children.

When Monty died in 1976, the pallbearers at his funeral in Windsor[12] consisted of five field marshals, an admiral of the fleet, a marshal of the RAF and Freddie. This was at the specific request of David Montgomery; indeed, it had been the plan for many years. He wrote later to Charles Richardson:

> One of the reasons why I was so keen to have Freddie in this role was because of the alleged rift between them. I felt that, if Freddie was there, this would demonstrate the extraordinary closeness of their relationship at various times over the years.[13]

Freddie was once again in very poor health at the funeral and had to be pumped up with drugs, with a guardsman walking close by in case he should need support. He himself died in Cannes only three years later.

It was, perhaps, unsurprising that many of the staff officers at Monty's HQs went on to have highly successful careers, both in the Army and outside it. Two followed Monty to the very top of their profession, Gerald Templer as CIGS in 1955 and George Baker as the re-styled CGS in 1968. Templer had particularly distinguished himself as High Commissioner in Malaya, where he oversaw the defeat of the Communist insurgency. As CIGS he succeeded John Harding, never a member of Monty's staff but certainly one of his long time protégés, who had beaten Brian Robertson to the job in 1952. Robertson, who was well qualified for the role, had been High Commissioner in Germany and C-in-C Middle East. On being asked by Churchill, once again Prime Minister, which of the two he recommended, Monty plumped for Harding on the grounds that a CIGS needed to have won a battle, and Robertson, albeit an extraordinarily gifted administrator, had not done so. Robertson subsequently went on to become the Chairman of the British Transport Commission and was created a life peer.

Also to serve on the Army Council were Sidney Kirkman as Adjutant General, becoming British Special Representative in Germany after his retirement in 1950 and then Director-General of Civil Defence, a vital job at the height of the Cold War, and Charles Richardson as both Quartermaster General and Master General of the Ordnance, at the end of a career which lasted until 1971. Many others reached general officer rank, including Gerry Duke as Engineer-in-Chief at the War Office, Gerry Feilden as Vice QMG, Bert Herbert, John McNeill and John Oswald, as well as David Belchem, who resigned his commission in 1953 and went on to have a successful career in industry and commerce. One of the most distinguished was John Sharp, who recovered quickly from his dismissal by Monty following the incident on the aircraft and rose to become Commander-in-Chief, Allied Forces Northern Europe. Had it not been for his untimely death in harness in 1977, he, too, might have reached the top of the Army. One of Monty's outstanding qualities was his ability to judge character and his decision in this case was thoroughly vindicated.

Many of the senior advisers who had already reached general officer rank well before the end of the war retired within the next few years. They included Meade Dennis, Drummond Inglis, Ricky Richards and 'Slap' White, the last of whom had, apart from a brief gap, served as Monty's Chief Signals Officer from El Alamein onwards. The Army was rapidly reducing in size, notwithstanding its commitments in Germany and Commonwealth countries, where independence was in a number of cases preceded by unrest. Whilst there were many exceptions, of whom Monty himself was the most prominent, it was time to bring in the next generation, whose members had been promoted much more rapidly than they might ever have hoped for and whose experience the Army wished to retain for the future.

By the end of the war the large majority of those serving in Main, Rear and Tac HQ's, and particularly the latter, were Territorial, Reserve or emergency-commissioned officers and, whilst some elected to stay on, most were only too keen to return to civilian occupations. Among those who left early from Main was Miles Graham, knighted for his services as Monty's MGA, who resumed his business career, becoming a director of Times Newspapers and a number of other companies and chairing the Greyhound Racing Association. Harry Llewellyn returned to his family's colliery business in South Wales, but his main loves were horse racing and show jumping. With his outstanding jumper, Foxhunter, he was in the team which won the bronze medal at the 1948 London Olympic Games and followed this with Great Britain's only gold medal in Helsinki four years later. He was knighted in 1977 and also succeeded to the family baronetcy.

Bill Williams went first to work for the UN Security Council Secretariat in New York, before becoming so exasperated that he returned to his true métier as a fellow of Balliol College, Oxford. In 1952 he became Warden of Rhodes House, having first visited all the countries from which Rhodes Scholars were selected. Later combining the role with that of Secretary of the Rhodes Trust, he eventually retired in 1980. He was knighted in 1973. He always kept in close touch with Monty and was consulted by him on a number of occasions.

Oliver Poole stood for Parliament and was elected Conservative MP for Oswestry. He resigned his seat in 1950 to pursue business interests, but combined this with acting as Head of the Conservative Political Centre and subsequently treasurer of the party. In 1955 he became the party chairman and was created a peer in 1958. Another Eighth Army and 21st Army Group stalwart to become a political party chairman and life peer was Frank Byers, who had worked in Staff Duties alongside Herbert and Baker; in his case he had been Liberal MP for North Dorset. The ranks of the former members of Monty's staff in the House of Lords were also swelled by two medical men, Arthur Porritt, who became Governor-General of New Zealand, and Bob Hunter, the former Tac MO, who became Vice-Chancellor of the University of Birmingham.

Two of Monty's LOs also became MPs: Carol Mather, later knighted for his services, as Conservative Member for Esher, and Dick Harden as United Unionist Member for Armagh. Bill Mather, also knighted, returned from the war to run the family company and become a prominent businessman in North-West England. Of Monty's other LOs, Dick O'Brien was knighted as Chairman of the Manpower Services Commission, whilst Tom Howarth, rated the most intelligent of the LOs by Toby Wake,[14] returned to his previous occupation as a schoolmaster and became successively Second Master of Winchester, Headmaster of King's School, Birmingham and High Master of St Paul's. Monty kept in particularly close contact with him and his son Alan,[15] who was one of two researchers who made a huge contribution to Monty's last book, *A History of Warfare*. Bigland was initially posted to the CCG; on leaving the army he became a stockbroker and then director of a number of wine and spirit companies. Wake returned to his family estate in Northamptonshire and followed numerous members of his family as High Sheriff and Vice Lieutenant of the county, in due course inheriting a baronetcy created in 1621. Paul Odgers returned to the Civil Service, in which he had a successful career, culminating as Deputy Secretary of the Department for Education and Science.

One of the more unlikely career moves was that taken by David Strangeways. He stayed in the Army until 1957, initially acting as a political adviser in both Germany and Greece and latterly commanding an infantry battalion in Malaya during the Emergency. When he left he entered a theological college as preparation to taking holy orders. After serving in several English parishes and as chaplain to the British Embassy in Stockholm, he became Chancellor and Senior Canon of St Paul's Pro-Cathedral in Malta. Llewellyn Hughes, Monty's favourite cleric during the war itself, was appointed Chaplain General to the Forces at the end of 1944 and went on to become Dean of Ripon. He remained a close friend and confidant of Monty.

Only Ray BonDurant of Monty's personal staff remained a soldier, in his case retiring as a colonel in the US Army in 1968. Trumbull Warren rejoined his law practice in Canada, where he was delighted to provide accommodation for Monty on his visits to that country, whilst both Dawnay and Henderson had highly successful careers in the City of London. Henderson was also High Sheriff and then Lord Lieutenant of Berkshire and performed a great service to British racing by setting up Racecourse Holding Trust, which saved Aintree, Cheltenham and a number of other racecourses which might otherwise have been taken over by property developers.

Henderson was another who remained in frequent contact with Monty, seeing him for the last time only two weeks before his death. He was the organizer of the Tac Reunion Dinners, which Monty used to attend even after he had given up dining out elsewhere. Later, Henderson was the instigator of the campaign to have a statue of Monty erected in a prominent position in Whitehall, where it stands alongside those of two other great soldiers of the war, Alan Brooke and Bill Slim. It was unveiled by the Queen Mother in 1980.

Chapter Twenty-Eight

Reflections

More has been written about Monty than about any other British general except Wellington. He cannot be readily compared with the Iron Duke, but he did emulate him in at least one respect, the use of relatively junior officers to obtain up-to-date information about what was happening on the battlefield. The similarities are striking. Like Monty, Wellington chose these officers personally and they were all young men, indeed many of them in Wellington's case were still in their teens. His senior ADC, Lieutenant Colonel Sir Alexander Gordon, was 22 when he joined Wellington at Corunna and 29 when he was mortally wounded at Waterloo, dying after the battle had been won. Wellington's sorrow at his death was no less than Monty's anguish at the loss of John Poston and Charles Sweeny, in each case souring a very considerable victory. Wellington's ADCs, all well mounted, carried much the same authority as Monty's LOs in their visits to divisions and brigades in the Peninsula and at Waterloo, giving him an unusual degree of control over the campaign and the individual battlefield. Each evening at dinner they provided a much needed safety valve for their commander, who enjoyed their company enormously.

It does not appear that Monty intentionally followed Wellington's example; indeed, well over twenty years later he claimed to the historian Antony Brett-James that this was 'an entirely new system of operating command'.[1] However, it was the same quest for tight control over the battlefield that caused the two men to arrive at an identical solution. Wellington was able to see his battles in person, but for Monty, in a completely different type of warfare, this was impossible. His answer was the Tac HQ, located as close as possible to the front, from which he himself could easily visit formations in action and send out his ADCs and LOs as circumstances demanded.

By the later stages of the war, Tac HQs were commonplace. Their value as mobile and flexible command posts in fluid campaigns resulted in their becoming the accepted practice in the armies and corps of 21st Army Group and, even after Monty had left, in Eighth Army in Italy. It was how Monty operated from his Tac HQ which was unusual. Dick McCreery, for instance, who succeeded Leese as commander of Eighth Army, used his Tac HQ almost every day when operations were taking place, as a forward base from which to visit his subordinate formations. However, he returned to his Main HQ each evening to confer with his BGS, other senior staff officers and the AOC of the Desert Air Force. Dempsey at Second Army also used to see his BGS daily, usually at his Tac HQ, but sometimes at his Main HQ. At 21st Army Group there was, by way of contrast, a serious and, as the campaign developed, a growing disconnection between the C-in-C and his Chief of Staff.

This had its roots in North Africa, where the use of Tac by Monty came in for some criticism, by Kirkman among others at Main HQ, but also by Maurice Chilton in his report towards the end of the campaign. This spoke of the 'intolerable strain' placed on Freddie, Graham and Williams, who were compelled to make frequent journeys by air to visit Monty. This was indeed, if nothing else, an inefficient use of time. In spite of his misgivings, Chilton understood the requirement for the army commander to be forward, but he thought that this would only be necessary in the circumstances of the highly mobile desert campaign, which were unlikely to be repeated in Europe. He was later proved wrong by the rapid movement experienced both in August and September 1944, following the break-out from Normandy, and in the weeks following the Rhine crossing. In the event, he himself had accepted the need for a Tac HQ well before that in his role as Second Army's BGS. However, he made sure that his communications with Dempsey were very good.

Whereas an army HQ employed hundreds, an army group HQ's personnel ran to several thousand, which impacted adversely on flexibility and mobility. Main and Rear HQs were organized on a fully mobile basis, but after Normandy they were always accommodated in buildings. The primary reason for this was not so much the disruption caused by frequent movement as the need for constant and high volume communication with the War Office and SHAEF, which was really only practicable with fixed telephone lines. As a result it proved impossible for Main HQ to find an acceptable alternative to Brussels until it was forced to do so by the ever lengthening distances from Tac and the advancing armies in the last weeks of the war. To be based at Main when it was so far away was rightly unacceptable to Monty, who wanted to be as close as possible to operations.

At 21st Army Group, as at Eighth Army, the main impact of the physical separation fell on Freddie, but it was much greater at the former. Whilst Freddie spoke to Monty by telephone every evening, this was never as good as seeing him personally. He was a frequent visitor to Tac, but was unable to go on a daily basis, as he had done for the critical parts of the North African campaign, because his varying responsibilities forced him to spend time not only at Main, but also at SHAEF and sometimes at the War Office.

Freddie had three roles. The first was to manage the activities of Main and Rear HQs. Because he was Chief of Staff and not BGS, or at 21st Army Group MGGS, Monty looked to him to handle everything, including logistics and human resources. This role he performed magnificently, taking full responsibility for all the detail, just as Monty required. He did so by choosing highly competent key subordinates and trusting them to carry out their jobs effectively, which by and large they did. Monty showed scant interest in what the staff were doing; as long as his intentions were converted into plans and actions, he was satisfied.

The second role was that of adviser to Monty himself. This was exceptionally difficult to fulfil, if only because Monty had total faith in his own judgement. If he looked for advice, it was on specific technical issues from experts like Kirkman, or on the administrative tolerances within which he would have to operate from Robertson or Graham, or on matters over which he had no control, the most important of which was what the enemy was doing. The last of these was why he accorded such importance to Bill Williams, on whose judgement Henderson thought Monty relied more than any other's. Freddie certainly used to present the options to Monty at Eighth Army, but Monty always made the decisions himself, usually without much debate. There were a few instances when Freddie and the staff were able to influence events, notably when the line of attack was changed for Operation SUPERCHARGE at El Alamein and when the left hook became the main focus at Mareth. In North-West Europe the staff did cause Monty to change his mind in mid-July 1944, when his proposed advance through the bocage was shelved in favour of Operation GOODWOOD, and a month later when the short envelopment was adopted at Falaise, but these were exceptions to the rule. In the case of MARKET GARDEN, he was totally deaf to any advice. He had a horror of staff being permitted to control operations, as he made clear to Eisenhower at the end of the Normandy campaign. In his eyes they were facilitators not decision makers, except as to the detail.

Freddie's third role was a new one for the campaign in North-West Europe, that of the main channel of communication between Monty and the man to whom he theoretically reported, the Supreme Commander. As the campaign developed after Normandy and differences on the issues of strategy and command began to dominate the relationship, it actually became the most important of the three roles, but it was not always successfully fulfilled and not through any fault of Freddie's.

The reporting line had never been an issue in the Mediterranean campaigns, in all of which Monty was immediately subordinate to Alexander. His scorn for Alexander's military abilities meant that he did not look to him for advice on operations, but relied on him for administrative support and used him as a buffer against higher authority. Alexander was content to play the game, and such frustration as this caused to his staff was smoothed over by Freddie.

This did not work with Eisenhower. Monty was exceptionally poor at keeping the Supreme Commander in touch with his operations, whilst doing exactly that for Brooke, who had no command role at all. His refusal ever to visit SHAEF, a matter of principle which arose from his philosophy of command, was nearly equalled by Eisenhower's reluctance to come forward to meet him. The result was that Freddie had to act as the intermediary and Freddie did not always have the full story. He also, as it subsequently became apparent, did not believe in the Northern Thrust, but there is no evidence that he did anything but advance its cause as best he could. It was not that but Monty's physical isolation at Tac which did the damage.

Tac operated for the most part in a little bubble of its own, which actually generated a strong *esprit de corps* amongst its officers and men. Contact with G (Ops) at Main was taken care of by Odgers, whilst one of Freddie's LOs visited daily to ensure that identical information was available on current operations in both HQs. Officers from Main came as required, but only a few ever saw Monty, who could not bear strangers in his own mess. Other than his personal staff, everyone was there by personal invitation. At both Eighth Army and 21st Army Group the number of people who were acceptable guests remained very small: essentially, a small number of officers from Main, notably Freddie, Belchem and Williams, with Robertson and later Graham when there was an important administrative issue to resolve, and Gannon on the subject of officer appointments and promotions. Churchill and the King were always welcome, as were Brooke and Grigg, whilst A. P. Herbert came on a number of occasions to lighten the atmosphere. Others were discouraged. Eisenhower visited only rarely and seldom stayed for the night,[2] and Bedell Smith came only twice during the entire campaign in North-West Europe.

This suited Monty down to the ground. It meant that he could focus on what he saw as the job in hand without external distractions, providing the necessary time to think about his immediate situation and the development of the campaign. It also allowed him time to relax. The personal staff, and to some extent the LOs, whom Monty admired immensely, became his family and a very happy family at that. This was immediately picked up by Bill Mather, when he arrived in Italy to take over the running of Tac from Dick Vernon, and was commented on by many others. Although Monty was always keen to provoke an argument in his mess, the atmosphere was very relaxed and there was much laughter. He also maintained a menagerie of animals, not only his dogs, but at various times cows, chickens, a turkey, at which he used to gobble, canaries, budgerigars, rabbits and the peacock which was quietly despatched by Henderson in Taormina. Like the mess dinners, these used to divert him from the inevitable strain of command.

One important feature of the mess was a betting book in which all wagers were recorded. Monty never proposed a bet himself, but was always ready to accept one. The bets, usually for amounts between £5 and £15, ranged from the date of the end of the war to the dates of the respective marriages of Henderson and Chavasse. Like a number of others, the latter was only resolved many years later, in 1950, but Monty never lost sight of them and could be counted on to ensure that they were settled.

The nature of the warm relationship between Monty and the very much younger members of his personal staff and LOs was queried by some. Nigel Hamilton, in his book *The Full Monty*, did not go as far as to conclude that Monty was a homosexual, but suggested that he established a 'homosocial bond' with them. The fact was that he found it very difficult to form close friendships with those of his own generation. There were exceptions, such as A. P. Herbert and Llewellyn Hughes, but on the whole he was a loner rather than a social animal when it came to his peer group. He also never really got on with women, with the very significant exception of his wife, but her death made him even more withdrawn as far as the opposite sex was concerned.

Hamilton's focus on Monty's sexuality drew a sharp response from Henderson, who pointed out in a letter that army and corps commanders invariably had ADCs who were much younger than them and that he himself had been with Monty around the clock for nearly four years without a hint of impropriety. Insisting that Hamilton was on the wrong track, he continued:

> You are right in saying that he was incapable of making friends with men of his own age. He wanted to command and be in the driving seat, he wanted to be in charge of any conversation – above all he wanted admiration … Where could he get this except from the young? His only relaxation was for an hour at dinner and he preferred being with the few of us holding court. He would invariably produce a subject as soon as we had sat down for discussion and hopefully for argument. He was a person who could relax with the young much better than with older people.[3]

Arthur Porritt thought that Monty worshipped his ADCs and LOs and, as the 'Pig Incident' demonstrated, Monty was certainly indulgent to them, allowing them to get away with actions which would be stamped on if others had tried them. The LOs in particular were very conscious of their importance to Monty. They never took liberties on operations, but they also understood that he would turn a blind eye if they let off steam on occasion when off-duty. Porritt, who was twenty years older, considered the B Mess at Tac a pretty riotous place, with a lot of smoking, drinking and 'blue talk'. The instigator of most of the high jinks was Poston, who could do little wrong in Monty's eyes.

Henderson, as Sweeny before him, was treated more like a son. Once he was well established he rarely saluted Monty or even called him 'Sir' and he could sail closer to the wind than anyone except Poston. On one occasion, when Monty visited a battalion of the King's Royal Rifle Corps, whose CO Henderson knew and in which Toby Wake was then serving, the CO remarked on how often Wake used to relieve himself each day and Henderson replied that Monty did the same. A bet was speedily made to see which man went the most often. Henderson, with the assistance of Monty's batman, Corporal English, ensured that Monty was kept permanently supplied with hot coffee on a very cold day and ran out the winner, by six to five. When Henderson eventually owned up, Monty was not greatly amused, but neither did he admonish him.

Monty's regard for his staff was reciprocated by them. He was universally admired and, when they got to know him, much liked, but their sentiments probably did not go as far as the hero-worship felt by Wellington's ADCs for their chief. Williams, in many ways the most thoughtful and without doubt one of the most intelligent members of the staff, expressed his own views thus:

> Did I like him personally? Yes, I did; I liked him very much. He was an exhilarating experience, as the rest of Eighth Army soon discovered … He was a high spirited character most of the time (though he could have his shrouded moods), indiscreet, vivid, and, if his humour was not infrequently barely banana skin deep, it reflected a resolute, betimes insensitively arrogant self-confidence which was quickly transmitted and buoyed one's own spirits far from home … Of course there were bits of him I didn't very much like. His idea of fairness, and more particularly of truth, did not always march in step with mine, would sometimes chill me inside and worry me, perhaps unduly.[4]

Monty did not like all his staff. For some reason he took against Harry Llewellyn, which may have been because Llewellyn was rather too obviously Freddie's protégé, keeping the Chief of Staff fully informed in a way that Monty himself did not always do. In Sicily he asked Llewellyn whether he would consider becoming a regular soldier after the war. The reply was 'Good heavens, no!',[5] after which Monty invariably and unusually called him by his surname and never 'Harry'. Yet when Henderson was asked what he proposed to do and answered that he did not want to be a soldier, preferring to go into the City and make a lot of money, Monty certainly did not hold it against him.

Monty followed the careers of many of the officers who had served under him very closely and was thus able to call on their services, either on the staff or in fighting formations, at the appropriate moment and usually to their mutual benefit. If he was close to someone, he would always have their best interests at heart. Some, like Poston, were sent off to Staff College to improve their career prospects, whilst Monty arranged for Warren to attend the college in Canada so that he could be near his newly born child. Others, including Belchem and the two Mathers, were encouraged to return to front line service, only to be recalled again later with the experience behind them.

The Main and Rear HQs of Eighth Army, and particularly of 21st Army Group, were too large to be able to generate the sort of *esprit de corps* experienced at Tac, but they were, nonetheless, good organizations in which to work. The tone was set by Freddie, who, according to Richardson, started in a low key following his appointment as BGS Eighth Army, but quietly assumed control, establishing 'a dominant but easy relationship with all the officers at Army Headquarters, including a number of personalities ... who had long experience of desert operations and were senior in age'.[6] It is clear that he was liked and respected in equal measure. The HQ officers 'would admire his quick brain, his sense of humour and his technique of quietly directing their efforts without in any way interfering with their activities.'[7]

Freddie relied heavily on an inner coterie of officers who were with him in North Africa and then accompanied him back to the UK in early 1944. On the operations side these were Belchem, Williams and Richardson. Belchem, in spite of his rank, which was junior to the several major generals in 21st Army Group HQ, was recognized as his deputy. Williams was particularly useful, not only for his sharp intelligence and sound common sense, but also, as a hostilities-only officer, for being able to tell Monty things which Freddie sometimes found it difficult to do, notably on the issue of the overall land forces command in North-West Europe. Richardson acted not just as a planner, but as a very senior liaison officer and trouble-shooter when one was needed, especially with the RAF.

On the administration side Freddie formed a very close relationship with Miles Graham, the two men seeing eye to eye on most issues. The relationship with Graham was social as well as professional, as he was one of a small number who were particularly keen on one of Freddie's great loves, gambling, which usually meant a game of chemin de fer. He and the other aficionados, who included Freddie's Military Assistant, Bill Bovill, would play on every possible occasion in their lodgings, caravans or the mess and, on one occasion, in a marathon game on the C-47 from the Sangro to Morocco at the end of 1943. When Freddie visited Tac and Monty had gone to bed, Henderson and Poston were enthusiastic players.

Such relaxation was vital to Freddie in the light of his two major persistent problems, his health and his relationship with Monty. Whilst Monty enjoyed extraordinarily good health throughout his campaigns, Freddie had to take sick leave on numerous occasions, both from Eighth Army and 21st Army Group. Gallstones were a recurrent complaint, but, as the war progressed, a more serious ailment was nervous exhaustion. Freddie was away at key moments, including the lead-up to Operation MARKET GARDEN and the post-Bulge press conference, when his wise counsel might have been beneficial.

The bigger problem, however, was the interface between him and Monty, which proved to be far from satisfactory once Tac had moved to Normandy. All might have been well if Monty had encouraged the inclusion of a senior officer at Tac, perhaps someone like Gerry Duke, who had provided the link with Vernon during the Sicily and Italy campaigns and was trusted by both men, to ensure that Freddie knew exactly what Monty was thinking. Monty was reluctant, however, and Freddie's insistence on the appointment of Russell, and subsequently of Kirke, failed dismally when they were marginalized. His instinct that something of this nature was required was the correct one, his choice of officer was not. Dawnay tried to keep Freddie abreast of what was happening, but his other responsibilities came first. The result was that Freddie never knew exactly what was in Monty's mind and was unable to function effectively as his mouthpiece to Eisenhower. That Monty conveyed his intentions and delivered his orders almost exclusively by word of mouth was a great strength in many respects, but it hampered full understanding when the only method of communication was a brief daily telephone call.

In retrospect, however, and in spite of its flaws, this was one of the great military partnerships, to be ranked alongside Napoleon and Berthier. Monty was always ready to acknowledge his debt to Freddie, writing in his *Memoirs* about the North African campaign: 'The first requirement in high command is to have a good Chief of Staff. Without de Guingand, I doubt if I could have done my part of the overall task';[8] and subsequently, of his move to 21st Army Group: 'I could not possibly have handled the task that lay ahead without the Chief of Staff who had been at my side since El Alamein.'[9] He trusted Freddie completely and was reluctant to lose him, invariably keeping his position open during the all too frequent absences on sick leave. Freddie, for his part, had no ambition other than to serve Monty to the best of his ability, which turned out to be considerable. He, in turn, was supported by a loyal and highly competent team, whose skill and dedication allowed Monty to achieve what he wanted without a moment's concern about the practicalities of its execution.

History inevitably focuses on commanders and on fighting men at all levels. It tends to ignore the work, often mundane, often tedious, certainly unglamorous, that is carried out by the staff, yet it is that very work which is so vital to success in the field. Monty, for all the criticisms of his detractors, was the most consistently successful British field commander since Wellington. He could not have achieved what he did without an outstanding staff.

Appendix I

Monty's Address to the Officers of H.Q. Eighth Army on Taking over Command

13 August 1942

1. I first of all want to introduce myself to you. You do not know me. I do not know you. But we have to work together: therefore we must understand one another, and we must have confidence each in the other. I have only been here a few hours. But from what I have seen and heard since I arrived I am prepared to say, here and now, that I have confidence in you. We will then work together as a team; and together we will gain the confidence of this great Army and go forward to the final victory in Africa.

   Now let me tell you the general lines on which we will work.

2. I believe that one of the first duties of a commander is to create what I call "atmosphere", and in that atmosphere his staff, subordinate commanders, and troops will live and work and fight.

   I do not like the general atmosphere I find here. It is an atmosphere of doubt, of looking back to select the next place to which to withdraw, of loss of confidence in our ability to defeat Rommel, of desperate defence measures by reserves in preparing positions in Cairo and the Delta.

   All that must cease.

   Let us have a new atmosphere.

3. The defence of Egypt lies here at Alamein and on the Ruweisat Ridge. What is the use of digging trenches in the Delta? It is quite useless; if we lose this position we lose Egypt; all the fighting troops now in the Delta must come out here at once, and will. <u>Here</u> we will stand and fight; there will be no further withdrawal; I have ordered that all plans and instructions dealing with further withdrawal are to be burnt, and at once. We will stand and fight <u>here</u>.

   If we can't stay here alive, then let us stay here dead.

4. I want to impress on everyone that the bad times are over. Fresh Divisions from the U.K. are now arriving in Egypt, together with reinforcements for our present Divisions. We have 300 to 400 new Sherman tanks coming and these are actually being unloaded at Suez now. Our mandate from the Prime Minister is to destroy the Axis forces in North Africa. I have seen it, written on a half-a-sheet of paper. And it will be done. If anyone here thinks it can't

be done, let him go at once; I don't want any doubters in this party. It can be done, and it will be done: beyond any possibility of doubt.

5. Now I understand that Rommel is expected to attack at any moment. Excellent. Let him attack.

I would sooner it didn't come for a week, just to give us time to sort things out. If we have two weeks to prepare we will be sitting pretty; Rommel can attack as soon as he likes after that, and I hope he does.

6. Meanwhile, we ourselves will start to plan a great offensive; it will be the beginning of a campaign which will hit Rommel and his Army for six right out of Africa.

But first we must create a reserve Corps, mobile and strong in armour, which we will train <u>out of the line</u>. Rommel has always had such a force in his Africa Corps, which is never used to hold the line but which is always in reserve, available for striking blows. Therein has been his great strength. We will create such a Corps ourselves, a British Panzer Corps; it will consist of two armoured divisions and one motorised Division; I gave orders yesterday for it to begin to form, back in the Delta.

I have no intention of launching our great attack until we are completely ready; there will be pressure from many quarters to attack soon; <u>I will not attack until we are ready</u>, and you can rest assured on that point. Meanwhile, if Rommel attacks while we are preparing, let him do so with pleasure; we will merely continue with our own preparations and <u>we</u> will attack when <u>we</u> are ready, and not before.

7. I want to tell you that I always work on the Chief of Staff system. I have nominated Brigadier de Guingand as Chief of Staff Eighth Army. I will issue orders through him. Whatever he says will be taken as coming from me and will be acted upon <u>at once</u>. I understand there has been a great deal of "bellyaching" out here. By bellyaching I mean inventing poor reasons for <u>not doing what one has been told to do.</u>

I will tolerate no bellyaching.

If anyone objects to doing what he is told, then he can get out of it; and at once. I want that made very clear right down through Eighth Army.

8. I have little more to say just at present. And some of you may think it is quite enough and may wonder if I am mad.

I assure you I am quite sane.

I understand there are people who often think I am slightly mad; so often that I now regard it as rather a compliment.

All I have to say to that is that if I am slightly mad, there are a number of people I could name who are raving lunatics!!

What I have done is to get over to you the "atmosphere" in which we will now work and fight; you must see that that atmosphere permeates down through the Eighth Army to the most junior private soldier. All the soldiers must know what is wanted; when they see it coming to pass there will be a surge of confidence throughout the Army.

I ask you to give me your confidence and to have faith that what I have said will come to pass. There is much work to be done.

The orders I have given about no further withdrawal will mean a complete change in the layout of our dispositions; also, we must begin to prepare for our great offensive.

The first thing to do is move our H.Q. to a decent place where we can live in reasonable comfort and where the Army Staff can all be together and side by side with the H.Q. of the Desert Air Force. This is a frightful place here, depressing, unhealthy and a rendezvous for every fly in Africa; we shall do no good work here. Let us get over there by the sea where it is fresh and healthy. If officers are to do good work they must have decent messes, and be comfortable. So off we go on the new line.

The Chief of Staff will be issuing orders on many points very shortly, and I am always available to be consulted by the senior officers of the staff. The great point to remember is that we are going to finish with this chap Rommel once and for all. It will be quite easy. There is no doubt about it. He is definitely a nuisance. Therefore we will hit him a crack and finish with him.

Appendix II

21st Army Group – Organisation of G Staff & Advisers

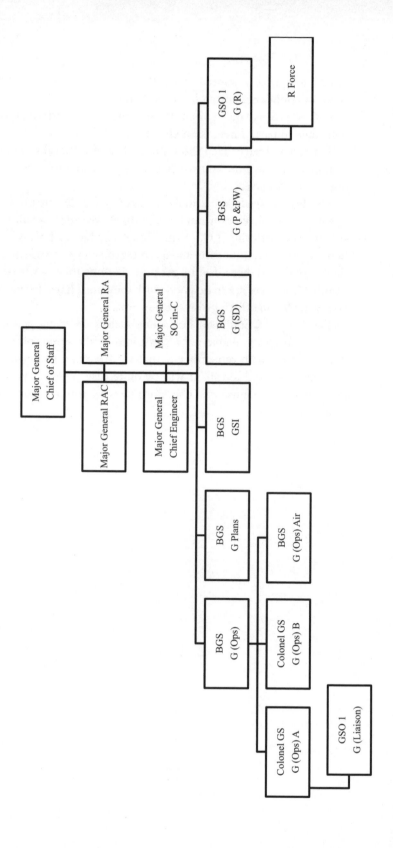

Appendix III

21st Army Group – Organisation of Q Staff

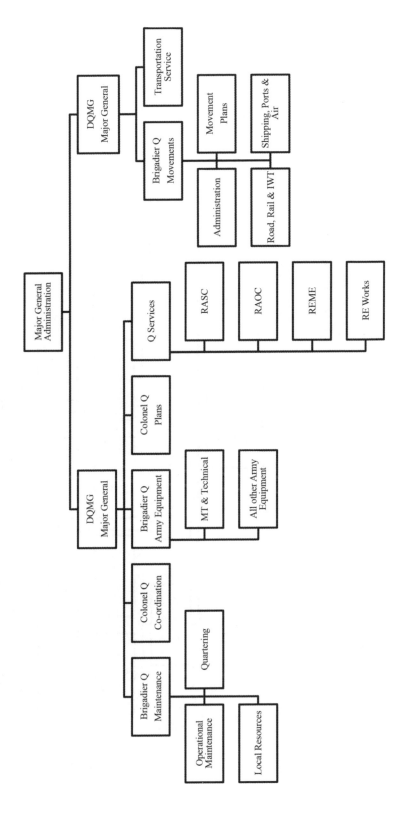

Appendix IV

21st Army Group – Organisation of A Staff

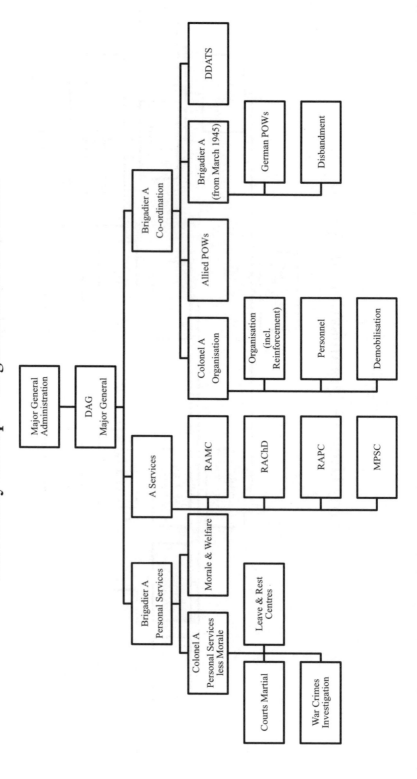

Appendix V

Officers of TAC HQ 21st Army Group

May 1944

C-in-C's Personal Staff

MA	Lt. Col. C.P. Dawnay OBE	Coldstream Guards
PA	Lt. Col. T. Warren	48th Highlanders of Canada
ADC	Capt. J.R. Henderson	12th Lancers
ADC	Capt. N.W. Chavasse	Middlesex Regiment
ADC US	Capt. J.R. BonDurant	US Army

G (Ops)

Col. GS	Col. the Hon. L.O. Russell OBE	Late Beds & Herts Regiment
GSO 2	Major P.R. Odgers	Ox & Bucks Light Infantry
GSO 2	Major K.J. Spooner	Norfolk Regiment
Major US	Major D.B. Whittington	US Army
GSO 3	Capt. F.J. Lawrence	Royal West Kent Regiment

G (Liaison)

Lt. Col US	Lt. Col H.A. Miller	US Army
GSO 2	Major L.G.S. Sanderson MC	King's Own Scottish Borderers
GSO 2	Major J.W. Poston MC	11th Hussars
GSO 2	Major J.R.E. Harden	Royal Tank Regiment
Major US	Major E.P. Prisk	US Army
Major US	Major D.K. Oliver	US Army
Capt. US	Capt. M.P. Frary	US Army
Staff Lt.	Lt D.C.M. Mather	Welsh Guards
Staff Lt.	Lt. D.T. Bourhill	Royal Artillery

GHQ Liaison Regiment

O.C..Det.	Capt. W.S. Mackintosh-Reid	Ayrshire Yeomanry

Signals

O.C. Det.	Capt. H. Oddy	Royal Signals
Cipher Offr	Capt. G. Compton-Rickett	Royal Signals
Cipher Offr	Lt. J.E. Brown	Royal Signals
2/Lt. US	2/Lt. W.D. Ford	US Army

<u>Camp Commandant</u>
Capt. (QM) W.H. Woodward   Royal Tank Regiment

<u>Transport</u>
Tpt. Offr   Lt T.G. Smith   Royal Army Service Corps
Tpt. Offr   Lt. L.T. James   Royal Army Service Corps

<u>Defence Troops</u>
C.O. Defence Pltn   Lt F.E. Appletree DCM   East Yorkshire Regiment
C.O. Armd Car Tp   Lt J.H. Mortimer   Royal Armoured Corps

Abbreviations

A	Adjutant General's branch
AA	Anti-Aircraft
AA&QMG	Assistant Adjutant and Quartermaster-General
AASC	Army Air Support Control
ACIGS	Assistant Chief of the Imperial General Staff
ACV	Armoured Command Vehicle
ADC	Aide-de-Camp
AFHQ	Allied Forces Headquarters
AFV	Armoured Fighting Vehicle
AFPU	Army Film & Photo Unit
ALFSEA	Allied Land Forces South-East Asia
ALO	Air Liaison Officer
AOC	Air Officer Commanding
AOC-in-C	Air Officer Commanding-in-Chief
AQMG	Assistant Quartermaster General
ATS	Auxiliary Territorial Service
BAOR	British Army of the Rhine
BBC	British Broadcasting Corporation
BEF	British Expeditionary Force
BGS	Brigadier General Staff
BRA	Brigadier Royal Artillery
BTE	British Troops in Egypt
BUCO	Build-Up Control Organization
CAO	Chief Administrative Officer
CB	Companion of the Order of the Bath
CBE	Commander of the Order of the British Empire
CCG	Control Commission for Germany
CCRA	Commander Corps Royal Artillery
CCS	Combined Chiefs of Staff
CGS	Chief of the General Staff
CIGS	Chief of the Imperial General Staff
C-in-C	Commander-in-Chief
CMG	Commander of the Order of St Michael & St George
CO	Commanding Officer
COS	Chief of Staff
COSSAC	Chief of Staff to the Supreme Allied Commander (Designate)
CRA	Commander Royal Artillery
CRE	Chief Royal Engineer

CSO	Chief Signals Officer
DA&QMG	Deputy Adjutant & Quartermaster-General
DAG	Deputy Adjutant General
DAQMG	Deputy Assistant Quartermaster-General
DCGS	Deputy Chief of the General Staff
DCIGS	Deputy Chief of the Imperial General Staff
DDATS	Deputy Director Auxiliary Territorial Service
DDMO	Deputy Director of Military Operations
DDMT	Deputy Director of Military Training
DMI	Director of Military Intelligence
DMO	Director of Military Operations
DQMG	Deputy Quartermaster General
DSO	Distinguished Service Order
DUKW	6-wheeled amphibious vehicle
FMC	Field Maintenance Centre
FUSAG	First US Army Group
G or GS	General Staff
GHQ	General Headquarters
GOC	General Officer Commanding
GOC-in-C	General Officer Commanding-in-Chief
GSI	General Staff Intelligence
GSO1	General Staff Officer Grade 1
GSO2	General Staff Officer Grade 2
GSO3	General Staff Officer Grade 3
HQ	Headquarters
I or Int	Intelligence
IWT	Inland Waterway Transport
KAR	King's African Rifles
KBE	Knight Commander of the Order of the British Empire
KRRC	King's Royal Rifle Corps
L	Liaison
LCT	Landing Craft (Tank)
LO	Liaison Officer
LOC	Lines of Communication
LRDG	Long Range Desert Group
LST	Landing Ship (Tank)
MA	Military Assistant
MBE	Member of the Order of the British Empire
MC	Military Cross
MGA	Major General Administration
MGGS	Major General General Staff
MGRA	Major General Royal Artillery
MGRAC	Major General Royal Armoured Corps
MI	Military Intelligence – as in MI5 or MI6
MO	Medical Officer
Mov & Tn	Movements & Transportation

MOVCO	Movement Control Organization
MP	Member of Parliament
MPSC	Military Provost Staff Corps
MS	Military Secretary
MT	Motor Transport
MTB	Motor Torpedo Boat
NATO	North Atlantic Treaty Organization
NCO	Non-commissioned Officer
OCTU	Officer Cadet Training Unit
OKW	Oberkommando der Wehrmacht (Armed Forces High Command)
Ops	Operations
OTC	Officers Training Corps
PA	Personal Assistant
P&PW	Publicity & Psychological Warfare
PLO	Personal Liaison Officer
POL	Petrol, Oil & Lubricants
POW	Prisoner of War
Q	Quartermaster General's branch
QMG	Quartermaster General
RA	Royal Artillery
RAC	Royal Armoured Corps
RAF	Royal Air Force
RAChD	Royal Army Chaplains Department
RAMC	Royal Army Medical Corps
RAOC	Royal Army Ordnance Corps
RAPC	Royal Army Pay Corps
RASC	Royal Army Service Corps
RE	Royal Engineers
REME	Royal Electrical & Mechanical Engineers
RN	Royal Navy
RTR	Royal Tank Regiment
SAS	Special Air Service
SD	Staff Duties
SHAEF	Supreme Headquarters Allied Expeditionary Force
SLU	Special Liaison Unit
SO-in-C	Signals Officer-in-Chief
SOE	Special Operations Executive
Tac HQ or Tac	Tactical Headquarters
TAF	Tactical Air Force
TURCO	Turn-Round Control Organization
VCIGS	Vice-Chief of the Imperial General Staff
W/T	Wireless Telegraphy
US	United States
USAAF	United States Army Air Force
VE-Day	Victory in Europe Day

Acknowledgements

I must start by expressing my deep gratitude to David Montgomery. Not only has he written a very generous Foreword, but, in spite of some misgivings about whether there was anything new to write about his father, he has been totally supportive throughout. He covered some of the same ground himself in the book he wrote in association with Alistair Horne – *The Lonely Leader* – so was an excellent sounding board. He had also met many of those I was writing about and, to my great envy, had visited every one of the twenty-seven sites of Monty's Tac HQ in North-West Europe.

The whole idea for the book came about when I was offered access to the papers of General Sir Charles Richardson, through the good offices of my daughter-in-law, Constance, who is Richardson's step-granddaughter. I must thank her uncle, Martin Richardson, for allowing me to take away the papers, including those which were used for his biography of Freddie de Guingand, together with recordings of interviews. Many of the photographs come from his collection.

I am very grateful to Lady Mather, whom I was able to interview, and to her son, Nicholas, who allowed me access to the diaries of his father, Carol Mather, and to the tapes of an interview he had given. I was particularly privileged to meet Major Sir Hereward Wake, the last of the LOs. Not only did Toby Wake give me what turned out to be a fascinating interview, but my visit prompted him into writing down for the first time his wartime memories, including his selection and employment by Monty.

The man who was physically the closest to Monty for the longest time – from November 1942 until July 1946 – was one of his ADCs, Johnny Henderson. Johnny's sons, Nicky and Harry, were most helpful, and Harry provided many of the photos in the book and some papers which were not otherwise in the main part of the Henderson collection at Eton College. At Eton I was greatly assisted by Michael Meredith, whilst Denise D'Armi facilitated the copying of further photos.

I never fail to be impressed by the National Archives, whose staff are the epitome of efficiency. I would also like to thank the staff at the Liddell Hart Archives for their assistance. Because the Montgomery Papers and the recordings of interviews are substantially in the Imperial War Museum, I spent more time researching there than anywhere else. Notwithstanding the enormous disruption caused by the museum being closed for refurbishment through much of the period, the Research Room remained open throughout, on the main site or in temporary premises, and the staff were unfailingly helpful. I must express my gratitude to Nigel Hamilton, who interviewed all the key members of the Eighth Army and 21st Army Group staff for his three-volume biography of Monty and deposited the tapes at the IWM.

I am most grateful for the support of Pen & Sword, particularly Brigadier Henry Wilson and Matt Jones, and for the light but expert touch of my editor, George Chamier. Finally, and as always, I would like to thank my wife, Sheelagh, and my sons, Tim and Rupert, for their constant encouragement. Rupert read and commented on the drafts of each chapter as they emerged and reduced to a minimum my tendency to prolixity!

Sources and Bibliography

Interviews

Lady Mather
Viscount Montgomery of Alamein
Major Sir Hereward Wake

Recorded interview of General Sir Charles Richardson by Mr A. Brett-James and Lieutenant Colonel P. M. Davies

Recorded interview of General Sir Charles Richardson by Miss Lucia Santa-Cruz

Primary Sources

The National Archives

Eighth Army HQ

WO 169/1011	A September–December 1941
WO 169/3910/11	Tac HQ Logs October–December 1942
WO 169/3914	Tac HQ September–December 1942
WO 169/3926	GS Ops & Rear HQ August–December 1942
WO 169/3937	GSI July–December 1942
WO 169/3938	A January–December 1942
WO 169/3939	Q January–December 1942
WO169/8494	GS Ops July–August 1943
WO 169/8495	GS Plans July–August 1943
WO 169/8496-9	GS Ops September–December 1943
WO 169/8414/5	Tac HQ Logs January–May & July–August 1943
WO 169/8519/20	GSI January–December 1943
WO 169/8521	A January–December 1943
WO 169/8522	Q January–December 1943
WO 201/432	Appreciation & plan for Operation LIGHTFOOT August 1944
WO 201/2501	Daily Diary November 1942–March 1943
WO 205/549	Report by Brig. M S Chilton on visit to Eighth Army March–April 1943

21st Army Group HQ

WO 171/103	Composition of Main HQ & Tac HQ
WO 171/127	G (Air) September–December 1944
WO 171/137-44	A January–December 1944
WO 171/3870-5	A January–June 1945
WO 171/3831	G (R) June-December 1944
WO 171/3868/9	R Force HQ January–June 1945
WO 171/3887/8	Civil Affairs & Military Government January–March 1944
WO 205/5B	Communication C–in–C & COS January 1944–May 1945
WO 205/5C	COS demi-official correspondence April 1944–May 1945
WO 205/5D	C–in–C demi-official correspondence February 1944–May 1945
WO 205/5E	C–in–C's personal signals June 1944–May 1945
WO 205/5F	COs' personal signals June 1944–May 1945
WO 205/44	War Establishment Civil Affairs & Military Government May 1944
WO 205/138	Move of HQ from Wentworth to Hammermith
WO 205/219	Report on potential Main HQ sites in Normandy July 1944
WO 205/306	Move of Main HQ to suitable site in Germany October 1944– April 1945
WO 205/330	Organization & functions of Tac HQ May 1944
WO 205/331	Move of Main HQ – instructions & composition September 1944–May 1945
WO 205/348-9	Move of Main HQ to Suchteln & Bad Oeynhausen March–June 1945
WO 205/400	Prospective sites for Main HQ after Brussels September 1944– May 1945
WO 201/586A	Standing Instructions for LOs Eighth Army & 21st AG October 1943–May 1945
WO 205/586B -602	Main HQ LO reports, June 1944–May 1945
WO 205/773	Organization of BUCO March 1944
WO 208/3575	Brig. E. T. Williams's assessment of ULTRA

Imperial War Museum

Montgomery Collection
BLM 41, 61, 63–4, 72–5, 77–84, 90, 97, 107, 110–14, 119–20, 123, 126, 140

Montgomery Ancillary Papers – Rt Revd C. Chavasse, Lieutenant Colonel C. P. Dawnay, Major General F. W. de Guingand, Colonel P. B. Earle, Lt. Colonel T. Warren, Contents of Monty's caravans, Monograph on Monty's beret, Notes for talk on Monty's caravans

Personal papers of Major General R. F. K. Belchem, Captain C Drury, General Sir George Erskine, Sir James Gunn, Brigadier R. W. Lymer, Sir Carol Mather, Major General C. H. Miller, Major General M. St J. Oswald, Major General G. W. Richards, Lt. Col. L. G. S. Sanderson, General Sir Frank Simpson and Major Sir Hereward Wake

Interviews recorded by Nigel Hamilton with Major General R. F. K. Belchem, Lieutenant Colonel T. S. Bigland, Air Chief Marshal Sir Harry Broadhurst, Major General Sir Francis de Guingand, Lieutenant General Sir Otway Herbert, Mr J. R. Henderson, General Sir Sydney Kirkman, Sir Carol Mather, Sir William Mather, General Sir Charles Richardson, Major General M. St J. Oswald, General Sir Frank Simpson, Mr P. R. Odgers, Lieutenant Colonel T. Warren and Brigadier Sir Edgar Williams

Other interviews with General Sir John Lawson, Sir William Mather and Canon D. I. Strangeways

Liddell-Hart Centre, King's College, London

Papers of Major General Sir Francis de Guingand, General Sir Sydney Kirkman, Captain Sir Basil Liddell-Hart, Major General J. H. McNeill

Eton College Library

Papers of J. R. Henderson

Other Sources

Dictionary of National Biography
London Gazette
The Times Digital Archive
Who's Who

Books

Alexander, Harold, *The Memoirs of Earl Alexander of Tunis 1940:1945*, London 1962
Anon., *The Administrative History of the Operations of 21 Army Group on the Continent of Europe June 1944–8 May 1945*, Germany 1945
Barnett, Corelli, *The Desert Generals*, London 1960
Barr, Niall, *Pendulum of War – The Three Battles of El Alamein*, London 2004
Baynes, John, *The Forgotten Victor – General Sir Richard O'Connor*, London 1989
Beevor, Antony, *D–Day – The Battle for Normandy*, London 2009
Belchem, David, *All in a Day's March*, London 1978
Bigland, Tom, *Bigland's War – War Letters of Tom Bigland 1941–45*, Liverpool 1990
Blaxland, Gregory, *The Plain Cook and the Great Showman – The First and Eighth Armies in North Africa*, London 1977
Bradley, Omar, *A Soldier's Story of the Allied Campaign from Tunis to the Elbe*, London 1951
Brett-James, Antony, *Conversations with Montgomery*, London 1984
Bryant, Arthur, *The Turn of the Tide – 1939–1943*, London 1957
Bryant, Arthur, *Triumph in the West – 1943–1946*, London 1959
Buckley, *Monty's Men – The British Army and the Liberation of Europe, 1944–5*, New Haven & London 2013
Butcher, Harry C., *Three Years with Eisenhower*, London 1946

Carver, Michael, *Harding of Petherton*, London 1978

Carver, Tom, *Where The Hell Have You Been?*, London 2009

Chalfont, *Montgomery of Alamein*, London 1976

Churchill, Winston S., *The Second World War*, Volumes II to VI, London, 1949–1954

Clark, Lloyd, *Arnhem – Jumping the Rhine 1944 and 1945 – The Greatest Airborne Battle in History*, London 2008

Cloake, John, *Templer – Tiger of Malaya*, London 1985

Connell, John, *Auchinleck*, London 1959

Danchev, Alex & Todman, Daniel (eds.), *War Diaries 1939–1945 – Field Marshal Lord Alanbrooke*, London 2001 & 2003

D'Este, Carlo, *Decision in Normandy*, New York 1983

D'Este, Carlo, *Bitter Victory – The Battle for Sicily 1943*, London 1988

D'Este, Carlo, *Eisenhower – Allied Supreme Commander*, London 2002

De Guingand, Francis, *Operation Victory*, London 1947

De Guingand, Francis, *Generals at War*, London 1964

Doherty, Richard, *Eighth Army in Italy – The Long Hard Slog*, Barnsley 2007

Donnison, F. S. V., *Civil Affairs and Military Government North-West Europe 1944–1946*, London 1961

Eisenhower, Dwight D., *Crusade in Europe*, London 1948

Forty, George, *British Army Handbook 1939–1945*, Stroud 1998

Fraser, David, *And We Shall Shock Them – The British Army in the Second World War*, London 1983

Gannon, Jack, *Before the Colours Fade*, London 1976

Greacen, Lavinia, *Chink – A Biography*, London 1989

Hamilton, Nigel, *Monty – The Making of a General 1887–1942*, London 1981

Hamilton, Nigel, *Monty – Master of the Battlefield 1942–1944*, London 1983

Hamilton, Nigel, *Monty – The Field-Marshal 1944–1976*, London 1986

Hamilton, Nigel, *The Full Monty – Montgomery of Alamein 1887–1942*, London 2002

Hastings, Max, *Overlord – D-Day and the Battle for Normandy 1944*, London 1984

Hastings, Max, *Armageddon – The Battle for Germany 1944–45*, London 2004

Henderson, Johnny, with Douglas-Home, Jamie, *Watching Monty*, Stroud 2005

Hesketh, Roger, *Fortitude – The D-Day Deception Campaign*, London 1999

Horne, Alistair, with Montgomery, David, *The Lonely Leader – Monty 1944–45*, London 1994

Horrocks, Brian, *A Full Life*, London 1960

Howarth, Tom (ed.), *Monty at Close Quarters – Recollections of the Man*, London 1985

Joslin, H. F., *Orders of Battle – Second World War 1939–1945*, London 1960

Keegan, John, *Six Armies in Normandy*, London 1982

Kershaw, Robert, *It Never Snows In November – The German View of MARKET-GARDEN, September 1944*, Shepperton 1990

Kirby, Norman, *1100 Miles with Monty – Security and Intelligence at Tac HQ*, Gloucester 1989

Lamb, Richard, *Montgomery in Europe 1943–45 – Success or Failure?*, London 1983

Lewin, Ronald, *Montgomery as Military Commander*, London 1971

Lewin, Ronald, *Ultra Goes to War – The Secret Story*, London 1978

Llewellyn, Harry, *Passport to Life – An Autobiography*, London 1980

Mather, Carol, *Aftermath of War – Everyone Must Go Home*, London 1992

Mather, Carol, *When the Grass Stops Growing*, Barnsley 1997

Montgomery, Bernard, *El Alamein to the Sangro*, Germany 1946

Montgomery, Bernard, *Normandy to the Baltic*, Germany 1946

Montgomery, Bernard, *The Memoirs of Field-Marshal Montgomery*, London 1958

Montgomery, Bernard, *The Art of Leadership*, Barnsley 2009

Montgomery, Brian, *A Field-Marshal in the Family*, London 1973

Moorehead, Alan, *Eclipse – Europe 1943–1945*, London 1945

Morgan, Frederick, *Overture to Overlord*, London 1950

Morgan, Frederick, *Peace and War – A Soldier's Life*, London 1961

Neillands, Robin, *The Battle for the Rhine 1944 – Arnhem and the Ardennes: the Campaign in Europe*, London 2005

Nicholson, Nigel, *Alex – The Life of Field Marshal Earl Alexander of Tunis*, London 1973

North, John, *North-West Europe 1944–5 – The Achievement of 21st Army Group*, London 1953

Paget, Julian, *The Crusading General – The Life of General Sir Bernard Paget GCB DSO MC*, Barnsley 2008

Parlour, Andy & Sue, *Phantom at War – The British Army's Secret Intelligence & Communications Regiment of WWII*, Bristol 2003

Porch, Douglas, *Hitler's Mediterranean Gamble – The North African and the Mediterranean Campaigns in World War II*, London 2004

Powell, Geoffrey, *The Devil's Birthday – The Bridges to Arnhem*, London 1984

Richardson, Charles, *Flashback – A Soldier's Story*, London 1985

Richardson, Charles, *Send for Freddie – The Story of Montgomery's Chief of Staff, Major-General Sir Francis de Guingand*, London 1987

Rolf, David, *The Bloody Road to Tunis – Destruction of the Axis Forces in North Africa, November 1942–May 1943*, London 2001

Rostron, Peter, *The Military Life & Times of General Sir Miles Dempsey*, London 2010

Ryan, Cornelius, *A Bridge Too Far*, London 1974

Ryder, Rowland, *Oliver Leese*, London 1987

Sanderson, Louis, *Variety is the Spice of Life*, London 1995

Sebag-Montefiore, Hugh, *Dunkirk – Fight to the Last Man*, London 2006

Stewart, Adrian, *Six of Monty's Men*, Barnsley 2011

Tedder, Arthur, *With Prejudice*, London 1966

Thompson, R. W., *The Eighty-five Days – The Story of the Battle of the Scheldt*, London 1957

Thompson, R. W., *The Battle for the Rhineland*, London 1958

Thompson, R. W., *The Montgomery Legend*, London 1967

Thompson, R. W., *Montgomery: The Field Marshal – The Campaign in North-West Europe 1944–5*, London 1969

Weeks, Ronald, *Organization & Equipment for War*, Cambridge 1950

Whicker, Alan, *Whicker's War*, London 2005

Williamson, David, *A Most Diplomatic General – The Life of General Lord Robertson of Oakridge*, London 1996

Wilmot, Chester, *The Struggle for Europe*, London 1952

Notes

Chapter 2

1. Richardson, *Send for Freddie*, p.67.
2. Robertson was not restored to the British Army List until 1945.
3. Richardson, *Flashback*, p.130.
4. He had been BGS to Alan Brooke at II Corps in France in 1940. Brooke remained his strong supporter throughout the War, although he considered that Ritchie had been over-promoted into Eighth Army.
5. He was Monty's Principal Staff Officer at NATO in 1951.
6. Belchem, *All in a Day's March*, p.103.

Chapter 3

1. Richardson , *Flashback*, p.77.
2. Brian Robertson, by now the DA&QMG, also rated a caravan, which he used to sleep in as it was designed, but he thought it tactful to keep it out of the C-in-C's sight.
3. Richardson, *Flashback* , p.103.
4. He went on to have a very successful career working for Eisenhower at AFHQ and then SHAEF.

Chapter 4

1. Letter from Montgomery to Williams, 7.9.62.
2. Franklyn was C-in-C Home Forces 1943–45.
3. Letter from Montgomery to Williams, 7.9.62.
4. Letter from Montgomery to de Guingand, 30.7.34.
5. De Guingand, *Operation Victory*, p.88.
6. Ibid., p.105.
7. Bryant, *The Turn of the Tide*, p.442.

Chapter 5

1. Montgomery, *Memoirs*, p.35.

Chapter 6

1. None of these would serve later on any of Monty's staffs, but all did well, McConnel and Nares becoming major generals by the end of the War and Hope a full colonel, who also rose to major general in due course.
2. Sanderson, *Variety is the Spice of Life*, p.25.
3. Dawnay, 'Inside Monty's Headquarters' in Howarth, *Monty at Close Quarters*, p.3.
4. Sanderson, *Variety is the Spice of Life*, p.89.
5. Letter from Monty to Dawnay, 20.8.40.
6. Letter from Monty to Dawnay, 25.8.40.
7. Letter from Monty to Dawnay, 20.9.40.

8. Ibid.
9. Montgomery, *Memoirs*, p.71.
10. On two later occasions Drury was to meet Monty in North Africa. On the first, he confessed that he was having some difficulties with his battery commander and shortly afterwards found himself posted to a much more suitable and congenial job in his division. On the second, he was waiting in a reinforcement camp after an illness; once again an order arrived very quickly for his future employment.
11. Warren interview by Nigel Hamilton (IWM 14098).
12. Letter from Monty to Warren, 11.3.42.

Chapter 7
1. Letter from Montgomery to Williams, 7.9.62.
2. Belchem interview with Nigel Hamilton (IWM 14092).
3. Montgomery, *The Art of Leadership*, p.247.
4. As it happened, the only response to what was, at best, a deep discourtesy, was a signal from Auchinleck to all corps and divisional GOCs, asking them to give their full support to the new Army Commander.
5. Richardson, *Flashback*, p.109.
6. De Guingand, *Operation Victory*, p.139.
7. Dancev & Todman (eds.), *War Diaries 1939–1945: Field Marshal Lord Alanbrooke*.
8. Whicker, *Whicker's War*, p.61.
9. The barrel was replaced by a wooden one, which released the space otherwise occupied by the breach and ammunition. The tank can be seen in the Imperial War Museum at Duxford.

Chapter 8
1. De Guingand, *Operation Victory*, p.146.
2. Richardson interview by Antony Brett-James and Lieutenant Colonel Philip Davies, 15/16.9.77.
3. Monty was sometimes held to be prejudiced against cavalrymen, on the grounds that they were essentially amateurs, more interested in equestrian sport than soldiering. He may well have thought this of individuals, but there was no general bar to cavalrymen serving under him, notably Harry Arkwright, his adviser on armour, and Johnny Henderson, his long-serving ADC, both from the same regiment as Lumsden.
4. Coningham was a New Zealander, whose original nickname was 'Maori', but this became corrupted to 'Mary', the name by which he was known to all.
5. Kirkman had been given a lower priority than Horrocks and he travelled the long way round, by flying-boat to West Africa and then across the Sahara to Khartoum and up the Nile to Cairo on the so-called 'reinforcement route'.
6. Kirkman interview by Nigel Hamilton (IWM 14096).
7. Richardson interview by Antony Brett-James and Lieutenant Colonel Philip Davies, 15/16.9.77.
8. Montgomery, *Memoirs*, p.114.

Chapter 9
1. In fact, the full title was Special Liaison Unit/Special Communications Unit ('SLU/SCU') which covered both the deciphering and communications staff, but in practice the shorter form was always used.
2. Note by Williams on the use of ULTRA, 5.10.45.
3. Ibid.

Chapter 10

1. The Jock columns were named after their inventor, Jock Campbell, a horse gunner who led 7 Armoured Division's Support Group and then the division itself, prior to being killed in a road accident. These groups of mixed infantry and artillery were used to harass the enemy in the early days of the war, then again during the advance after Operation CRUSADER and finally during the early battles on the Alamein Line.
2. Sir William Mather interview in 1995 (IWM 15326).
3. Mather, *When the Grass Stops Growing*, p.178.
4. This was an empty threat, as Casey was neither British nor a politician, although he had sat in the Australian Parliament and been a member of the Government there. He went on to be Governor of Bengal and the first Australian to be the country's Governor-General.
5. Mather, *When the Grass Stops Growing*, p.187.

Chapter 11

1. Francis Tuker of 4 Indian Division claimed that it was an old British dummy minefield; if so, it should have been known about.
2. The lesson was learnt, and in future scouting for a new HQ site was not entrusted to the GSO1s, but to a Rhodesian major, Bob Long.
3. Llewellyn, *Passport to Life*, p.131.
4. Spooner continued to serve in Operations at Main HQ. In 1944, he would be one of a small number of GSO2s (Ops) who would go to Normandy with Tac HQ.
5. Transportation by rail effectively ended at Tobruk. There were two small lines out of Benghazi, to Barce (108 km) and Soluch (56km) respectively, but neither of them were of much value.
6. Richardson, *Flashback*, p.136.
7. Others present included James Gammell, GOC-in-C Eastern Command, John Swayne, GOC-in-C South-Eastern Command and William Morgan, Paget's CGS.
8. Dawnay, 'Inside Monty's Headquarters' in Howarth, *Monty at Close Quarters*, p.8.

Chapter 12

1. 'Spud' Murphy was still well regarded by Monty and had been commended to Brooke as a trainer for Home Forces or a senior role at the War Office. In due course he became BGS(I) at Second Army in North-West Europe.
2. Ewart had actually been posted back to the UK, but his departure was delayed by a month.
3. Operation MARKET GARDEN in September 1944, claimed as 90 per cent successful.
4. Richardson interview with Anthony Brett-James and Lieutenant Colonel Philip Davies, 15/16.9.77.
5. In an interview with Nigel Hamilton (IWM 14064), Broadhurst described Monty as being in 'a terrible state'.
6. Richardson interview with Lucia Santa-Cruz, 1969.
7. The new SASO was Air Commodore Claude Pelly, who was known to Freddie and much liked by him.
8. Wallace was to be killed just before the end of the campaign in a South African Air Force Boston, to be succeeded by McNeill, now promoted to Lieutenant Colonel.
9. The highest ranking General Staff officer in an army was almost always a brigadier. This was certainly true of First Army in North Africa, Second Army in North-West Europe and Fourteenth Army in India and Burma. However, not only Freddie, but also his successors at Eighth Army under Leese and McCreery, were major generals.

10. Brigadier Chilton, in his report on Eighth Army's HQs, described Training as Oswald's 'real job', but this was never the case. WO 205/549.
11. In an interview with Nigel Hamilton (IWM 14096), Kirkman expressed his antipathy to the use of a Tac HQ.

Chapter 13

1. The American planning team was called Force 343.
2. Letter from Monty to Freddie, 29.4.43.
3. Richardson , *Flashback* , pp.151–2.
4. After a brief spell in the wilderness, Gairdner was appointed to advise Auchinleck, by then C-in-C India, on armoured warfare. He then replaced Lumsden, who was killed in a kamikaze attack, as Churchill's Personal Liaison Officer to General MacArthur. Remaining in Japan after the surrender as Attlee's PLO, he was later Governor of Western Australia and then Tasmania, retiring as a full general with a knighthood.
5. There were several deception operations, designed to make the Axis powers believe that the invasion would be mounted in Greece or Sardinia. The most famous was Operation MINCEMEAT, the planting of false documents on a corpse ('The Man Who Never Was') washed up on a beach in Spain.
6. Simonds was a very recent appointment: his predecessor as GOC of 1 Canadian Division, together with the GSO1 and AA&QMG, had all died in an air crash on their way to Cairo for a briefing on the plan.
7. HMS *Antwerp* was formerly a passenger ferry on the Harwich to Antwerp run; it had been commissioned into the Royal Navy in 1940.
8. De Guingand, *Operation Victory*, p.292.

Chapter 14

1. Montgomery, *Memoirs*, p.190.
1. Letter from Monty to Richardson, 1.9.43.
2. Chavasee was the nephew of Captain Noel Chavasse, who won a VC and bar in the Great War – one of only three men to do so.
3. 1 Airborne Division returned to the UK, but was replaced by 2 New Zealand Division.
4. Montgomery, *Memoirs*, p.198.
5. Danchev & Todman (eds), *War Diaries*, pp.499–500.
6. It was drafted by Henderson, but amended by Monty.

Chapter 15

1. Marshall was still promoting it vigorously at Casablanca in January 1943.
2. The acronym was used not only for the individual, but also for his whole organization.
3. Morgan, *Overture to Overlord*, p.69.
4. Ibid., p.70.
5. Wentworth subsequently became the Rear HQ of SHAEF until after the Normandy breakout, whilst the underground bunkers constructed there continued to be used as a Signals Centre for 21st Army Group.
6. An early proposal was that Paget would do a direct swap with Monty, which he considered would be a demotion. The matter was resolved by his appointment as C-in-C Middle East, *vice* Jumbo Wilson, who succeeded Eisenhower as Supreme Commander in the Mediterranean.

Chapter 16

1. IWM BLM 72.
2. Freddie remained a major general, whereas Morgan had been and remained a lieutenant general. This was at the insistence of Monty, who believed that there would be unmerited expectations of promotion from more junior officers as a result.

3. Both men moved to good appointments, Morgan as GOC-in-C Southern Command and thereafter Chief of Staff to Alexander in his capacity as Supreme Commander in the Mediterranean, becoming Supreme Commander himself after the end of the War. Kimmins became Director of Plans at SEAC.
4. Somewhat unusually, Lloyd was a Territorial Army officer, with a background in education.
5. Montgomery, *Memoirs*, p.222.
6. A much more serious victim of this policy was General Andrew McNaughton, the C-in-C of the Canadian Forces Overseas, who wanted to visit 1 Canadian Division. He, too, was banned and never forgave Monty.
7. De Guingand, *Operation Victory*, p.191.
8. Henderson, 'Morning, Noon and Night' in Howarth, *Monty at Close Quarters*, p.41.
9. Henderson, *Watching Monty*, p.57.

Chapter 17
1. Richardson, *Flashback*, p.172.
2. Herbert interview by Nigel Hamilton (IWM 14072).

Chapter 18
1. There were a number of these, the most successful of whom was Juan Pujol, codenamed 'Garbo', who purported to the Germans to have a whole network of agents.
2. Danchev & Todman (eds), *War Diaries*, p.538.
3. Dawnay 'Inside Monty's Headquarters' in Howarth, *Monty at Close Quarters*, p.14.
4. IWM BLM 73/1.

Chapter 19
1. Bob Long, the Rhodesian who had been responsible for reconnoitring Main HQ locations after the Mainwaring debacle, was also asked for, but elected to remain with Eighth Army, possibly because he would otherwise be moving even further from his home.
2. WO 205/330.
3. One of Odgers' fellow GSO 2s was Ken Spooner, who had been Monty's ADC when he arrived in Egypt.
4. These are all now housed at the Imperial War Museum at Duxford.
5. Odgers, *A Tac Chronicle*.
6. These words of Montrose, together with a quotation from *Henry V* and the prayer of Sir Francis Drake before the attack on Cadiz, had been pinned up in Monty's office caravan since just after the Battle of Alam Halfa.
7. Mather, *When the Grass Stops Growing*, p.247.
8. 12 according to Mather, 30 according to Sanderson!
9. Sanderson, *Variety is the Spice of Life*, p.260.

Chapter 20
1. Richardson, *Flashback*, p.178.
2. There were good reasons for this. Although Major General Urqhart of 1 Airborne Division would have preferred to go in by day, the RAF and USAAF commanders insisted on a night-time operation and on the chosen night there was only a quarter moon. Moreover, Leigh-Mallory was unable to obtain any assurance from Ramsay that the aircraft would not be fired on by the fleet of Allied ships.
3. Monty was well aware of the continuing deficiencies of the Allied tanks, but keen to suppress any public mention of this, lest morale in the armoured divisions should be adversely affected.

Chapter 21

1. Kirby had a degree in French and German from London University.
2. When Monty himself became CIGS, he called for the file and had it destroyed!
3. Montgomery, *Memoirs*, p.257.
4. De Guingand, *Operation Victory*, p.398.
5. The fatalities included Lieutenant General Lesley J. McNair, Commanding General US Ground Forces, who had come to observe the operation. He was the highest ranking Allied officer killed in North-West Europe.
6. As late as 14 August OKW was still calling for an offensive towards Avranches.
7. Montgomery, *Memoirs*, pp.254–5.

Chapter 22

1. Ibid., pp.267–8.
2. De Guingand, *Operation Victory*, p.411.
3. Williams interview by Nigel Hamilton (IWM 14100).
4. Danchev & Todman (eds.), *War Diaries*, p.586.
5. He had been appointed a Chief Commander of the Order in August 1943.
6. It is now better known as Europa and is the seat of the European Council.
7. XII Corps – Rouen, Abbeville, St Omer, Ypres, Ghent, Antwerp. XXX Corps – Vernon, Amiens, Douai, Tournai, Brussels.
8. The building was found to be in poor shape, wrecked by the Germans who had been billeted there.

Chapter 23

1. Also called the Maas–Scheldt Canal.
2. Montgomery, *Memoirs*, p.298.
3. 1 Airborne Division's most reliable communication with the outside world was between its Phantom detachment and the one at Tac, although it was still sporadic at best.
4. Richardson, *Flashback*, pp. 187–8.

Chapter 24

1. This was the name of a German patriotic song, which was particularly popular during the Franco-Prussian and Great Wars.
2. Llewellyn, *Passport to Life*, p.167.
3. Mather, *When the Grass Stops Growing*, p.284.
4. This had been a threat since the beginning of the German offensive, when enemy soldiers in Allied uniforms were sent to wreak confusion behind the lines and were rumoured to be out to kill senior commanders.
5. Signal to Brooke 28.12.44. Montgomery Papers IWM.
6. De Guingand, *Generals at War*, p.111.
7. Ibid., p.112.

Chapter 25

1. Mather, *When the Grass Stops Growing*, p.295.
2. Bryant , *Triumph in the West*, pp.425–4.
3. De Guingand, *Generals at War*, p.156.
4. Ibid., p.158.
5. Major General Tom Rennie, the GOC of the Highland Division, who had restored its fortunes comprehensively after its failures in Normandy, was killed during the operation.

He was one of only a small handful of British general officers to be lost in action during the war. He was replaced by Gordon MacMillan, who had served in the division in North Africa and commanded two other divisions in North-West Europe. He had been one of Monty's students at Camberley and was very highly regarded by him.

Chapter 26
1. Signal to Eisenhower and Brooke 27.3.45, Montgomery Papers IWM.
2. A *Wehrkreis* was a German Military District, corresponding almost exactly to a British Corps District.
3. I Corps took on some officers from R Force, whose deception activities now came to an end. Strangeways was given the job of running the Ruhr Intelligence Office, responsible among other things for denazification.
4. *The Times*, 27.4.45.
5. One result of Wake's wound was that he was unable to salute Monty other than with his left arm!
6. *The Times*, 15.5.45.

Chapter 27
1. It was to remain so until 1954, when it moved to Rheindahlen.
2. Llewellyn, *Passport to Life*, p.169.
3. Letter from Monty to Freddie, 31.5.45.
4. Letter from Freddie to Monty, 2.6.45.
5. He was allowed to retain the honorary rank of major general.
6. *Ten Years with Eisenhower*.
7. 'The Sparks Fly Upwards' was his preferred title for the book, but he was persuaded not to use it by his publishers.
8. Montgomery, *Memoirs*, p.16.
9. Letter from Henderson to Charles Richardson , 9.4.86.
10. Eisenhower, *Crusade in Europe*, p.314.
11. Ibid.
12. Monty's former personal staff and LOs sat either side of the coffin during the service.
13. Letter from David Montgomery to Charles Richards, 3.11.86.
14. Interview with the author, 30.8.12.
15. Later a Conservative MP, Government Minister and Life Peer.

Chapter 28
1. Brett-James, *Conversations with Montgomery*, p.112.
2. On one early occasion at dinner in his mess, Eisenhower was brusquely ordered by Monty to put out his cigarette, so his reluctance was understandable!
3. Letter from Henderson to Hamilton, 21.11.2001.
4. Williams, 'Gee One Eye, Sir' in Howarth, *Monty at Close Quarters*, p.28.
5. Llewellyn, *Passport to Life*, p.148.
6. Richardson, *Send for Freddie*, p.69.
7. Ibid., pp.69–70.
8. Montgomery, *Memoirs*, p.167.
9. Ibid., p.205.

Index